S0-ARX-578

SETTLERS

SETTLERS

being extracts from the
journals and letters of
early colonists in

CANADA, AUSTRALIA
SOUTH AFRICA
AND NEW ZEALAND

Edited and introduced by
JOHN HALE

FABER & FABER LTD
24 Russell Square
London

First published in mcml
by Faber and Faber Limited
24 Russell Square, London, W.C.1
Printed in Great Britain by
William Clowes and Sons Limited
London and Beccles

Prefatory Note

I have tried to leave as few traces of my hand as possible on this book. Notes have been kept to a minimum, on the principle that a moment's pause inside the text is better than a moment's glance outside it. The historical introductions are simply to help locate each writer in the broad picture of his country's history as a whole. They contain nothing that is not in standard works and I should be most happy if I felt they were being passed over.

I feel no need to Apologize for this anthology, though this, perhaps, is a break with convention. For too long the emphatic voice of the traveller has tended to obscure the quieter tones of the men and women who cleared the forests and raised the farms. The writings of actual settlers, indeed, are still somewhat hard to come by, and there is no convenient social, domestic background to colonial history.

In attempting to provide one I have included some writers, like Lady Anne Barnard, who were not strictly settlers but who were anxious nevertheless to identify themselves with the countries they resided in. This fact, coupled with the intrinsic value of their records, will, I hope, justify their inclusion.

The writers here have been chosen to cover as wide an area of country and occupation as possible during the first decades of settlement, and those who have had experience of compiling source books will understand how charmed I was to find that all these men and women emerged clearly as individuals, some remarkably eloquent ones. This is another reason for editorial reticence. I should like, however, to repeat an appeal made from time to time by Historical Associations in different parts of the Commonwealth. Much of this type of material remains in private hands, possibly unsuspected. If any reader fancies that he is in possession of letters or diaries comparable with or surpassing in interest what follows and would like to feel that they were being made use of, I would be pleased to refer him to persons competent to deal with them.

Oxford–Harvard

Contents

Contents

South Africa

New Zealand

Appendix

Illustrations

Maps

Note on Texts

Original spelling and punctuation preserved.

To avoid frequent interruptions of the text omissions are not signified.

Sources are mentioned at the end of each biographical note.

With very few exceptions individual sentences have not been broken. When this has been done, ... are inserted.

. . . means cuts made in sources by their editor.

CANADA

Canada, principally to illustrate the movements of Henry

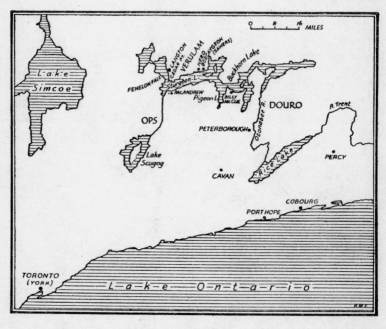

Part of the Newcastle District of Upper Canada, showing names
mentioned by Mrs. Stewart, Need and Langton

Permanent settlement in Canada dates from the earliest years of the seventeenth century. Families came across from France and built houses along the banks of the St. Lawrence, the only highway through wild land. Often they did not trouble to cultivate more than a fraction of their deep, narrow farms. France did not need their produce, Quebec and Montreal, though dependent on the surrounding countryside, were but small ports and their markets hardly affected cultivation. The urge for expansion was not to come from this quarter.

Yet though these conditions did not change, a hundred years later French names reached out across the map to Louisiana in the south and over the Great Lakes in the west; in 1743 La Vérendrye reached the Rocky Mountains. The British, whose American colonists were hemmed in by the Alleghenies, contributed no notable names to this vast movement. Nor were they stirred by the motives that sent the French so far afield: the desire to find a water route clean across the continent, to missionize, and, finally, to develop the fur trade.

For furs were a crop for which no land had to be broken and no seeds sown. They had only to be collected; most of the trapping was done by Indians. And they fetched extravagant prices at home. The early history of Canada, apart from the settled area on the St. Lawrence, is largely a history of the fur trade.

The first rivalry from Britain came in 1670, when the Hudson's Bay Company was chartered and given a monopoly and an authority over all the land drained by rivers flowing into Hudson Bay and Hudson Strait. Soon, from an area about the size of western Europe, but mostly unexplored, Indians began to bring their furs to the Company's trading posts, like York Factory, and for nearly a century their enormous profits flowed home without serious threat, save from an occasional French military expedition.

[13]

Meanwhile, the result of wars with Louis XIV and Louis XV, which were fought in America as desperately as in Europe, was the complete substitution of British for French rule. But though the problem of conquest was over, that of government was only just beginning, for the French Canadians were persons as distinct from any others as the South African Boers and greatly outnumbered their conquerors. As a result of this their support was reckoned on when the armies of the American Revolution, in their struggle for independence from British rule, were looking about for allies. They confidently invaded Canada in 1775, taking Quebec and besieging Montreal. But the strength of the British, under Sir Guy Carleton, was greater than they had anticipated, and they had to withdraw.

Not only was this attempt at forcible union a failure, but by driving thousands of those who had no desire to see America independent to Canada they confirmed a cleavage which has remained final. The United Empire Loyalists, as these men were called, were, with their families, of the utmost value to a country overweighted with subjects of French descent and stocked by colonists of a not too worthwhile type. Many Loyalists, it is true, went home or to the West Indies, but the majority settled in Canada, where they were given cheap land and every inducement to remain and prosper. They completely transformed the character of Upper Canada (or Ontario), for though fewer of them went there than to the Maritime Provinces (Nova Scotia and New Brunswick), they filled up a country almost empty of Britons, and were of a class more suited to the stern and distressful incidents of pioneer life. The nature of the change was recognized at home by Parliament's passing of the Constitutional Act dividing the country into Upper and Lower Canada, now Quebec and Ontario.

By this time there was a ding-dong battle in the interior between rival fur traders. La Vérendrye had shown how the Hudson Bay territory could be tapped, and hardly had the French Empire in Canada fallen than speculators were on their way from Britain to Montreal to set up rival establishments. After an inedifying period of free-for-all competition, the North-West Company was formed in 1784, and rivalry between these two great concerns gradually sent traders and trading posts further and further west. For it was no longer any good waiting for Indians to bring in their furs: traders had to hasten to the source of supply, trying all the time to get in one another's rear, and moving therefore slowly across the continent.

One of the richest areas was round Lake Athabasca, and it was from here that Alexander Mackenzie, in the employ of the Montreal company, set out to explore the river which bears his name, and to reach, on another expedition, the Pacific, the first white man to cross the continent north of Mexico. When ALEXANDER HENRY came to write his diary the North-West Company had little more to fear from its rival, especially when the struggle with the short-lived but vigorous X.Y. Company (also of Montreal) had been settled by the amalgamation of 1804. Of the evils and horrors of this most successful trade Henry can speak for himself.

But there is a tragic postscript to be added to this tale of rivalry, for the land Henry described was to see a still more unnatural strife. In 1812 the Earl of Selkirk brought over a party of impoverished Highland peasants and planted them on the Red River, where he thought they might have chances of success they were denied at home. To arrange this he had to work with the Hudson's Bay Company, who held the title to the land, for the Red River ultimately, and under another name, ran into their Bay. This philanthropic scheme was interpreted as a threat to the Montreal company, who turned an army of half-breeds on the settlement, urging them to get rid of the invaders of 'their' land by any means they liked to choose. During some years of theft, plotting and murder, most of the settlers were killed or frightened away. But Selkirk always kept up the battle, sending more men and supporting them as best he could up to his death in 1820. His death, however, meant that opposition to an amalgamation between the North-West and Hudson's Bay companies came to an end, and it took place in the following year.

*   *   *

For some time Canada did not attract emigrants. There was an abortive scheme of assisted emigration in 1815, but it was quickly

[15]

whittled down to a system of free grants of land to those who
wanted to pay their own passages. There was, it is true, a constant
stream of people crossing the Atlantic, but most of them preferred
the United States, where there were openings for the skilled
worker, the town-dweller. Canada still wanted agriculturalists,
men who could chop down trees and clear the land. But from time
to time numbers of people went, either at their own expense, or
assisted by poor-law guardians, or under schemes organized by
individuals, like Selkirk's experiment or the novelist Galt's successful settlement round the town he founded at Guelph, west of
Toronto. In one way and another families arrived, and the
population of Ontario, which had been under 20,000 in 1791, rose
to 150,000 in 1824, and in twenty years more had trebled again. It
was all very unsystematic. THOMAS NEED shows, for instance, the
dangers of granting away too much low-priced land, and the consequent speculation which held up the working of the land while
it was being juggled with, from one ledger to another.

From his record and from those of FRANCES STEWART and JOHN
LANGTON we can get a very comprehensive idea of the growth of
one particular area, Peterborough Settlement in the Newcastle
district. The first parties to reach it went north from Cobourg
through forests crossed hitherto only by survey parties, round
Rice Lake and up the Otonabee River. That was in 1818. One of
the members of a party in the following year, Adam Scott, built
a mill on the banks of the Otonabee and remained until 1825 the
sole occupant, with his assistants, of the land on which the town
was to be built. Scattered along the rivers and lakes about 500
others accumulated.

But in 1825 the Government at home sent over a large party
under the charge of the Hon. Peter Robinson, chiefly from the
south of Ireland, and five times more numerous than the existing
inhabitants. Each family was given a hundred acres of land,
together with 'a cow, an axe, an auger, saw, hammer, 100 lbs
nails, cooking utensils, 5 bushels of seed potatoes and 2 gallons of
corn.' This varied provision encouraged them to build a town, and
Mrs. Stewart describes how on the arrival of the Governor, Sir
Peregrine Maitland (who disappointed her because he did not 'in

[16]

the least degree look like a person who had made an elopement'), the town was named after the leader of the emigrants. When Need and Langton arrived it was flourishing, though most of the surrounding country was still ungrazed by the cows and unbowed by the axes.

The number of emigrants to Canada was gradually increasing. The Government, in order not to lose good material to the ungrateful Americans, began to publicize the northern country, and a stream of handbooks, usually moderate and well informed, were printed to encourage and sustain the nervous passenger during his six to eight weeks on the Atlantic. The storm described by BRIDGET LACY was by no means the greatest risk she ran. Before the Statute of 1835 conditions on emigrant ships were extremely bad. Lord Durham's comment that they could be known by their smell alone at gunshot range would have rung true enough to the inhabitants of a place like, say, York (as Toronto was called before 1834), suffering from the miasmas of their own swamps as well as the infections brought by parties of newly arrived immigrants.

Still, the inhabitants could get their revenge by passing on a virus of their own, that of party strife, which was having as unfortunate effect in Upper Canada as racial antagonism in the lower province, where agitators could always make mischief between rulers and subjects. As a result Lord Durham was sent out. The upshot of his celebrated Report on the situation was an Act joining Upper and Lower Canada, and gradually establishing, not only for Canada, the principle of responsible self-government.

*   *   *

That the fur trade had never ceased to fill an important rôle in Canada's history is seen in ALEXANDER HUNTER MURRAY's account of his founding a trading post on the Yukon for the Hudson's Bay Company. If Langton's letters show how inconvenient uncertain boundary lines could be to anyone contemplating building a house, the subsequent history of Fort Yukon shows how infuriating uncertain frontier lines could be to any concern trying to set up a trading station. That the Russian rivalry he feared did not turn into open warfare was possibly due to the fact that the

s.—2   [17]

Russians were not sure whether the fort was really on their side of the frontier or not. (Alaska was not bought by America until 1867.) A survey taken in 1869 led to the reluctant vacating of the station by the Company, who founded another which later on was declared, in its turn, to be on the wrong side, when more accurate astronomical observations were taken. So a third, Rampart House, was built safely east of the line separating Alaska from the Yukon on our maps to-day.

Alexander Henry

Alexander Henry was typical of the men produced by the cut-throat competition, the constant danger from Indians, the isolation from military or legal protection, that marked the fur trade. Hard, dispassionate and observant, his diary shows that the brutal circumstances of a life of continual improvisation had not destroyed his eye for the unusual or merely delightful in the scene about him. He gives the barest record of facts, but it is a means of bringing episodes like the burnt herd of buffalo or the Tongue River massacre before us with uncomfortable clarity.

He was the nephew of a pioneer fur trader and joined the North-West Company himself about the year 1792. After sixteen years mainly in southern Manitoba, he moved west into Saskatchewan, and in 1813 was sent further yet to Astoria on the Columbia, which now forms the frontier between the States of Washington and Oregon. Here, two years later, at the river's mouth, he was drowned.

The original of the diary is lost. The text used in *The Manuscript Journals of Alexander Henry and of David Thompson, 1797–1814*, London, 1892, 2 vols., by the editor, Elliot Coues, is the 'Coventry Copy' in the library of Parliament at Ottawa. He decided to 'take what grammatical liberties with the text' he saw fit, and to condense it.

Panbian River = Pembina River.

[19]

Derouine   = To go 'en derouine' was to conduct or
                encourage trade in places other than
                recognized trading centres.
Beat meat   = Pounded meat.
Grand Wabbano = An important Indian ceremony, though
                inferior in solemnity to the 'Grand
                Medicine.'

May 17th 1801. I went up to Panbian river on horseback to find a proper spot for building. I got there at twelve o'clock, crossed Red river with Desmarais, planted my potatoes and sowed a few garden seeds on the spot where Mr. Grant's fort stood. We recrossed, and, after examining the ground, pitched on the north side of Panbian river, at the point of land between that and Red river, about 100 paces from each. The ground was so encumbered with large fallen trees, and the underwood so intricate, that we could not see ten yards before us; however, I drew out the place as soon as possible. Between this spot and the plains on the W. are great numbers of fine large oaks, very proper for building, and on the N. side, between this and a small rivulet, are plenty of fine large bois blancs, proper for flooring and covering. The stockades must be hauled from some distance below, where there are fine patches of poplar.

Aug. 22d, 1801. We arrived at the forks of the Assiniboine; sent on the canoes; took the horse myself, and, with two men, proceeded by land up the Assiniboine three leagues to the Grand Passage, where we crossed, having the water up to our saddles. Came on, and slept at the passage on Sale river.

Aug. 23d. Early we were on our horses; saw numerous herds of buffalo in the grand traverse, and at sunset reached Panbian river, where we found camped, near the fort, 55 men bearing arms —the same people we traded with last winter, with a few more Saulteurs from Red lake. Not an Assiniboine or a Cree has been here during the summer. The former are doubtful of the behaviour of the Saulteurs toward them; the latter have made several trips to the Assiniboine, and purchased a number of horses, for guns and medicines. I found the stockades erected, and our houses and stores nearly finished. My people have been alarmed the whole summer, our Indians telling them almost every day that they saw the enemy. These alerts, however, always proved to be false—merely schemes to shelter their indolence, as they have done nothing, not even providing any provisions, though buffalo have been very numerous, commonly in sight of the fort. Ten packs of furs and skins have been brought by the Indians from Red lake, etc. On the 28th my canoes and bateaux arrived. I gave the Indians a present of ten kegs of mixed liquor and as many fathoms of tobacco, for which I did not receive one penny; still, several were displeased and asked for more.

21st. Mr. J. Crébassa arrived with two canoes and ten men for the X.Y.; they build also below me; none of them dare build above me for fear of the Sioux.

25th. Sent J. B. Desmarais and five men in a canoe with 15 pieces to build at Rivière au Gratias.

Oct. 1st. My fort and buildings finished. Sent men to make hay on the E. side of Red river.

13th. Chamanau arrived from the hills, bringing his deceased wife on a travaille to be buried here. It cost me a large keg of mixed liquor, a blanket, three pots, and a quarter of a pound of vermillion to cover the corpse. A few Assiniboines, Crees, and Sonnants begin to come to our mountain house to trade.

22nd. I had a watch-house built fronting the X.Y. door; placed St. Germain and Le Duc to watch their motions. Terrible fires all over the plains. Wayquetoe's wife died of the wounds of last winter, when her husband shot her.

Oct. 27th. I sent to the Hair hills for earth to whitewash my houses, there being none near Red river. The white earth generally lies in the open plain, covered with about a foot of black soil. It is sometimes in strata a foot thick, intermixed with black soil and sand, and, again, is simply covered with the black soil, under which it is pure and white, like lime, and answers the same purpose in setting our buildings.

Nov. 1st. Snow fell about six inches in depth. I went to the mountains to meet the Stone Indians. Old Frog and his band have ten tents. I settled with them, and they made great promises to hunt well.

22nd–24th. Snow continued. Men making sleighs. The Saulteurs at the Hair hills have joined the Stone Indians, and are all camped together in idleness, singing, dancing, smoking, and trading medicine for horses.

28th. The men put up a flag-staff—an oak stick of 75 feet, without splicing. I gave them two gallons of high wine, four fathoms of tobacco, and some flour and sugar, to make merry.

30th. Men begin to use sleighs and dogs.

Friday, Jan. 1st, 1802. This morning the usual ceremony of firing, etc., was performed. I treated my people with two gallons of high wine, five fathoms of tobacco, and some flour and sugar. My neighbors came visiting, and before sunrise both sexes of all parties were intoxicated and more trouble than double their number of Saulteurs; the men were fighting and quarreling all night. Joseph St. Germain and others returned from a derouine with 200 skins, all good—the best derouine ever made from Panbian river.

3rd. People continually en derouine to Indians' tents: arrivals from and departures to the different outposts, and men hauling home meat from the hunters' tent. Buffalo near the fort: I killed two with one ball.

10th. Hunters running buffalo, with which the plains are covered;

at the fort heard them fire, and saw the cows fall; they killed 23.
The beasts were bellowing all night.

Jan. 13th. Before daybreak I set off with two men for the Assiniboine, by way of Rivière aux Gratias. Each of my men had a train
of two dogs, with my baggage and provisions, and I a train drawn
by three stout dogs. Snow very deep; my men were obliged to beat
all the way on snowshoes.

Mar. 14th. In a drinking match at the Hills yesterday, Gros Bras
in a fit of jealousy stabbed Aupusoi to death with a hand-dague;
the first stroke opened his left side, the second his belly, and the
third his breast; he never stirred, although he had a knife in his
belt, and died instantly. Soon after this Aupusoi's brother, a boy
about ten years of age, took the deceased's gun, loaded it with two
balls, and approached Gros Bras' tent. Putting the muzzle of the
gun through the door the boy fired the two balls into his breast
and killed him dead, just as he was reproaching his wife for her
affection for Aupusoi, and boasting of the revenge he had taken.
The little fellow ran into the woods and hid. Little Shell found the
old woman, Aupusoi's mother, in her tent; he instantly stabbed
her. Ondainoiache then came in, took the knife, and gave her a
second stab. Little Shell, in his turn taking the knife, gave a third
blow. In this manner did these two rascals continue to murder the
old woman, as long as there was any life in her. The boy escaped
into Langlois' house, and was kept hid until they were all sober.
Next morning a hole was dug in the ground, and all three were
buried together. This affair kept the Indians from hunting, as
Gros Bras was related to the principal hunters.

Saturday, May 1st. I set fire to the E. side of the river. We sent
our horses to graze in the plains on the W. side.

2nd. Langlois and some others came *en baggage* down Panbian
river in three skin canoes; one had upset and some property been
lost—sugar, beat meat, axes, etc. The current had drawn her
with such violence against a tree as to turn her over. The river

[23]

Indians are camping and all drinking hard—men, women, and children.

3rd. Arrived and camped four Assiniboines, with the Saulteurs—the first that have come here to trade and drink. They are very suspicious of the Saulteurs, and always on their guard with guns, bows, and arrows in their hands. The young Saulteurs would fain insult them during their drinking matches, but we prevented it.

4th. Indians all arrived. I gave them their spring presents; to some, clothing, to others large kegs of mixed liquor.

Oct. 5th. Wayquatchewine, in a drinking match, stabbed another Indian on the shoulder blade, but the knife was arrested by the bone, and the wound was not mortal. At the same time he stabbed a woman in the breast; it appears to be an ugly wound, but not very deep, as the knife went in slanting and made a great gash.

Nov. 2d. Sent trains for meat. Buffalo in abundance. I hired Le Bœuf as hunter. This man is supposed to be the best among the Saulteurs and other strong, wild animals; his name is derived from his superior capacities in hunting the buffalo. He has often, even in seasons when there is no snow, approached a herd, and then, when on his firing they ran off, chased them on foot for a long distance, loading and firing rapidly, and keeping in the thick of the herd until he killed as many as he wished. He came in to-day with a loup-cervier that he had caught in the plains in a fair chase and killed with his small ax; he certainly is an extraordinary runner. He is a tall man, spare and lean, of a mild disposition, but wicked when provoked to anger.

Nov. 24th. A day so dark that I was obliged to use a candle to write at midday. We had a heavy fall of snow and hail, with tremendous claps of thunder and lightning, which continued most of the day, and a strong N.E. wind. About 18 inches of snow fell in 12 hours. The river froze again.

Nov. 26th. One of my men, who was much in debt, offered me his services as long as he could perform any duty, on condition I would clothe him and allow him to take a woman he had fallen in love with; for himself he asked nothing but dressed leather to make a shirt, capot and trousers, all the year round, and a little tobacco. He is an able-bodied young man. This proposal did not surprise me, having seen several people as foolish as he is, who would not hesitate to sign an agreement of perpetual bondage on condition of being permitted to have a woman who struck their fancy.

Nov. 27th. We cannot stir out doors without snowshoes. Buffalo are very numerous; I shot three cows. The cold was so severe that I froze all one side of my face, which was soon an entire scab and very painful.

Dec. 25th. Buffalo passing in droves within 100 yards of the fort. My winter stock complete.

January 1st, 1803. Plagued with the ceremonies of the day—men and women drinking and fighting, pell mell.

Mar. 19th. I saw nightingales, a gull, and a hawk. We take from 30 to 50 fish daily.

25th. Heavy rain; snow all gone; wild fowl in abundance, Red river clear of ice. Water very high. Women making sugar. Very few drowned buffalo drift down this spring.

27th. The plains are covered with water from the melting of the snow so suddenly, and our men suffer much, as they are continually on the march, looking after Indians in every creek and little river. The water is commonly knee deep, in some places up to the middle, and in the morning is usually covered with ice, which makes it tedious and even dangerous travelling. Some of our best men lose the use of their legs while still in the prime of life.

30th. One of my men undertook to make a real pair of wheels on the plan of those in Canada; he finished them to-day, and they were very well done. I made him chief wheelwright, and we shall soon have some capital carts. A man gave a large stout dog a kick in the side, of which the poor beast died instantly.

Apr. 8th. Plains on fire in every direction. We began to fear the Assiniboines and Crees might steal our horses; they have seemed honest thus far, but they are all horse-thieves.

13th. Men making blockhouses to protect the fort. We pretend it is on account of the Sioux, but I apprehend much less danger from them than from the Saulteurs, who are getting numerous, and at times insolent.

14th. Men working at the new ground, and manuring the garden. Indians arriving daily and drinking the proceeds of the spring hunt.

19th. The men began to demolish our dwelling-houses, which were built of bad wood, and to build new ones of oak. The nests of mice we found, and the swarms of fleas hopping in every direction, were astonishing.

20th. Indians drinking. Le Bœuf quarreled with his wife and knocked her senseless with a club, which opened a gash on her head six inches long and down to the bone. She laid so long before she recovered her senses that I believed her dead.

May 6th. Indians arrive daily and drink continually.

7th. I planted potatoes, turnips, carrots, beets, parsnips, onions, and cabbage-stalks for seeds. Sowed cabbage seed.

12th. My beau-père desired me to take his second daughter, saying one woman was not sufficient for a chief, and that all great men should have a plurality of wives, the more the better, provided they were all of the same family. He set a striking example of this himself, as he had for wives three sisters at that time.

Jan 6th, 1804. Lagassé arrived from Rivière aux Liards with news of Mr. Cameron's death; he expired on the 3d inst. at 7 p.m. As he was sitting on a stool, he fell on his face upon the floor, and died instantly, without uttering one word.

7th. Long before day I was on the way up to Rivière aux Marais. The cold was very severe, and weather blusterous. Two of my men had their faces badly frozen. My sleigh and dogs were of no use, the cold being too severe to ride; I was obliged to walk and run to keep from freezing to death. I got there at two o'clock. On the 8th I dispatched three men with a train and six dogs for the corpse.

9th. I took an inventory of the property, both of the company and of the deceased, but found there had been some foul play and embezzlement, particularly in the wearing apparel of the deceased. I recovered all I could. I gave Cadotte charge of the place, but the establishment will turn out a heavy loss—a great quantity of goods gone, and very few packs of furs on hand. I could find no account book, either of Indian debts or the men's advances. I suspect foul play in this case, and that the book has been committed to the flames.

10th. I returned home; weather very severe. On the 12th one of my men gave a mare that cost him, G.H.V.P. currency, equal to £16 13s. 4d., Halifax currency, for one single touch at a Slave girl. Another of my men, who was out with the hunter in a leather tent last night, got up in his sleep and fell into the fire with his buttocks foremost; he is much burned, and cannot walk.

13th. I sent two men to make salt above Park river.

15th. The men arrived with the corpse on a train, wrapped in a Russia sheeting and two parchment skins. They had attempted to bring it in a coffin, but it was too broad for a train. This was a melancholy day for us all. Langlois had arrived from his place, and was just sitting down to his dinner, when the corpse was announced. What a sudden change! Only a few days ago he was

[27]

merry and cheerful, as we were riding along cracking jokes and running races, and little did he believe himself so near his end. He was a good-natured, inoffensive, zealous, and sober young man.

16th. Having got a coffin made, we buried Mr. Cameron alongside his deceased wife, attended by all the men, women, and children of the fort. His easy, affable manners had won the esteem of all.

Feb. 22d. I started Mr. Hesse and his wife for Red lake to bring down sugar and bark; with him go two men. Grande Gueule stabbed Perdrix Blanche with a knife in six places; the latter, in fighting with his wife, fell in the fire and was almost roasted, but had strength enough left, notwithstanding his wounds, to bite her nose off. He is very ill, but I don't suppose he will die.

April 1st. I went to the upper part of Tongue river to meet a band of Indians returning from hunting beaver, and fought several battles with the women to get their furs from them. It was the most disagreeable derouine I ever made; however, I got all they had, about a pack of good furs; but I was vexed at having been obliged to fight with the women. It is true it was all my neighbor's debts.

April 2d. I returned with the furs I had so well purchased. The grass begins to point out of the ground in the burned prairies. Fire in the S.W. Of my men, some are making wheels, others carts, others sawing boards and squaring timber; the smith is making nails, others sturgeon nets; some are smoking tongues; the most active and capable are gone with the Indians to hunt beaver and take care of the furs.

Sept. 21st. The war party arrived; they had been no further than Schian river and seen no Sioux.

23d. Indians daily coming in by small parties; nearly 100 men here. I gave them 15 kegs of mixed liquor, and X.Y. gave in proportion; all drinking. I quarreled with Little Shell, and dragged him out of the fort by the hair. Indians very troublesome, threatening to level my fort to the ground, and Tabashaw breeding mischief. I had two narrow escapes from being stabbed by him; once in the hall, and soon afterward in the shop. I perceived that they were bent on murdering some of us and then pillaging. I therefore desired all hands to keep on their guard, and knock down the first Indian who should be insolent. The fellows soon saw we were ready for them, and dropped away. I would not give out one drop more rum, and all was soon quiet.

Nov. 25th. I found it necessary to visit a band of Mr. Langlois' Indians, who were hunting beaver and bear in the mountain about the sources of Salt river. I set off with one man on horseback at midnight—light rain and very dark—most favourable weather to escape the X.Y., who were on the watch. At daybreak we met a band of Assiniboines going to Mr. Langlois with bear's meat, grease, etc. Plains burned in every direction and blind buffalo seen every moment wandering about. The poor beasts have all the hair singed off; even the skin in many places is shriveled up and terribly burned, and their eyes are swollen and closed fast. It was really pitiful to see them staggering about, sometimes running afoul of a large stone, at other times tumbling down hill and falling into creeks not yet frozen over. In one spot we found a whole herd lying dead. The fire having passed only yesterday these animals were still good and fresh, and many of them exceedingly fat.

Jan. 1st, 1805. An express arrived with a packet from Montreal, containing sundry circular letters informing us of the coalition which had taken place. It certainly was high time for a change on this river. The country being almost destitute of beaver and other furs, and the Indians increasing in number daily from the Red Lake and Fond du Lac country, the X.Y. had been lavish of their property, selling very cheap; and we, to keep the trade in our own hands, had been obliged to follow their example. Thus, by our obstinate proceedings, we had spoiled the Indians. Every man who killed a few skins was considered a chief and treated accordingly; there was scarcely a common buck to be seen; all wore

scarlet coats, had large kegs and flasks, and nothing was purchased by them but silver works, strouds, and blankets. Every
other article was either let go on debt and never paid for, or given
gratis on request. This kind of commerce had ruined and corrupted the natives to such a degree that there was no bearing with
their insolence; if they misbehaved at our houses and were
checked for it, our neighbors were ready to approve their
scoundrelly behavior and encourage them to mischief, even offering them protection, if they were in want of it. By this means the
most notorious villains were sure of refuge and resources. Our
servants of every grade were getting extravagant in their demands,
indolent, disaffected toward their employers, and lavish with the
property committed to their charge. I am confident that another
year could not have passed without bloodshed between ourselves
and the Saulteurs. This would certainly have caused a critical
situation, as those fellows are all so connected that to injure one
is to injure the whole. Of this I was well aware, and always avoided
pushing matters to extremities, at the same time not allowing
myself to be imposed upon.

In the month of May all the Indians were camped at our fort,
drinking and making the grand wabbano; they were as troublesome and extravagant as usual, the principal cause of which was
my neighbor. Crébassa persisted in telling them that the report
concerning the coalition was false, and that next year the X.Y.
would be stronger than ever, with double the number of canoes,
etc. In this manner he played the cheat to the last moment, when
he was obliged to send all the remainder of his property, utensils,
horses, and summer men over to my fort, on the embarkation. The
consequence of this mean dissimulation was that he got himself
despised by the natives, and in the end he had a narrow escape for
his life from Pegouisse, who certainly would have murdered him
had I not interfered.

Fifteen tents of Assiniboines followed Mr. Langlois from the
hills this spring and encamped at my fort with the Saulteurs. In
the first drinking match a murder was committed in an Assiniboine tent, but fortunately it was done by a Saulteur. L'Hiver
stabbed Mishewashence to the heart three times and killed him

[30]

instantly. The wife and children cried out, and some of my people ran to the tent just as L'Hiver came out with the bloody knife in his hand, expecting we would lay hold of him. The first person he met was William Henry, whom he attempted to stab in the breast; but Henry avoided the stroke, and returned the compliment with a blow of his cudgel on the fellow's head. This staggered him; but instantly recovering, he made another attempt to stab Henry. Foiled in this design, and observing several coming out of the fort, he took to his heels and ran into the woods like a deer. I chased him with some of my people, but he was too fleet for us. We buried the murdered man, who left a widow and five helpless orphans, having no relatives on this river. The behavior of two of the youngest was really piteous while we were burying the body; they called upon their deceased father not to leave them, but to return to the tent, and tried to prevent the men from covering the corpse with earth, screaming in a terrible manner; the mother was obliged to take them away.

May 25th. Embarked for the Forks.

22nd. Sent the brigade off, and Mr. Harrison. Went on horseback to Rivière la Souris. Made three trips to Portage la Prairie. Delayed embarking until June 9th, when I left the Forks in a light canoe, with six men, and on the 29th arrived at Kamanistiquia, after a passage of only twelve days. This was extraordinarily expeditious, and I shall always suppose that a single well-mounted canoe can make the voyage in a shorter time than several canoes together. Notwithstanding all their hurry and bustle, I overtook my brigade below the last rapids, at the storehouse; had I been an hour later, they would have got in before me.

Aug. 1st. Embarked with a fair wind, which blew a gale from the N. but kept under sail—about three feet hoisted.

2nd. In the afternoon, arrived at Panbian river, having had an extraordinary breeze all the way. This may be called a passage of 22 days from Kamanistiquia, and I believe that, with such lading, it is impossible to perform the voyage in less time.

Canada

Here I received the unwelcome news that the Sioux had fallen
upon a small camp of my Indians on Tongue river, not many miles
from the fort, on the 3rd of July, and killed and taken prisoners
14 persons—men, women, and children. My beau-père was the
first man that fell, about eight o'clock in the morning. He had
climbed a tree, to see if the buffalo were at hand, as they were
tented there to make dried provisions. He had no sooner reached
the top than two Sioux discoverers fired at the same moment, and
both balls passed through his body. He had only time to call out
to his family, who were in the tent about 100 paces from him,
'Save yourselves! the Sioux are killing us!' and fell dead to the
ground, his body striking several branches of the tree as it
dropped. The noise brought the Indians out of the tent; when,
perceiving their danger, the women and children instantly ran
through the plains toward an island of wood on Tongue river,
about a mile distant, and on a direct line toward the fort. The
men took their arms and made off also, keeping in the rear of their
women and children, whom they urged on. The four surviving
men had not gone more than a quarter of a mile when they saw the
main body of the war party on horseback rushing down upon them.
Crossing Tongue river, and in a few moments coming up with
them, the Sioux began to fire. The four men by expert manœuvres
and incessant fire prevented the enemy from closing in on them,
while the women and children continued to fly, and the men followed. They were within about 200 paces of the wood, and some
of the most active had actually entered it, when the enemy surrounded and fell upon them. Three of the Saulteurs fled in
different directions; Grand Gueule escaped before they were completely surrounded, but the other two were killed. The one who
remained to protect the women and children was a brave fellow—
Aceguemanche, or Little Chief; he waited deliberately until the
enemy came very near, when he fired at one who appeared to be
the chief, and knocked the Sioux from his horse. Three young girls
and a boy were taken prisoners; the remainder were all murdered,
and mutilated in a horrible manner. Several women and children
had escaped in the woods, where the enemy chased them on horseback; but the willows and brush were so intricate that every one

[32]

of these escaped. A boy about 12 years old, whom a Sioux pursued, crawled into a hollow under a bunch of willows, which the horsemen leaped over without perceiving him. One of the little girls who escaped tells a pitiful story of her mother, who was killed. This woman, having two young children that could not walk fast enough, had taken one of them on her back and prevailed upon her sister-in-law to carry the other. But when they got near the woods and the enemy rushed upon them with hideous yells and war whoops, the young woman was so frightened that she threw down the child, and soon overtook the mother; who, observing that the child was missing, and hearing its screams, kissed her little daughter—the one who relates the story—saying, with tears streaming from her eyes: 'Take courage, my daughter! try to reach the woods—and if you do, go to your eldest sister, who will be kind to you; I must turn back and recover your youngest sister, or die in the attempt—take courage—run fast, my daughter!' Poor woman! she actually did recover her child, and was running off with both children, when she was felled to the ground by a blow on the head with a war club. She recovered instantly, drew her knife, and plunged it into the neck of her murderer; but others coming up, she was despatched. Thus my belle-mère ended her days.

The surviving man having reached the fort, my people went out the next day to the field of battle, where a horrible spectacle was presented. My beau-père's head was severed from his body even with the shoulders, his right arm and left foot were cut off, his right leg from the knee stripped of the skin, and all carried off. In the plain lay the bodies of the women and children, within a few yards of one another, and the remains of Aceguemanche, he who had fought so bravely, lay near his wife and children. The enemy had raised his scalp, cut the flesh from the bone, and taken away the skull for a water dish; his limbs were severed from his body, and only the trunk remained, with the belly and breast ripped up and thrown over the face; his private parts had been cut off and crammed into his dead wife's mouth. She was also butchered in a shocking manner and her children were dismembered and thrown in different directions. All the bodies were stuck full of

s.—3 [33]

arrows, and there were found also many old knives, two or three broken guns, some war clubs, broken bones, etc. The bodies of the other men were found at the entrance of the woods, butchered in the same shocking manner. There was a spot of ground in the long grass near the remains of Aceguemanche, where it was plain to be seen that a person had fallen from his horse and lay bleeding for some time, but the body of this Sioux could not be found.

On my return all was grief and lamentation; and at sight of me it broke out afresh with such sobs and cries that I almost wished I had not been so expeditious on my voyage. The Saulteurs were assembled, preparing for war and only waiting for the Assiniboines and Crees to join them; a number of Saulteurs are also awaiting them above this place; they will form a party of about 300 men, mostly mounted. I gave them a nine-gallon keg of gunpowder and 100 pounds of balls, to encourage them to revenge the death of my beau-père and his family. At this they said among themselves that I had 'almost as much sense as an Indian'; and if I had added a few kegs of rum I should have been considered fully as wise as themselves. This manner of comparing a white man to an Indian is the highest compliment they can pay. Let no white man be so vain as to believe that an Indian really esteems him or supposes him to be their equal. No—they despise us in their hearts, and all their outward professions of respect and friendship proceed merely from the necessity under which they labor of having intercourse with us to procure their necessaries.

On the day after my arrival, I went out with Mr. Langlois to view the field of battle, and collected the bones in a heap. My beau-père was the only one buried; his body, having laid in the shade, was not in such a state of corruption as those in the plain, exposed to the hot sun. When my people first came here they could not approach the bodies to inter them. The wolves and craws, therefore, answered that purpose. I gathered up the remaining bones of my belle-mère in a handkerchief. We followed the Sioux road until we came to the place where they had stopped to divide the spoils, put on new shoes, and prepare for flight. We found the camp very extensive, and by the number of small painted sticks, such as they generally leave behind after a fight, we judged the party to have consisted of about 300 men, with a great many horses. Many old, worn-out shoes were lying about.

Apr. 5th. My man finished two new carts and made a wheel-barrow.

11th. The North West Annual Winter Express arrived from Athabasca. L'Hiver hamstrung his young wife to prevent her gossiping about; the rascal cut the tendons on both heels, and made several gashes across the wrist, while she attempted to defend herself.

12th. Express off for Leech lake, with William Henry and four men. Men making blockhouses.

13th. Dreadful snowstorm.

23rd. Ice broke up in Red river.

14th. One of the H.B. boats off; sent one of my boats also, with the first trip of 122 bags of pemmican. I sowed three quarts of oats.

23d. William Henry arrived from Leech lake, with a cargo of sugar. Indians all camped. Pishaubey arrived with Washegamoish-cam in two wooden canoes from Pelican river, with 300 beavers and 40 prime otters. They had seen Sioux repeatedly, but always avoided them.

26th. Assiniboines arrived and camped.

28th. Red Lake Indians arrived—Grand Noir and his son-in-law, the scoundrel who killed one of our men last spring, at Red lake—an American named Hughes. The Indian came on purpose to kill George Simpson, who was in charge. Hughes, who was standing by the door, saw that the Indian was inclined to do mischief. He therefore caught up a tent pole and gave the fellow a blow on the head, which staggered him; but the Indian, on recovering himself, shot Hughes dead. This was the second affair of its kind at this place, two years in succession; in each, an Indian intended to kill the master, but the blow fell upon another man. Grand Noir brought a paqueton of beavers, to induce me to show charity to his son-in-law. All the principal men in camp came with him, but the murderer was not to be found. I kicked the skins out of the house and would listen to none of their speeches, telling them that if I could see the murderer he would be a dead man, and that no number of skins could pay for the blood of one of our murdered servants.

This day I sent off my boats and canoes for the Forks, so heavily loaded they could scarcely swim.

Frances Stewart

Frances Stewart's father, the Reverend Francis Browne, 'was a man of refined tastes and had prepared several works for the press, which, however, were never published.' He died in 1796 when she was two, and the next literary influence that came her way was one that shone, and in print, in no such uncertain fashion. In the care of her great-uncle, she used to spend a good deal of time as a child at Edgeworthstown, and used to act there in the plays which her cousin, Maria Edgeworth, used to write for birthday occasions. And when the cousins grew up, the author of *Castle Rackrent* never lost touch with Frances, as she gratefully acknowledges.

In 1816 she married, and Maria wrote: 'I can congratulate Mr. Stewart more upon your having such a temper as you possess than I would if you had brought him ten thousand a year.'

The six years that followed were pleasant and uneventful, save for the regular arrival of children. She played the piano, sewed, and read so much that her friends were concerned for her eyesight. These same friends called her 'docile' and 'reasonable' in their letters. Certainly there was nothing in this existence that could have stood her in good stead, one would have thought, for the hardships of pioneer life. Save, perhaps, that we get a hint in an early letter from her mother: 'Your fame, dear Fanny, is spread far and near as a child that can bear a good deal of pain with firmness and temper.'

[37]

The need for these qualities arrived in 1822, when Thomas Stewart (referred to as T. in his wife's letters) failed in business together with his brother-in-law and partner, Mr. Reid. Both men decided to emigrate with their families in the hope of rebuilding their fortunes, and on June 1st left Belfast for Quebec on a ship, the *George*, which was sunk, like many another emigrant ship, on the passage home.

What followed is told movingly enough in Frances' own words, and her complaints, the lack of a church, the inability to escape to her books from the 'everlasting, always-increasing piles of needlework,' make her fortitude the more sympathetic, as does the little vanity she shows on the occasion of the Governor's visit.

Only one of her children died, the Elizabeth whose end is described here. She herself lived to a good age among the numerous offspring of the surviving ten.

The text is in *Our Forest Home, being Extracts from the Correspondence of the late Frances Stewart*, Montreal, 1889, edited by E. S. Dunlop.

A.M. = Her eldest daughter, Anna Maria, b. 1817.
Ellie = Her daughter Eleanor, b. 1819.
Sir Peregrine Maitland was Lieut.-Governor of Upper Canada 1818–1828, being succeeded by Sir John Colborne.

August 8th 1822. On Thursday night about eleven o'clock we reached Kingston; it was so late we could not find any house open to procure lodging, so we spread our matresses on the top of our chests, wrapped ourselves in blankets, and slept in the boats; and although the dew was so heavy that our pillows were perfectly wet except just where our heads had been, none of us took cold. What reasons we have to be grateful, for nothing but prosperity has attended us since we entered this country.

The town or village of York looked pretty from the lake as we sailed up in a schooner, but on our landing we found it not a pleasant place, as it is sunk down in a little amphitheatre cut out of the great bleak forest. The lake in front is full of rushes which have been cut and left to decay in the shallow water, causing it to be very unhealthy. It is not a healthy town (fever and ague are common), and it is said to be much fallen off within the last two years; a deadness hangs over everything. Kingston is much preferred as a place of residence. We were advised to apply for a grant of land instead of purchasing a farm; a petition therefore was laid before the Executive Council asking for twelve hundred acres for each of the gentlemen. It was read at the Council and the next day Mr. Stewart received this satisfactory reply: 'Colonel Foster to-day called upon Major Hilliar, secretary to Gen. Maitland, your business being the subject of conversation, Major Hilliar said that the Governor was so anxious to give you every advantage that he would, without reserve, grant everything you may ask within the bounds of reason.' This is great encouragement. Besides the land we were given permission to chose the situation in any part of the Province we please, and the Township of Douro was advised, as an unbroken place, to draw our large grant.

Feb. 10, 1823. The time has now come to remove to Douro. Mr. Bethune has provided us with teams; we feel much parting with our kind friends. We are taking one maid and one man-servant with us.

[Later]. Our journey lay through the townships of Hope, Cavan, and Monaghan, at this time thinly settled; starting as early as we could we made but little progress the first day. On the second we travelled nine miles without seeing a house or clearing. This day the horses were urged on and at ten-o'clock on the evening of the 12th we arrived at Scott's Mill; the only house on the plains. The Little Lake which we were to cross was frozen over, but not being considered safe yet for teams we were obliged to walk across, our children and baggage being carried by our servants and some men who kindly assisted. Our friends had sent an ox-sleigh to the edge of the lake to meet us.

The snow was about two feet deep, and late in the night when we were in the dark forests it began to snow again. The progress was much more difficult than I ever expected; the sleigh, being heavily loaded I was obliged to walk. Our lantern, unfortunately,

became filled with snow and the candle so wet that it could not be
re-lit with the tinder box. At last a light appeared and we soon
reached our log house. The light proceeded from a large wood-
fire which rejoiced our hearts. We found our house in a very unfinished state; the door had not yet been hung nor any partitions
erected. Where the chimney was to be was a large opening in the
roof; the intense frost had stopped the mason-work when about
half completed. Finding things thus rather puzzled us, not knowing where to lay our children at this late hour of a weary day, the
floor being coated with ice and mortar. However we soon discovered some shavings in a corner, these we spread on the ice, on
them laid our mattresses and cheerfully and thankfully lay down
to rest after a supper of tea, bread and butter, and pork. Being
very weary we slept soundly and on waking up in the morning
I saw the stars looking down through the aperture left for the
chimney.

April 5th. We are better pleased with our new estate here. The
buds are all swelling now and of late I have heard one or two new
birds, but they remain so high up in the trees that I have not been
able to see what they are like. I have not heard a *singing* bird yet;
they have either a wild whistling sort of note, or else a mere
chirp.

We have numbers of dear little tom-tits and a few sparrows and
crows; these I used to despise at home, here I delight in them for
they are like old acquaintances. I have been surprised at the nice
green herbage that is under the snow wherever it has been deep
enough to preserve the plants from the frost. A.M. every day
fetches me handfuls of little plants. They are almost all new to me
and I am very impatient for the appearance of their flowers.

There are several beautiful lichens and mosses besides some
pretty ferns. The depth of snow has delayed us very much in clearing our land, but next week we are to have five men to cut down
trees. 'Choppers' they are called here. It is quite a sublime sight
when a great hemlock nearly a hundred feet in height begins to
shake its dark head, then to fall, slowly at first, then as it comes
lower increasing in rapidity, tearing branches off its neighbours

[40]

and shaking all the trees around; coming down at last with such a crash that the whole forest re-echoes the sound.

I should have liked very much to have been here at the building of our houses because they are larger than log-houses usually are, and the logs are very large. Those which form the foundation are of cedar which is a very heavy and lasting wood, and will, I think, keep it perfectly firm and steady as long as we shall want it. In a few years T. intends to build a good stone house for we have plenty of excellent lime-stone on our land. T. is going to manufacture potash; the process is simple and as it sells well he thinks it will pay the expense of clearing the land. One must pay high for labour. The common wages for a chopper are twelve dollars a month.

We have no great variety in our food as pease-soup and boiled pork make our dinner every day. We have no potatoes yet, as all we can procure are left for planting. At first it seemed odd to dine without them, but boiled pease, pea-soup, bread and sometimes turnips do very well. We have excellent bread, and in this respect are much better off than many people at first setting up in the woods, for I have heard of two or three families in our own class, who, for the first six months had no food of any kind except salt pork for breakfast, dinner and tea, without even bread. We have excellent milk, and plenty of it.

But with all this interest and pleasure we have one great want here, that of a church. It is dreadful to be without a place of worship.

There is a most skilful doctor who lives about fourteen miles off. He visits every family in the neighbourhood once a fortnight, and appoints places where he can receive messages. Our names are down on his list; every one he visits in this manner pays him *three dollars a year*! He is a Scotchman, young but clever.

May 7th. The house is still in a very unfinished state. The boards for flooring were laid down in their rough state to season so that they are now quite loose; and, from the heat of the fire in the winter and that of the sun now they have separated from each other, in some places an inch. But they are not to be laid properly

[41]

until our cellar is made in the autumn; there is to be a well in the cellar too.

When this is done we will paper and carpet our little sitting room which at present serves as our bedroom.

We breakfast at seven, dine at noon, have tea at eight and to bed at ten or eleven. On Sundays we are always an hour earlier and have prayers in the kitchen morning and evening.

May 23rd. My last letter was despatched on 11th April, since which time nothing very remarkable has occurred in our colony except that Mr. Reid went to York to complete the business of our grant which could not be done until this township was surveyed. The survey was only finished about three weeks ago, when, one very wet day I saw two men walk past my window; one had a blanket about his shoulders, a pair of snowshoes in his hands and a small fur cap on. The other was dressed in ragged sailor's clothes. I took the foremost for an Indian as they generally wear blankets about them but to our surprise we found this was Mr. Birdsall, a very smart young Englishman who is the surveyor of the township in this district, and his assistant; they had five other men with them as chain-bearers etc. I found that they had all been living in the woods for the months of March and April which accounted for the ragged and weatherbeaten appearance of the whole party. After another week's work the survey was finished and then it became necessary for one of our gentlemen to go to York to protect our claims and secure our acres. The roads were in such a state that no waggon could go.

Mr. Reid therefore went on foot from here to Cobourg where, as the ice prevented any boating, he hired a horse and rode to York accompanied by Squire Burnham.

June. My time is very completely filled up here so that I never feel the want of visitors, though I do not like giving up society too much. I have numberless things to attend to and a great and never ending store of needlework going on, but I make a little time every day for reading that my mind may be employed while my fingers are the same. I often wish for a pianoforte; in the evenings I have some spare time and I often look over my old music books now piled in a corner; but I hope in a few years I shall be able to have this delightful amusement again.

T. works very hard. He is up at a little past five, comes in to breakfast at seven, works again till twelve when we dine, afterwards he rests till about two, then works again till about eight o'clock when I summon him to tea or coffee. He sometimes wonders at how much he can do; he says he has not felt so strong since he was first lame. Indeed we have great reason for gratitude to God, for we are all remarkably healthy. We are very cheerful too though I cannot say that much 'merriment' has crept into our circle yet. T. has made one deal table, three stools, and a rough sort of bedstead. I shall feel very grand when we can get a dozen chairs.

July. This place is so lonely that in spite of all my efforts to keep them off, clouds of dismal thoughts fly and lower over me. I have not seen a woman except those in our party for over five months, and only three times any one in the shape of a companion.

Our friend Mr. Faulkner paid us one visit and I am in hopes of seeing him again. He is a very pleasing, agreeable, well informed man, whose conversation improves as well as pleases. But alas! till sleighing comes we cannot hope to see this friend or anyone, for we have no roads fit for waggons, and boating is too tedious for the ladies of this housekeeping country.

August. We observe the holy day in the following manner:—The Reids come about eleven in the morning, T—— reads the lessons for the day and Mr. R. the prayers. Bad weather never prevents as many of them as can do so coming.

T——'s health is very good. At the beginning of the summer I was very thin and weak from the heat. My occupations in this country are not of a kind to interest the *mind*, and, alas for my perverseness, I am fonder than ever before of reading—the greatest indulgence I can give myself is to devote half an hour to a book or writing home. There are so many calls on my time—the superintending of the household, the care of the three children, and the everlasting, always-increasing piles of needlework. This last I

[43]

sometimes think I can never hope to get through; a year of wear and tear and no shops from which to procure anything obliges me to plan most carefully.

Early in the spring the land in front of the log house was cleared as much as possible to make room for a flower and vegetable garden. T—— had hired some Highlanders who had settled in the township of Otonabee to do the work of chopping, piling wood into heaps, and burning. It was all a hurried time; however, we have some good potatoes, turnips, and oats to repay us. All grow well on the new ground. My flowers are very fine; holly-hocks grown from seed I brought with me; mignonette which fills the air with sweetness; a grove of fine bright sunflowers; and scarlet-runners at one side of the house. I assure you it looks quite gay. The river in front of the house is most beautiful and so swift, too much so to allow of fishing, but further up in the eddies we catch excellent bass. The Indians, coming in their canoes, bring also fish and venison which they exchange for pork or flour. Our workmen shoot numbers of partridges which, unaccustomed to any disturbance, come quite close to them when at their work. Wild ducks are also plentiful from the same reason.

[Her daughter Bessy contracts dysentery.]

I was quite ignorant of the treatment of this disease and there was no doctor within reach, the nearest, Dr. Hutchison, living eighteen miles away in Cavan. We had as yet no canoes on the river and were dependent upon a chance visit of the Indians for a passage to the other side; but now in our deep need our faithful Highlander Donald, seeing how very ill our darling was, volunteered to swim the rapid stream and walk through the woods to the doctor, saying that if I wrote the particulars he would bring the necessary medicine. He started early in the morning of a cold October day and returned about midnight with some powder and a message that the doctor would come the following day. I gave the medicine but no improvement followed; the day passed in great anxiety for Dr. H. did not come. But to our relief on the third day he arrived; he left home at the time appointed but lost his way in the woods for some time, hence the delay. When he saw our darling she was sleeping; he left medicine but would not have her disturbed, giving us hope of a turn for the better. The next day she appeared more lively but would not eat the arrowroot or sago which I prepared for her. She cried for *bread*, and of this we had none, not having been able to procure flour for some time for any money. It was a bitter trial, not having the thing for which she seemed to crave. The next day she fell into a stupor and about midnight the little angel spirit passed away to the immortal land. It pleased the Almighty to call our beloved child to Himself. Oh, gracious and almighty Father grant me thy grace to resign my darling infant to Thee. Thou gavest and Thou hast seen fit to take her. Oh God, thy will be done. Let not my turbulent heart rise, for Thou knowest best what is merciful. 'Ye have sorrowed *now*, but I will see you again and your heart shall rejoice and your joy no man taketh from you.' What comfort in these words.

May 1824. The Reids and ourselves are still the only European inhabitants of this township. All behind us are wild forests untracked by civilized feet hitherto, except for the surveyors who were here last spring; but I understand that a tide of settlers is to set in next autumn. Being so far back as we are has great disadvantages and we have felt many of them. The want of a place of worship and a clergyman is the greatest.

Our poor child is still unbaptized. If I could leave home I would take her to Cobourg but that is impossible just now.

I am still without a maid. For some time Mrs. Reid lent me one of her daughters but they are all required at home now so that for three weeks I have been working away at everything my own self. But these are hardships to which every new settler is liable and we are under the care of that great and good God who is able to support us under every trial. His arm has kept us from sinking. Do not call it heroism, my dear partial friends; it is not our merit indeed, for we are weak in ourselves.

This winter we have gone through what at home would have half killed us. We were nearly five months without a drop of milk. The children living on salt meat and potatoes for dinner; their breakfast and supper being very weak tea and bread. Sometimes I give them boiled rice or barley, but not very often. I drink nothing but tea for I cannot touch 'punch' which is our only other beverage.

Now I am doing work to which I never was accustomed; cooking, washing, nursing, house-cleaning, etc., and I am able for all.

During all this time the children have continued fat, strong, and healthy. I am very awkward about some parts of the housework so that at times I find myself very much hurried, yet it is not nearly so hard as I expected, nor have I suffered in any way from it.

We have never seen a bear here, though four were tracked in our neighbourhood last winter, and wolves are, I am sorry to say, coming about us. Last week they ate up Mr. Reid's two sheep and a lamb. They committed this depredation quite close to his house. A sad loss.

July. There are two or three things for which I do long. I do not mention the hope of being again with you all, for that is of course my most ardent wish and prayer, perhaps too much so. But I allude to lesser things. I do long to have the house a little more comfortable and convenient and to be able to pursue the former occupations and amusements to which my heart still clings, and to which I wish to draw the tastes of my little A.M. and Ellie. I long for a nice garden and the smile of roses and primroses, and oh, for the green hedges and fields of my own native land! It is now three years since I saw a red rose. One day two years ago when we were some leagues from Quebec, T—— went ashore and got me some white ones. But how very childish I am to indulge in these humours. I have great reason to be happy so why regret these little pleasures?

I must return to a subject which constantly occupies both our thoughts and conversations—Maria Edgeworth's great kindness. It is so good of her when she is in constant intercourse with remarkable people, brilliant from talent, or fashion, or rank, to think so much of me living in the backwoods of Canada in the most remote place. I can never express how T—— and I feel towards her.

Our crops look well except the pumpkins and melons which have failed. There are many uses made of the pumpkin in this country. It is excellent food for cattle. It makes very good pies when boiled and mixed with eggs, milk, etc., and many people make molasses from it; to do this it is cut into pieces, boiled till pulpy, then the juice is pressed out and boiled till it is thick and dark coloured like treacle; it tastes rather *acid* and rather *sweet*; I think it very bad. The Americans call it 'Punkin Sass.' We have a great deal of maple molasses which is very nice.

Dr. Hutchison was here some time ago and told me that Mr. Sheppard of Quebec, who is going to publish a 'Canadian Flora,' wrote to ask him to request 'Mrs. Stewart of Douro' to lend him her countenance and assistance, to feel interested in his work, and to endeavour to procure him specimens. I should be very glad to do so had I time.

December 1825. I often think how much greater happiness it would be to return home, than it is to live as we do here in a never-ending scene of bustle, turmoil and hard work. Now but three years are over and though we have a fine, wide, light opening in the woods, ten acres of promising wheat under the snow, plenty of land ready for crops, and the stock increasing, yet there is a degree of anxiety and wearying hurry for ever, which prevents inside comfort. Hiring men to do the work Mr. Stewart cannot do himself obliges us to do without many comforts, such as furniture, etc., but you know the old saying that 'When things come to the worst they must mend.' The arrival of the poor immigrants from Ireland has given us some variety. They are encamped on 'The Plains,' a place about two and a half miles off. Their huts look very odd, being made with poles standing up and interwoven with boughs or branches of trees, with mud plastered over all. They live in these till log shanties are ready for their families in Douro. These huts already cause 'The Plains' to be called a village. The emigrants are under the care of Mr. P. Robinson, a native of this country, very pleasing and gentleman-like, of good property, and a member of Parliament. He is a great acquisition to us, he and Mr. Stewart are always together. The poor emigrants have suffered much, and many have died. They are principally Roman Catholics. A priest also lives here. There seems to be a total want of religion, I feel unhappy about it, the awful consideration of how they plan and scheme for this world without thinking that we may be called away at a moment's warning appals me.

1826. [No month] On Saturday last the Governor and his suite arrived. T—— and Dr. Reade were very busy making preparations for his reception and accommodation. All the immigrants were desired to assemble at the village to welcome His Excellency. After dinner all the men and boys of this house set out, though it was a very cold, windy, snowy day, so bad that I said Sir Peregrine would not come, but T—— was sure that he would, because he never travelled on Sunday. T—— took his bugle with him to sound when he first came in sight to give notice of his arrival. It was growing dark, and he had actually set out on his way home, when a gentleman said that the grand party was advancing, so back T—— went and sounded his bugle. The immigrants formed a line on each side of the road for a quarter of a mile, and as soon as his sleigh came in sight ten men took off the horses, fastened basswood ropes on and drew him to Government House where a great fire was blazing to welcome them. . . . He had a large party with him—five sleighs. All seemed very pleased and gratified— Sir Peregrine very much so, and Mr. Robinson and his brother, the Attorney-General, particularly so. T—— says Mr. Robinson shook his hand almost off and expressed strongly his approbation of all the arrangements. Sir Peregrine settled that he would go to the Cavan Church the next day. So T—— went off immediately after breakfast intending to get a place in one of the sleighs. I thought no more about them and set myself down to my own reading, when, after some time, a note was brought from T—— saying that the Governor requested I would dine there and that he would send his own sleigh for me, William and his nurse. You know to this I could send no refusal. A little while later T—— came home, he came for me. The Governor's sleigh had broken down and could not come; but he had borrowed another.

You may imagine what a fine fuss this put me into. How should

I dress myself? That was my first thought. I knew none of the company would expect me to be fine, living as we do here, so I thought I had better put on whatever would take the shortest time. T——'s opinion on the very important subject of dress was a great comfort to me. We soon agreed that a very pretty Irish tabinet which I had never yet worn would be the best. In a short time, all my curlings, etc. having been completed, we set out. We went first to Dr. Reade's, as we were going together. After a little time up drove Mr. and Mrs. Rubidge. We all laughed and talked for an hour when the gentlemen agreed to let us have quiet possession of the parlour to adorn ourselves. They went to the Doctor's medicine shop, and we ladies spent one good hour in dressing our beautiful persons. I had but little show in the business as I had only my head to dress. Mrs. Rubidge and Mrs. Reade went without caps. Mrs. Reade had a large wreath of artificial flowers in her hair and wore a brilliant geranium coloured tabinet which did not suit her. Mrs. Rubidge had on a white striped gauze trimmed with pink satin. When we set out T—— and Mrs. Reade, Dr. Reade and Mrs. Rubidge, Mr. Rubidge and myself all walked, and in the same routine entered the drawing-room of the Government House, which is nearly opposite to Dr. Reade's. You must know that all these houses which sound so grand are merely log houses and little better than the cabins are at home.

Sir Peregrine Maitland is not at all a striking looking person; he has nothing military in his appearance or deportment, nor does he in the least degree look like a person who had made an elopement. He is remarkably quiet and retiring in manner, his countenance sweet and placid, but too calm and composed for a general. In his appearance he is much more like a clergyman than an officer, but is very pleasing. He talked to me a good deal both before and after dinner as he thought proper that I should take precedence, and consequently I sat between him and Mr. Robinson. He talked about the country and the immigrants, and then a good deal about planting and gardening, giving me some good, useful hints about transplanting young trees. After tea he retired to write letters, and we repaired to Dr. Reade's little *hotel d'amitié*, where we were all to bundle in, at least a great many of us. Mr. and Mrs. Rubidge slept in the parlour. Mrs. Reade, her two little girls, Willy and I, five precious souls, all slept together in a tiny room divided by a little board partition from the parlour. There was no door, so that the partition was only a screen. Dr. Reade, T——, and Father Crowley all slept on the floor of the little shop. The next morning after breakfast we returned home.

Bridget Lacy

These two letters are the only ones in this book of which the authenticity is in any doubt. They occur in a collection of Canadian letters written home by relatives and friends of the editor, the Reverend T. Radcliff, who has a footnote: 'The name of this correspondent is the only fictitious one introduced. The facts, however, are correct.'

Thirteen members of Radcliff's family went to Canada in the spring of 1832 and one of them, his son William, took 'Bridget Lacy' as servant and nurse. After the stormy passage described, with its 'groaning, and raching, and willy wombling,' they arrived safely and on July 23rd 'were fortunate enough to procure *the only* private lodging in York!—furnished, and comfortable, for one pound a week' (Mrs. Wm. Radcliff).

Bridget's master bought 400 acres at 10*s.* in the Huron Tract, Adelaide township, and on his wife's recovering her health went to live on his land. The Radcliffs were the first to build in this township, and their wives and servants the first white women to visit it.

So much can be deduced from other letters in the collection. What happened afterwards I do not know. Nor do I know why Radcliff senior introduced a fictitious name, but I suspect that it was because he was unable to resist making a few judicious alterations to heighten the comic effect of letters that no doubt already contained much that was 'beyand the beyands (as the saying is).'

Canada

Text in *Letters from Upper Canada*, edited by the Rev. T. Radcliff and published in Dublin, 1833.

To Mary Thompson, Ireland.

York, Upper Canada, August 1832

Dear fellow Servant, and fellow school-fellow,

For we were educated together, and printiced out together—and my blessing on the Committee of fifteen, and my blessing on them that taught us to read and write, and spell, that you may know all about me, and I about you, though there are rivers, and seas, and woods, and lakes between us—and my blessing on the mistress that taught us to work, and wash, and make ourselves useful, so that while health stands by us, we may earn honest bread in any country. And sure enough, dear Mary, you shall hear all the good and bad that happens me, and I hope to have the same from you.

And now that I am on land, it is only good natured that I should give you some account of my doings since I set out.

If I had you with me, I would have been easier in my mind; but still my mistress was very good, and I got on bearably, barring the shocking sickness, such as no one in the cholic, or the breeding way, or after hippo, or after squills, ever felt before or since.

If you were only to have seen how smooth we floated down the River, and out of the Bay, and away to Wicklow, where I was born, at the back of the murrough, near Tinnakilly, you would have said, away you go—eating, and drinking, and laughing, and cracking jokes; but my jewel, before the second day was over, we were all knocked of a heap; and then if you were to hear all around you as I did, groaning, and raching, and willy wombling, and calling for water, and nobody to bring them a sup, and wishing themselves at the bottom of the sea; in troth, Mary, you would have pitied a dog in the same taking. The hold was full of people, mighty snug and decent, with money in their pockets, going out to make their fortunes; and most of them Protestants, that found home growing too hot for them; and that they had better save their four bones,

[52]

and their little earnings before it was too late, and sure enough, I believe they're right. There are mighty good people among them, and mighty pretty girls, that when they arn't sick, sing psalms in the evening, very beautiful; and there's one Jenny Ferguson, from the north, that I am very thick with, and she has a voice like an angel. In troth there are none of them bad, and its mighty sweet upon the sea.

Well, my dear, when the singing is over, they're all very merry; and there are some gay lads, and great fun, and a little courting, but all in a civil way; and I sometimes make one; and between you and I, Mary, but don't say a word at all at all, I think there's a servant-boy of a Mr. Jackson's, one Benson, that's throwing a sheep's eye at me—but nothing *certain*, barring a sly pinch here and there, and other tinder tokens that may end in smoak after all.

They say a girl will soon get a husband in this country. Some will, and some will not. I'd be sorry to be trusting to them.

The boy I have told you of, may be settled near us, and if he is as sweet upon me then, as he is now, he may put some of their noses out of joint. To say the honest truth, I would not like to be beholden to them; though they say they're civil enough in Canada, not all as one as in the States, where they have the impudence of Old Nick, in making free with their betters.

You would not believe, dear Mary, the forwardness of them Yankees.

Sure, I heard a gentleman, after coming from Philadelfy, in the United States, telling my mistress of there going some journey there in a cart, and the horses tiring and stopping to sleep at a farmers, and when he had got into bed, and was falling asleep, was roused by one over him, saying, 'I guess I tumble in here,' when the greasy carter that drove him, stretched his ugly carcass along-side him, and began to snore in three minutes. Now think of that Mary. If it was my case, not a pin in my pincushion but he should have the full binifit of, the impudent mohawk.

That's liberty and quality as they call it—a nice bed-fellow indeed—instead of his own pretty wife, who was put to sleep with the young woman of the house, to make room for this scurvy Gee-ho-dobbin.

[53]

The only accidence we had on the voyage was an old woman that died, and a child born in the hold, and a little girl choaked with a potatoe, and two doctors on board—but no blame to them—they weren't called till all was over—and the Captain, long life to him, put the old woman decent in a coffin, saying that the sherks should have a mouthful of sawdust before they got at her old bones.

Oh! but I had like to forget the chief sport. Sure we had a boxing match, Mary, which I must tell you of, by and by. But what banged all was the storm. That was what was near settling us for life. Oh! Mary, Mary, it was tremenduous—but I can only tell you the beginning of it.

Now, Mary dear, how will I describe it to you?

Do you remember when we were little girls in the school—and the carpenters working in the yard, and a great long board, and we and the other girls playing weighdy bucketdy, and we going up in the air and down again to the ground. Well then, there's the way it began, but in troth, my dear, it was only a beginning—for before you could thread a needle, up went my heels as straight as a ladder, and then down again, that though I was lying on the broad of my back, I thought I was standing on my two feet on the bottom of the sea.

Then came on the whillaloo from above, and the cracking of masts and ropes, and dear knows what—and off I dropped in a swoon, I suppose, for I never saw or heard any thing more till all the danger was over.

I just remember calling out oh, my jewell, take the child—and when first I opened my eyes, what should I see, but my own little darling, Miss Mary, tied in her own mahogany chair, and that same tied to the bed, and the little dear laughing heartily; and no wonder, Mary, for you'd have laughed yourself, as I did, and couldn't help it, when, with a toss of the ship, we saw every thing big and little, mugs, jugs, and porringers, &c. all hunting each other about the floor.

Well, well, well,—I believe this letter will never end; so that I'll say nothing about the journey from Quebec to York, only that it was mighty pretty; and beautiful steam-boats, and rumbling

coaches, and bad inns, and fine rivers, and plenty of trees; and
here we are at York, and here we have been for a month, living as
bad as in a cholera hospital, for the whole town was nothing else;
and every day, every day, we never thought we would get over the
next night safe. But we could not run away, for my mistress was
brought to bed of a little girl, as fine a creature as ever you see.
But we are all well now; and when my master comes back from the
waterfall of Niggeraga, (the say they were all Niggers here once,)
we are to set out for the estate he has bought in the Huron Tract;
and whatever comes across me there, Mary, you shall know the
particulars of it, as it may be a temptation for you to come out
yourself next year, with your own black eyes, to throw yourself in
the way of the same good fortune. They say no girl, barring she is
old and ugly, will stand two months.

My Mistress says an officer will take this free, with her own.

So dear Mary no more (and I'm sure no more would be agreeable,) at present, from your loving schoolfellow,

and friend,
Bridget Lacy.

To the Same.

Addalad, Dec. 1832.

My dear Mary,

We are at our journey's end at last. I hope you got my letter
from York town; I have a great deal to say, and but little time to
say it in, as Mr. G. is going back to York, and will carry this, and
send it free too, from that, if he can.

It's I that would be long sorry to put you to charges for my
foolish prate;—and send your's Mary, to the old master, and I'll
get it by some one comming out.

For to go for to tell you all we had to bear since I wrote last,
would take a choir, and in troth I've no great time on hand, for
sure enough, dear Mary, I have *changed my situation* since I came
here. Now I know what you'll say—aye do I—as well as if I was at
the inside of you:—'Oh ho! I knew what the tinder whisper and
the loving pinches aboord the ship would come to—and I wish you
joy, *Mrs. Bridget Benson.*'

[55]

Troth then, my dear, your'e out in your guess—for it's no such thing, but *who knows?* Would you believe it, *he's* living within four miles of me at Bear's Creek, and comes over to church of a Sunday, and to see me, and to eat a bit before he goes; and now Mary *the butter is coming out of the stirrabout,* being that my *change of situation* is nothing more or less than my change from childeren's maid to *cook,* and a happy change too, Mary, for instead of that poor streeleen thing I was, leaving home, I am now growing plump and fat, and well to look at—and so Benson tells me, and that I look better and better every time he comes over; and Mary, dear, there's a wide differ betune the nursery and the kitchen—and isn't it a great thing to be able to give a friend, and *such a friend,* a savoury toothful, when he's so oblidgeing as to go for to come so far to see you, and he a fine young lad that hasn't a nick in his horns yit, as the saying is, whatever he may live to have, and has the whole township to choose from. And Mary, dear, we're no ways stingy of our vickels in this country, and its he that likes the Venzon. Why, my dear, they're as plenty with us as goats on the Wicklow mountains; and Mary, you'd like it greatly, and so do I: and sure enough it does'nt go into an ill skin.

But what made this changification? you will ask. Why this way—the mistress thought the other life was too asy for me: and so it was; and as I dressed a dish or two that plazed the master, she said, she'd put me into the kitchen, where I might show my talons.

While my master was building this house we lived above a month at a farmers, and a quare place it was, but I larned a great deal while I staid, and the woman of the house was no bad warrant to tell me how to do a thing.

But what flogged all that I had ever seen, was making sugar out of a tree, Mary—not a word of lie do I tell you; you take a big gimlet and make a hole in the tree, (the *maypole* I think they call it,) and out comes the shuggar, like sweet water thick like, and you boil it, and you—but where's the use of my telling you any thing about it, as you have no sugar trees at home.

I remember when you and I thought a shuggar stick, a mighty good sort of a thing, never thinking I'd lay my eyes upon a *sugar tree.* I'm told there are such things as butter trees too, but seeing's

believing, and they shan't take me in that way, but there's one
tree I'm sure of, and that's a plumb tree, wild in the woods, for I
pull'd with my own hands more than I could eat and carry away,
and we boiled them with the maypole sugar, and a fine parcel of
jam we had, all for nothing but our trouble, which was only a
pleasure, not to say anything of having it to the fore.

When I was pulling them, it come into my head, that if there
was shuggar trees, and tea trees, and butter trees, and bread trees,
which I read of at school, the wood would be a very nate place for
a tea party, and the plumbs, and the rawsberries, and currents,
and strawberries would be a good *sace*,—was'nt this a funny
conseat? But I'd want something after all, and that would be *you*
Mary alongside of me, and a pair of handsome lads to make us
merry—and sure enough the woods aren't without that same, only
that their pelts are all red, with roasting themselves I suppose at
them big fires in the woods at night. Some of them without any
manner of doubtification, are very fine Ingines, but that's our
share of them, for they say they won't mix, and may be all for the
better, for I'd rather die an old maid than be called a squawl, and
have a porpus tied on my back, rolled up like a salmon in a hay-
rope, on the Wexford Coach; and more than that, to be made to
do all the druggery by land and water, in the shanty and kinnoo,
gutting all the fish, and dressing all the birds and beasts, for never
a hand's turn will them fine haroes do, but hunt, and shoot, and
fish, and eat plenty, and drink hearty, like any gentleman. Fond
as I am of cooking, Mary this would be beyand the beyands, (as
the saying is)—but while I'm on the subject, I must tell you how
much I'm coming on; and would you believe it? I bake all the
bread, for there's no bakers or huxters here to send in the fresh
loaves every morning; but we must have all *within ourselves*.

One day there came two women to the farmers to buy cabbage,
for my dear, they'd sell any thing here, they're so fond of the lucre
of gain; but says one of the women to my mistress, that was standing in the firhandy, 'Why then, ma'am,' says she, 'I'm sure you're
the lady my daughter was telling me about, that she said, she was
sure was an Irish lady.' 'Why do you think I'm Irish?' says my
mistress. 'Well then, I'll tell you that—because you're fat, and

you're fair, and you're comely, and you're handsome.' And true for her, for she's all that, and *good* into the bargain.

Well, Mary, that was the day but one before we came away; and its well that ever we got to this place, with them roads, and the floods, and the cricks, and the axes going, and the wagging knocked about, and the horses tired, and the dark night coming on us, and the mistress almost destroyed, and the children as bad. But God be praised, here we are all, safe and sound.

You have plenty of *Whitefeet* with you, Mary; but here they were a scarce article till we came. My master's brother's wife's were the first female whitefeet that ever stepped upon the town of Addalad. Then came on my two fellow 'prentices, and then my mistress, and then myself, that's as white as the best of them, as Benson the rogue told me yesterday.

But now, lo and behold you, there's hundreds and hundreds all about us, and houses growing out of the woods every day.

But after all, its an awful thing to be living in the woods. Oh! them terrible wolves, if you were to hear them. I never got a wink of sleep the first fortenight. I'd be shockingly in dread, they'd spoil our *tea party*. Such yowling, and growling, and yelling, and pellmelling, as no Christian ever heard. They say its hunting the deer they are. Set 'em up with venzon the bastes!

Well isn't it surprizing with all I have to do, I could find the time to write so long a letter, by fits and starts—but do the same to me, and I tell you again and again, and be sure to come to Addalad, (isn't it a comical name? maybe there's *something* in it,) and by the time you come, I'll know who's who, and what's what, and will direct you for the best.

You know I told you, I had *two* strings to my bow. May be one of them might make a noose for *you*.

Good night dear Mary. 'Early to bed, and early to rise.'

Your affectionate School-fellow,

Bridget Lacy.

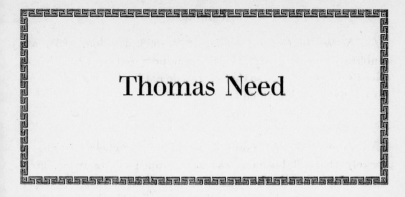

Thomas Need

Thomas Need is not a particularly attractive person. A little priggish and a little unfriendly—a neighbour complained that he kept no spare blankets for strangers—his record of life in the Newcastle district of Upper Canada is valuable far more for the points at which it supplements those of Frances Stewart and John Langton than for the personality it reveals.

His father was connected with Walker, Parker and Co., well known as manufacturers of patent shot, and Thomas, intending to enter one of the professions, went up to University College, Oxford, whence he graduated in 1831. But by this time he had changed his mind and decided to emigrate to Canada, and this, with financial help from friends, he did.

After some experience of farming, and having despaired of making a living by it, he started a saw mill and set up a store at Bobcaygeon, as 'In consequence of so large an influx of settlers in the Autumn, I had thought it prudent to lay in a considerable store of flour and pork, which proved extremely beneficial to my neighbours, and returned me a considerable profit. In this country, a gentleman may, if he chooses, keep an open shop or store without derogation, and it is no uncommon thing to see a man of education and acquirement standing behind a counter.' And at this point we lose sight of him.

His book, *Six Years in the Bush, or Extracts from the Journal of a Settler in Upper Canada*, 1832–1838, London, 1838, was published anonymously. The text was prepared by a friend from Need's rough journal, so that entries do not in all cases correspond to the dates under which they appear.

Late June, 1832. At Toronto, we found the cholera raging so fiercely that all business was at a stand; so we immediately resumed our seats in the waggon and set off down Yonge street, on an expedition to lake Simcoe. For some miles the farms on either side the street or road were well cultivated; and here perhaps, of all places in the Province, ought the mere practical farmer to settle, as the proximity to the capital gives him a safe and steady market for his produce, and the means of obtaining in return many of the comforts of life. At an inn on the road side, I met with a young farmer from my own county in England; he was altogether hopeless and desponding, a thing in itself by no means uncommon with settlers of his station in life during the first two or three years, their minds being generally too contracted to look far into the future, or to bear with patience present hardship, that good may come; but from what little I saw of my co-compatriot, there was no room to hope that his prospects would brighten as time advanced; for instead of business he had evidently turned all his attention, since his arrival in the Province, to the study of Yankee manners and idioms, which, disagreeable as they are, he certainly managed to render more offensive by his unpleasant caricature; cool impertinence he mistook for independence; and a swaggering jaunty air for an easy manner; of cause he 'guessed and calculated', but to my inquiries respecting his prospects, and what information he had gained, and where he meant to settle, he was utterly unable to give a straight forward reply:—doubtless he will soon be a bankrupt here, as he probably has been already in England, where, if he has friends or credit left, he will return, 'seven times' more worthless than when he came out. I do not know any thing more degrading than an affectation of Yankee airs and idioms in a newly-imported English settler; whether yeoman, or, as I fear, sometimes ('*proh pudor*' be it said), gentleman.

[60]

The English emigrant, like the ancient Roman, should carry with him to the colony the manners, habits, and principles of the mother country; he ought to glory in the title of *Englishman*, and esteem it as much a privilege as ever did Roman that of *Citizen*; but too often the reverse is the case. The Anglo-Canadian copies the worst and most prominent features of the American character, and the British settler in his turn caricatures the copy. I have no quarrel with the manners of the real American, which are for the most part essentially good, inasmuch as they are civil, friendly, and obliging; but they are peculiar, and there is certainly nothing in them for an Englishman to be enamoured of, much less to imitate. Policy also might teach us to avoid this error; for England, and especially English settlers of the better class, may rest assured, that if they do not their utmost by precept and example to maintain the national character, and foster a love for British institutions in the colony, the growing amalgamation which this base imitation is producing between the States and the Province, will eventually unite them in other respects also; and then, what will our domination be but a name, which the first opportunity will blot from the map? At present, the hatred excited by the last war in some degree checks the tendency to republicanism, but with the passing generation this will pass; and then, if the present taste be encouraged, will come the startling question, *what else have we to trust to?* No, if we would not realize the American boast that monarchy cannot thrive on the new Continent, let the English settler take pains to prove its real superiority to any other form of government; so that whenever, in the course of years, this thriving Colony is able to go alone, its constitution and form of government may be modelled on those which have raised the mother country to her summit of glory.

July 2. Lunched at Newmarket. All that we saw in that settlement put us in high spirits; which, however, were in some measure checked a few days afterwards, by the opinion of two intelligent gentlemen I met at the Lieutenant Governor's table at Toronto; to the effect that it was impossible to realize any considerable property by farming in Canada, though an English gentleman of small capital and some experience might live in comfort, and bring up a family respectably.

July 9. On our return from lake Simcoe, we found the cholera still raging at Toronto, and his Excellency very busily employed in doing all that humanity and policy could suggest to arrest or mitigate the evil. By his recommendation, we again started on an expedition to Seymour, a then unsettled township of much reported promise on the river Trent. Our first halting place was Coburg, a small but rapidly increasing town, situated on the lake, about midway between Toronto and Kingston. A stage passes through the town daily, and the steam boats always touch. It has also a post office, two bank agencies, several good stores and private houses, and is in many respects a desirable place to settle near. From hence to Percy on the Trent the road was execrable, though we were of course assured that it was in *contemplation* to make it better.

On leaving the growing village of Percy, we were quickly buried in the woods of Seymour Township: an entirely new settlement, if *settlement* it could be called, where nothing was *settled*; the day was spent in wandering through the forest and discoursing with our guide on the nature and quality of the land: we were not however tempted by what we saw; and after passing an uncomfortable night in a wretched shanty, returned to Cobourg in order to visit Rice Lake, and some of the Townships on the Otanabee river.

October. . . . I took a careful survey of Verulam township, and finally decided on purchasing a lot of 3000 acres, as a first investment of capital. This resolution made, we sped merrily back across the Shallow lakes, to Peterboro'—then steamed down the dull Otanabee, and duller Rice lake, and reached Toronto in safety, a few days before Christmas.

January, 1833. The necessary forms for the completion of my purchase in Verulam were proceeding as fast as the Government regulations would permit, so that by the end of the month I found myself proprietor of 3000 acres of wild forest land, at the easy cost of a dollar per acre, or £750 provincial currency. All crown lands in the Colony are obliged to be sold by public auction—a system which works extremely ill in practise, though in theory it may seem a safe provision against jobbing and corruption on the part of Government agents.

When an intending settler has determined on a lot of land, and ascertained the market value, he must give notice to the Crown agent, who proceeds to advertise the lot for sale in the provincial journals, for one month; afterwards, at the next Government sale, it is put up to public competition at the price named by the proposed purchaser, to whom if no advance be made, it is of course knocked down; but very frequently the public auctions are attended by men of straw, with the express intention of out-bidding the real man, on the chance of transferring their bargain to him at a premium; or, failing in that, of throwing it up, which they are at liberty to do when the first instalment is called for, thus equally injuring the Crown and the settler.

When a sale is computed, one fourth of the purchase money is required by law to be paid down, and the remainder in four equal annual instalments, bearing interest at 6 per cent.

Happily, Verulam Township was then too little known to attract the attention of adventurers of this description; and I had so arranged matters, that immediately after the completion of the purchase I was prepared to bid farewell to the capital, and move with all my effects towards the woods. No accident occurred on the road, if I except the upset of a sleigh, with the consequent dispersion of its freight in the deep snow; and on the evening of the sixth day from leaving Toronto I reached in safety the little town of Peterboro', where my head quarters were to be until the spring advanced and the ice broke on the lakes.

February 14. Attended a sale of land in the adjoining township of Ennismore, under a distress warrant for non-payment of taxes. The day was very beautiful, and a fresh fallen coat of snow had made the sleighing excellent. Dr. Johnson has expatiated on the delight of rapid travel in a chaise and four; Lord Byron, on that of being borne along on the back of a fleet courser; but had either of them experienced the glow of health and spirits imparted by the motion of a sleigh, and the music of the bells, they would have given it the preference. Uncleared lands are subject to a light impost of one penny in the pound, which, if not regularly paid, is suffered by Government to accumulate for eight years; but at the expiration of that period, a distress warrant is issued by the sheriff, for the sale of such portion of the property as will cover the arrears. Nothing can be more equitable than the process:— ample notice is given; and at the time of the sale the question is put, for how many acres any one will pay the Crown dues? The bidder of the lowest number is of course successful, and the acres specified are made over to him, subject always to redemption on the part of the proprietor, within a year, on payment of £20 per cent interest on the money advanced. In this manner considerable sums have sometimes been realised by land speculators, though on the present occasion the extravagant sum of £3 per acre was obtained. After the same, I returned to Peterboro' to dine with the Government agent, upon a noble muskalongy and a haunch of forest venison, assisted by an excellent wine: a luxury which the settler ought rarely to indulge in in this country, where the price of a bottle of wine is about equivalent to that of an acre of forest land.

February 28. The good people of Peterboro' have been in a state of considerable excitement for some days past, in consequence of an attempt on the part of a few low radicals to get up a 'grievance' meeting, as seditious assemblies are here denominated. Placards were pasted on the walls, and advertisements in the journals duly announced the expected arrival of an arch-agitator to take part in the proceedings; but, at the appointed time, the honest and loyal part of the community mustered in such overwhelming force, both as regarded numbers and respectability, that the malcontents saw no chance of carrying their resolutions, and fairly slunk off the field with their leader, without showing fight. There may be a few inconveniences which want redress; but I confess I can find nothing like a real grievance in this colony, nor indeed room for any other than the most cordial feeling of gratitude and love to the mother country, under whose domination it is so steadily prospering.

April 17. Having laid in a good store of axes and other necessaries for the use of the men, I returned to the settlement.

April 26. The next few days were occupied in building a shanty, or rude hut, which an appearance of change in the weather seemed to render advisable. The month of May set in cold and wet; but I was obliged to go to Peterboro' to lay in fresh stores. The voyage was altogether miserable; and in addition, I had the vexation to discover that my new boat was good for nothing: on returning, however, it was a great satisfaction to find my mansion finished, and ready for occupation.—It consisted of one apartment, 14 feet by 12 feet in the clear, and contained, in the way of furniture, a camp bedstead, a chest of drawers, and a well-filled bookcase; it had also the somewhat unusual luxury of a chimney, pegs for the suspension of guns and fishing implements, and shelves for my scanty kitchen utensils: a hole in the planks served to admit light, and air found free entrance through numberless cracks and crevices; sure as it was, however, it served my purpose well; and when the evening closed, I used to light my lamp and sit down to my books with a great feeling of comfort. Several of the classics, which on their shelves at Oxford were rather looked *at* than *into*, were now treated with the attention they deserve; and in the solitude of the Bush, it was no light pleasure to re-peruse scenes and passages, every one of which was pregnant with some cherished association of school or college.

July 1. I received a letter, stating that I was appointed a Commissioner for the improvement of the inland navigation of the Newcastle district, and requesting my attendance at a meeting to be held at Peterboro', where I immediately went to meet my brother Commissioners at their board: several plans and estimates were proposed and taken into consideration, and one or two important improvements ordered to be carried into effect. On my return, I visited some recent settlers in Douro township, and also an enterprising young man who was building an extensive saw mill, and laying out the ground plan of a village, which he hoped soon to see erected and peopled on his property. The site was well chosen, and very beautiful, but not more so than my own; and I could not help dreaming, that in a few years my own lonely hut might be surrounded with a thriving village, and the now idle waters of the cascade be diverted to turn a mill. It was a dream, perhaps, but Canada is the land of dreams, and what seems a 'baseless vision' one day, is a reality the next.

July 20. The air is much cooled and very pleasant. Some Indians crossed the lake in their canoes, one of whom brought me half a buck; I am now becoming acquainted with these aboriginals, and mutual attentions and civilities pass on both sides; they are honest and civil, and always ready to do me any service. On one point alone, that of hunting furs, they are said to be as tenacious as English landholders of their game; and as some white men, who have gone out for the purpose, have never returned, there are grounds for suspecting that they do not always confine their remonstrance to angry words or sulky looks. Each family possesses an hereditary hunting ground, which is marked by bounds, well known to the tribe, and on which a trespass is highly resented. A skilful Indian will sometimes obtain in the course of the season furs to the value of £100.

August 20. Went to Peterboro'; where a rapid improvement had taken place during the summer—new houses had been built, new shops opened, and a large influx of inhabitants had arrived. I had been so many weeks absent that I had forgotten to change my half-Indian costume before I left the woods, consequently my old acquaintances recognised me with difficulty, and especially as the sun had sadly changed my complexion, even the boys in the streets hooted as I passed.

Oct. 6. A Land Surveyor arrived to-day to lay out the ground plan of a village, which some projected public works on our chain of lakes is likely to call into existence on my property. We measured several lots, and in many instances had bidders for them immediately. One person proposed to open a tavern; which, if respectably conducted, will be very useful to the infant settlement.

The intention of Government (sanctioned by the Legislature) is to cut a canal between Lake Sturgeon and Pigeon Lake, for the purpose of avoiding the present dangerous river and rapids, and connecting the navigation of the two Lakes. Such an undertaking I had in some degree anticipated when I selected my lot of land; but I had not imagined that it would have been so soon executed, or that the interests of our rude district could so soon have attracted public attention. From this time I may fairly consider the value of my property in the market quadrupled.

March 26, 1834. To-day, news arrived that the provincial Parliament had granted £100 to our township, towards the expense of erecting a bridge over the river between us and Peterboro', and in addition £20. towards the formation of a practicable road. This act of liberality will bring us within easy reach of the district capital, and also of the civilized world.

April 8. The anniversary of my departure from England: I had now been nearly two years in the Colony, and in many respects my most sanguine expectations had been realized. A fine climate, fruitful soil, and the easy recreations afforded by the lake and the forest, had suited my tastes, and atoned for the seeming monotony of my existence. I had also enjoyed to the utmost good health, and even spirits—that chiefest, perhaps, of all blessings—the " mens sana in corpore sano," and had reason to believe that there was before me a fair prospect of rising in wealth and importance in this land of my adoption. On the other hand, experience and due consideration had convinced me that farming was not the road to wealth in Canada, and that I might employ my capital in many other ways to more advantage. I therefore determined to let my present house and clearing as soon as an eligible tenant offered, and devote my future attention to general business. Subjoined is a statement of the outlay expended on purchasing, clearing, and cropping twenty acres of land, and building a loghouse and other necessary appendages—

[total was 849 dollars or £212 5s.]

Of the returns I cannot speak so clearly: a wet harvest, and a great

[67]

scarcity of hands (the usual complaint of a new settlement) having combined to injure the crop, which did not amount to more than fourteen bushels of wheat to the acre, or at the then price of wheat (a dollar per bushel) about £42 for the 20 acres. I do not however give this as a general return, but simply as my own:—doubtless many settlers have been much more fortunate, but still the first crop is liable to many accidents and difficulties, and the settler ought not to depend much upon it. With a capital producing from sixty to a hundred pounds a year, independent of the farm, a gentleman of education and active business-like habits may live very comfortably and attain to rank and consideration in the colony, which circumstances might preclude him from reaching at home: but with less than this he will find it hard to get over the first difficulties, and will probably have many years of laborious uphill work to surmount, before he can expect to be comfortably settled.

January 1836. Logging and fixing, and other 'Bees,' having been of frequent occurrence in the township since its rapid increase, it was proposed by a new settler to summon his friends to a 'house-warming bee,' on new year's day. The party assembled in force, and in high spirits, for all of us had parted on kindly terms with the year that was gone, and were full of hope and expectation from its successor. The mansion of our host was rudely built, and more rudely furnished; but if our comforts were few, our cares were fewer; and what with toasting 'British connexion—Sir John Colborne,' and other provincial toasts, in addition to the old English stock which it would have been sinful to have passed over, I fear the heads of many of us were as light as our hearts before we took our blankets and stretched ourselves before the fire.

January 4. This being the first Monday in the year, a public meeting was called according to law, to appoint parochial, or rather township officers: no difficulty was raised or party spirit shown, and well-qualified persons were generally elected to serve.

Among other signs of the growing importance of the township, a court of requests was now opened for the recovery of small debts. I took some pains in having it established, for it seemed to afford security both to debtor and creditor, and to save vexatious law expenses, for no attorney is allowed to practise in these courts, and the award of the presiding commissioners is always final. A good sleigh road was also opened to Peterboro', which will make us in future independent of the state of the lakes.

September. In the back woods, marriage by civil contract, in the presence of a magistrate, is permitted, where a clergyman does not reside within a prescribed distance. Individually, I have always persuaded parties to go to a clergyman from religious scruples; but one morning a young Indian of my acquaintance entered my house in the midst of a pouring rain, and sat himself down with great composure: at length he thus addressed me:—

"Well, Mister, I guess you pretty good man to Indian."

"Yes, Jacob, when he behaves well."

"Oh me! Jacob always behaves well; (after a pause) they tell me you a magistrate."

"Well, Jacob, what can I do for you then?"

"Oh, never mind; (after another pause) I want something."

"Indeed; let me hear it then."

"Well, then, I believe Jacob wants to get married."

"Oh, that's your belief, is it? but how am I to assist you?"

"Oh, Mister a Magistrate—Magistrate marry Jacob very quick, as quick as parson."

"Well, perhaps in your case, Jacob, I might, but where is your squaw?"

"Oh, she outside."

And accordingly looking out I beheld the dripping beauty, with two young companions, waiting patiently the result of our conference, in the heavy rain. I instantly begged them to come in, whilst I prepared the certificate, and everything being found proper, the knot was tied. The bride and her friends instantly withdrew, but not so the happy Benedict, who lighted his pipe, and quietly resumed his seat, to wait, as he said, until the rain was over.

[69]

October 27. A prodigious quantity of snow fell this week, and the lakes were entirely frozen over, a circumstance which had not occurred so early in the season within the memory of the oldest settler: early in November, however, it all melted away, and we had fine clear weather to the end of the year.

January 1837. The court of requests was held to-day, for the second time in our township; I was much disappointed to find the business considerably on the increase, and a great deal of knavery attempted by parties summoned; indeed its establishment, instead of proving a security to the settlers, threatens to be a vast injury, by tempting store keepers to give credit inconsiderately, and consumers to obtain goods without regarding the means of payment. When redress was difficult and expensive, the trader was cautious for his own sake; but now he appears to give credit without hesitation, relying on the court for recovery. People also thus brought before a court of law aquire a litigious spirit, and I cannot help regretting extremely the haste with which several of us concurred in promoting the establishment of it in our neighbourhood.

September. In this month a highly important meeting of the influential settlers of the district was held, to deliberate on the practicability of running a steam vessel through our lakes—several spirited resolutions were passed, a committee of management formed, and a capital of between two and three thousand subscribed in shares. This was a promising beginning, and left no room to doubt that ere another year a steam vessel will regularly pass the very door of my clearing, and the spot, where scarcely six years ago I had first stepped out in the primeval forest, be continually thronged with men and merchandise.

As travellers and intending emigrants may be interested in knowing the cost of a journey from England to the Upper Province, I subjoin a statement of my travelling expenses from Peterboro' to Liverpool, which would equally apply to Toronto:

Thomas Need

	£	s.	d.
Fare from Peterboro' to Cobourg .	0	10	0
Steam boat to Rochester . .	0	7	6
Canal boat to Utica . . .	1	10	0
Railroad to Albany . . .	0	7	6
Albany to New York . . .	2	15	0
Two days detention at New York .	1	0	0
Fare to Liverpool	30	0	0
	£33	17	6

Maintenance is included in these prices, which are not likely to vary, excepting the fare from Albany to New York, which a strong opposition had reduced below a remunerating price.

Thus a traveller may reach the capital of Upper Canada, from any part of England within moderate distance of Liverpool, for about £40 allowing himself leisure to see all that is remarkable in the route, and every year these charges will become less, as greater intercourse incites competition.

John Langton

Between 1805 and 1825 Pestalozzi, the great Swiss educationalist, lived and taught at Yverdun, on the Lake of Neuchâtel. Here he entertained a cosmopolitan stream of visitors, among whom Talleyrand and Mme de Staël were only two of the most distinguished. There were few English at first because of the Napoleonic wars, but his ideas had spread beyond the Channel, and as soon as peace came an elderly English merchant boarded a ship and hurried his children across to entrust them to the reformer's care.

Thomas Langton had earned a sufficient fortune abroad to enable him to retire to England, where, at Blythe Hall, near Ormskirk in Lancashire, he settled down in 1802 and devoted all his interest to the rearing and education of his children.

Two years in Switzerland prepared William, Anne and John for three more under the care of tutors in France, Italy (where a drawing showed them all to have determined chins), and Germany. At this point rumours of financial disaster brought them home, though the threat was not fulfilled for another six years.

As a result, John had to be helped through Cambridge (he was at Trinity) by an aunt, and in 1833, at the age of twenty-five, emigrated to Canada.

Here his high spirits and energy overcame all the initial difficulties so satisfactorily that in 1837 he invited his father and mother to join him, together with Anne, whose own letters, published in 1904 as *Langton Records*, serve as a domestic supplement to his own.

While living on Sturgeon Lake he saw a good deal of Thomas Need, to whom he had been given an introduction, and whom he called 'a very doubtful and uncertain person,' and in 1833 went to call on Mr. Stewart, Frances' husband, who 'still lives in the original loghouse, but it is made as comfortable and ornamental as any cottage in England, and he has a fine clearing.'

In 1845 he married Lydia Dunsford, daughter of a clergyman living on Sturgeon Lake, and shortly afterwards became more interested in speculation and local government than in farming, becoming Warden of Peterborough and its representative in the Legislature, Vice-Chancellor of the University of Toronto, and finally Auditor-General and Deputy Minister of Finance. By this time he had left his farm and lived at Toronto, where he died in 1894.

These letters to his father and, from 1837, to his brother are taken from *Early Days in Upper Canada. Letters of John Langton from the Backwoods of Upper Canada and the Audit Office of the Province of Canada*, Toronto, 1926, edited by the late W. A. Langton.

August 2nd 1833. To-day, after looking about the town [York], I waited upon the Governor and had great difficulty in avoiding giving him a promise to go through the western townships before finally settling, it being his policy at present to send all respectable emigrants there; but, from all I have heard from those who have been there, I do not think they would suit me, and time is too precious to waste in merely looking about me.

There are several reasons which induce me to give a preference to the Newcastle district. It is the most English of all the districts and the society of a superior caste; lands are to be purchased there cheaper than in any part at an equal distance from a market; there is not that want of water that has caused such great loss in many of the inland townships; instead of being shut up on all sides by the forests, you may obtain a healthy, airy frontage to some of the numerous lakes, which, besides making the situation more pleasant, and, I should think, healthy, enables the settlers to burn, when in the confined clearings in the heart of the forest there is not a breath of air stirring; mill sites are of course more numerous; labour is cheaper; and, lastly and principally, they have an extent of internal navigation unparalleled in any part of the world, I should think.

The upset price of Government, as you know, is 10/-; but I am at present partly in treaty for certain U.E. rights, which I can procure at 3/9 to 5/-, and, if I come to any arrangement upon the subject, the cost of my land will be materially diminished. The origin of these rights dates from the Revolutionary—I beg the Yankees' pardon—the War of Independence; when tickets for so many acres were given to the United Empire Loyalists, as they were called, for their services, and to their children afterwards. Thousands of these rights have been bought up and settled, the price in the olden time being somewhere about 5*d*. or 6*d*. per acre, and some few yet remain unlocated. The cause of their being so much lower in price than government land is, that, by the grants, they must be settled and ten per cent. cleared in two years, which keeps the speculators in a great measure from purchasing them. A similar condition is annexed to the other lands indeed, but Government is not very strict, except in the case of these rights, against the transfer of which they set their faces as much as possible; to an actual settler, however, such a condition is of no moment.

Immediately after the sale I mean to proceed up the Lakes again, to inspect some of the situations more minutely; which I shall be able to do now, as I have taken a copy of the government surveys, by which, with the assistance of a compass, I can find out exactly what lot I am upon—a very difficult matter before; and, as I shall pass through York before the next sale, and shall there get permission to look over the surveyor's field notes, I shall be more prepared with knowledge of the nature of the land I am buying than I can be now.

Cobourg, Aug. 23, 1833. In conformity with my promise of writing to you as soon as I had fixed on the spot where I am to spend my life, I seize the first vacant moment since my purchase to inform you that on Tuesday last, the 20th Aug., between the hours of eleven and twelve, I became, for the first time in my life, a Lord of the soil.

Now look at the map of Upper Canada. Do you see the Bay of Quinté, upon which Kingston is situated? Well—the river Trent runs into this bay as you will see, and, if you will take the trouble to follow it up for some twenty or thirty miles (which you must do on foot, for it is not navigable), you may then get into a boat and sail up into the Rice Lake. You will admire it very much for the beauty of its banks and islands, though at this season of the year the wild rice beds give the lake itself more the appearance of a grass plot than a sheet of water, but I would not advise you to stay long admiring the scenery or you will probably catch the ague; but go at once to the town of Sully (where you will find one house), whence you may take a steamer which will carry you twenty-five miles up the river Otonabee to Peterborough.

After the specimen of Canadian towns which you will have seen at Sully and at two others on the river—Howard containing a shanty, and Cambleton a loghouse without windows—you will be surprised to find Peterborough a very pretty, picturesque, thriving village, with about 2,000 inhabitants and near thirty genteel families within visiting distance; but you will be more surprised to find that in 1825 scarcely a dozen white men had ever trodden the woods where it stands.

From hence you may continue to ascend the river and will enter some very beautiful lakes; but, as the Otonabee is scarcely navigable for canoes above the town, I would recommend you to turn your face towards the N.N.W., and walk six miles till you reach the Chemong or Mud Lake at Bridgenorth (Population 1). This individual will lend you a boat which you may row five miles north to the Indian village.

Of course one so well acquainted with Uncas, Chingachgook, Magua, etc., knows what to expect in his Indian guide; but, nevertheless, you will be surprised again, upon being introduced to Stephen Elliot, James McQue, Joe Bullfrog, Joe Muskrat or any other of the fraternity, to behold a handsome young man with long black hair, dressed respectably in hat, shirt, coat, waistcoat and trousers, and with all the other outward and visible signs of a Christian man. Even my most respectable friend Capt. Nogy, the chief, I will engage shall not at all remind you of the great Sagamore of the Mohicans. They are all a most peaceable, sober set of men; I doubt if any of them ever saw human blood, except old Bedford who killed his wife: but that, as he says in excuse, was a long time since. I cannot, however, say as much for their industry; some of them would sooner fast twenty-four hours than take the trouble to cook a meal. All this and more you will have had time to observe before any of the aforesaid gentlemen will have made up their minds whether they will take you up or not.

However I will suppose you in a canoe, moving lazily up into Pigeon Lake, and thence, through the rapids called Bob Cajwin, into Sturgeon Lake. I forgot to say that at the rapids you passed the town of Verulam (Population 0), but on the Lake you will find six settlers. Certainly this is not many, but then four of them have been at an university, one at the military college at Woolwich, and the sixth, though boasting no such honours, has half a dozen silver spoons and a wife who plays the guitar.

Now look at the map again. You will observe that the Sturgeon Lake runs east and west for about ten miles and that it then divides into two branches; the one running south leading into a settled township called Ops, the other leading north towards Cameron Lake. Up this last you will please to sail along the eastern coast for about two miles, when you will see a stony beach lined with cedar, hemlock, birch and pine, and immediately behind that the brighter foliage of the oak, maple and basswood. If you look very narrowly at this shore, in about a month, you will see a very small clearing, and near a brook you will perceive a wigwam composed of birch bark and cedar boughs. Pray step on shore and walk in; you will find an old friend who can at any rate promise you some salt pork and unleavened bread, with a cigar and a glass of whiskey; and it is more than probable that a fine bass or maskinonge, fresh from the Lake, or a couple of wood ducks, as fat as

ortolans, may be added to the repast; who knows whether a
haunch of venison or a sirloin of bear may not be forthcoming. A
fire before the entrance of the wigwam will serve the treble purpose of giving warmth, light to eat your supper, and of keeping off
the mosquitoes, and a bed of cedar boughs, with a buffalo robe for
a covering, you will find no despicable lodging. This and a welcome
is all I can offer you; but in the morning I will lead you through
the woods to see all the wonders of my estate. You shall behold a
swamp, into which however you cannot penetrate until the frost
gives you firm footing; you shall see a beautiful hill gently sloping
down to the lake and from which there is a beautiful view—if the
trees were out of the way—and where a mansion will some day
stand; and a brook—or creek as we call it—which will be the site
of a mill. Then I will take you to an old settlement of the Mo-
hawks, who were massacred about fifty years ago by the fore-
fathers of your respectable friends Joe Muskrat, Joe Bullfrog, etc.
After this I will paddle you in my canoe to Cameron Falls, about
six miles off, where you may see Niagara in miniature; the fall is
only twenty-two feet high, but the body of water is very great and
the shape exactly that of Niagara.

Beyond this all is wilderness, though the speculators have
bought a good deal of land. Jameson, if he comes to settle this
winter, will be both my nearest and my last neighbour. At present,
I am the pioneer of the township, for, though Jameson has begun
a clearing, it is deserted again, and I fear I shall have no one there
till the spring. But, as soon as the ice breaks up in the spring, a
steamboat will pass my door, and who shall say that I am then
beyond the precincts of civilization?

When this steamer, which will be finished next week, can get
through the locks now building at Bob Cajwin, I shall have only
six miles of land carriage to Peterborough, and thirteen miles from
the Rice Lake to Cobourg, to bring me upon Lake Ontario. I shall
then be in *uninterrupted* water communication with upwards of
150 miles of coast, along these back lakes and rivers. Yet, with all
these advantages, I get a block of excellent land, with half a mile
frontage to the lake, and with a mill site upon it, at a price
averaging 8/- an acre. Land which has far less advantages is now

selling at £5 an acre; the very mill site alone, if near Peterborough, would sell for much, much more than I gave for all the land. *If* it was near Peterborough, you will say—but, I answer, land near Peterborough might, three years ago, have been bought at even a less price; and why should not land on Sturgeon Lake increase in value as well as on the Otonabee. Good land, in good situation, is now getting very scarce; and, when the new lands are all bought up, the old ones must rise rapidly in price.

All these speculations as to the rise of land are *entre nous*; though I am convinced of the eligibility of my situation, I will not talk of it till it comes to pass; but bear in mind that the 16th lot in the Xth, the 16th and 17th in the XIth concessions of Fenelon, and the 17th in the Ist of Verulam, containing 500 acres, more or less, only cost £200, and ask five years hence what they are worth.

I don't know of anything else that would prove very interesting to you from this quarter of the globe, lots and concessions being the only subject of conversation here.

Sept. 12th. Arrived at Peterborough I commenced enquiries for choppers, but, as no decent men could be found, I was advised to wait a week till the harvest was fairly over and the poor settlers were ready to leave their farms for a winter's job. Accordingly I set out with my former companion McAndrew for Sturgeon Lake, intending to spend the time usefully in looking at our land again and fixing upon the points for building our houses and commencing our clearings.

7th. Early in the morning McAndrew and I borrowed Capt. Sawers' boat and performed a pretty hard day's work, rowing upwards of thirty-five miles and scrambling through the bush not far short of ten; but what made it worse was that from half past five to nine o'clock in the evening we had nothing to eat but two small biscuits, one for tea and the other for dinner. To this sad fare we were reduced by Capt. Sawers who obstinately refused to give us any pork or flour or even to lend us a pot in which to boil some potatoes we had begged—to punish us, as he said, for coming unprepared from such a land of plenty as Peterborough to sponge upon the poor backwoodsman at Bob. We first landed at the mouth of my creek and pushed on, along its course, for about a mile, through an almost impassable cedar swamp,—not so much impassable from the wet as from the thousands of trees which encumber the ground in every direction, sometimes five or six deep, in every stage of decay.

To you, I dare say, a swamp conveys no very pleasant ideas, but I look upon that bit of land as the best I have; in the first place the cedars (though not red cedars) are very valuable for posts, rails and sundry other purposes; there is at least a foot of vegetable matter at the top and a good alluvial soil at the bottom, and there cannot be any difficulty in draining it. If the creek were cleared from the decayed trees, which choke it up everywhere, the fall is such that it would drain the land without any further expense; and this will not be difficult, for, if a cedar swamp is well chopped and the fire put in at a good time, it will not leave a particle of inflammable matter behind; indeed it only burns up too much. The cedar stumps, it is true, will not rot out in two or three generations, but, if fire is put into them in a year or two, they will burn down below the surface and leave you perfectly clear meadow land, though certainly ill adapted to the plough; and for the former purpose such land is for other reasons the most proper, as in spring and autumn it will be liable to flood.

We next landed at a pretty point, attracted by the sandy beach, which is rather a rare thing along these lakes, and found excellent land close down to the shore; but what pleased me better, we stumbled upon a brook, running merrily over a gravelly bottom, the mouth of which is imperceptible from the lake. Where it comes from and whether it may not be another mouth of the former one I cannot tell, for the ground was covered with a kind of nettle, growing very high, which, though not so painful as our English nettle, made nothing of stinging through our trousers. Near this is to be my shanty, there being every advantage; dry and good land, excellent water, a sandy beach for my canoe, and a fine open view down the lake.

My land is at any rate well watered, for, besides the two larger streams, on my former journey I discovered a small one, which

[79]

may indeed be the same as this last, but, where I crossed it, it was running in an opposite direction; but in my next letter I shall be able to give you a better account of the topography of my land.

Again we landed and went back on another part where there is a hill, which will undoubtedly be the situation for a house, some dozen years hence, if matters prosper with me. But now comes the worst of the business. In surveying a township the surveyor only marks the boundary lines and the concession lines, which in Fenelon run north and south; and, as my shore runs in the same direction, of course my boundaries are the side lines, which are merely imaginary lines which none but a surveyor can find; so I am in the most pleasing uncertainty whether any of these three points is in my land. By guessing at the distance from Sturgeon's Point and Cameron's Falls, and by the bearing of a creek on the opposite side of the lake, I thought that I could find my front, which is a mile in extent, and my creek I considered an infallible guide; but since I have found two where only one is marked, I begin to doubt whether the cedar swamp is not to the north of me. Again, if that is really my creek, the hill is so near my other boundary that I dare not begin clearing there; and as for the other creek,—I yesterday found out a nasty little broken front of ten or twelve acres, barely perceptible on the map, which comes exactly in the middle of my frontages and which I vehemently suspect to be the identical spot where the creek falls into the lake. This however I will buy on Tuesday, at all costs, and then I think I may be certain of being on my own land.

After leaving my part of the lake, we crossed to search for McAndrew's land; but, after a three hours' search, we could not even find the boundary of the two townships, such is the uncertainty in which we poor pioneers are left. I have since seen the surveyor of Verulam, who will be up there next week, and has promised to mark the boundary. This will set McAndrew at ease, but, as to me, the running of my lines will be a tedious and, I am afraid, an expensive job, and at any rate he has not time to do it now, being engaged to lay out the town at Bob-cajion-unk, which is to be called St. Albans.

An Indian and his Squaw

Canadian Log Hut

Peterborough, Oct. 31. I am much obliged to you for the fishing tackle. I fear that much of it will be of little use to me upon our lakes, neither salmon nor trout making their appearance so high up; but the lines at any rate will be useful to me, and the rest perhaps to fishers on the lower lakes.

Our fish are the maskinonge—a most excellent species of pike, as fat almost as an eel—and the eel itself; the sunfish I believe we have, but I have never seen nor tasted any; the whitefish abound above and salmon trout below. The bass is our staple commodity, and a most excellent one it is; if you are on the lake, tie a line, baited with a piece of red cloth, round your wrist and proceed on your journey, and it is ten to one that, before you have got a quarter of a mile, you will feel your prize. In some parts of the lake, if you are short of meat for dinner, you may put the potatoes on to boil and, before they are done enough, you may have ten or twenty bass on the gridiron. Maskinonge and eel are generally speared, a very difficult matter till one has studied the laws of refraction a little. I have bought some seine twine and mean to net a net this winter which I expect will supply me pretty well with fish next summer; and I do not know whether it may not be worth while to take up an old pork barrel with the brine to Lake Kinashgingiquash, some vacant week in the summer, and bring back a cargo of whitefish, which, salted in that manner, are almost as good as herrings. At any rate I cannot afford salt pork at present prices; I am selling it to my choppers at £4-12-6 p. barrel of 200lb., and I do not make a half-penny by it.

For game—we have abundance of venison, which is becoming more plentiful as the clearings increase, affording them more food and driving off the wolves; you may buy it of the Indians at $1\frac{1}{2}d$. p. lb., and sometimes for less. Partridge and rabbits are pretty plentiful, but the former difficult to get without a dog. Ducks, in thousands and tens of thousands, frequent the rice beds at the mouth of the Scugog, about four or five miles from me. These, together with a bear, two wolves, martens, racoons, muskrats and squirrels are my only acquaintance as yet.

I believe I have now fully answered your letters and may go on with my journal from somewhere about the 12th September.

I believe I added, as I was leaving Peterborough, that I had been detained by the unexpected arrival of the Governor. Indeed the whole town was in as great a ferment as if His Majesty himself had been expected. Militia men turned out and the guard mounted before a loghouse, dignified by the name of Government House. By the bye, the said house is so full of bugs that they dared not invite his Excellency to sleep in it and had rigged up a tent near it, under which his bed was prepared. However, as I said before, Col. Brown and his men were parading about for two days, and one whole day was spent by nearly half the town in erecting a flagstaff. The second day it was considered certain he would come, and we all, except one or two cunning ones, put on our clean shirts, etc. Troopers were galloping about in all direction, watching all the avenues by which the enemy might approach; and a man was stationed on an elevated point, with orders to keep his eyes fixed on the bridge and to fire a shot the moment the great man crossed it. At last, about noon, every thing was ready; the colonel had drawn out his forces so as to make the best possible show, the dozen who had uniforms being posted in conspicuous situations, and a reserve of ragged Irishmen being drawn up behind the cow house to fire a salute. And, after all, they ended by saluting our parson, or rather his horse; for the reverend gentleman, finding the animal which had been sent forward to bear the honoured weight of the Governor, mounted him and rode forward with the news that he was not coming at all. Some of the officers, who had their uniforms on, were very indignant; those who had made everything ready to slip them on at a moment's warning laughed; but as for our worthy little Colonel—for a full minute it was doubtful whether he would not cry. Mr. McDonell, the government agent, bore it with the greatest philosophy,—he merely observed, 'Well, well, then we'll eat the little pig ourselves.' Nevertheless it was no small inconvenience to me, for the boat was stopped to carry the Governor up our Lakes, and I could not get off by it after all, for the captain, when he found he had been made a fool of for three or four days, set off in a pet, without giving anybody notice.

Finding I could not get it till Monday the 23rd, I sent enough luggage, to serve for my first settlement, to go on that day, and took that opportunity of going up to Sandy Lake on Saturday the 21st, with a Mr. Mudge of the Navy, who is settled there, and with a Lieut. Hay, R.N., who was on the lookout for land.

We had expected to be in time to catch the steamer in Buckthorn Lake, but, in consequence of a deer hunt which kept us some time, we were too late, and had to sleep at a house there. The next morning, the 24th September, we started by day-break in my own canoe. The mist was so thick that I could scarcely find my way to the nearest house on the shore, where we intended to breakfast. Upon arriving there, we found them all ill of the ague, and no eatables; so we were obliged to push on to Billy McQue's. There nobody was at home but we took possession, and, thinking the spade looked cleaner than the frying pan, I broiled some venison we had with us on it; finding some ears of corn we roasted them also and made an admirable breakfast. As we were finishing one of the lads came in and offered us some potatoes, which we, thinking we had some way to go and as it was already afternoon, accepted; whilst they were boiling we broiled some more venison and after our dinner started again and reached Bob-cajion-unk pretty early, where we slept on shavings in a loft at Sawers'.

Early on Wednesday morning, the 25th September, I found out the two men I had engaged to chop for me and, upon consulting with them, found that their boat and canoe were insufficient to take up our luggage, so I borrowed a scow and four men at 3/6 a day, from the canal which is cutting, and, after several hard hours' work, they got my load up the rapids. About two o'clock they reached Sawers', and thence Hay and I went on in the canoe and had a fire ready for them to cook their dinner at Need's. From thence I got them off about four o'clock, and, as it was a beautiful afternoon and we had a moon, I intended to work at it all night. About five we set off to follow them and overtook them at sunset, when the weather became menacing, and soon after a tremendous thunderstorm came on which forced us to land at the nearest point we could make. This, in the dark, happened to be a swamp— and here I must leave us for the present, endeavouring, for a long time ineffectually, to light a fire.

[83]

Oct. 31st. I left us, as you will no doubt know before you get this, endeavouring to light a fire upon a little ridge in a swamp by the lake side, and you must now imagine us successful notwithstanding the rain, and fancy Mr. Hay and myself, six men, a woman and a half-starved wretched little baby sitting round the fire, some drying themselves, the rain having abated, and some cooking supper. Here we determined to sleep, and, after supper, the woman and baby were put under the boat, Mr. Hay and myself stretched ourselves side by side near the fire, with our knapsacks as pillows and my blanket and water-proof cloak over us, and the men each crept under a bush or tree as best he could; one poor devil, not knowing how far he was going, had not even brought his coat with him.

As I have mentioned the baby, lest your compassion should be too much excited by it, it may be as well to observe, that though the most miserable puny little creature imaginable a month since, it is now, thanks to the air of the woods, at least half a year older in appearance and more noisy than is at all agreeable.

It rained all night, but, thanks to my waterproof, Hay and I remained dry; but, about three or four in the morning, such a storm commenced that we were obliged to fly for shelter to a hollow tree where, notwithstanding our cramped position, I slept most soundly till day-break. It having cleared again a little, we breakfasted and started about seven (26th Sept.), but we had barely proceeded a mile when a storm more awful than any I have seen in Canada commenced, and Hay and I made with all speed for a sandy beach, and there, upsetting the canoe, we crept under and lay there till noon, without ever daring to peep out and see what had become of the scow. I don't think I ever saw such tremendous rain. About noon, having exhausted all our topics of conversation and having slept as much as we could, we got tired of our situation and, there being no chance of its clearing up, we emerged from our hiding place and launched our canoe. The scowmen were not far off, under a cedar tree; we roused them up and got once more under way, Mr. Hay and I in the canoe, and the woman and child and her husband in the boat, going on before to my land to light a fire, etc.

There we landed about three o'clock, completely drenched, and prepared to light a fire when we discovered that my fool of a man had brought no means of procuring a light. Now I, who, for the last four or five years of my life, never stirred out without tinder and flint and steel in my pocket, happened on this occasion to have left them behind; and, the only gun we had with us being a percussion one, we could get no fire from it; so we were obliged to send the man back in the boat to meet the scow, and, after near two hours vain endeavours to warm ourselves, we at last got a good fire up and supper cooked, just as the scow arrived. The evening having become fine on a sudden and the wind being fair, I determined upon sending the men back in the scow, much against their inclination. Just about sunset, however, the bad weather returned, and, as the poor devils did not get back till three o'clock the next afternoon, they have given me a bad name, averring that I only gave them four meals in three days, which is strictly true, but then they forgot to say that they had already breakfasted the first day and that I offered them at parting as much pork and potatoes with them as they liked, which they in a pet declined. However I have learnt two things from the days' adventures—never to stir twenty yards from my own door without flint and steel, and I have also got a light axe made to carry at my belt, and it has served me many a good turn since; the other thing—never to turn any man from my house at night, and God knows I should have been hospitable enough upon this occasion, as the house I then kept was an open house. This same house, to which we retired when the men were gone, consists of three cedars and a butternut, covered with wild vine,—very picturesque truly and very airy, and there it shall stand unharmed, if possible, amidst the general havoc, as a memento of my first landing; but as the road line, I find, runs over my very hearthstone, I may perhaps be compelled to have it down.

As soon as we had got our suppers, we got the canoe up to the fire and made it our roof. I gave Hay, as my guest, my best blanket, my waterproof and the choice of his bed, and I believe he slept pretty well; but as to myself my lair was on an inclined plane, so that as soon as I fell asleep I rolled out, and, instead of sleeping under the canoe, I slept under the drip of the canoe; as the fire had gone out, when I woke about one, and my blanket was very thin, I felt considerably cold. I woke up the men and made them get another fire, and for an hour or two I amused myself toasting potatoes at it till I got dry, when I went to bed again and again acted the part of gutter to the roof till morning, though as Hay's snoring kept me a good deal awake I continued to keep up my position rather better than in the earlier part of the night. But I must not grumble at Hay's comfortable sleep, for, though he had the better berth, he caught a cold and I did not.

From the 29th Sept., when I arrived, to the 11th October, when I left Peterborough, I have nothing to record but that, on the 6th, McAndrew and I walked up to Selby, about nine miles off, the intended site of a flourishing village, and were much pleased with the beautiful rapids, upon which it is built; and that Hay, not being able to get land in my neighbourhood suitable to his wishes, has settled on Sandy Lake; for which I am sorry, as I was much pleased with him.

On Friday, the 11th, we set out to Mud Lake, being obliged to leave many things behind us, and got to the rapids at Bob-ca-je-won-unk (that is the spelling I think I shall adopt, *a* and *j* having the English pronunciation) that night. Here McAndrew and I found that the government scow we had intended to use was removed, so we volunteered our services and those of our men to assist Jameson up, if he would lend us his scow afterwards. Accordingly on Saturday morning (the 12th) we commenced unloading her of about seven or eight tons of goods, and got thirteen hands from the works, who, with us eight, had hard work getting her over the fall; above this we loaded her again, when it appears the hands from the canal wanted $16.00 for the whole job of getting her up the rapids, which for three-quarters of a day we thought a most exorbitant charge; so Jameson paid them $4.50 for what they had done, and we all turned into the water, resolving to get her up ourselves; but, after having been an hour working hard up to our middles in the water, we were obliged to give it up, and Jameson had to go over again and cry peccavi; the contractors, like the Sibyl of old, sent us only eleven men but still charged the same $16.00 in addition to the $4.50. We felt our-

[86]

selves however in their power and were obliged to submit; but we now got up gloriously, as we all, being already wet, continued to help in the water. About the middle however the channel suddenly deepened so much that I was left behind, unless I had taken to swimming. My first notice was seeing McAndrew, who is six feet two, put his watch in his mouth (mine had long been there) and the next moment I was up to the shoulders. Not relishing a swim, I left them and went on to prepare for their reception above, where I lighted a glorious fire in an empty shanty into which I effected an entrance *via* the chimney.

The next morning, being Sunday (the 13th), we wasted several valuable hours in shaving and such luxuries, and did not get off till ten—with our own party only—and as we unfortunately struck upon some rocks in the rapids, we had to jump out again; then the wind being very wintry, there arose a sort of contest who should take the oars to warm ourselves. However, what with the wind and what with our exercise, we were tolerably dry by the time we reached Cedar Point, where we resolved upon camping, about an hour after dark. Here we experienced the wisdom of the Indian custom of encamping before sunset, for it was so dark, that we lost much time in procuring suitable wood, and were half an hour in getting a light, all our punk being wet in our pockets. At last, with the assistance of gunpowder, we lighted a fire, but to me, as flint and steel bearer, it was at the expense of one whisker and both eyelashes. After an excellent supper of stewed duck and potatoes, we slept most soundly, McAndrew and I occupying a bed of cedar boughs near the fire, with a buffalo robe for mattress and another for a counterpane.

Next morning (the 14th) we roused Jameson and got him on one and a half miles to my land and breakfast. Here McAndrew and I stayed behind looking at my land, and then followed to Cameron's Falls, where the scow was unloaded, and with our two men we brought her down, with a fair wind, to my place for dinner. Starting again at four, we reached Sandy Point soon after sunset; taking the precaution of calling at Cedar Point to carry away some of the embers, which were still smouldering from our last night's fire.

Next morning (the 15th) we were up before daybreak and pulling against a stiff breeze at sunrise. We reached the head of the rapids at ten and left our large scow there, going down to borrow a small scow from the works to bring up our luggage in two or three trips. McAndrew, with four hired hands, undertook the scow, whilst I remained getting a second load ready. Eight times they got round an island out of sight, and as often the current carried them back almost to their starting place; but at last they accomplished it and took up a second load. That night we slept in a bed and were so comfortable that we never were conscious till morning that our shanty, twenty by sixteen feet, contained twenty-three other souls.

On Wednesday morning (the 16th) we got up another load, and, with four extra hands, took the large scow up to McAndrew's to sleep.

The next morning (the 17th), with two of the extra hands and Dan, I set off for my own land, and, after ranging my luggage under some cedars for the remainder of that day and half of the next, we employed ourselves in cutting a road from the landing, making my chopper's shanty our lodging.

By noon next day (the 18th), I had fixed upon my situation, which is at some distance from the Lake on the side of a hill; the shore being too much exposed and too low.

On Saturday (the 19th), the logs being all cut, we raised the walls; and on Sunday evening I set out with two men in my canoe to McAndrew's, who in the meantime had got on a little faster than I, having no road to cut. After breakfast he and I set out in my canoe to proceed up the Scugog into Ops to buy boards and potatoes. For two or three hours we were engaged searching for the mouth of the river, which at last we found—about two and a half miles from where it is laid down in the maps, and, as we had fourteen to go up the river to the mills, it was dark when we arrived there.

Next day (Monday the 21st), having bought our lumber and potatoes and arranged for their conveyance down, we returned, shooting ducks by the way, and slept at McAndrew's.

On Tuesday I returned home alone to breakfast and found the

roof on my shanty; and on Wednesday we got the walls chinked and my luggage brought up. On Thursday the logs for the other shanty were cut, but for want of help we could not raise it. That same Thursday the 24th October I slept for the first time under a roof of my own.

From my own house Jan. 9th, 1834. First let me wish you all the compliments of the season, and then apologize for the long period of my silence. The post, as you must be aware, does not stop at my door, and it is a long walk to go forty miles through the snow to put a letter in the Post Office at Peterborough. One opportunity indeed I had when I sent my man down, about three weeks ago, but I hastened his departure for the sake of giving him company on his journey, and, though I still had two days' notice, this must serve as my excuse—I had just got into my new house and, as the thermometer stood at ten degrees, I was naturally extremely anxious to put in windows and doors before the cold increased; and, not to mention that I had no table, I had nothing but iron pens, in which the ink froze so fast as to render the writing even of a short note a work of considerable time and labour. However, to drop excuses, I am resolved to be ready for any chance opportunity to Peterborough, though at present in perfect ignorance how this is to reach any civilized portion of the province.

I never was very fond of potatoes, but now I have an almost Cobbettish horror of the 'Lazy root.' Yet a requisite quantity of fat pork cannot be turned down without some vegetable matter to qualify it; and unleavened bread, baked in a frying pan, is but a sorry substitute for bread.

As I am on the subject of eating, you may wish to know how we live in the backwoods. In the summer fish, ducks and venison are rather plentiful, but in winter, that is from November to April inclusive, salt pork is the standing dish for breakfast, dinner and tea; and a most expensive one it is, each member of my establishment consuming at the rate of one and a quarter pounds per day at 6d. p. lb. To make this pork go further I deal much in soups— potato soup is the favourite and is so much relished by my men that it has become the ordinary dish at breakfast. Should you wish to introduce it into your establishment, the following is the receipt. Take a lump of pork and, having peeled fifteen or twenty potatoes, put the whole with an onion into a pot and boil it until it has acquired the desired consistency. You may laugh, but I can assure you my potato soup is so celebrated that McAndrew desired me to bring my boy over one Sunday to teach his cook the mystery of the concoction. My pea soup is not so much admired, being merely hard black pease floating about in weak greasy broth. We tried a plumb pudding at McAndrew's on Xmas day, but it was a decided failure; the currants and suet were scarce, the eggs entirely wanting, and flour by much the preponderating ingredient. Nevertheless, notwithstanding these our Canadian luxuries I have not forgotten an English dinner, and I am almost ashamed to say that visions do sometimes float before my imagination of the dinners I shall eat when I pay you a visit in Europe; but more especially with Prince Hal in Shakespeare 'I do remember that creature, small beer.' Before that time indeed I may have become exclusively enamoured of salt pork and wedded to the use of lake water and that detestable stuff Canadian whiskey. Custom does a great deal, as in the case of tea. Being short of sugar, McAndrew and I agreed to stop it to the men, and to set an example gave it up ourselves; and as to milk,—pray never mention the word goats to me—milk was a thing we never dreamt of; but on Christmas we resolved to enjoy ourselves, produced the sugar and sent three men to get a pint from a neighbour, I don't know how many miles off; we tried with both milk and sugar, and then with each separately, but finally unanimously resolved that pure unsophisticated tea is the best.

I have been rather lengthy upon the subject of eating, but without some allusion to that most important function I should have given you but a poor notion of my situation; and moreover because matters of cookery have assumed an additional degree of importance with me from my having officiated as cook myself for three weeks. I certainly did once roast a duck to charcoal, and once burned the pea soup so much it was necessary to give it to the goats, but, upon the whole, when I handed over the frying pan and

potato kettle to my boy Willie, I did it with the conviction that
nature intended me for a great cook; great, first because I have a
genius that way, and secondly because I never could overcome my
aversion to washing up dishes, etc.

York, February. To-day, (the 4th), I have been to see our provincial Parliament, who certainly are not an imposing body and do
not seem to be more celebrated for talking to the point than their
prototypes at home; but in one thing they have effected an improvement upon our English forms: when a division takes place,
the Ayes stand up in their places and a little boy calls out their
names in order, each sitting down as his name is called, the Clerk
at the table taking their names down; the same is repeated with
the Noes, and the lists are then handed to the Speaker, who
declares the majority. Another plan is good:—each member has
his own seat with a small desk before it.

Since I mentioned the Parliament before I have paid our legis-
lators another visit and have heard a long rigmarole from the two
leaders of the Opposition; one of them commenced as follows:
'Several Honourable gentlemen has rose in this 'Ouse'—a very
fair sample of the whole oration; I feel myself fast growing a Tory.
There is a singular incongruity in the *tout ensemble* of the House;
the court dress and sword of the Sergeant at Arms and the cocked
hat of the Speaker (instead of a wig) all seem as if intended to look
imposing; but the appearance of the members themselves, writing
their letters or reading their newspapers at their several desks,
whilst a little boy is running about, bringing them plates of sand-
wiches, etc., reminded one much of a coffee house. During the
whole of the five or six speeches I listened to, not a single
member appeared to think of anything but his own business;
and, when one speaker sat down and another rose, very few
even condescended to look up from their papers, to see who it
might be.

April 25. Unless some radical change is made in the money matters
of this country it will not be a country to live in. Property there is
in abundance but no representative of it, and the former increases

in much more rapid proportion than the latter, so that we are getting worse every day. A metallic currency I am afraid cannot be established amongst us yet as the balance of trade is so decidedly against us with the States, but a much more extended paper currency must be issued or there will soon be a stop to all business. The bank issues are not half sufficient for the wants of the country, and they are under great restrictions in this respect from Government, but above all they are a monopoly. When they are refusing discount to every one else, the directors and their friends find favour in their sight; they are a monopoly, not by statute but by the circumstances of the country. There are few men in Canada with capital sufficient to establish a private banking house of any extent and these few have their capital so locked up in mills, steamboats, land-speculations, etc., that they cannot attempt it. And as for joint stock banks that was tried and failed last session. It passed the lower house indeed but a majority of the Legislative Council are either bank directors or shareholders and they threw it out. A private bank—or more—must be established with English capital and I think the country holds out the fairest prospects to them. Property, as I said before, there is in abundance— much more property and more generally diffused than in England in proportion. There is scarcely a man in Canada who has not tangible property of some kind and our Register offices prevent any fraud in this respect, as no deed or mortgage is valid that is not registered. During several years that Mr. Bethune was cashier of the Cobourg branch, though the discounts were then much more freely given than of late years, delay indeed frequently occurred, from the want of a circulating medium, but during the whole of that time the actual loss upon discounted bills was only £200 or £300. When the risk is so small, six per cent. offers, I think, a temptation. Then, if a low rate of interest were allowed on deposits, all that specie which yearly comes out from England with the emigrants to be locked up in their chests would be deposited with any substantial bank and all the remittances to and drafts on England would pass through their hands. The exorbitant profits on exchange which the bank exacts have thrown all that business where practicable into the hands of the Montreal merchants. When exchange was at five per cent. at Montreal not more than one and one-half or two could be obtained at Cobourg and in one case I know that only par was obtained. The bank have found their monopoly pretty profitable, twenty-six per cent. having been divided last year. I do not wonder at the Legislative Council throwing out the Bill for establishing a joint stock bank at Cobourg.

Feb. 18th, 1835. I can only say at present that we have had a very gay winter; several parties from Peterborough and the neighbour-hood have been up to see the back lakes and observe how we back-woodsmen live, and we in return, besides coming down for the Bachelors' Ball, which took place on the 27th ulto., are now under-going a round of dancing, etc., which has kept us from home for a week already and promises to detain us a day or two more. Balls in Canada are no joke; when one comes forty miles to dance one does not like to make such a journey for a trifle and one takes a spell of dancing sufficient for an average winter at home. We commence at seven or eight and, as the roads are hardly safe for the ladies to drive home by in the dark, we contrived, on the 27th at least, to keep them employed till daylight. We had about forty dancing ladies present and when I came to reckon up in the morning I had danced with all but two and with some of them two and even three times. On the 13th inst. we had a grand ball at Major Shairp's which we kept up till half past five; last night at Col. Brown's we stayed till two, and to-night at Major Hamilton's we are going to keep it up as long as we can find any one to dance with. My share of the dancing will not however be so great as usual as I am engaged in the capacity of butler, etc. Besides these more formal parties we from the back lakes spend all our vacant evenings at Major Hamilton's where we generally of late have contrived to get up a dance. They are an extremely pleasant family with no non-sense or formality, but I have not yet been able to make up my mind with which of the three eldest daughters I am in love. Neither do I hear that McAndrew or Macredie have as yet made up their minds, though all the world of Peterborough are of the opinion that we are three couples elect. In fact marrying and giving in

marriage proceeds rapidly this year. Last year we had but one
bridal party but this autumn we had two of our ladies carried off,
one of them the belle of the district; and this winter two of my
pleasantest partners have made their appearance at our balls as
brides . . .

Oct. 16th. I must however acknowledge receipt of the two pack-
ages, all the contents of which were very welcome, but the stock
and waistcoat might have been dispensed with as they are articles
of attire which I never wear. I couldn't help smiling when I unpacked them, so strongly did they contrast with my usual dress,
viz., white trousers, or such as were white on Sunday morning, a
red shirt open at the breast and tucked up above the elbows—
et voilà tout—a coat never comes over my back except at Peterborough, or when I call on Mrs. Frazer. I do however carry a
coat about with me—a blanket coat, the most comfortable and
lasting wear I know, but it is seldom used except to sleep in at
strange houses though very useful to kneel on in my canoe.

Toronto, July 13th, 1836. In my last letter concluded at Peterborough I brought my motions down to the time when I was starting for the election. Tom Macredie was left at my house in charge,
though with the exception of weeding potatoes there was nothing
to take charge of, and Wallis, Dennistoun, Gawin Hamilton and I
went down in Wallis's new gig.

Before I get you any farther on the road I must introduce you
to the Calypso, who will cut a prominent figure in the events of the
ensuing week.

The Calypso, (for you must know that the whole naval arma-
ment belonging to Fenelon Falls whether canoes, scows, skiffs or
boats are all named after some of the characters of the Archbishop
of Cambray's epic), the Calypso I say is a two-oared gig brought
out by Wallis from Glasgow, and, though being built solely for
speed she is much too light to carry a load or be of general use in
such a rough country as ours, she is extremely convenient to go
down to Peterborough in and she will serve as a model by which
our boat builders may improve.

As the Calypso was destined to carry the honoured weight of
our candidate McDonell it became necessary after she had carried
us to Mud Lake that we should carry her to Peterborough; and as
the road had been newly ploughed (a manner of equalizing the ruts
and holes which is called turnpikeing in this primitive country),
and there had been heavy rains for a week before, I can assure you
we had no sinecure. We picked up three volunteers by the way
and they occasionally gave us a spell, but nevertheless we were
unanimously agreed that though very light in her own element the
Calypso is confoundedly heavy on a ploughed road, a truth to
which two black patches on my shoulders testify to this day. The
old steamer on the Otonabee which had been sunk last fall below
Peterborough, having been raised and refitted to carry down our
voters, was now ready and was starting the next morning for the
Rice Lake to tow up two large scows to serve in the same cause;
but unfortunately as the steamer, like everything else here, was in
debt and the creditor was a leading Radical below, a report was
spread that she was to be seized at the Rice Lake and Wallis was
requested to take down his crew in her for the double purpose of
throwing the bailiff into the lake if he ventured on board and of
keeping an eye on the Captain who was too well known as a
Radical to be trusted so far alone. We four accordingly with T.
Fortune, a younger brother of J. B. F., and Wallis's servant went
down in her well armed with shilelaghs, and after a tedious navigation of a day and a night returned without even the satisfaction of
meeting a bailiff to duck.

On Monday morning at five o'clock we started with the steamer
full of voters and the Calypso in tow until we came within six or
seven miles of Sully on the Rice Lake where the election was held,
when we took McDonell with Messers. Shaw and Kirkpatrick on
board, and Dennistoun and I pulled them on to Sully, beating the
steamer by half a mile—or rather keeping our distance for we got
nearly as much start of her. We stayed on the ground till all the
speeches were over and then rowed off to Spoke Island about a
mile and a half from Sully in the middle of the lake, which we had
fixed upon for our encampment and which for the future, in honour
of the cause, has been named Constitution Island.

[95]

Canada

We had brought down with us a large marquée which had served as a hospital tent during the emigration of '25 and '26, and as a raft touched at the island in the afternoon we impressed sundry boards which made us a long table and benches. The island is about twenty or thirty acres in size and beautifully situated to command a view of the other islands and the whole extent of the lake, and, being covered with natural grasses and only a few oak trees and shrubs scattered about it, it made an excellent situation for an encampment. Our party consisted besides ourselves of Shaw and Kirkpatrick,—Wallis's man attended as cook, etc. We each brought from Peterborough lots of cold prog; this with venison and fish which we got from the Indians afforded us good living and we always had half a dozen guests, either of our friends at Peterborough or of the gentlemen who came up to vote from other parts of the country, besides our candidate who usually spent the evening with us, and we often had very good speechifying. We spent a very pleasant week altogether, and if our presence was not very useful to the cause (Wallis being the only voter) we certainly added much to the animation of the scene. The beautiful little Calypso with her flags flying and her crew all dressed alike in striped guernsey frocks, white trowsers and low straw hats with blue ribbands, and each a British ensign as a scarf, rowing to and from the island and taking out the candidates every morning to address the electors as they came in the steamboat, was a sight that Rice Lake had never seen before—I guess.

All this is very ridiculous on paper, but in the midst of an election it is another thing.

On the Friday we pulled to the head of the lake which is about four miles from the polling booth for the County of Durham where I gave my vote, but for this solitary vote which was not wanted we lost all the fun at Sully, the Radicals having given in during our absence, McDonell and Ruttan being 176 ahead and 65 voters in possession of the polling booth. Upon hearing the news we hurried back and by our haste lost the fun at Durham likewise, the Radicals there giving in half an hour after.

The Constitutionalists throughout the country have gained a glorious victory.

Langton's Original House at Blythe

Crossing Bell River

Blythe, March 10th, 1837. Parliament is prorogued and we now know the results of the session. They certainly have been very Tory altogether; there is no fear of any alteration in the constitution from them and the most important question of all, the Clergy Reserve question, they have left as they found it. This has been almost the only question upon which any main principle has been discussed; there has been discussion however enough in all conscience, but its only object has been to decide who should get the greatest share of the public money. The old Parliament did nothing in the shape of improving the country, the present one I fear has been doing too much. To every public work which was proposed they have granted a charter and advanced money till towards the end of the session it began to be a question whether half the money could be raised; and consequently to meet this difficulty clauses were introduced into all the money bills, at the eleventh hour, suspending operations until the governor in council should authorize the works to commence. I cannot say I like this, it gives too much power to a person wholly irresponsible to the parties granting and paying the money. We for instance have got £77,000 for the Trent, subject to the above condition; suppose only half the sums granted can be raised, what is to hinder Sir Francis from stopping our work altogether and laying out all the sum granted on the Hamilton railway or some other work. We shall have however £16,000 spent on our lake and at Peterborough without any such clog, and we have been formed into a new District, called Colborne, of which Peterborough is the capital. These are the two measures which principally affect us.

Oct. 21, 1844. The complaints are universal of the difficulty of making a living by farming, and I feel no doubt, after giving it a fair trial, that in the present state of affairs it is not to be done. Still I cannot bring myself to think of giving up the farm, for the chances will certainly improve every year and in time even farming alone will probably become more profitable. Were there any other means of making a little money to help the farm, the kind of life is one which I should prefer to any other, and though agriculture alone is a poor prospect, you may live better on a small sum on a farm than anywhere else. The question is what other means of money-making there are, and it is a question which I have asked myself and others five hundred times without getting any satisfactory answer. Ways of making money there doubtless are, but almost any I can think of involve the necessity of moving to a more civilized neighbourhood and it is exactly this which I want to avoid. A steamboat would have the advantage of improving the country more perhaps than anything, but the chances of profit are not very encouraging and the risk and capital to be expended are great. At present the thing is out of the question because the public works from want of funds are at a standstill and it will be probably two years before the whole line will be opened. A distillery on my own creek in connection with the farm, and a store principally intended to buy grain for the distillery would I believe produce enough, but there are objections even in the way of this. My mother is most decidedly and most strongly opposed to it on the score of morality, as she thinks a facility of procuring whiskey would be an injury to the country. Besides this a bill has been introduced into our House of Assembly for imposing an excise of sixpence per gallon on whiskey (about thirty per cent. on its value), which will have the effect of throwing the business into large establishments.

I think I have before said to you that I know of no money-making business in Canada except the Law, storekeeping, tavern-keeping and perhaps I may add horse-dealing. The two latter we will altogether omit. Storekeeping is decidedly the most money-making and is carried on with very little capital, but it appears to me that those who make it pay are invariably those who have started with next to nothing and have gradually crept up in the world, increasing their business as their capital, custom and experience increased; I hardly recollect an instance of any who have succeeded in planting a full grown tree.

Alexander Hunter Murray

In 1818 Alexander Hunter Murray was born in the little Argyll-shire village of Kilmun, facing the mouth of the Clyde. While still young he emigrated, choosing the United States in preference to Canada. There he travelled widely for the American Fur Company.

Restless, he left Texas and Louisiana for the north, joining the Hudson Bay Company as a senior clerk, and being sent by them to the Mackenzie River district. On his way, north-west from Lake Winnipeg to Lake Athabasca and by the Great Slave Lake to Fort Simpson, he met the daughter of a prominent local trader and was married to her by the special contract used in the backwoods, where there was no clergy. Together they went on to Fort McPherson.

In 1844 John Bell had explored the Porcupine River up to the Yukon, and his report having been satisfactory the Company decided to establish a post there. It was for this purpose that Murray set out in 1847, and a description of his choosing a site and erecting Fort Yukon is contained in the journal, with its vigorous pen-and-ink sketches, which he composed there for the benefit of his employers.

He was transferred to the Pembina in 1853 with the rank of Chief Trader, though, in the words of a friend, 'the adventure on which he most prided himself, evidently, was his having founded the most remote post of the company, Fort Youcon, in Russian America, situated within one or two degrees of the Arctic circle.'

[99]

He later retired with his family to a cottage just across the Red River from Henry's post; he called it 'Kilmun'; and died there in 1876.

The text was edited from a copy of the original by L. J. Burpee in *Journal of the Yukon* 1847–1848 *by Alexander Hunter Murray*, Ottawa, 1910.

Lapiers House = La Pierre House.
Batture   = Part of a river bed showing above the surface.
Battishe   = Thongs across a snowshoe.
Castor   = Beaver skin.

25th June, 1847. I must say, as I sat smoking my pipe and my face besmeared with tobacco juice to keep at bay the d——d mosquitoes still hovering in clouds around me, that my first impressions of the Youcon were anything but favourable. As far as we had come (2¼ miles) I never saw an uglier river, everywhere low banks, apparently lately overflowed, with lakes and swamps behind, the trees too small for building, the water abominably dirty and the current furious; but I was consoled with the hopes held out by our Indian informant, that a short distance further on was higher land.

Saturday 26th. I left with three men and one of the Indians to explore the banks of the river for a site for our Fort, and was guided by the Indian who seemed to take great interest and pride in showing us the best places, and in describing the banks of the river above and below. We found the land all too low, and with marks of being overflowed, except two places to which he took us. The one chosen is decidedly the most eligible, and answers *well* only for the scarcity of timber; it is a ridge of dry land extending about 300 yards parallel with the river, and 90 yards in width; the banks are here as they are everywhere else as far as we have seen, sandy and undermining, but there is a large batture in the river in front, and above that an island of about a mile in length, which sets the current out, and prevents it except perhaps in high water, from cutting away the banks. Behind us is another and larger ridge of high land, but it is too far from the river. The other place mentioned is about a mile further up on the same side of the river, where there is still higher land, but the banks are composed of pure sand, the wood still scarcer than here, and the small channel opposite, which passes behind the island, nearly closed up and in the fall quite dry. Having made the best choice I could, we returned, and tracked the boat up to our final encampment, had the goods and everything taken ashore and placed in security for the night. After the Indians were informed that we had decided on building here, two of them left to inform their friends of our arrival in their country, the two others remained with us, one of whom is a leader of a small band of fourteen men, who, he says, obey him like his own children.

27th. The Sunday was spent by the men in preparing little bark cabins for themselves, and by the interpreter and I in talking with the Indian leader, who gave very direct answers to our numerous questions about the country, the natives, the Russians, etc. He was one of four Indians from the place that had seen the Russians the previous summer, and described them as did the others at Lapiers house, as being all well armed with pistols, their boat was about the same size as ours, but, as he thought, made of sheet iron, but carrying more people. They had a great quantity of beads, kettles, guns, powder, knives and pipes, and traded all the furs from the bands, principally for beads and knives, after which they traded dogs, but the Indians were unwilling to part with their dogs, and the Russians rather than go without gave a *gun* for each, as they required many to bring their goods across the portage to the river they descended. The Indians expected to see the Russians here soon, as they had promised to come up with *two boats*, not only to trade but to explore this river to its source.

This was not very agreeable news to me, knowing that we were on their land, but I kept my thoughts to myself, and determined to keep a sharp lookout in case of surprise. I found that the population of this country was much larger than I expected, and more furs to be traded than I had goods to pay for. Mr. McKenzie and I divided the night watch between us, a rule laid down and strictly adhered to when Indians were with us.

28th. About 4 o'clock in the morning we were aroused by reports of fire arms from the point below, and everyone was on his feet in an instant, three shots were fired by us in return, twenty canoes hove in sight around the point and soon paddled up along shore until close to our encampment, all the Indians joining in songs and most unearthly shouts. They remained in their canoes without attempting to land until the Indian leader spoke to them; as soon as they had collected on the bank (there were fifteen men with their wives and families in all about forty) their chief, a young man, commenced to harangue, but it was addressed to the Peels River Indian, who replied at great length in his own defence. The Loncheux of Peels river and the Indians of the Youcon were at war a few years since, and are not yet on the best of terms, it was concerning this and not us that the chief was talking. I gave each of the men three inches of tobacco to smoke before we commenced with the *speechifying*. They immediately formed into a circle and began to sing and dance at a *furious rate*, expressive of their joy at seeing us, they then brought from their canoes some fresh meat and a quantity of dried fish, and laid it at the door of my tent and traded it willingly for powder, ball and tobacco. As advised by the interpreter I deferred saying much until the principal chief arrived with another band which one of the Indians had gone after. During the day two more Indians arrived from the opposite side of the river, and in the evening another salute of five guns was heard from below. Not approving of the practice of wasting ammunition I ordered the men not to fire, but one Indians monitor (the young leader) said it was the custom with them, when they came in peace, to discharge their guns, and if we did not return the salute, they might consider us to be enemies. Five shots were then fired in answer to theirs, which was responded to from the fleet of canoes, now close at hand, by yells and shouts that might have 'struck terror to the soul of Richard,' but *we* knew it was that of rejoicing. There were eighteen men also some women and children in this party. They hauled up their canoes a short distance below, and formed on the bank in 'Indian file,' the chief in front, the women and children in the rear, and danced forward by degrees until in front of the tent, where they were joined by the first party, formed into a large circle, with the two chiefs in the centre, and continued dancing and singing without intercession for upwards of half an hour. A small piece of tobacco, the same as before, was given to each of those last come, and a larger piece to the chief, easily distinguished from the others by his eagle feathers and a greater profusion of beads on his dress. Some more fresh meat was brought forward and traded as before for ammunition and tobacco. The principal chief then shortly addressed the Peels River Indian, supposing him to be our interpreter, and concluded by saying, he 'waited to hear the White Chief speak.' What I had to say was all 'cut and dry' and delivered by the Interpreter in sentences, and after their own fashion. I commenced by bringing to their remembrance Mr. Bell's visit to this river three summers ago, when they were all absent. We had heard so much from other natives about their being a brave people and friendly to the whites, and their country reported so good for furs and provisions, that we had come with the intention of building a Fort and remaining among them. We had sent messengers by the men of the lakes, last winter, to warn them of our intention, but these people had not told them the truth, they were angry at our bringing so many things into this country, because it would prevent them from trading the furs at so low prices—that we had come a long journey, and had much trouble in bringing the goods across the mountains, still we would trade with them at the same rate as at Peels River and other parts of the country. I told them we were a different nation from the *Whites* some of them had seen farther down the river last summer, these people only came once a year to take away their furs, and cheat them with useless goods, what we brought were good, guns, knives, and everything else, and we meant to live always amongst them, but this year, we had only brought a few goods on trial, and if they brought us plenty of good furs, and were able to supply us with food, that more goods and more men would be sent next summer, and we would build a large Fort and reside always in their country, and supply them with guns at twenty Beaver each, instead of twenty-five and thirty which they had been giving to other nations, and the same quantity of beads for six Beaver for which they had given the men of the lakes twelve and fifteen. After enumerating the articles we had, their excellent qualities, and the rate at which they were traded, I concluded by asking if they wished us to remain and build here (several of the young men, regardless of Indian etiquette, replied *aha*, *aha* (yes, yes)), and if so, if they would bring their furs to us instead of taking them to the other whites (the Russians).

The principal chief, after being spoken to by several others, walked to the front and *made a speech*, the longest I ever listened to, except, perhaps, a *cameronian sermon*, and some parts of [it] equally far from the text.

I told them that I was pleased to hear them talk so well, we had heard that they were *great hunters*, and we had brought little to eat, depending on them to bring us meat. That we much wanted dressed moose skins for shoes, for we had brought none with us. Battishe for snowshoes in winter, parchment for windows of our houses, deer skins and sinews, etc. That we would trade all good furs made in winter or spring but not those killed in summer. We had this year very few beads and guns, and would only give them for Martens, Beavers, Black and Silver Foxes. That anything else we had, would be given for all other furs, except Rats and Marinots. I then advised them to turn their attention to making provisions and those things we so much required, and as an 'earnest of future favors' some tobacco ready cut up on a board was presented to them; very few of them had pipes, and I noticed several chewing the tobacco and even swallowing the juice. After smoking until several were completely intoxicated, the young chief 'par example' could not get up until a drink of water was given to him, he said they were now very happy and wished to have a great dance, but they had only black paint at present, if they had some red it would make them look much *prettier*. A little vermilion and a present of a comb and looking glass was given to each of the chiefs. They retired to where the women had prepared an encampment with branches and in a short time issued forth arrayed in all

[104]

their fineries, and commenced a regular *Break Down*, all joining. Thirty-seven men and a lot of women and children, only two of whom had before seen the *Whites*. They danced a variety of figures accompanied always with songs, and continued at it for nearly two hours. I am partly wrong in saying *figures*, with one exception they danced always in a circle, the only difference in their steps, gestures, and songs, of which latter they have a great variety. After the *ball* was finished they retired to their own encampment, but the singing was taken up, at intervals, until morning.

Undated entries.

Having already formed great ideas of the country, I determined on building a Fort worthy of it, we are in an isolated corner of the country and cut off from all communication with other posts at least for assistance, and surrounded by hostile Indians, the Rat Indians are enraged at our being here, the 'Gens-du-fou' reported ditto, also those down the river with whom the Russians have been trading, the Russians themselves might give us battle, and I concluded on making a convenient and substantial Fort, though it might take longer time.

We were seldom without visitors, and they did not often come empty handed, we had always *plenty to eat* and plenty to do so that none were allowed to weary. Geese and duck were always passing, and now and then a Beaver would clap his tail 'en passant' before our levee. The woods behind abounded in rabbits and partridges, and go which way one would, if a good shot, he need not return without something for the kettle.

We lived on good terms with the natives and feared nothing, except to see two boat-loads of Russians heave round the point on a nocturnal visit from the Gens-du-fou.

The natives on whose lands we are number about ninety men, and are divided into three bands, the chiefs or leaders of each with a number of their followers were here in June as I have already noticed at length, the others were soon made aware of our arrival, and in a month afterward I believe they had all been here, and all were alike pleased to see us. They soon brought us their furs, principally Beaver and Martens the greater part of which had been brought up by the leaders and a few of the *rich* men of the nation who were preparing to meet the Russians down the river. Beads and guns were always demanded and I had few to give them, and was anxious to distribute what I had as equally as possible among them. But they were not satisfied with this mode of trading, they say when the others go to trade with the Russians they get what they ask for and expect the same here, while we had what they required. Notwithstanding the explanations and reasons given we had some difficulty in pleasing all, they were however satisfied with our prices. Blankets, axes, knives, powder horns and files went off readily enough, but it was hard to dispose of the clothing, as they consider their own clothing much superior to ours both in beauty and durability, and they are partly right, though I endeavoured to persuade them to the contrary. I could not give them the reason for bringing so few goods, that we had brought only a few on trial, but more would be sent next year, which was the only way to prevent them disposing of their furs elsewhere.

Not many days after [November 27] the young chief arrived in the evening and informed us of the arrival of two Indians from the lower bands with men from the Russians. They had been sent to the Indians here with messages from the Russians who were passing the winter at the mouth of the river they descended, had a large stock of goods with them, were trading at much better prices than formerly, and had better goods than us. The Russians were trying to incite the Indians here against us by telling them that it was on account of our being in their country that so many of them had died in summer, that we were bad people, etc., and inviting the Indians to go to them with their sick friends as they had medicines to cure all diseases, that they were sorry they had not been able to keep their promise with the Indians here and visit their country in summer, they had been unfortunate in having necessary boats built, but next summer they would meet them farther up the river with plenty of goods. The Russians had taken the most effective plan to work upon the credulity of the Indians here, and I was greatly mortified to hear from the young chief that some of his followers believed what they had said and intended to go down with their furs by the first open water. I sent for one of these Russian Indians who was remaining with the lower band and heard a repetition of the whole story before several other Indians.

I had a long talk with them in presence of the stranger, and took care to give the Russians a 'lick back' in their own coin. I explained particularly the motives that induced our opponents to send these messages, the cause of their lowering their prices, and succeeded in persuading them of the absurdity of the idea of our causing the death of their people, instead of that we were their best friends, and had brought medicines to keep them from dying, etc. etc. etc., as for taking their furs below in spring they were their own masters, and could dispose of them to the Russians if they chose, but if they did so they would be sorry for it afterwards, assuring them that no more goods would be brought here in summer. The Indians present seemed willing enough to hold on until next season, still a few days afterwards, a lot of beaver were sold to the Russian Indians for fancy beads, an article they could not procure from us and which they value above everything else.

I have been accustomed to the *strongest kind* of opposition while in the south, and would like nothing better, as I love a row, than to have it again, but I would wish also to have the means of competing.

But here we are far across the Frontier, and with little but promises to give the Indians.

I received the [outfit?] by the return of my men from Lapiers House on January 5th and must say, that I was greatly mortified to find so limited a supply of the articles most needed (beads and guns) being sent; I notice that there are only a quarter of a box of beads (16 lbs.). I would have been better satisfied had none at all been sent, as I could then have settled with the Indians alike, without displeasing one more than another. I am now at a loss what to do. There is one man of the upper band who has between 90 and 100 skins in martens and beaver which he is keeping *all* for beads on our return. *Two men* would take more than what are sent, and how am I to settle with 300? I know you could not be aware at the time the outfit was made up of what was required here, and moreover that it requires a certain time too, if you have to depend on goods coming from England, perhaps three years, before an

[107]

extra supply of goods for this addition to your district is received at Fort Simpson, you might not have had the means to send more, still I did expect at least two boxes of beads and two of guns. Now I have got into a scrape, or at least will get into one on my return; the Indians all expect a larger outfit, I have promised it to them and what excuse can I give? There is not an Indian here, and very few even at Peels River but wear fancy beads, that is blue and red of various sizes, they cost the Indians nearly double what they pay for the common white beads, all these fancy beads are traded from the Russians, or by the Peels River Indians from the 'Gens-du-fou' and natives of this quarter. To trade here successfully, there ought to be for one year's outfit four boxes of common white beads, one box of red (same size) and one box of fancy (blue of various sizes and colors and necklaces), this quantity it will perhaps be difficult to procure at York factory, but there is a great quantity sent to Red River, there every common woman wears them, the Company may perhaps receive one shilling for each necklace, if they were sent here they would be worth at least 30 shillings each. For the small shells, a few of which you sent me at Peels River, they are most valuable, every Indian wears them, as nose and ear ornaments, for hair bands, etc., and a small quantity might be sent annually from the Columbia without a great deal of trouble. Except cloth and capots which can only be disposed of when there is nothing else, cloth not even then, everything else can be traded here, some brass arm bands and neck ornaments, medals and larger sized ear rings could be disposed of advantageously, also some fancy handled knives. I would most urgently advise, if you would wish this settlement to prosper, that an extensive and suitable outfit be sent, even though some of the old established places should be more scantily supplied for a season. We cannot begin to compete with the Russians as to prices, nor can I tell what the result will be after the full force of the opposition will be felt.

June 16th. I am now on the voyage to Lapiers House, encamped amongst the rocks in the Ramparts of Porcupine River.

I left Mr. V. McKenzie and four men at the Youcon, and gave

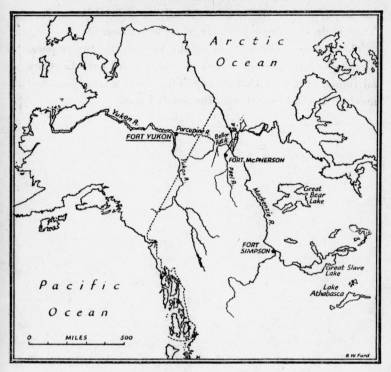

North West Canada, to illustrate Murray's journal

instructions for the summer's work, and there is plenty to keep them all employed. Our spring operations are pretty well forwarded considering the great distance all the wood had to be brought. *Two* new boats are built each 30 feet 8 in. keel and 9 feet beam.

We have subsisted all spring until the day of our departure upon fresh moose meat, and there is left, well packed with snow in the cellar fresh provisions more than will support the people left till our return. With one thing and another I have been able to make the two ends meet, and saved the greater part of the pemmican brought with me.

Guns and beads, beads and guns is all the cry in *our* country. Please to excuse me for repeating this so often, but I cannot be

[109]

too importunate, the *rise* or *fall* of our establishment on the Youcon depends on the supply of these articles.

The returns of the first year of the Youcon, are twelve packs of furs, and a half ditto of deer skins, also a small box of castors, in all valued at £1557.15.3 stirling. This is not a large sum, but as much as I could collect with the goods I had.

AUSTRALIA

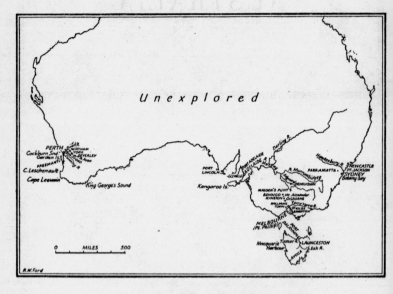

Australia and Van Diemen's Land

In April 1770 Lieutenant Cook, in the *Endeavour*, discovered and entered Botany Bay. His ship, the first visitant from the civilized world, hove to alongside a party of natives preparing a meal by a fire on shore. They evinced no surprise. The anchor was dropped and echoes rolled over the water of a kind never heard there before. The aborigines continued with their cooking. It is one of History's most delightful moments, for seldom can her processes have been greeted with a more complete indifference. Even the discharge of the greatest marvel of all, that wielder of portable thunder the musket, only caused one of the natives to jump and drop his spear, which he immediately picked up again.

The place was named after the activities of the ship's botanists, one of whom, Sir Joseph Banks, came to be the instrument of its settlement and to earn the title 'Father of Australia.'

For the continent was ignored for years after Cook's voyage. It was not until the American War of Independence made it impossible for England to get rid of her surplus convicted felons by shipping them across the Atlantic that it was forced back into public notice. The gaols were crammed; they overflowed into old hulks moored along inland waterways; and then the hulks overflowed. The problem of the disposal of the wicked became desperate. Suggestions were not lacking. The East Indies, the West Indies, the Falklands, Canada, Nova Scotia, and Florida, all were considered, until before a committee which reported to the House of Commons on April 1st, 1779, Banks made the suggestion that two or three hundred felons should be sent to Botany Bay.

But the committee seemed more interested in Yanimarew, 'situate about 400 miles from the mouth of the river Gambia,' and seemed encouraged by Dr. Thomas Walker's evidence to the effect that 'all Europeans upon their arrival had a fever, which was called a Seasoning Sickness; that out of 210 convicts he did not apprehend above a sixth part would die of it; that those who recovered from that disorder were usually very healthy afterwards.'

Not until December 6th, 1786, did an Order in Council appoint 'the eastern coast of New South Wales [Cook had thought it looked like Glamorganshire] or some one or other of the islands adjacent' as the destination of transported criminals.

Next year the First Fleet sailed from Portsmouth. It consisted of the frigate *Sirius*, the tender *Supply*, six transports and three store ships, a total tonnage of less than 4,000 tons. On board were 778 convicts and 695 free persons, marines, sailors and their families. Before them lay a voyage of eight months to their destination, a piece of coast which had only been sighted once before and lay some 16,000 miles away, at the centre of a largely unexplored ocean. A romantic episode, it was an emergency solution to a problem in social sanitation, and there is scanty evidence that in the heads of more than one or two individuals were visionary prospects of Empire.

Two years later ELIZABETH MACARTHUR was taken by her husband to Port Jackson (which had been preferred as a place of settlement to Botany Bay). She witnessed the hardships inevitable when a few shiploads of criminals and their gaolers are tipped into an untamed wilderness with few implements and scant ability to cultivate it. But thanks to the wisdom of Phillip, the first Governor, the settlement survived, and, as a few free settlers tentatively came to take advantage of the offer of land and convict labour, extended over the site of the future city of Sydney and up along the rivers.

Macarthur himself became famed as the founder of the wool trade. He was fortunate in being able to secure some merinos from the Escurial flocks which had been presented by the King of Spain to the Dutch at the Cape. With these he bred sheep whose wool was enthusiastically received in England. Continental supplies no longer were available for the ever-multiplying looms of the industrial revolution, and Australia's prosperity was assured.

Politics in New South Wales, meanwhile, were running an erratic course, and a climax came when Bligh (of the *Bounty*) arrived as Governor in 1806. A successful revolution led to his being set afloat again, on this occasion in the Bass Strait, but Macarthur was forced to retire to England for a time.

His claim to be the founder of the Australian wool trade has been challenged on behalf of SAMUEL MARSDEN, the colony's chaplain. But Marsden was more important for the mission he established in New Zealand and for the constant fight he kept up against the physical as well as the moral evils of the convict settlement. These were great, though there is no space to consider them here, and sprang from two main causes, the immense consumption of spirits and the complete disproportion between men and women; to which a third, an uncreative and savage discipline, may be added. The result was a reputation that tended to keep settlers away from the colony until the success of the wool trade was established beyond doubt and land far from the actual penal concentrations made available. In 1812 George Blaxland crossed the Blue Mountains and was the first to look down into what seemed an illimitable expanse of grassland and forest. The beginning was to be slow, but he had set moving the advance of the squatters, opening up the continent as they drove their flocks continually onwards, heedless of the agitated twitterings of Government about the official limits of a little colony in the south-east.

*   *   *

Van Diemen's Land (called Tasmania from 1853) was early included in the penal scheme, and one of its settlements, at Port Arthur, provided an extreme of brutal misery for those convicted of crimes after their arrival in Australia, a distinction it shared with Norfolk Island, about 900 miles east by north of Sydney. Transportation to New South Wales stopped in 1840, to Van Diemen's Land in 1853.

By the time WILLIAM BARNES arrived to get rich quick as a brewer, a dismal tragedy had been played out. The aborigines of Van Diemen's Land were of a race even more ancient than those of the mainland, whose predecessors they are thought to have been. Intercourse with Europeans in Australia did not necessarily imply civilization, and in this case it meant extinction. The aborigines as a whole were a strange people, living in terms of a remote antiquity. It was difficult to bridge the gulf and imagine them as fellow human beings, and for some time it was not attempted. Like

[115]

the bushmen in South Africa, they were hunted as noxious animals, even poisoned by means used to get rid of wild dogs. An attempt to save them was made, indeed, in Van Diemen's Land before it was too late. At Governor Arthur's instigation every available man on the island was to help form a human chain some hundred and fifty miles long, which, slowly moving south, would drive the blacks back to the coast, where they could be captured and segregated. The result was that four and a half thousand men, at a cost of £30,000, rounded up a small boy and an old woman; all the others had slipped through. But eventually, in ones and twos, they were rounded up and put together on Flinders Island, in Bass Strait. And here they gradually sickened till by 1847 only forty-four remained. Thirty years later the race was extinct.

* * *

Van Diemen's Land had been occupied originally to prevent the French from getting there first, and the same motive led to the dispatch in 1826 of an expedition from Sydney to King George's Sound, on the south-western tip of the continent, and a settlement survived there to join up with the larger settlement on the Swan River, which was organized direct from England. GEORGE FLETCHER MOORE came over with the first parties in 1830. But the promoters of the scheme lost most of their money. So much land was given away so cheaply that the settlers lost touch with one another, and, besides, the land was not so spontaneously fruitful as it was in the east. Many settlers threw in their hand and left. From 4,000 the population dropped to 1,500 in 1832. Twenty years later it had only passed the original number by a thousand. Paradoxically, for they had at first prided themselves on their insulation from the felonous east, they were forced to ask for convict labour, and by 1867 numbers and wealth had so much increased that Western Australia was secured from decline, and transportation, having done its work, was brought to an end.

* * *

Five years before Moore came out, JOHN BATMAN made his famous treaty with the aborigines at Port Phillip. The land in

[116]

what was to be called Victoria was already believed to be good, but the authorities in New South Wales were against an undue scattering of population, and the south coast was unvisited in the main save by whalers from the Strait. But in 1835 Batman sailed with a few companions and some Sydney aborigines to Port Phillip. Here, by means of his own natives, Batman persuaded Cooloolook, Bungarie, Yanyon, Moowhip, and three Jaga-Jagas to grant him and his associates over 600,000 acres, including a large part of the modern Melbourne. His story is gravely beset with inconsistencies and it is perhaps difficult to believe that he was acting in good faith with savages who had no notion of private property, whether or not they could understand a lot of legal rigmarole as transmitted by blacks whose dialect was different from their own. Government refused to acknowledge the deed, but in the nature of things settlement was inevitable; the land was good and, after this, widely publicized. Two streams of immigration, one from Van Diemen's Land and another overland from New South Wales, brought a large and vigorous population.

*   *   *

The founding of South Australia provides a complete contrast to the haphazard methods employed in Victoria. Plans were carefully laid at home under the guidance of Edward Gibbon Wakefield, whose ideas have coloured all subsequent thinking about *The Art of Colonization*. In the book of this name and in another still more vigorous, the *Letter from Sydney*, written while serving a prison sentence for abduction, he claimed that the fault that had spoiled all previous attempts at colonization was letting the land go too cheaply. The result was a horde of petty masters with no one to work for them. Tack a 'sufficient price' to the land and poor emigrants would have to work for some time in cultivating someone's property before they could afford to buy themselves. They in turn would be able to find labourers saving up to buy, and so on. After many obstacles had been overcome a 'South Australian Company' was formed to carry out a plan of settlement. The first ships sailed in 1836, taking MARY THOMAS and her family with them. Notions about the country were so vague that they expected to find the best land on the largely barren Kangaroo Island. Adelaide was finally settled upon, but the price charged for land was still not a 'sufficient' one, and Wakefield's theory was again proved for the edification of future colonists, as we shall see when we come to deal with New Zealand. Speculation was rife, but the fields remained untilled, and the colony was in a sad way, crippled with debt and no longer attracting settlers, when George Grey came out as Governor in 1841. Thanks to him, the colony was firmly established when he left, four years later.

*   *   *

Much of its thunder was stolen, however, when gold was found in Victoria in 1851. It had been known for many years that there was gold in Australia, but the authorities were afraid that it would divert too much attention from agriculture. This attitude was abruptly changed when the Californian gold rushes started drawing thousands of men away altogether, and it was as much to save her own population as a matter of luck that gold was found in several places, notably in the hills north of Melbourne. Ballarat, Mount Alexander, and Bendigo suddenly became famous names. Diggers came swarming in from outside as well as from every part of Australia. There were nuggets of 2,000 ounces, weekend fortunes of £10,000; for spectacular successes and growing violence the Victorian did not yield to any gold rush in the world. The population doubled, then doubled again, till that of New South Wales was passed. Even JOHN DAVIES MEREWEATHER, highly principled clergyman as he was, was nearly swept off his feet and admitted that 'the sight of a quantity of rich virgin gold just taken from the surrounding mould agitates the nerves strangely.'

All our writers, in fact, saw their states established and prospering, and those who dared to prophesy good things were true prophets.

Elizabeth Macarthur

Elizabeth Veale was born in 1768. Her father was a country gentleman of means, and on his property near Holsworthy, by the Cornish border of Devon, she lived, a dreamy and poetical girl, until she was twenty-one. Then came marriage and metamorphosis. John Macarthur, soldier and farmer, was a high-tempered and imperious man, and it is not surprising that she should relate that her friends did not think 'that either of us had taken a prudent step.'

In 1789 Macarthur, who had obtained a commission in the newly formed New South Wales Corps, took his wife to Australia, only two years after the sailing of the First Fleet.

The farm he built on his 200-acre grant near Parramatta he named after her, and here they lived a genteel but vigorous pioneer life, while he became involved in sheep breeding and local politics with increasing absorption until a crisis came under Bligh and he was forced to return to England until matters were smoothed over in 1813.

Meanwhile Elizabeth had adapted herself so well to marriage and pioneering that after twenty years he could write: 'I am perfectly aware, my beloved wife, of the difficulties you have to contend with, and fully convinced that not one woman in a thousand, (no one that I know) would have resolution and perseverance to contend with them at all, much more to surmount them in the manner that you have so happily done.'

[119]

She died in 1850, outliving him by sixteen years. The care of eight children probably made the rendering of Foot's minuet remain the apex of her prowess at the piano, but we have no means in print of knowing how much longer this charming dilettante badgered Mr. Dawes for an alternative art or science to amuse her leisure hours.

These letters to her friend, Miss Kingdon, in England are printed in *Some Early Records of the Macarthurs of Camden*, Sydney, 1914, edited by Sibella Macarthur Onslow.

Sydney, Port Jackson, N.S. Wales, March 7th, 1791. At length we have a prospect of communication once more with our friends by letter. The *Gorgon*, so long wished for, and so long expected, is not yet arrived, and by her unaccountable delay, has involved us all in the most mysterious uncertainty, and clouded our minds with gloomy apprehensions for her safety. I hope you will have rec'd my letter, dated August, 1790, which I sent by the *Scarborough* transport, by way of China.

I told you of the unfortunate loss of the *Syrius*, a King's ship, that had been stationed here from the first settling of the Colony. She was wrecked on Norfolk Island. The ship's company, who all escaped with life, but not altogether without hurt, remained on the Island, and the *Supply*, a small brig, that sailed from this place with the *Syrius*, returned with the news of her sad fate.

The provisions of the Colony, at that time, being at a very low ebb, it was deemed necessary to take some step lest supply might not arrive from England in time to prevent a threatened famine. Every individual of this Colony was reduced to a very short allowance, and the little brig was dispatched to Batavia under the command of Lieutenant Ball, there to take up a Dutch ship, and purchase a certain quantity of provisions for this place, with which it was to be freighted and dispatched hither with all possible expedition. A few weeks after the *Supply* sailed, the first ship, *Lady Juliana*, arrived, and brought an account of the loss of the *Guardian*, occasioned by falling in with islands of ice. The ship arrived on the 3rd June, and came timely to prevent very great distress.

On the 21st June the *Justiana* arrived, a store ship, and on the 29th our fleet was safely anchored in the Cove. As all these ships were under contract to return by way of China to take home Tea for the East India Company, and there being at that time no ship stationed here, no way was left to convey a relief to the inhabitants of Norfolk Island, but by ordering some of those ships to touch there on their way to China. The *Justiana* and *Surprize* received orders, for that purpose reimbarked a certain proportion of provision for the island. We had every hope that the supplies might arrive in time to prevent any fatal consequences; yet, as we could have no certainty of that, and till some ship should first arrive here that might be dispatched to know the particulars of their fate, our minds were never perfectly easy on their account. At that time there was, with the *Syrius's* company, the Marines, and convicts, near 700 persons on the Island, and I can truly say that for upwards of six months I never passed a day without reflecting on them with pain and anxiety. Week after week stole away, and month after month with little diversity. Each succeeding sunset produced among us wild and vague conjectures of what could be the cause of the *Gorgon's* delay, and still we remained unsatisfied—indeed all our surmises have nearly worn themselves out and we are at a loss for new ones—time the great resolver of all events alone can determine this seeming mystery to us.

On the 20th October a general cry prevailed through the Garrison of the Flags being hoisted (which is a signal of a ship appearing off the Harbour). I was preparing myself to receive Mrs. Grose and Mrs. Paterson, being fully persuaded it was the *Gorgon*, however I was soon undeceived, as it proved to be the *Supply* from Batavia; she had a very quick passage but had experienced a very sickly one.

On the 21st of January the *Supply* was sent to bring hither the *Syrius* ship's company, and learn the state of affairs at that place. She returned on the 25th of February with the officers and men in health, and brought a good account of the health of every individual left behind. This circumstance removed some considerable

[121]

anxiety from our minds; but it proved our fears had been but too well grounded, as when the *Supply* arrived they had not more than ten days' provisions in the store, at a full allowance, and from the 14th of last May, till the 18th of July, they were reduced to the scanty pittance of 3 lbs. of flour and 1½ lbs. of beef for a week. At this time a most merciful relief came to their assistance. It had been observed on a high hill in the island (which they have named Mount Pitt) that many seabirds frequented it. An endeavour was made to take some of them, which was successful, and by attending more particularly to the time of their appearance and their favourite haunts they were discovered in the greatest abundance. It was the season in which they laid their eggs, and both birds and eggs were taken in such quantities as occasioned the small allowance of meat they had issued before to be stopped, and, however wonderful it may appear to you, yet true it is, that those birds for many weeks, were the chief subsistence of seven hundred men, and they were so easily taken that after sunset it was impossible to walk on the Mount without treading on them, and sometimes towards evening, they have been observed hovering in the air in such innumerable flocks as considerably to exclude the light from admiring spectators. But now the melancholy truth of their decrease became more and more apparent. Their flights were directed to other quarters and at length few remained. But before hope was quite extinguished, a ship appeared and brought them a long expected supply. Believe me, my dear friend, that in writing these faithful traits of the pitiable situation of the inhabitants of Norfolk Island, a chill seems to overpower my faculties; my mind has so truly entered into their distresses that a dread comes over me, which I am unable to describe, but it is succeeded by so firm a reliance on the merciful dispensations of an Almighty, whose hand I think we may here trace without presumption, that I can only admire in silence.

I shall begin my relation now of things more immediately occurring to myself.

We passed our time away many weeks cheerfully if not gaily—gaily indeed it could not be said to be. On my first landing everything was new to me, every Bird, every Insect, Flower, etc.; in short, all was novelty around me, and was noticed with a degree of eager curiosity and perturbation, that after a while subsided into that calmness I have already described. In my former letter I gave you the character of Mr. Dawes, and also of Captain Tench. Those gentlemen and a few others are the chief among whom we visit. Indeed we are in the habit of intimacy with Captain Tench that there are few days pass that we do not spend some part of together. Mr. Dawes we do not see so frequently. He is so much engaged with the stars that to mortal eyes he is not always visible. I had the presumption to become his pupil and meant to learn a little of astronomy. It is true I have had many pleasant walks to his house (something less than half a mile from Sydney), have given him much trouble in making orreries, and explaining to me the general principles of the heavenly bodies, but I soon found I had mistaken my abilities and blush at my error. Still, I wanted something to fill up a certain vacancy in my time which could neither be done by writing, reading, or conversation. To the first two I did not feel myself always inclined, and the latter was not in my power, having no female friend to unbend my mind to, nor a single woman with whom I could converse with any satisfaction to myself, the Clergy-man's wife being a person in whose society I could reap neither profit or pleasure. These considerations made me still anxious to learn some easy science to fill up the vacuum of many a solitary day, and at length under the auspices of Mr. Dawes I have made a small progress in Botany. No country can exhibit a more copious field for botanical knowledge than this. I am arrived so far as to be able to class and order all common plants. I have found great pleasure in my study; every walk furnished me with subjects to put in practice that Theory I had before gained by reading, but alas, my botanical pursuits were most unwelcomely interrupted by Mr. Macarthur being attacked by a severe illness. In December he got better, and in January we removed into a more convenient house.

I shall now tell you of another resource I had to fill up some of my vacant hours. Our new house is ornamented with a pianoforte of Mr. Worgan's, he kindly means to leave it with me, and now, under his direction, I have begun a new study, but I fear without my Master I shall not make any great proficiency. I am told, however, that I have done wonders in being able to play off 'God Save the King,' and Foot's minuet, besides that of reading the notes with great facility. In spite of musick I have not altogether lost sight of my botanical studies. I have only been precluded from pursuing that study by the intense heat of the weather which has not permitted me to walk much during the summer. I have seen very little rain since my arrival, indeed I do not think we have had a week's rain in the whole time, the consequence of which is our garden produces nothing, all is burnt up; indeed, the soil must be allowed to be most wretched and totally unfit for growing European productions, though you would scarcely believe this, as the face of the ground at this moment, when it is in its native state, is flourishing even to luxuriance, producing fine Shrubs, Trees, and Flowers which by their lively tints afford a most agreeable landscape. Beauty, I have heard from some of my unlettered countrymen, is but skin deep. I am sure the remark holds good in New South Wales, where all the beauty is literally on the surface, but I believe I must allow it has symetry of form also to recommend it, as the ground in all the parts that have been discovered is charmingly turned and diversified by agreeable vallies and gently rising hills; but still, these beauties are all exterior.

Of my walkes round Sydney the longest has not extended beyond three miles, and that distance I have, I believe, only ventured upon twice: once to a farm which Captain Nepean has for his Company, to which we sent our tea equipage and drank tea on the turf, and once to a hill situated between this and Botany Bay where I could command a prospect of that famous spot. Nor do I think there is any probability of my seeing much of the inland country until it is cleared, as beyond a certain distance round the Colony there is nothing but native paths, very narrow and very incommodious. The natives are certainly not a very gallant set of people, who take pleasure in escorting their ladies. No; they suffer them humbly to follow Indian file like. As I am now speaking of the natives, I must give you an account of how we stand with them. In the winter, 1789 (which you will recollect is summer in England) a dreadful small pox was discovered amongst the natives. Amongst the unhappy objects that were discovered was a Boy and Girl. These were brought in, and from the humanity of the Clergyman, who took the Girl, and of the principal surgeon, Mr. White, who took the Boy, they were both saved. After they began to learn English and to make us understand them, it was immagined from their communication that if a man or two could be brought to reside with us, that some valuable information might be obtained respecting the interior parts of the country. With this view the Governor left no means untried to effect an intimacy with them, but every endeavour of that sort, as before, proved ineffectual. They accept of his presents as children do playthings; just to amuse them for a moment and then throw them away disregarded. Despairing to gain their confidence by fair means, the Governor ordered that two men should be taken by force. This was done; the poor fellows, I am told, exhibited the strongest marks of terror and consternation at the proceeding, believing they were certainly meant to be sacrificed. When they were taken to the Governor's house and immediately cleaned and clothed their astonishment at everything they saw was amazing. A new world was unfolded to their view at once. For some days they were much dejected, but it soon gave way to cheerfulness. They were then admitted to the Governor's table, and in a little time ate and drank everything that was given them. They now walked about the settlement as they liked, only with a man who was appointed to attend them that they might not escape into the woods, but, as they showed no apparent inclination to do that the vigilance of their keeper by degrees abated, which the older of the two (named Coleby) soon observed, and in a very artful manner one night made his escape. The one who remained, and called himself Bannylong, till May, 1790, and then took himself off without any known reason, having been treated with the most uniform kindness, and appeared highly pleased with our people and manners, taking it a great compliment to be called White Man. On the 7th Sept., Captain Nepean and several other Gentlemen went down the Harbour in a boat, with an intention of proceeding to Broken Bay to take a view of the Hawkesbury River. In their way they put in at Manly Cove, a place so called from the spirited behaviour of the natives there at

[125]

the Governor's first landing. At this time about 200 natives were assembled feeding on a whale that had been driven on shore. As they discovered no hostile intentions our party, having arms, went up to them. Nauberry was in the boat and was desired to inquire for Bannylong and Coleby, when behold both gentlemen appeared, and advancing with the utmost confidence asked in broken English for all their old friends at Sydney. The Governor lost no time, but as soon as he was acquainted with the above circumstances, ordered a boat, and accompanied by Mr. Collins, the Judge Advocate, and a Lieut. Waterhouse of the Navy, repaired to Manly Cove. He landed by himself unarmed, in order to show no violence was intended.

Bannylong approached and shook hands with the Governor, but Coleby had before left the spot. No reason was asked why Bannylong had left us. He appeared very happy, and thankful for what was given him, requesting an hatchet and some other things which the Governor promised to bring him the next day. Mr. Collins and Mr. Waterhouse now joined him, and several natives also came forward. They continued to converse with them with much seeming friendship until they had insensibly wandered some distance from the boat, and very imprudently none of the Gentlemen had the precaution to take a gun in their hand. This the Governor perceiving deemed it prudent to retreat, and, after assuring that he would remember his promise, told him he was going. At that moment an old man advanced whom Bannylong said was his friend, and wished the Governor to take notice of him. At this he approached the old man with his hand extended, when on a sudden the savage started back and snatched up a spear from the ground and poised it to throw, the Governor, seeing the danger, told him in their tongue that it was bad, and still advanced, when, with a mixture of horror and intrepidity, the native discharged the spear with all his force at the Governor. It entered above his collarbone, and came out at his back nine inches from the entrance, taking an oblique direction. The natives from the rocks now poured in their spears in abundance so that it was with the utmost difficulty and the greatest good fortune that no other hurt was received in getting the Governor into the boat. As soon

as they returned to this place you may believe an universal solici-
tude prevailed, as the danger of the wound could by no means be
ascertained until the spear was extracted, and this was not done
before his Excellency had caused some papers to be arranged lest
the consequences might prove fatal, which happily it did not, for
on drawing out the spear, it was found that no vital part had been
touched. The Governor, having a good habit of bodily health, the
wound perfectly healed in the course of a few weeks. Since then a
convict game keeper has been killed by a spear, but it seems in
some measure to have been owing to his own imprudence. Bannylong came many times to see the Governor during his confinement,
and expressed great sorrow, but the reason why the mischief was
done could not be learnt, since that period the natives visit us
every day, more or less.

My spirits are at this time low, very low, to-morrow we loose
some valuable members of our small society and some very good
friends. In so small a society we sensibly feel the loss of every
member, more particularly those that are endeared to us by acts
of kindness and friendship. From this circumstance and my
former letters you may be led to question my happiness, but this
much I can with truth add for myself, that since I have had the
powers of reason and reflection I never was more sincerely happy
than at this time. It is true I have some wishes unaccomplished,
but when I consider this is not a state of perfection I am abundantly content.

Elizabeth Farm, Parramatta, 1st Sept., 1795. By the capture of a
ship off the coast of Brazil we were left without any direct intelligence from Europe for twelve months. We firmly believed that a
Revolution or some national calamity had befallen Great Britain,
and we should be left altogether to ourselves, until things at home
had resumed some degree of order, and the tempest a little subsided. These fears, however, have by a late arrival proved without
foundation.

This country possesses numerous advantages to persons holding
appointments under Government. It seems the only part of the
Globe where quiet is to be expected. We enjoy here one of the

finest climates in the World. The necessaries of life are abundant, and a fruitful soil affords us many luxuries. Nothing induces me to wish for a change but the difficulty of educating our children, and were it otherwise, it would be unjust towards them to confine them to so narrow a society. My desire is that they should see a little more of the world, and better learn to appreciate this retirement. Such as it is the little creatures all speak of going home to England with rapture. My dear Edward almost quitted me without a tear. They have early imbibed an idea that England is the seat of happiness and delight; that it contains all that can be gratifying to their senses, and that of course they are there to possess all they desire. It would be difficult to undeceive young people bred up in so secluded a situation, if they had not an opportunity given them of convincing themselves. But hereafter I shall much wonder if some of them make not this place the object of their choice. By the date of this letter you will see that we still reside on our farm at Parramatta, a native name signifying the head of a river, which it is. The town extends one mile in length from the landing-place, and is terminated by the Government House, which is built on an eminence, named Rose Hill. Our farm, which contains from 400 to 500 acres, is bounded on three sides by water. This is particularly convenient. We have at this time about 120 acres in wheat, all in a promising state. Our gardens, with fruit and vegetables, are extensive and produce abundantly.

It is now spring, and the eye is delighted with the most beautiful variegated landscape. Almonds, apricots, pear and apple trees are in full bloom. The native shrubs are also in flower and the whole country gives a grateful perfume. There is a very good carriage road now made from hence to Sydney, which by land is distant about 14 miles, and another from this to the river Hawkesbury, which is about 20 miles from hence in a direct line across the country. Parramatta is a central position between both. I have once visited the Hawkesbury, and made the journey on horseback. The road is through an uninterrupted wood, with the exception of the village of Toongabie, a farm of Government, and one or two others, which we distinguish by the name of Greenlands, on account of the fine grass, and there being few trees compared with the other parts of the country, which is occasionally bushy, and more or less covered with underwood.

The greater part of the country is like an English park, and the trees give it the appearance of a wilderness or shrubbery, commonly attached to the habitations of people of fortune, filled with a variety of native plants, placed in a wild irregular manner. I was at the Hawkesbury three days. It is a noble fresh water river, taking its rise in a precipitous range of mountains, that it has hitherto been impossible to pass; many attempts have been made, although in vain, I spent an entire day on this river, going in a boat to a beautiful spot, named by the late Governor, 'Richmond Hill,' high and overlooking a great extent of country. On one side are those stupendous barriers to which I have alluded, rising as it were immediately above your head; below, the river itself, still and unruffled; out of sight is heard a waterfall whose distant murmurs add awfulness to the scene. I could have spent more time here but we were not without apprehensions of being interrupted by the natives, as about that time they were very troublesome, and had killed many white people on the banks of the river. The soil in the valley of this river is most productive, and greatly superior to any that has been tilled in this country, which has induced numbers to settle there, but having no vessels there is at present much difficulty in transporting the produce to Sydney. Our stock of cattle is large; we have now fifty head, a dozen horses, and about a thousand sheep.

Mr. Macarthur has also set a Plough at work, the first which has been used in the country, and is drawn sometimes by oxen and at others by horses. The ground was before tilled with the hoe. These details I am sensible have no other interest than as far as they serve to show the progressive state of this yet infant settlement.

Mr. Macarthur has frequently in his employment 30 or 40 people whom we pay weekly for their labour. We have but two men fed at the expence of the Crown, altho' there are persons who contrive to get twenty or more, which the Governor does not or will not notice.

You will wonder how a return is made for the daily expence which it must appear to you we incur.

In the first place some thousands of persons are fed from the public stores, perhaps between three or four thousand, all of whom were formerly supplied with flour from England to meet the demand for bread. But since so many individuals have cleared farms and have thereby been enabled to raise a great quantity of grain in the country, which at the present time is purchased by the Commissary at 10s. a bushel, and issued for what are termed rations, or the proportionate quantity due to each person instead of flour. In payment for which the Commissary issues a receipt, approved of by the Government; and these receipts pass current here as coin, and are taken by Masters of Ships and other adventurers who come to these parts with merchandise for sale. When any number of these have been accumulated in the hands of individuals they are returned to the Commissary, who gives a Bill on the Treasury in England for them. These bills amount to thirty or fourty thousand pounds annually. How long Government may continue so expensive a plan it would be difficult to foresee. Pigs are bought upon the same system, as would also sheep and cattle, if their numbers would admit of their being killed. Beef might be sold at 4s., if not 5s. the lb. A good horse is worth £140 to £150. Be it ever so bad it never sells for less than £100. A cow is valued at about £80. An English cow that was the property of Colonel Grose sold for £100. From this statement you will perceive that those persons who took early precautions to raise live stock have at present singular advantages.

We have fattened and killed a great number of hogs in the year, which enabled us to feed a large establishment of servants. These labourers are such as have been convicts, and whose time of transportation has expired. They then cease to be fed at the expence of Government, and employ themselves as they please. Some endeavour to procure a passage home to England; some become settlers, and others hire themselves out for labour. They demand an enormous price, seldom less than 4s. or 5s. a day. For such as have many in their employment it becomes necessary to keep on hand large supplies of such articles as are most needed by these people, for shops there are none. The officers in the Colony, with a few others possessed of money or credit in England, unite

[130]

together and purchase the cargoes of such vessels as repair to this country from various quarters. Two or more are chosen from the number to bargain for the cargo offered for sale, which is then divided amongst them, in proportion to the amount of their subscriptions. This arrangement prevents monopoly, and the impositions that would be otherwise practised by masters of ships. These details which may seem prolix are necessary to show you the mode in which we are in our infant condition compelled to proceed.

I have had the misfortune to lose a sweet Boy of eleven months old, who died very suddenly by an illness occasioned by teething. The other three, Elizabeth, John, and Mary are well.

How is it, my dearest friend, that you are still single? Are you difficult to please? or has the war left you so few bachelors from amongst whom to choose? But suffer me to offer you a piece of advice: abate a few of your scruples, and marry. I offer in myself an instance that it is not always, with all our wise foreseeings, those marriages which promise most or least happiness prove in their results such as our friends may predict. Few of mine, I am certain, when I married thought that either of us had taken a prudent step. I was considered indolent and inactive; Mr. Macarthur too proud and haughty for our humble fortune and expectations, and yet you see how bountifully Providence has dealt with us. At this time I can truly say that no two people on earth can be happier than we are.

Samuel Marsden

Born in poverty and apprenticed to a blacksmith, Samuel Marsden became an important figure in the early history of Australia and a still more important one in that of New Zealand; while his features, in a couple of unpleasant but indefatigably reprinted engravings, will be familiar to anyone who has opened an illustrated history of either.

He was an intelligent child and was assisted through Cambridge, where, before taking a degree, he was persuaded by William Wilberforce to accept a chaplaincy in New South Wales. Marsden left the university, married, and went out to Sydney in 1794.

He found an exceedingly difficult situation waiting for him. Apathy and dislike of his cloth he might have expected, but what really hurt was the hostility in high quarters. Governor Phillip had left in 1792, regretted by all well-intentioned persons, and before the arrival of his successor, Hunter, there was an interim of three years presided over by Major Grose and Captain Paterson of the New South Wales Corps. Their favouritism towards the military and their indifference to the moral welfare of the population had aroused the anger of the otherwise mild chaplain, Johnson, but his remonstrances had only exacerbated evils he had neither the authority nor the personality to cure.

Marsden worked hard without very much effect. Macarthur referred to him as 'that arch-hypocrite,' and it is true that his dual position as magistrate and chaplain made for embarrassment. But his experiments with woolled sheep and his labours on his farm during this time caused another estimate to be made of him, this time by Governor King, who called him the 'best practical farmer in the colony.'

But the farmer never had more than one eye on the harvests of this world. Ships often brought Maoris across from New Zealand, and during his conversations with them Marsden determined to combat the violence and cannibalism of the islands. He went back to England to find missionaries, but tales of horrors had gone before him and he could persuade no clergyman to come, only Hall, a shipbuilder, and King, a maker of twine.

Back in Australia he found relief from the discouragements around him in continuing preparations for his mission. He sold some of the precious flock to help pay for a ship, and in December 1814 visited New Zealand himself for the first time. In all he made seven of these missionary journeys, dying at last at Windsor, New South Wales, in 1838, an object of reverence, irritation, and pity.

These letters to his friend, Miss Mary Stokes, of Cheapside, are printed in *Some Private Correspondence of the Rev. Samuel Marsden and Family*, 1794–1824, Sydney 1942, edited by George Mackaness, O.B.E., M.A., Litt.D., F.R.A.H.S., who owns them. Other letters, along with Marsden's journals, will be found in the edition by J. R. Elder.

Parramatta August 24th 1794. We are now pretty comfortably settled at Parramatta and shall not be removed to Norfolk Island while Major Grose is Lieut. Governor. I am resident about 14 miles from Mr. Johnson and have to preach at several places, but have no church at any of them. I bless God my congregation is constantly increasing, and two or three have begun to enquire what they must do to be saved.

Things are better upon the whole than I expected to find them among such abandoned people. I am not surprised to see them cast such contempt upon God and Religion knowing the human heart to be so full of enmity to Christ and his Gospel. What gives me the greatest uneasiness is the unhappy differences which prevails between Mr. Johnson and the Lieut. Governor. I cannot describe our situation: it is such an uncommon one. All the higher ranks are lost to God and Religion, and you may so form an idea of the characters of the lower orders.

While we were at Mr. Johnsons their house was broken open and a good quantity of sugar was stolen belonging to Mrs. J. and 70 lb. of Coffee belonging to me—I had also 6 pairs of shoes stolen from me by Mr. Johnsons servant. We do in a literal sense dwell amongst lions.

October 26th 1795. The enemy hath so completely possessed himself in the minds of all ranks and orders here, that it is a matter of doubt with me that His Power will be ever seen in this place to fall like Lightening from Heaven. I wish the unfortunate Convicts were the greatest enemies to the Cross of Christ we had to encounter. Satan hath his Agents everywhere, and generally some persons of influence and authority in the world. To do my Duty here as a Minister is extremely hard and burdensome. When I compare what I do with what I think I ought to do the whole of my work seems daily neglected. I am ashamed & confounded before God for all my shortcomings. A Physician hath no business when all the inhabitants around him are whole. This is exactly my case. I do not know one person that wants the great physician of Souls. I often wonder how some of your great preachers (your Newtons and Fosters in London) men of sound piety and real godliness would feel if they had to preach for six months, and knew that they had not for that space of time two persons to preach to who ever made the enquiry 'Where is God my Maker' or had the smallest concern for their souls. I should like to know what effect this supposed situation would have upon their great minds, though I believe they could not tell me. I know this situation hath produced a very odd and I may add a very unpleasant effect upon mine.

Government hath not provided me any place to perform public worship in yet neither do I know when they will. I am going to preach at the Hawkesbury settlement on Sunday next, twenty miles distant from home, and I know no more where I shall sleep

or perform divine Service than you to whom I am writing. And
what is much more trying I expect the people will absent themselves, as soon as they know I am coming. These things render a
ministers duty painful and difficult.

With regard to temporals our situation is much better than
would be expected. Articles of comfort are often very dear, but we
are seldom without them. I paid a guinea a pound for the last Tea
I bought here, and three pounds a dozen for red and white wine.
When I was at Norfolk Island about four months ago Tea sold
there for 27/- per lb. and Tobacco 10/- Candles 3/- Spirits £1/5/-
per Gallon, and all other articles which would be procured from
the ship that was there were equally extravagantly dear. Though
this is the case we have no cause to complain of our outward comforts taking them all together. If everything was equally agreeable
we should be well situated. I have great reason to be thankful that
I am happy in my own family; I believe few more so. As you are
married I may mention this to you without risk of being laughed
at. Did you know what sad feelings I sustained on account of Mrs.
M. in my late voyage from Norfolk Island, for nearly a fortnight
together when every day and night too I expected to be buried in
the Great Deep, you would not have dropped that kind hint in Mr.
Johnsons letter 'Tell Mr. M to be kind to Mrs. Marsden.' Your
admonition is highly gratifying to me, as it only enjoyns a repetition of what I take pleasure in. I should have been wretched and
miserable here without a wife, now I am happy and comfortable.

Our little daughter (whom probably you may have heard of)
grows a fine girl and affords a little amusement for Mrs. Marsden.

December 3rd 1796. We feel ourselves greatly indebted to you for
your kind remembrance of us in this distant port. News from old
England come from whom it may is welcome and much more if it
comes from a lover of Jesus. We have many things to struggle with
here which have a natural tendency to deaden our affections and
stupefy our souls.

You mention in your letter you would be glad if I would collect
you some seeds and plants from Norfolk Island. I was there better
than a year ago, but I do not know when I shall go again. I will

write to an acquaintance who lives there and endeavour to obtain some for you. Anything that this country affords and that I can obtain shall be very happy to send you. I think it probable I shall be able to collect you some seeds such as you never have yet received as I sometimes visit different parts of the settlement at the distance of forty or fifty miles from Sydney. Such as I can obtain you shall have, though I do not profess any great botanical knowledge myself.

I have much to occupy my time and a great variety of duties to perform. I am a Gardener a Farmer a Magistrate & Minister so that when one duty does not call me another always does. In this infant colony there is plenty of manual labor for every body. I conceive it a duty for all to take an active part. He who will not work must not eat. Now is our Harvest-time. Yesterday I was in the field assisting in getting my wheat. To-day I have been sitting in the civil court hearing the complaints of the People. To-morrow if well must ascend the pulpit and preach to my people. In this manner I chiefly spend my time. It may appear strange but it is necessary situated as we are. You can form Madam no idea of our state. I wish to be found faithful to act like a Christian Minister. I can say this that I do not eat the bread of idleness. It is my opinion that God will ere long visit New South Wales with his heavenly grace. Out of these stones he will raise up children unto Abraham. There has not been any shaking yet among the dry bones, but the Son of Man is commanded to prophecy and I hope by and by the Lord will command the wind to blow. Stir up thy strength O God and come amongst us.

My little family are all well. Mrs. M. has not time to write by this conveyance she enjoys her health well. I take more care of her probably than you are aware of. I beg my kindest respects to Mr. Stokes. Inform him our crops are immensely great—we have the greatest abundance of wheat now. Could maintain some thousands more people if we had them in dry provisions. We could also make plenty of wine if we had persons who understood the operation properly. Would be very thankful if you could by any means send me out a few Hop-cuttings. I think they would grow if they were packed properly with a little mould in a case and nailed down.

[136]

And also a little hop seed. Hops would be a general good to this Colony.

Feby 22nd 1800. I am busy in building a Church at Parramatta. Shall be happy to see it completed. I think it would never be done if I was to leave the settlement. I can only say it is my present intention and wish to quit the colony yet my times are in the Lords hands, it will be enough if I am found faithful when my work comes to be done. The building of an Orphan house is another object which lies near my heart. I shall feel uncommon satisfaction in having it carried into execution. The number of poor children in the colony I pity who have either no parents or would have been better at this moment if they had never known them. I shall say nothing of the monopolies extortions and oppressions of the great, and the wickedness poverty and ruin of the lower ranks of the inhabitants of N.S.W. You will hear of these things from other quarters. They will and must become a national concern speedily or you will hear of the murder of the greatest part of us by and by.

April 27th 1803. Last Easter Sunday I consecrated my church at Parramatta. This building proves a great comfort to my mind as I can now perform a divine service in a manner becoming the worship of Almighty God. At Sydney there is no place of public worship and I fear will be none for a long time to come. I do my duty with great reluctance there and few attend for want of accommodation. It is surely one of the most shameful neglects of Government that perhaps was ever known since we became a nation professing Godliness.

Government have granted one of the Roman priests who was sent a prisoner from Ireland permission to perform the Catholic service here. I am apprehensive this toleration will be productive of some serious evils. Satan has still his friends in the world and maintains his cause in every quarter. I did not expect to see his kingdom strengthened among us by the addition of the Roman religion.

I am surprised no Clergyman comes out in the place of my former Colleague Mr. Johnson. He tells me he has no inclination to visit us again and that none has been appointed to succeed him.

I labor hard but the toils of the day makes rest sweet at night so that the morning finds me ready for my task. My spirits and strength seldom fail me. I should be happy in a colleague as I am constrained to travel from Sydney to Parramatta every Sabbath which is 16 miles and preach in both places. Another clergyman would ease me in this respect and some others.

I am making great progress in my Orchard and Garden. I have got many hundred of different Fruit Trees and great abundance of some kinds of fruit. I made more than 60 Gallons of Cider this year which promises to be very good. This was made from peaches, though we have apples they are not of the cider kind. I have Hops also growing now well. The vines have run more than two feet.

March 13th 1804. The seeds you wrote for Mrs. Marsden has put up in a small box with some others, which I hope you will receive safe. I have sent them by one of the officers of the Calcutta, to whom I refer you for information of this Colony. This gentleman can give Mr. Stokes a particular account of the wild cattle, he having paid two visits to the cow pastures. Mrs. Marsden has visited them once about a month ago. Where the wild cattle feed, it is the finest country the imagination can conceive, the hills and vales are so beautiful. It was my intention to have sent you a good collection of seeds by the Calcutta, but have been prevented from collecting them by the Irish rebels, they have given us some trouble lately and put the Colony in much danger. I hope they are subdued for the present—they had laid a plan for a general insurrection, fortunately for us it did not succeed. I wish you would inform me particularly what you want, & if I can get it here, you shall have it—the great difficulty is to get an honest man to take what we wish to send without stealing it. My private letters are sometimes stolen, and if not stolen, opened by some person unknown. The greatest rogues come and go from this Colony. If you ever get a letter it must be a chance business.

[Undated] I shall be happy should I ever live to see religion flourish amongst us—there is no prospect of this. I often think the Gospel, if we may judge from appearances in the settlement, was only intended for children, the common soldier, & the convict in irons. The military officers will march the soldiers to the church door, & then return, the gaoler will unlock his cells & turn his prisoners out to public worship, but has no idea of attending himself.

Nov 26th 1811. The Cow I sent out has brought me two female Calves, and is now in Calf again, and that I bought from the officers one. I shall soon have a find herd of English cattle. I have got most of the artificial grasses now growing which are cultivated in England. One field all English grass, I have mowed and made into hay. Were you now to visit us you would imagine you were in England, excepting the pleasure you would feel in breathing a pure air.

By the Admiral Gambier I have sent to England 4,000 to 5,000 lbs. of wool. This will be the beginning of the commerce of this new World. Many think nothing of these things now. They cannot see any advantage to be derived to them, their children, or this settlement by improving the fleeces of our sheep. But I anticipate immense National wealth to spring from this source of Commerce in time. The ant though it is a small creature, yet we see their numbers uniting together raising large hillocks, particularly here. The Bee can carry but little honey, but in time the Hive is filled. When I consider we have not much less than 50,000 Sheep in the settlement, and that these 50,000 sheep will produce while I sleep or wake as many fleeces of wool. It is a National object to attend to them. Should their fleeces be worth no more than as many dollars, yet the slave condemned to the mines must sweat and toil and dig for a long time before he can drag from the bowels of the earth so much wealth.

I think you will hear of wheat and other kinds of grain being grown in New Zealand before two years are over. My friend one of the chiefs who had lived with me and acquired a knowledge of agriculture will introduce cultivation among his countrymen. This will add greatly to their civilization and comfort and prepare the way for greater blessings. I may be too fond perhaps of the garden, the field and the fleece. These would be the first object of my attention was I placed among a savage nation. The man who introduced the potato into Ireland and England merited more from those nations than any General who may have slain thousands of their enemies.

Divine goodness has intimated that a time shall come when men shall beat their swords into plough shares and their spears into pruning hooks. Then agriculture will be the principal occupation of mankind. I think we should enjoy as much of this promise now as the world will allow us. Men who can, should all beat their swords into plough shares, and follow the simple life found only in the field and garden. I have attended to your recommendation with respect to enclosing my grounds and have fenced in more than 100 acres since my return.

I had almost forgotten to mention the bearer of this letter, Mr. Grant. He was transported to this country some years ago in consequence of firing at a gentleman whom he had challenged and who had refused to fight him. The difference originated about a young woman to whom he was attached. His case was always considered a hard one in this Colony. He was sent out for life but his pardon has been obtained from the governor.

October 8th 1814. With respect to this Colony it improves fast and must in time be a great Country. The Mountains have lately been crossed which hitherto had prevented all communication between the present settlements and the Country beyond them. A number of men are now employed making a road over the mountains as a pass has been found. The country is said to be very fine beyond them. One Gentleman travelled more than 100 miles after he had passed the Mountains and found the Country very good, and a fine river running through it towards the west and abounding in fish. I have no doubt but when we get into the Country beyond the Mountains we shall find some of the finest ground and very probably some large rivers which may empty themselves into the Sea on the west side of New Holland.

We are getting on with good schools for the Children in all the districts. I am now putting a roof upon a Female Orphan House at Parramatta which will contain about 200 girls. It is a noble building. If the young girls are only taken care of and kept from vice the Colony will prosper as it will be the principal means of checking the growing national sins by checking the vicious inclinations of young men. No young man need be afraid to marry here lest he should not be able to provide for a family. In a new country like this there are always plenty of means at hand for a man to support himself & those belonging to him.

William Barnes

William Barnes must remain largely his own spokesman. These short letters, however, provide as good an impression as we can demand of this excited and ingenuous self-made man, so anxious that nothing should happen to spoil his success and so sure of his own ability to extend it.

He evidently thought he was the pioneer of brewing in the island. But we see that he was mistaken from a footnote in Goodwins's *Emigrant's Guide* of 1823: 'Mr. Gatehouse has established a brewery at Hobart Town, where strong beer is now to be had at 4*s*. per gallon, table beer at 1*s*. 6*d*. per gallon, and yeast at 1*s*. per quart, from which 25 per cent. discount is allowed to licensed retailers.'

But Barnes may well have driven him out of business, for nothing seemed to stand in the way of his growing prosperity. In Henry Widowson's *Present State of Van Diemen's Land* (London, 1829) appears this paragraph: 'Mr. Barnes, an extensive brewer, has a small quantity of arable land on the hill to the west [he is looking down the valley from Launceston], which slopes gradually to the water's edge. This gentleman has six thousand acres at the back, the generality of which is extremely bad.' It may have been bad, but it was more than he had had in 1824.

In 1830 he found time to marry Anne Sharland, gaining a doctor and a surveyor as brothers-in-law. By this time he was a justice of the peace and a director of the Cornwall Bank and was beginning to think that the brewery upon which he had lavished so exclusively his time and care was, after all, only the means to an end. In 1835 he leased it to others and, in the words of Mr. P. L. Brown, to whom I am indebted for the information in this paragraph, 'apparently settled down as a landed proprietor.' Thirteen years after his arrival in Van Diemen's Land he was chosen among all the citizens of Launceston to present their farewell Address to Governor Arthur on his retirement.

The originals of these letters belong to Mr. John Manifold of Purrumbete, Victoria, and are published in *The Narrative of George Russell with Russellania and Selected Papers*, Oxford, 1935, edited by P. L. Brown.

Launceston, Van Diemen's Land, 5th May, 1824. As there are two vessels advertised to sail directly for England I shall commence a Letter to you, as I do not intend to allow a single opportunity to escape me if I can possibly avoid it. I have already written to you two letters: once via Sydney, and on the 15th March by the 'Woodlark', which sailed for London. In both these letters I advised having drawn a Bill on you @ 90 days' sight in favor of John Wyld Esqr, for £157-17-6, and have already stated fully my object for so doing. I trust therefore you will honor the Bill, otherwise my credit and prospects (which are now excellent) will be ruined for ever here. However, after what you have done for me, I feel confident you have my welfare at heart and will not hesitate respecting it.

Since my arrival here I have been completely occupied from daylight in the morning to dark, and have great reason to be thankful for the progress I have made through strict attention and the assistance of a most valuable friend who has been particularly kind to me. This friend is Lieut. Kenworthy, son of Mrs. K. of Parkgate, who is Civil Engineer and Inspector of Public Works here, and has always at his command from 250 to 300 government men. He is universally respected and esteemed. It was through his influence with the Commandant of Port Dalrymple

[143]

(Col. Cameron) that I obtained the Land on which I have built my Brewery. It had been reserved hitherto for government purposes, and frequently refused; it is considered well worth £300. Lieut. K. has also assisted me with Timber and the labour of government men, which has enabled me (altho I have only been here about two months) to have Buildings nearly finished of the following dimensions—viz.: Brewhouse 30 feet by 15, 12 feet high; Malt Barn 36 feet by 16, with a Granary over it; and a kiln 12 feet square and 16 feet high. The Kiln is built of bricks, and the other buildings of sawed Timber, boarded and shingled.

There is a great advantage attending the situation in having a fine navigable River with 6 yards from the front wall, and being so close to the Soldiers' Barracks is a most excellent protection. I have already got the Malt Barn floor layed, and as soon as it is dry shall commence operations. I have also erected a small Cottage near to my other Buildings, which in the course of another week I expect to occupy. It is most delightfully situated on rising ground, and a most beautiful River (the Tamar) seen front meandering for many miles, with a fine Rich country on both sides, terminated by mountains. I do not intend to finish my Cottage at present, but shall get into it as soon as it is covered in. The general way of building here is a frame of sawed Timber boarded outside and lined with a Brick in bredth in side, and Plaistered. House Rent is enormously high here: I have been obliged to pay at the rate of 30/- a week for the small place I occupy; and as to Lodgings, there are none. My present establishment consists of half a dozen plain Chairs, an old Sofa & round Table (borrowed), and a few White Plates. Living at an Inn is ruinous, the Charge as follows: for Bed (which is generally a Wool Mattress laid on the floor and swarming with fleas) 2/6 a night; Breakfast 2/6; Dinner 5/6; Tea 2/6; and for any thing in the shape of wine, Beer, or spirituous Liquor, their charges amount to extortion. For instance, 2/6 for a Quart of Porter or Beer, and 2/6 to 3/- for a Glass of Spirits.

There is a very foolish custom prevalent in both these colonies of giving servants Tea and Sugar morning and evening; so that a man who has been transported for a Robbery, or even Murder, gets daily $1\frac{1}{2}$ to 2 lb Bread, $1\frac{1}{2}$ lb Meat (generally fine fresh mutton)

South View of Sydney

every day, with 3 ounces of Tea and a pound Sugar every week. If he is a Mechanic, or in short any kind of tradesman, he can make his 3 Pounds a week with ease by working over hours. Those prisoners who are not assigned to Settlers work for Government till 2 o'clock, and the remainder of the day they have to them-selves. You have a very erroneous idea in England of the situation of Convicts transported to this place. There is not one of them (if he is steady and industrious) but might become independent in a few years. Several emancipated convicts possess great wealth; for instance, there is a man of the name of F—— residing here who has about 3000 head of horned cattle and from 3000 to 4000 sheep, and this man was a Prisoner not many years ago. We are not in that dread of the Convicts as you imagine. They will, to be sure, rob you if they can; but murder is very rarely committed, and I would as soon ride 20 miles at night here as I would from Chester to Bromborow. In short, I have no sort of apprehension in that respect. The Police is very strict, and any Prisoner who commits an offence is tryed in a very summary way. He is first examined by the Magistrate of Police, Mr. Mulgrave, who has the power of flogging and Imprisonment to a certain extent; but, if he conceives the offence to deserve more than he has the power to inflict, he commits them to a Bench of Magistrates which sits every month, and they have the power to Transport him to the New Settlement, Macquarie Harbour, for life, where is worked in chains and very indifferently fed. For any capital offence (such as murder, sheep stealing, &c) we have now a criminal court established here, which has the power of life and death. The Judge and Attorney General are only recently arrived from England, and the first court will be held at Launceston on the 15th June, when, I have no doubt, some executions will ensue. These are principally for stealing sheep, which in this Country is generally punished with death.

I have three assigned servants. One an old Welshman from Denbigh who follows my Cart and Bullocks; a young man of the name of Dod, who says he comes from Nantwich in Cheshire and was transported for stealing a Horse at Shrewsbury; he says he has an uncle now living in that neighbourhood—at some Hall; but I forget the name of it. The Third is an Irishman.

s.—10   [145]

The servants are generally great Rascals, and will rob you if they can. I have been twice robbed since I arrived in this Island. First, my writing desk, which I had put on board the Brig 'Ann' for security, to bring round from Hobart Town, was broken open and rifled of its contents, and then thrown overboard, with all my Letters, papers, &c rent adrift; the Desk was afterwards picked up empty. The next Robbery took place on the evening of the King's birthday, when the Magistrates, officers, and first men on this side the Island dined together. I was invited to the dinner, and whilst there a pane of glass was taken out of my window, which was then lifted up, and my dressing box, two coats, my new Hat, and several other things. Fortunately, they were heard, or I would have been stripped of all the clothes I had. The Dressing Box was found next day hid among some Bricks, but rifled of its contents.

You can form no opinion of the depravity of some of the Prisoners. They all drink to excess, generally raw spirits, very seldom less than a half pint of Rum at one time. It is no uncommon thing for one of them to expend in drink from £20 to £40 of a night; and some of the small settlers are little better in that respect; they are most of them in the hands of the Publicans. I hope my Beer will in some degree induce them . . . [the rest of this letter is missing].

Do not make my Letters public,
   which I know is the Custom
      in Cheshire.
Launceston, 9th September 1824. In my last I stated to you that I had drawn for £100 to enable me to purchase Hops. I trust you will honor it. My Brewery far exceeds my most sanguine expectations; in short, if I could get a regular supply of Hops, a very few years would give me a fortune far superior to what I ever possessed. I am doing so well that I am afraid to tell you for fear you would not believe me. In short, with the small means I brought out, I am even astonished myself.

The demand for my Ale is already so great that I am obliged to extend my Premises; even at present my sales are equal to 400

Hogsheads of 63 galls each a year. All I fear is being in want of Hops.

I assure you once more that I am in a fair way to make a very rapid fortune, and only want a little assistance for the present. After this year I fully expect to able to pay off all I owe, as I do not estimate my profits this year at less than £500, and I consider that the property I possess in the Colony well worth £2000. I have got a most desirable grant of 1000 acres, with a reserve of 500; and 2000 acres for you beside me, and 700 for Capt. Crear on the other; all on the banks of the South Esk. Besides this I have 400 acres within half a mile of Launceston, on the River Tamar, opposite where the vessels lay in port. This I purchased for £112, and I could now get for it £350; but in a year or two, I have no doubt, it will be worth twice that sum.

I have engaged a young man who has had charge of a very large Brewery in Scotland; he perfectly understands his business. In short, there is proof of it, for we cannot brew it fast enough for the demand. I charge six pounds five shillings, or 25 Dollars, for 63 galls, and for any smaller quantity 2/6 p. gallon. I assure you that I frequently feel astonished at my great success, so much so that I scarcely fancy it can be real. I have got my cottage nearly finished, and am now building an additional Malt Barn, with a Granary over it, 60 feet long by 20 wide. All I want are the Boilers and constant sup of Hops, and I do not fear selling a thousand Hogsheads a year. The Ale we brew is so much superior to what the warm climate of Sydney will enable them to brew, that, independent of the demand here, any quantity would sell there. In short, I have already refused two orders, not being able to do more than supply my customers here. *Keep all this to yourself, whatever you do*; for at present I have no competition, and I do all I can to make it appear an unprofitable concern.

If I do not write you so often as you could wish, you must excuse it; for I assure you I have not a moment's time. It is said from the Governor to the lowest person in the Island that no person ever did so much in the same time as I have done, especially when they acquainted with my slender means. However, I now consider myself so firmly established that should you come out (which I more than expect you will) I know you will not be a little gratified by the reception I shall be enabled to give. I am delighted with the Country, and the Society at Launceston is very good; there are six or eight families that I could dine with every day if I chose; but I never go out but on Sundays. I visit none but the very first people, and dine frequently with the Commandant. At present no person's Credit can stand higher than mine does here, and will continue to do so, provided the two Bills I have drawn on you are paid. If they are dishonored I shall suffer most dreadfully; but, from your kind assurances to me, I feel confident you will not allow my Credit to be ruined for so small a sum.

Lieut. Kenworthy and myself continue most intimate friends, and he has been a friend indeed to me; in short, without his Interest I could have done no good. If you can pay Mrs. K. any attention, pray do so on my acct., for her son's intimacy has been worth at least £1000 to me.

Launceston, Christmas Day 1824. No man in the Country stands higher than I do. I associate with the Governor and very first people. I dined with His Honor a few days ago, and he expressed great satisfaction with the Beer from the Port Dalrymple Brewery. He and Mrs. Arthur and Family are now here at Launceston for six weeks; he has been twice down at my concern, and has promised me every support. He is very much pleased with this side of the Island, and means to spend five or six months here every year.

Great Improvements are going on; a new Church, Court House, Mill, and several other public Buildings; and the Town encreases so fast that I am sure it is nearly twice as large as when I first saw it, and there is nothing but new Houses building wherever you turn your eye. It must in a very few Years become a place of very great importance indeed.

We have had rather an unfavourable season for vegetation, in consequence of a long Drought, and the corn crops are expected to be short in consequence. There is now a market in the Brazils and the Ile of France for all our surplus produce, which has stimulated many of the small as well as principal Farmers to exert themselves. Some of our first rate Settlers live like Nabobs; they have their

5000, 6000 or even 8000 acres of Land, with a good House & building, horned Cattle, sheep, &c, almost innumerable. The Country is fast filling up, and, unless some new districts are discovered, there will be a scarcity of Land. I still retain the 2000 acres for you; but I shall not press you to come out, as I mentioned to you that I would not. It certainly is the Land of my adoption; still, if things go on well with me for three years, as it is now likely, I mean to take a trip Home for a short time. But it will certainly be to return here.

Should any of my Friends (particularly my very kind Friend Orford) accuse me of neglecting them, assure them to the contrary, and I hope to make up for all very soon. My Ideas are so taken up with my business that it is even at present almost painful to sit down to write to you.

George Fletcher Moore

Born in 1798, George Fletcher Moore was a member of a large, well-to-do Irish family. He studied law and was called to the Irish bar, but was unable to settle down to legal practice and playing the flute, and emigrated to West Australia. The opportunity was a good one. The British Government was then offering large tracts of land to anyone who would settle in that part of the country, but it was nevertheless against the advice of his friends that he finally left Dublin in 1830.

He was prepared for, and they had regretted, a hard, rough life mainly of manual labour. He got it, but he also found employment for his brain with its special training. He became Advocate-General and even for a while Colonial Secretary. And not content with collaborating with Governor Hutt in preparing a *Descriptive Vocabulary of the Aboriginal Language* he wrote the song which he claimed (though very tentatively) established the colony's name as 'Western Australia.' On his return in the '60s, he was holder of 'twenty-four thousand acres of land in fee simple, as well as several allotments in towns.'

These letters, sent home to his family, particularly to his brother Joseph, were sent back later to Australia, where they were published in *The West Australian*, and thence reprinted by himself, the newspaper having cut out a good deal, in *Diary of Ten Years Eventful Life of an Early Settler in Western Australia*,

London, 1884. Part of this work (up to 1834 or pp. 1–207 of the 1884 ed.) was previously published as *Extracts from the Letters and Journals of George Fletcher Moore Esq., now filling a judicial office at the Swan River Settlement*, London, 1834, edited by Mr. Martin Doyle.

Nov. 12th, 1830. I seize the opportunity of almost the first leisure moment which I have had here, to give you a hurried account of my proceedings and prospects up to this time.

We anchored in Cockburn Sound on this day fortnight, and on the evening of the same day landed on Garden Island, where the first thing that struck me was the very unpromising appearance of the soil (which seemed to be little else than white sand) and the singularity of tolerably good crops, or rather patches, of peas, barley, turnips, radishes, &c., which it produced.

On Sunday we reached the mainland, where (on the beach) the embryo town of Fremantle is situated.

I was anxious to see the governor without loss of time, and therefore proceeded to Perth, about twelve miles up the river, in the boat of Mr. Brown, the Colonial Secretary, from whom I have received the kindest and most hospitable attention.

One of our natives slept with his head on my knee in the boat, but not till he had asked permission, which I gave him; first taking the precaution of spreading paper on my trowsers to save them from the grease and red earth with which his hair was dressed.

I next went up the Canning River, my object being to obtain a grant without loss of time, and to take my people to it, but I find it difficult to get one. The only land available for present purposes is on and near the banks of the rivers: all this is now allotted on both sides of each river, almost to their source; but an offer is frequently made of giving one half to a new settler on condition of his performing the location duties sufficient to secure the whole. I have an offer of this kind on the banks of the Swan River, and think of accepting it; if I do not, I must explore beyond the mountains, where a fine country is said to have been discovered twenty-five miles to the south, where three rivers fall into a lake, and thence into the sea, or still farther to the south to Port Vasse, or Cape Leschenhault; or it may be to Cape Lewin, where the soil and climate are good and the harbour is excellent. These, of course, are my unarranged notions on the subject, not grounded yet on any firm foundation; for I have not been long enough here to form any decided opinion as to soil, situation, or probabilities. In general, the higher you go up the Swan River, which is an estuary, the better is the adjacent land, which is overflowed in winter, and like all alluvial soil productive for summer pasture.

Much disappointment has been felt by many over-sanguine persons here, who thought they had nothing more to do than scratch the ground and sow. But there are many difficulties to surmount; the proper seasons for sowing are scarcely yet ascertained; from this circumstance many have failed altogether in their crops, which throws them on their capital for another year, and but few have been able to raise as much as is sufficient for their own consumption.

Our vessel was the first that came during the season; and being just in time, everything sold enormously high. If this colony be supported as it ought, during the trying time of its infancy, I am convinced, from all I hear, that it will succeed. Cockburn Sound is an excellent harbour in winter; Gage's Roads in summer. From the nature of the coast, the climate, and the relative circumstances of the interior, it is unlikely that another harbour so good will be found in this quarter. All the rivers in this neighbourhood seem to be small, and to have bar harbours. A river has lately been discovered, beyond the range of hills running to the north-west. Beyond those hills, the interior, for forty or fifty miles back, has an undulating appearance, and is then succeeded by plains good for pasture. On this side, the only good pasture is on the alluvial flats, which are flooded every winter. Those who speculate on keeping large flocks speak of going next summer over the hills, which are of trifling elevation, and present no serious obstacle to carriage, or the formation of roads, when the colony is strong enough to make or require them. The expense and labour of conveying goods up the river, at present, is very great; boats in summer must be unloaded, and dragged over the flats, but above these the water is deep, and the navigation only occasionally impeded by fallen trees, which may easily be removed. Every settler should have a boat, and learn how to manage it.

Friday 19th.—I wrote the foregoing observations at the house of Captain Irwin, from whom I have received the greatest kindness. I have since been up the Canning River, about a mile above the navigable part, to look at some grants which are undisposed of. The country there is beautiful, covered or rather studded with magnificent trees, but the substratum is ironstone, the clay strongly impregnated with it, hard and unmanageable, and having very little grass on it, which (for immediate use) is the chief requisite. Besides, the river there is salt in summer, and fresh water it is difficult to find. The Canning (with this exception) is located up to the mountains. It is intended to build a town near its source, where there is some fine ground.

About Fremantle, where I am now sitting, in my tent, the land is mere sand; but we must not judge of this by similar-looking places at *home*, for all vegetables flourish on it, and cattle thrive on the herbage, scanty though it be.

Until you have gone above Perth, the ground is of the same nature; it changes to alluvial flats, and the higher grounds consist of sandy loam of different qualities. Brick and pottery clay is abundant, and they are making bricks in many places, which will soon supersede wood as a material for building. I saw a wooden house burned down some nights ago, and have therefore a dread of one—a mud edifice for me. The great mistake committed by settlers has been bringing too many articles of machinery and implements, which are not necessary, or suited to the soil. Some ploughs, cars, saws, and mill machinery are lying even yet on the beach.

25th.—I have taken half of Mr. Lamb's grant; it is nearly at the head of the navigable part of the Swan River; how it may look after enduring the heat of the summer I know not but it had a fine appearance when I was there. There are several very respectable persons settled near it, and there is now a party of soldiers stationed there. Since I wrote the first part of this, two vessels have arrived from Van Diemen's Land, with provision, which has caused a most beneficial effect on prices;—other ships are expected soon, so that we shall have plenty; but it is evident that, until the colony is able to produce something substantial for its support, we must depend on contingencies and have a fluctuating market. That it *will* succeed ultimately, I have not the least doubt; but we shall have two or three years of hard struggling to contend with. The servants I brought with me are all happy, contented, and healthy, and it must be my care to keep them so. As to myself, with the exception of several scrapes, cuts and bruises on my hands from dragging, carrying, and other works (for I have not spared myself), I never was in better health—thanks to the beneficent Giver of it. I have not as yet suffered any difficulty or privation, which I think worthy of mentioning. I hope to get all my luggage and articles to Perth on Monday; paying £5 for taking one boat-load so far, and I must then push them over the flats.

8th December. A vein of good soil has been discovered on the banks of a river called the Avon, behind the hills, on which many of the settlers are selecting their grants. I have got one upon the river towards the south.

All the lands up the Swan and Canning have been long since granted; but some of the grantees have left the colony, and their lands may be resumed by the Government, if not occupied, at the expiration of the year. I have spoken to some practical farmers, who have not the slightest doubt that the colony possesses every *capability*, both for agriculture and grazing, and though the pasture lands on this side of the hills are not extensive, there is an unlimited tract behind them and at no great distance.

Two or three vessels have come in since I first wrote, and the prices of provisions and clothing are now moderate.

Cattle are very dear, though we daily expect arrivals from Hobart Town. Good cows are as high as £25, though some have been purchased for £12. It is not advisable to bring stock from England; freight and casualties make them come too expensive.

At present I am unwilling to take the responsibility of advising any one to come out; but I have met with no difficulties for which I was not prepared.

I went out some days ago, about four miles off, to hunt kangaroos; we huntsmen saw five, but the dogs never got sight of them. I went astray returning, and no wonder, for nothing is more perplexing than walking in the bush; you have no object to steer by, except your shadow or a compass; the one is always changing with the day, and the other may mislead, unless you keep your eye constantly upon it. The country is most singular, but does not possess those features of extreme interest which I expected; there is (as far as I have seen) great sameness in the scenery, and several parties which have been beyond the mountains (perhaps to the distance of 100 miles) report the scenery to be of the same character—undulating ground and extensive plains; but no very striking object, no large rivers no lakes of any extent—and the low lands are subject to floods in winter. The river on which I have my grant from Government has been but lately discovered, and is not, I believe, navigable; it runs strongly in winter, and forms a series of pools and shallows in summer; its course is to the north-west, the more northerly part being nearest the Swan River, but the better ground along its banks lying more to the south; on this has been laid out the site of three towns; Northam—said to be about twenty-eight miles from the head of the Swan; York—ten miles further, and Beverly—(close to which is my grant), ten miles more; this I know only from an unfinished map.

We are to have a monthly conveyance by boat for our goods, up to the head of the river. A store has been established at Guildford, a few miles from this, where we are sure of procuring a temporary supply of the necessaries of life, when it may be inconvenient to obtain them from Perth. Prices are now moderate. I have bought sugar at sevenpence, rice at twopence-halfpenny, and coffee at eightpence per pound, arrack at six shillings and sixpence per gallon; rum is a dearer article, generally twelve shillings and sixpence per gallon; it is allowed as a daily ration to the servants, who have got into the habit of demanding it, and grumbling if refused.

August 22nd, 1831.—Dined after church service yesterday on delicious kangaroo soup, a fine haunch of ditto, lamb, a pair of fowls, ham and sausages, turnips, lettuce, onions, fruit-pies, and plum and custard puddings. Just think of such fare on the Swan River, and confess whether your organs of taste can resist an extra humidity 'from bare imagination of the feast.' You know, however, that I care little for these things, and detail them merely to show that we have not *always* hard fare.

It falls frequently to my lot to settle disputes about boundaries: the *Dii Termini* are very troublesome divinities to me; this day I have been arbitor in a case of this nature, besides one on a disputed point concerning a sale of horses.

I have to finish a certain memorial to the Home Government, to attend an agricultural meeting on the second of next month, and to prepare for an exploring expedition over the mountains on the fourth, and have just written for Mrs. Tanner a song about this colony, of which she wishes to send her friends a copy; but I have not time now to transcribe it, but must do so at some other time.

I have a song in my mind, suggested by that of a bird's notes; and if I can get my flute mended, shall set it for you. I mean to try the system of robbing my own potatoes—viz., taking away the large ones from the roots, which is practised here with good effect.

23rd.—You will think me a most dissipated dog when I tell you that I have dined with the same large party three successive days!

Servants' wages are extremely high, and all work proportionably so; £2 10s. per month for inside servants; from 5s. to 7s. per day (without diet) for labour. At present the cultivation of new ground will not pay where there is any difficulty beyond mere ploughing, and that can only be performed in cleared flat meadows. The quantity of stock is still insufficient to support a shepherd. There are not yet more than a dozen persons possessing large flocks, but we are in daily expectation of arrivals of sheep from Van Diemen's Land. I am within the limit when I tell you that for even a small establishment like mine, where everything is to be purchased, it is necessary to have between £200 and £300 a year.

George Fletcher Moore

Our means will be greater and our wants less as our gardens and crops become productive. My stock of shoes for myself and people is already exhausted, and the price is 18*s.* per pair. Clothes and provisions, as in all infant societies, are of course our chief wants, but in some things *money* goes a great way. Wine, tea, and sugar are cheap. F—— talks of sending goods here on commission—an excellent speculation; in shoes alone a profit of 150 per cent. might be effected.

As to clothing, black and blue clothes are the most saleable. Our medical men, lawyers, clergymen, and those in mourning, as among you, wear black; and there are persons here of each of the learned professions. The Government officers and naval and military men wear blue cloth coats with gilt crown buttons, and blue frocks and trousers—on great occasions, white duck trousers; but there is some hazard in this speculation, unless on a small scale.

Substantial clothing seems to be the taste of our sensible people, who are good judges of such matters. Blue striped shirts, shoes, boots, buskins, and corduroy trousers, meet with ready sale. We are in great want of light black beaver hats, which every one who can get them wears; but we can procure no male head-pieces here, except some villainous-looking silk ones of an old-fashioned shape. In the country, or in undress, little attention is paid to mere ornament; but in company, or on state occasions, we are a very well-dressed and *particular* people.

As to the ladies—I suppose you have hitherto been in the habit of mistaking them for Hottentot dames, and consider them suitably appareled in linsey-wolsey, or "in druggets drest of thirteen-pence a yard;" but our fair ones of the upper grades are of a very different class indeed: but, alas! alas! I cannot enumerate any of the thousand articles which they may wish for, from the *bustle* (no allusion to the Hottentot ladies, I assure you) to every other appendage of the person:—pray interest yourself to have a well-selected cargo sent especially to them. Among the common necessaries which would sell well in this colony are starch, blue, candles of every kind, glass, *flannel*, and soap, which now brings (and sold as a special favour) 2*s.* 6*d.* a pound.

[157]

Masters here are only so in name; they are the slaves of their indentured servants. In my absence, —— does nothing, and if I speak to him—exit in a rage. I could send him to gaol, but I do not like this extremity, and yet I cannot afford to loose the advantage of his time, and pay £30, besides diet, to another in his place. Letty, however, continues faithful.

Perth, Sept. 3rd.—I must tell you all about the *great doings* since the last entry in my logbook.

Yesterday I came down here for our market, and meeting of the Agricultural Society, and for the Governor's ball.

The ball was kept up with the greatest spirit until six in the morning; and the dancing almost without interval—contre-dances, quadrilles, Spanish dances, and gallopades. I never before witnessed such gaity at a ball, nor ever before danced so much in one night; four rooms and an arcade were all filled, and connected with the verandah; a superb tent was fitted up, decorated and festooned with naval flags, and in this we had supper—an elegant and abundant one. The gentlemen from India were astonished, for they had heard the most gloomy reports; and the invalid confessed that when coming ashore he had been considering with the captain, the expediency of sending some provisions from the ship, as a preventive against starvation; his amazement at seeing ample supplies of butter, eggs, vegetables, poultry and butcher's meat, may be guessed at; he purchased freely and paid liberally; he has rented a house for some time, and is now recovering; indeed he was actually frolicksome all the evening.

WESTERN AUSTRALIA FOR ME.

Sung by me at the first ball given by the Governor, Sir James Stirling, in Perth.—G. F. M.

Air—'Ballinamona oro.'

From the old Western world, we have come to explore
The wilds of the Western Australian shore;
In search of a country, we've ventured to roam,
And now that we've found it, let's make it our home.

[158]

And what though the colony's new, Sirs,
And inhabitants yet may be few, Sirs,
We'll see them encreasing *here too, Sirs,*
So Western Australia *for me.*

With care and experience I'm sure 'twill be found
Two crops in the year we may get from the ground;
There's good wood and good water, good flesh and good fish,
Good soil and good clime, and what more could you wish.
Then let every one earnestly strive, Sirs,
Do his best, be alert and alive, Sirs,
We'll soon see our colony thrive, Sirs,
So Western Australia *for me.*

No lions or tigers we here dread to meet,
Our innocent quadrupeds *hop on* two feet;
No tithes and no taxes we now have to pay,
And our geese *are all* swans, *as some witty folks say.*
Then we'll live without trouble or stealth, Sirs,
Our currency's all sterling wealth, Sirs,
So here's to our Governor's health, Sirs,
And Western Australia *for me.*

Nov. 1st.—I am at a sad loss for furniture, having scarcely a table, chair, press, or shelf, except what I brought with me, and I have no *doors*—mere contrivances in place of them. More of servants' whims! I have just heard of one who demands four glasses of rum per day! Really, there is no enduring the insolence of this class here; they soon find out their value and act accordingly. Any one bringing out servants should accurately enumerate in their indentures every article, and how much of it each should get. Many, who on landing would have been startled at the idea of taking four glasses of spirits every day, soon reconcile themselves to this excess, if they be indulged by their masters: in laborious and warm work, however, such as mowing, a large allowance of grog is not unreasonable.

I exchanged two pair of small linen trousers (which had been made for the boy who came out with me) for a cock of hay, and have a grand project in my head of bartering some chickens (when hatched) for a kid which one of my neighbours *expects* soon to have born to him.

4th.—I am helping Mackie to cut an avenue from his place to mine; many settlers are doing the same kind of thing, which makes our houses appear much closer than we before supposed.

Dec. 4th.—After the expiration of the time which my servants have to remain with me, I should be glad to have others bound for five years, and would advance their passage money, giving them £5 a year with clothes and diet, or £10 a year without clothing; but retaining in my hands their wages until the passage money be cleared, and with a contract that their servitude should continue until this debt be fully discharged—a bonus of two glasses of rum per day.

7th.—Great visitings among the neighbouring servants; seven or eight of them patrolling about; and all this is sure to end in drunkenness and mischief—they talk of forming a *club*! They have too much control over their masters already; and club-law would be a terrible exercise and increase of their power.

10th.—How different my rural life from that which I had imagined it would be! Instead of being demi-savage and romantic, it is civilised (often ceremonious) and uniform; with less of privation and more of occupation for mind and body than I had anticipated But where are all the flocks and herds?—Where?

It cost me £32 to get a cow and a calf, and the cow is dead. Sheep are £3 each; so that it would take all my capital to possess a flock—even less than the patriarch's—such as would afford the keeping of a shepherd. From one sow I have had thirty pigs—the only stock that has multiplied with me—and a much larger number I could not support. It is easy for a person at home to say, "You can keep pigs and poultry without limit as to numbers," but they must be fed in summer at considerable expense; and as our

The Universal Pamphleteer.

EMIGRATION TO THE SWAN RIVER.

A COMPLETE HISTORY

OF THE

SWAN-RIVER SETTLEMENT;

DESCRIBING ITS

Soil, Climate, & Natural Productions,

AND PARTICULARLY THE ADVANTAGES IT POSSESSES, COMPARATIVELY
WITH OTHER COLONIES, AS A

PLACE OF EMIGRATION;

WITH

MR. FRASER'S REPORT

ON ITS BOTANICAL PRODUCTIONS,

As Read before the Linnæan Society;

THE OUTFITS REQUISITE FOR EMIGRANTS;

AND THE COST AT WHICH THE NECESSARIES AND COMFORTS OF LIFE MAY
BE OBTAINED;

The Terms offered to Emigrants by Government,

&c. &c. &c.

TO WHICH IS ADDED, THE

LATEST AND MOST CORRECT INFORMATION

As to the Progress of the First Settlers, and the Present State of the Colony.

THE UNIVERSAL PAMPHLETEER,

Consisting of Scarce, Instructive, and Entertaining Tracts on all Subjects, comprises—
Lives of Remarkable Men—Facts and Romances from History—Tales and Legends—
Extraordinary Trials, Adventures, Phenomena, and Crimes—Abstracts of Acts of Par-
liament—Arts and Treatises, &c. &c.

Each Pamphlet contains eight closely-printed octavo pages; and the Work is embellished
with superior illustrative Embellishments on Wood.

An Emigration Handbook

fences are generally bad, the pigs eat down the wheat and destroy the gardens, and the poultry soon devour their own value in grain. These are among our checks; however, I am giving you the worst side of the picture—the features of the reversed one you will trace through the sketching lines of my whole journal.

The truth is, I hate high colouring in these cases, which may mislead, and therefore strip the portraiture of all adornment and exhibit the naked truth, "which when unadorned is adorned the most." An awful responsibility would rest on me were I to hold out inducements to any one, when success depends so much on the taste, physical adaptation, amount of capital, &c. It costs a considerable sum to bring out and to support the emigrant until he can support himself. Land must be purchased—if from government at 5*s.* an acre; and if servants be brought out, the expense of maintaining them is considerable; and what can a solitary individual do if he do *not* bring them? Two or three stout hard-working brothers, or a father with a family able and willing to assist, with *some money*, are sure of establishing themselves in rough comfort and plenty in a very few years; but there must be no squeamishness as to fare. In short, it is a plodding, matter-of-fact, and hard-working sort of life, until you become settled; with very little of the romance and adventure about it which is so tempting and alluring to your minds. Yet it has its pleasures too; but people should prepare themselves for what it really is, and therefore I show more of the unfavourable side, and expose the truth in its most undisguised and unflattering state, leaving people to draw their own inferences. There is one point which I recommend to every one coming out; namely, the purchase of cattle from the Cape. Good ponies are very reasonable there also.

Jan. 12, 1832. Our colonists are complaining that their friends and connexions at home have made so little exertion to assist them through the first difficulties. It might have been obvious that an infant settlement could not altogether support itself independently of extrinsic aid. Vessels have not been encouraged to come here, and those that have arrived have brought scarcely any provisions. We have at present no more than a few weeks' supply of flour, and are totally without rice, maize, peas, barley or oats: we may have as much wheat as will serve for six weeks, with great economy; but it is already selling at 25*s*. per bushel. Vessels have been expected daily for the last three months, and we are now sick of hope. The state of the colony at present is dispiriting; but we hope it will not long continue so, and that we shall rise above every difficulty and discouragement. A helping hand is now greatly needed; and a little extra aid from the Government would enable us to procure working cattle, milch cows, and sheep, and would place us beyond the chance of poverty or privation. This is a country where there are few natural productions that are edible, but it produces crops inferior to none in England, and with less trouble: indeed the soil is capable of producing any crop, and its herbage is abundant for the support of cattle. I should not, perhaps, have touched on this point, had it not been the subject of conversation in a company which I have just left; and, indeed, this point is the general topic of conversation in the colony at present.

Feb. 17th.—I was on this day sworn in a commissioner of the civil court in Western Australia, which will open early next month. This court is almost without limit as to jurisdiction; juries may be called for, if the parties will pay them; and appeal lies to the Governor and Council in cases beyond a certain amount; short forms to be used, with few technicalities. I have had rare work cutting down long declarations into small compass, making forms of conveyance, leases and mortgages, pruning of all redundancies, and reducing all to an alarmingly small size. You remember I had rather a taste for this, and I have entered on my occupation *con amore*.

27th.—Busy, in Perth, making arrangements with respect to the court; and I have bought a town allotment in Perth, with a house partly built on it. The situation (on the river) is beautiful, and about £20 will be sufficient outlay for putting the house into repair: it will be valuable. The allotment is thirty-three yards wide, and ninety-nine yards long. It cost £11 5*s*. 6*d*. to fence the front, with the regulation-post and rail fence made of mahogany; the railing at the sides is of split wood.

March 4th.—Prices have risen to a very serious height just now, and there is consequently a great outcry in the colony. Some of our friends appear to think that we are so well off that we cannot possible want for any thing; and others probably imagine we are so far gone, that it is hopeless to send us any thing; so we fall *between the two stools.* Can you picture to yourself a new colony? You cannot. It is impossible for one, in the midst of the luxurious refinements of the old country, to conceive the actual state of a new one. Not that there are intolerable hardships, nor even great privations; but people's fancy will play them the trick of sup- posing that from throwing seed into the ground we can ensure a crop without any further trouble; whereas our culture, and all our operations, are most laborious: my two men have been now nearly a month *looking* for thatch and putting it on two houses, which are not near finished yet. As to breaking ground, it is easy when you have cattle; but, generally speaking, we are not so provided. It occupies a man twenty days to break up an acre with a hoe, from its wild state, though this could be done easily with cattle. But, as I have already observed, we have few of them, and the neighbouring colonies will not send them, either from jealousy or fear; and individually we cannot afford to charter vessels and import them, and we are not yet strong enough to form a company. What can we then do?—two or three hundred of cattle, and two or three thousand sheep, would be purchased by us, if they were sent by government at a fair rate; and this would establish the colony.

August 6th.—I was induced to leave my plough this day for the sake of training my young dog at the kangaroo chase, and caught one after a long run. Have I ever detailed this chase to you? I believe not. You advance silently, watching in every direction, and when you see a kangaroo, you immediately run in the direction of him, hallooing on the dogs, which follow the game by view as far as the ground is clear. The sportsmen then wait patiently, half an hour or an hour, until the return of the dogs, which is sooner or later according to the length of the chase. The dogs are examined in the mouth to see if they have fur or blood, or the *smack* of kangaroo, which is something like that of bay leaf: if the indications of murder be upon them, they are desired to "show" the game, and in "showing" it the excellence of the dog is exhibited. One of ours being desired to "show" set off at a trot. We all followed at the same pace in a straight line for a mile, at the termination of which he brought us to the dead kangaroo. But I expect some lucky day to be at a nobler hunt than this—a bull chase—as a wild bull was caught and killed the other day. The meat, (sold at 1*s*. 6*d*. per lb.), produced nearly £50; and a great sensation has been created by a rumour that thirty-six head of wild cattle has been seen. I doubt the truth of the report. Really this kangaroo-hunting is very important to the settlers in their present circumstances. Some of my friends have had fresh meat of this animal for three months together, when it would have required three casks of pork, at £10 each, to have supplied their establishment during the same period. Thus have their dogs saved them £30.

9th.—A soldier coming up yesterday from Perth was attacked by natives; he says that he shot two of them. It will be prudent on my part, when I set out to-morrow morning at day-break, to arm myself with a double-barrelled gun and ball cartridges.

19th March 1833.—While wandering about to-day with a gun on my shoulder, I met a gentleman who informed that the natives killed a valuable mare belonging to Mr. Tanner, at Woodbridge, yesterday, in revenge it is supposed, for some imaginary cause of offence. The same people were perceived on Friday behind my place (soon after the hay was destroyed) on the look out, in all probability, for my flock; but I keep a steady watch, and shall take my gun with me every day, and observe the precaution of putting a brace of pistols in my belt. We have been on good terms with them every where, so that I cannot imagine the occasion of this mischievous outbreak.

June 8th. 9 *o'clock at night*.—These plaguy natives have stolen one of my pigs. They are sad hypocrites; those very four who were here were, I suspect, privy to, if not active in, the theft. It is difficult to ascertain the real fact. I wish it was either peace or war between us; but now we must not touch them, for by proclamation they are declared under the protection of the law, as British subjects.

March 7th 1834.—A very warm day. Some natives have been here before sunrise begging some grease to smear themselves for a battle. One of them was afterwards slightly wounded in the side by a spear. One young woman was speared through the arm and in the leg, and that was the extent of all the mighty business. I shot some birds for them and killed two at one shot, which raised a shout from both armies—about 40 men.

9th.—Again troubled with natives all day. There is a singular belief supposed to be general now among the natives that we are the spirits of their deceased friends, and they call many by the names of men long dead. Of one old man who is fast declining, they say that he will soon become a white man, and then he will have plenty of bread. They hold opinion with Pythagoras as Gratiano says, of the transmigration.

15th.—I got paid to-day for a pair of slippers by a piece of iron-hard cash! and another wishes me to take a pig for some other things. Mr. B—— wants me to take a goose! These are the modes of payment. There is not any news; but the natives are becoming everywhere more bold, the colonists more uneasy, the Government more puzzled, and I fear a rupture if the offending natives be not removed wholesale to some island—which might be done.

Tuesday, March 18th—Yesterday being "St. Patrick's Day in the morning," the Messrs. Burgess invited me to dine with them. A pleasant day it was, marked by one appropriate feature—they had tried and succeeded in distilling a small quantity of "potheen," which was our beverage.

Monday, June 1st. 1835.—This is the anniversary of the foundation or establishment of this colony, and is to be celebrated in Perth by rustic sports and gambols, as running after pigs with soaped tails, jumping in sacks, &c. I was trepanned into subscribing a pound for it, as the Government officers were expected to contribute.

Jan. 28th. 1839.—Yesterday one of my boys succeeded in catching a young emu alive. It is a wonderfully tame, even silly thing—like a young turkey; by the way, the same boy also succeeded in shooting a turkey, which I had to-day at dinner. It was delicious.

March 28th.—I have been so much occupied of late, and so little at this place which I call my home, that I have got out of the habit of writing a daily journal as heretofore. Every morning, when I am in Perth, I devote a couple of hours with the Governor and the interpreter to the formation of a vocabulary of the native language. Our progress is slow, but deliberate. We have discovered a tolerably regular conjunction of their verbs, consisting of present and past tense and participle,—for instance, booma, booma-ing, boomaga, respectively stand for beat, beating (or beat), beaten. We are also trying to collect and arrange all the minerals of the colony, and have made a tolerable show already. Mr. Preiss, a German, has discovered, in the Toodyay district, something of a fossil nature, which, I think, is an 'encrinite,' and is the first of the transition or secondary formation (if it be of one or the other) which has been found here. This gives hope of coming to a coal formation. The Governor has offered a grant of 2560 acres to anyone who may first discover a coal field.

April 1st Friday night.—I am very tired. Have just come from Perth after a rather severe week's work. On Tuesday we sat in Executive Council till five o'clock; on Wednesday our sessions commenced, and I was engaged till six in the evening with a very heavy calendar. On Thursday I was at work at six o'clock in the morning, preparing for Council, as we had an adjourned meeting of our Executive Council at 10 o'clock, in order to prepare for Legislative Council at one o'clock. Only think of sitting in Executive Council to discuss and settle the heads of a Bill at 10 o'clock, which was to be read a first time in the Legislative Council at one o'clock on the same day. We had barely time to change our dress, and then we sat down in Legislative Council till five o'clock. I thought I had done a pretty good day's work, and had gone home with the intention of getting some dinner, when I was sent for to conduct a heavy prosecution for burglary at the sessions; so I hurried to the court. The case had just commenced, and was not finished till after ten o'clock at night.

July 13th.—I have fallen out of my habit of regularity, and find it difficult to recover it. We have advanced here to such a pitch of civilization as to have private theatricals. The play of "Love, à la militaire" was performed on Tuesday night to a fashionable audience, among whom not the least delighted spectators were the young folks of the town and vicinity of Perth. Most of them having never seen a play, were wonderfully amused.

Mary Thomas

Mary Thomas was nearly fifty when she emigrated, and was never able to reconcile herself to the discomforts of pioneer life, let the profits (and they were considerable) be what they would. A Southampton girl, she married Robert Thomas, a man who had already emigrated, though it was only from Montgomeryshire to London. He was a moderately successful publisher and law stationer in Fleet Street.

He had been dabbling with the idea of going to Australia for some time before 1836, when he was finally persuaded by a friend who was private secretary to the first Governor, Captain Hindmarsh, and he arrived with his portable press in time to print the first Proclamation of the infant colony. He was given an epitaph in 1860 by Sir George Grey, which would serve for a multitude of his fellow colonists: 'He was a fine example of the earnest, able, energetic pioneer colonist; a man of great natural ability and singular force of character.'

But our regard is for his wife, who wrote so many unhappy poems, who wanted so much to go home, but died at last to be buried beside him in that atmosphere which made it necessary to dust the furniture three or four times each weary day.

The MSS. of these letters to her brother are now in the Archives Department of the Public Library, Museum and Art Gallery of South Australia. They are published, with certain omissions, in *The Diary and Letters of Mary Thomas* (1836–1866), Adelaide, 1915, edited by Evan Kyffin Thomas.

Adelaide, October 14, 1838. I will now tell you some of the reasons which induced us to leave England. In the first place, the lease of our house had nearly expired. It was greatly out of repair, partly owing to the next house above having been pulled down and rebuilt a short time before. This caused ours to give way, though I could not make Mr. Thomas believe it was in so bad a state as it really was. I knew if we stayed to the end of the lease we should have heavy dilapidations to pay for. I also knew this would put him in a terrible rage, as I estimated them to be at least £200, and to prove that I was right in my conjecture Mr. Baugh has since informed us that the repairs took £300. Added to this, Robert wished to go abroad, and William was not likely to be placed to any business. Mr. Baugh wished very much to have him as an apprentice, and I did not like to see him idle away his time at home. The scheme of this new colony happened to be started just at the time. We first heard of it from Dr. Inman, of Portsmouth, who came up to London to purchase some land in it for one of his sons, who is now here. It was thought to be an excellent opportunity for young men of talent to try their fortunes, especially as the plan on which this colony is founded is considered to be superior to all others; and as neither of my boys is deficient in genius or education I flattered myself that, with attention and industry, they might become at some time or other possessed of considerable property. Besides this, Frances's health, which was never good in London, I hoped might be improved by a sea voyage and change of climate. These were the principal reasons which made me encourage rather than otherwise Mr. Thomas's inclination to become a landholder in this new Province. Accordingly, he purchased 134 acres, each at twelve shillings per acre, which also entitled him to two in the principal town, and these were purchased several months before we left England.

You shall now have a short account of our voyage. We left Fleet Street, having disposed of the business and the remainder of

[169]

the lease, at Ladyday, 1836, and took lodgings at Fish Street, near St. Paul's, for three months. There Mary and Helen had the scarlet fever just before we left England.

You may suppose what a situation I was in, never at sea before, and unable to procure many comforts which we might have had on land, a very inattentive doctor, and unaccommodating captain. Neither the captain nor his wife inquired if I wanted anything, or offered the smallest nourishment for the children out of the cabin stores, although they had plenty of everything. We were in the intermediate, there not being room in the after part of the vessel for our family, and we did not choose to be where they could not be with us. So we engaged two cabins in the intermediate with two berths in each, and so far were as comfortable as we could expect. We paid thirty-five pounds per head, and the captain was to find us in everything. This was little more than hard biscuit and salt junk, not very digestible food for the children recovering from a dangerous illness; and yet in the cabin they had fresh meat every day. I sat up with William five nights in the dark, as no one is allowed a light on board a ship, and with constant attention and some medicine, which I procured from my own doctor before I left London lest I should have occasion for it, he recovered, and without the disorder spreading to the steerage. This I was most apprehensive of, as there the passengers were more crowded. Thus it was nearly another three weeks before I could get a comfortable night's rest, though I can hardly say that I had that during the whole voyage, especially in rough weather. The expectation that the children would be tossed out of their berths generally kept me awake, and sometimes I was up the greater part of the night.

I forgot to mention that while we were at Chalton Mr. Thomas engaged two of Mr. Martin's men as agriculturists—Jacobs and Windebank—and I also engaged Mary Lillywhite, of the same place, as servant and companion, for she lived with us the same as my own family. Unfortunately, however, she was too much of the fine lady to give me much assistance. They all came up to London the day before we sailed. We also engaged two printers—one a journeyman, and the other a turnover apprentice—and two other young men, we being entitled by the money we paid for the land to take out ten labourers or servants, free of expense, who were bound to remain for one year, but we have not one of them now. Jacobs and Windebank left us after some months, as the land could not be taken possession of so soon as we expected, and we had no employment for them suitable to their inclinations. About twelve months ago Mary Lillywhite married our printer, whose name is Fisher, and they both left us, but still reside in Adelaide. Since then I have been without a servant, having no accommodation for one in my present habitation unless I allowed her to sit at my table and sleep with the girls, which I will never submit to, especially here, where the servants are becoming as saucy and independent as they are in America. Both servants and labourers being scarce, they get too much wages by half.

We reached the mainland, our final destination, on the 10th, and Mr. Thomas, the two Hampshire men, and William went on shore and pitched our tents. On Sunday, the 13th, it being a very calm day, we all landed, having been on the water exactly eighteen weeks. We had to walk about a mile from the beach. We found Robert well. He had arrived with the Surveyors a few weeks before. With the exception of the tents of the surveyors, there was not, when we landed, a human habitation in South Australia but those which had been raised by the passengers of the *Africaine*. These, of course, were all canvas. The swamp, too was so high that we were obliged to wade through it up to our necks, and no trace of a human footstep could be seen.

This place is called Glenelg, and here we remained for several months. On December 28, the Governor, Captain Hindmarsh, arrived in the *Buffalo*, and he remained for some time at Glenelg, in a rush hut which had been prepared for the family, as the site of the capital had not then been fixed upon. Soon afterwards it was decided in favour of the present situation of Adelaide.

(*Diary*, Dec. 28, 1836. Early in the morning it was announced that the *Buffalo* had arrived from Port Lincoln, accompanied by the *Cygnet*, which had gone thither to escort the Governor, Captain Hindmarsh, to Holdfast Bay. This made us all alive, and soon after Mr. Thomas received notice to attend at the tent of Mr.

[171]

Gouger, the Colonial Secretary, where His Excellency the Governor was expected to be at 3 o'clock to read his Commission and proclaim the colony. Mr. Thomas then went to the Company's store and soon returned with a request that he would procure a ham, as Mr. Gilbert was not provided with one, which was done, and a fine Hampshire Ham was dressed for the occasion. It was also requested that we would prepare ourselves to meet the procession, as all who could were expected to attend. We went accordingly, and found assembled the largest company we had yet seen in the colony, probably two hundred persons.

The Governor's Private Secretary read the Proclamation under a huge gumtree, a flag was hoisted, a party of marines from the *Buffalo* fired a *feu-de-joie*, and loud hurrahs succeeded. A cold collation, of which we partook, followed in the open air.

The Governor was very affable, shaking hands with the colonists and congratulating them on having such a fine country. After the repast he mounted on a chair and gave the first toast, 'The King,' which was received with three times three, and followed by the National Anthem, led by Mr. Gilles. The old royal appellation of 'George' was so natural to Englishmen, after four successive reigns of Kings of that name, that it was forgotten at the moment that a 'William' was now on the throne, and the first line was sung as formerly, 'God save great George, our King,' which excited a smile. Yet I believe that William the Fourth has not more loyal subjects throughout his wide dominions than those who were there assembled to welcome the first Governor of South Australia. The health of His Excellency was then proposed and drunk with loud and universal cheering, followed by 'Rule, Britannia.' Then 'Mrs. Hindmarsh and the Ladies' was proposed by Mr. Gilbert, and also received great applause, as did several other toasts.

The Governor then gave the following:—'May the present unanimity continue as long as South Australia exists,' which made the plain ring with acclamations. At about 5 o'clock His Excellency and lady departed to the ship, and some officers and others followed in another boat. They all seemed highly delighted with our village, as I may call it, consisting now of about forty tents and huts, though scattered about without any regularity. Everyone fixed his present abode wherever he wished, knowing it would not be of long duration.)

In March, 1837, the remainder of the town land was sold by auction in acres, of which Mr. Thomas bought eight, in addition to the two preliminary ones he already possessed, at from six to eight guineas per acre. All these are in good situation and likely to increase in value. As a proof, a few days ago he sold for two hundred guineas a quarter of one of them, the whole of which cost him less than ten.

Adelaide is about six miles from Glenelg, or Holdfast Bay, as the anchorage there is called, and somewhat further from Port Adelaide, another part of the coast, which place I have never yet seen, and perhaps I never shall, as I seldom go out, especially since I have been without a servant.

We came here on June 1, 1837. Mr. Thomas and the boys came up some time before, as the printing press was obliged to be set up here, and resided in the tents until September while this building was finishing. Since then we have been within these walls, which are built of mud, and the roof is of boards. We have a stone house in progress, and when we remove into it I hope it will be the last remove we shall make till we return to dear old England!

Mr. Thomas, who is perfectly infatuated with this country, does not seem to anticipate such an event, but I do, and so do the girls, and I feel confident that, please God, at some time or other such will be the case.

This is certainly a very fine country, and capable of the highest improvements. Doubtless those who are born and brought up here will think of it as we do of our native country, that there is no other like it in the world; but to those who know what England is, and recollect the comfort there enjoyed, it never can bear a comparison, notwithstanding its luxuriant plains, its magnificent trees, its ranges of lofty hills, and scenery often sublime. The soil, too, can doubtless be made to reproduce nearly all the fruits and vegetables of the known world. We have a garden in which we have abundance of the latter and some of the former in cultivation, but the vegetables have not the sweetness of those in England, and generally run to seed before they have attained half their size. This

[173]

may, perhaps, be remedied by proper management, the plants being, like ourselves, not yet acclimatised.

All our goods had to be brought from the beach by hand, as no such animal as a horse or a bullock was then in the colony. Now there are thousands of both, with carts and every convenience for carrying baggage and passengers, and lodgings either at inns or private houses; and yet those who have been accustomed to English comforts will find themselves very deficient of them in many respects, unless they reckon among them hundreds of rats and mice, thousands of fleas and flies, millions of ants and mosquitoes, and many other such annoyances.

I must now think of bringing this long letter to a close, which I have been nearly a week in writing. I have so little time to spare that I could not sit to it long together. Since I began it Mr. Thomas has let a quarter of an acre, which cost him ten guineas, on a building lease for ten years for forty pounds a year, and the tenant is to leave all building thereon at the expiration of the lease.

You were kind enough to offer to do anything you could for us. It is only a childish whim, for I fancy I could relish a bit of Hampshire bacon more than anything to be got here, and if you can prevail on Mr. Kinggate to pay you for two flitches out of my money from the bank interest I would be glad to have them. They should be well packed in a strong case, for the meat here in summer is flyblown before it is cold, and next day crawling with maggots.

I forgot to tell you that our population exceeds four thousand, and several more ships are expected. Streets are rapidly forming in all directions in regular lines, for the city is laid out on a particular plan, which cannot be deviated from, and in a few years this will be a magnificent place. We have already a church built of stone and of considerable dimensions, and a clock has lately been fixed in it. This we find of great use, as all our watches are stopped, influenced, I suppose, by the climate. This is a general complaint. Mr. Thomas is making bricks on his country sections. These are in great demand, and are now used in preference to mud. When we built our house stone was the only thing to be had. Of course our fuel is wood, which I fear will soon become scarce. It is already

very dear, owing to the great consumption, and although we have
plenty on our lands the carriage is expensive. No doubt this
country contains much coal, which will be very profitable to anyone who may discover it. We have abundance of goods of all kinds,
almost as cheap as in England, but provisions are dear. Fresh
meat, 1*s.* per pound; fresh butter, 3*s.* 6*d.*; salt butter, 2*s.* 6*d.*; and
bread 1*s.* 8*d.* per loaf; all of which have been much more. We sometimes get fish. The water is not so good or so plentiful as in
England. Neither is the air so bracing or refreshing. Frequently
there is a hot and scorching wind, which, while it lasts, is almost
past endurance. With all the advantages of this fine country it will
never bear comparison with dear old England, where I hope to end
my days in peace and comfort. This is all I desire, for I have no
ambition to be rich, and though we may wish, with the blessing of
God, to obtain a competence here, we must go to England to enjoy
it.

February 7, 1839. At present I must content myself with giving
you some account of the natives, which may not be uninteresting.
They are for the most part a harmless, inoffensive people, but
extremely ignorant, and rank among the lowest of the human
people. They seem to have but little intellect for improvement or
imitation, which is proved by their never attempting to build
themselves substantial houses, notwithstanding the example
which we have set before them, and the assistance, with an abundant supply of tools and material, which would be afforded them
if they had either the ingenuity or the industry to avail themselves
of them. But they (the men) are naturally indolent and averse to
labour of every kind. They leave what little work there is to do,
such as carrying burdens, their young children, and such-like,
entirely to their women, and will encumber themselves with
nothing but their warlike weapons, which you may be sure are
rude enough, consisting of long spears pointed at one end, and,
since the arrival of the whites, studded about two or three inches
from the point with broken glass. They have no tools whatever,
nor, so far as I have ever heard, any kind of domestic utensil.
Consequently, they cook their provisions, consisting chiefly of

kangaroos, opossums, iguanas, lizards, snakes, etc., on the bare
coals, without divesting them, I believe, of either skin or entrails—
at least the small animals. Birds are deprived only of their feathers.
They likewise eat several kinds of roots and herbs. The men are
generally tall and well made, but most of the women are the most
abject-looking beings you can imagine. The latter are diminutive
of stature and are always stooping, from their habit of carrying
everything at their back. Soon they have all the appearance of old
age.

There is one thing more which I must mention, and that is the
correctness with which they pronounce our language, though at
first, when we came among them, it was only by repeating what we
said. For instance I said to a woman,

"What is you name?" to which she replied, with great accuracy,
"What is your name?"

I made answer, "My name is Mary Thomas," and she again
replied,

"My name is Mary Thomas."

But now they are rather more enlightened (I speak of the tribe
about Adelaide), and some of them have learned what is said to
them tolerably well, and to give, in some instances, rational
answers. There are some white persons who have likewise studied
their dialect so far as to make themselves understood by them.

February 17. I believe I did not tell you that we had been at
Glenelg about a month before we saw any of them. Then a man
and a boy were discovered by a person of the name of Williams,
a fellow-passenger with us, while out shooting about five miles
distant. They did not observe him. He therefore reloaded his gun
and then called to them, at the same time advancing. They immediately started up (as they were in the act of making a fire) and
seized their spears. Mr. Williams held out his hand with a biscuit,
whereupon they cautiously came forward to meet him, and signs
of mutual friendship having been exchanged he induced them to
accompany him to the tents at Glenelg. He went round the village,
as we may call it, with them. It did not appear that they had ever
seen white people before, judging by the astonishment they

expressed at all they beheld. They peeped into the tents and examined everything that came in their way with perfect good humour, and highly delighted. They shook hands with everyone, male and female, without being at all abashed. They were both stark naked, but we thought it most prudent not to appear shy, especially in the first interview. They were afterwards taken to the Commissioner's stores and clothed with a pair of trousers, a flannel shirt, and a woollen cap each, as a great many of such articles were sent out expressly for the natives. No monarch in his robes could be prouder than they were of their dress. This man and boy remained with Mr. Williams three days, sleeping at night by his fire on the bare ground, and before he left he again brought the boy to our tent. I endeavoured to excite his wonder by showing him such things as I thought he had not seen. He was greatly astonished at the opening and shutting of an umbrella, the effect of a lucifer box, and seeing the water run out of a filtering machine. But what most of all surprised him was a large telescope drawn out to its full length, which he at first took to be a gun. He said "Boof!" meaning that it would make a noise. But I shook my head and said "No boof!" Then with some difficulty I persuaded him to look through it, when he expressed his astonishment by lifting up his hands and exclaiming "Mawny! Mawny!" which is their word for anything wonderful.

Those who have learned a little English generally make use of that phrase "very good" to whatever is said to them, and consequently one of them, who, it was supposed, had killed a white man, on being told that he would be hanged for it, replied as usual, "Very good."

They have committed some depredations, such as spearing a few sheep and such-like. Otherwise their conduct has hitherto been peaceful and orderly, and they very logically exculpate their own misdemeanours by saying, "White man come kill black man kangaroo. Black man kill white man sheep. Very good."

But the greatest mischief they have as yet done the settlers is not from any design on their part to injure us, but from a custom they have of burning the grass during the hot weather in order to drive the kangaroos where they may be caught and to force the

s.—12   [177]

snakes, which are part of their subsistence, out of their holes. Frequently they set large trees on fire in order to catch the opossums, in the hollows of which these animals generally live. Many trees are found still standing, with cavities burnt out in this way large enough to contain eight or ten persons. Their fires on the hills are quite awful. We have frequently seen fires this summer which have reached for twenty or thirty miles in circumference, for they light them at distances so that they shall enclose a large space, and the grass being so exceedingly dry, it may be truly said to burn like wildfire. We have seen three or four such fires as these on the hills, which are about five miles away, at the same time, so that Adelaide has been nearly ambushed with flames. Some of these fires have done much damage to the stock stations by destroying the grass on which the bullocks and sheep were pastured, and which, as we had a very dry summer and nearly five months of hot weather, is rather scarce. Consequently the stock-keepers have been put to great inconvenience.

I have now given you a long account of the native inhabitants, whose appearance, though disgusting in the extreme to an European, calls for our pity and compassion, and whose condition, though not as yet greatly amended by their intercourse with white men, yet I trust will be undoubtedly so in time. They are considered as British subjects, and have all protection from injury quite equally with any person in the colony. They are provided with anything they may require by applying to the Protector of the Aborigines, either for their comfort or advancement, and it is intended to impress on their minds that they must not do an injury to white men, as none will be allowed to hurt them. But there is some difficulty in making them understand the principle of justice as distinguished from retaliation, which they consider as indispensable. When two black men in one of the neighbouring colonies were hanged for murdering a white man, the other natives could not be brought to comprehend why two men should suffer for one, though both were concerned in the matter.

We shall have another newspaper to print, 'The Port Lincoln Herald,' as you will see advertised in last week's 'Gazette and Colonial Register.' Port Lincoln is now all the talk as being one of the finest harbours in the world. Several gentlemen have already gone there to form a settlement, and a great deal of land has been sold, which already bears a high premium. The first number is to appear on the 27th of this month, and in consequence of our having it to print we shall want more hands.

Mr. Thomas desires me to say that if you know of any good compositors who are desirous of emigrating, steady and sober men, they will be sure here of good wages and constant employment. If they have families, so much the better, as their children, whether boys or girls, will get employment likewise as soon as they are able to earn anything. Indeed, for mechanics and labourers of every kind a new field is here opened for their exertions, which, if well directed, cannot fail with the industrious and persevering to realize an independence. But to those who have been accustomed to something superior to a life of labour it offers little encouragement in the way of comfort, though prosperity may be equally within their reach.

I cannot say that I much relish working so hard as I do now at my time of life, especially as I see little prospect at present of its being otherwise, for the climate is such that cleanliness and comfort, according to English ideas, are entirely out of the question and incompatible with the country altogether. For I cannot call any place comfortable where the clouds of dust cover all your furniture three or four times a day, driving through every crevice; where you are incessantly hunting fleas and bugs and are overrun with ants, spiders of an enormous size, and flies or some other teasing insect, and where the water, which in England is generally plentiful and delicious to drink, is here both scarce, comparatively speaking, and never palatable as a beverage without an infusion of some kind. In short, I am determined, if ever I have it in my power, to quit this country and return to my native land, and I trust that Heaven will grant me this petition if it be only that I may lay my ashes with my native dust.

August 11, 1840. If you have received the parcel I mentioned you have got a view of our two houses. On the top of the larger one there is a lofty flagstaff to signalize the vessels as they arrive in the

Bay, about six miles distant, and clearly seen with a glass, so that every ship as soon as it comes in sight is announced by a ball, either red, white, or black, according to what she is supposed to be. This has so delighted the colonists that they come to us far and near for explanation when any signals are flying, and it is seldom a day passes without one or more, the flagstaff being sometimes decorated with three or four different colours at the same time. Although another belonging to the Government is stationed at a short distance, ours generally gives the first and most accurate information.

We still have wet weather and the streets are so muddy it is almost impossible to wade through them. As much of the soil here consists of clay and sand, without any gravel to bind them together, the streets in the rainy season are rendered almost impassable. As we are now going to have a Mayor and Corporation I hope that some of the deficiencies at present complained of will be remedied, for the town is now fast rising into importance.

John Davies Mereweather

John Davies Mereweather graduated from Oxford—where he had been at St. Edmund Hall—in 1844. Where he lived before that and what he did immediately afterwards I do not know, but in 1850 he emigrated to Australia.

He wrote an account of the voyage out, and it was published at home two years later as *Life on Board an Emigrant Ship* and encouraged him to become a literary clergyman. But before he appeared in print he had commenced a diary, which, in spite of its pulpit antitheses and unhappily respectable vocabulary, gives a brisk picture of life around Melbourne at a particularly interesting time.

He left Australia in 1853 owing to the obstacles put in the way of his pastoral work there, and returned to England before going abroad again, this time to Venice, where he became English Chaplain.

The air of the lagoons nourished the author in him with such effect that in 1867 he produced *Semele, or The Spirit of Beauty*. Lest the title by itself should give a false impression of the nature of the work, I give the author's own explanation of his purpose, which is of considerable interest, for in the same year, it will be remembered, Pater published his essay on Winckelmann, who had written 'sehnlich wünschte ich zur Kenntniss des Schönen zu gelangen':

'To lay before my countrymen a sketch of what Venice is,

[181]

according to my own impression, to intersperse that sketch with
thoughts and reflections naturally arising from the object immediately under consideration, and to rectify misunderstandings
which may have arisen in many minds with regard to many things
connected with that wonderful city, has been the object of the
following Tale, the heroine of which seems to have fallen into a
fault, which, in this material age—amid this "positivisme des
mœurs modernes," as a French writer expresses himself—will
assuredly find no imitators—that of loving Beauty and Art, Spirit
and Embodiment, with a frenzied enthusiasm, excluding all
rational consideration of human duties and every-day life.'

Life on these terms was indeed too much for his heroine, who,
finding the strain of combining respectability of conduct and
frenzy of sentiment unbearable, fell into a decline, went staring
mad and—but the author should be allowed to give the dénoue-
ment in his own words:

'Five months after the terrible catastrophe, and on the same
day of the month, she voyaged into the Untried Land on a soft
midnight under the earnest, loving gaze of the sympathizing stars,
not with despairing shriek or agonized gesture, but tranquilly and
smilingly, as sinking into a happy sleep, prelude to a gladsome
rising, and murmuring always in musical undertone, "Addio!
Addio! O venezia, la bella, la diletta."'

He himself passed to the Untried Land in 1895.

His diary is printed as *Diary of a Working Clergyman in
Australia and Tasmania* 1850–1853, London, MDCCCLIX.

June 17th, 1850.—To-day, though in mid-winter, we have a
glowing sun, modified by a balmy breeze. All the deck is confusion,
for the emigrants, who go no further than Adelaide, are getting
out their baggage. I, at the request of the passengers, drew out a
testimonial for the doctor, which was unanimously signed; and he
deserves this mark of attention, for, professionally, he has been
most assiduous, and socially, he has behaved as a gentleman
should. Many of the surgeons on board of emigrant ships are

disreputable characters in every way. In the course of the day I went with two passengers to Adelaide. We travelled in a public conveyance, which was a Whitechapel cart, drawn by two horses, tandem fashion. The drivers of these vehicles carry as many passengers as they can get. We were said to be lucky, for there were only six besides us three. The road, which passed through a desolate tract of country, was full of large holes, which by recent rains had been converted into round ponds; these ponds we had to coast round, making a great half circle, so that instead of travelling seven miles, the distance between Port Adelaide and Adelaide, we travelled at least ten miles. On our way we met and passed innumerable bullock-drays, drawn by eight, or ten, or twelve, patient, hard-tugging bullocks. We also saw several of the aborigines, clothed in dirty blankets and kangaroo and opossum-skins; they looked half-starved, like the dogs that followed them, and were hideously dirty and ugly. Adelaide strikes me as a very miserable, squalid place. Wide streets are laid out, but there are few houses in them, and those few are mean and wretched: the roads are full of holes, receptacles of dust in summer and mud in winter; public houses abound, and drunkenness seems everywhere prevalent. There is a substantial Change for the merchants to congregate in, but all the business of Adelaide seems done at a noted public-house, kept by a man called Coppin, or Choppin. Here is to be seen a strange mixture of merchants, newly-arrived immigrants, squatters, bullock-drivers, shopkeepers, loose characters, trafficking, blaspheming, laughing, singing, yelling, and drinking innumerable nobblers. Everybody goes there, for every business rendezvous is made at Choppin's. As I could get no conveyance to the port in the evening, I slept at an inn there. Each bed-room has three very plain sofa-couches; and I was told that if I didn't wish companions, I must pay for all three. The guests here live table-d'hôte fashion, and their breakfasts, dinners, and teas, are served with a monotonous prodigality. At every meal there are beef sausages, mutton chops, beef steaks, roast mutton and boiled beef, good potatoes, and most delicious bread; and of these three substantial meals the guests partake with the most persevering elasticity. The table-talk is of bullocks, highly-flavoured with oaths, and each person seems bent on making his fortune as quickly as possible. I can imagine the early Puritan settlers in North America to have been a very different set of persons. A young person at table, speaking contemptuously of some newly-arrived immigrants ('Jimmy Grants,' I think, was the slang term she applied to them), I asked her how long she had been out herself? 'Oh,' she said, 'I have been out six weeks, and I feel quite colonial already.' I told her I could well believe her. But the affectation and pretension of these people is to me very extraordinary. To hear them talk, you would suppose they had held important social positions in their fatherland, instead of which, three parts out of four have been driven out of it by hunger, or by crime.

July 8.—Steamed up the Yarra Yarra, whose banks are very ugly. They are low, covered with sad-looking, short scrub, and studded with boiling-down establishments, which circumfuse most fetid odours. In about a couple of hours arrived at Melbourne, a considerable town, sufficiently well situated on two hills and the intervening valley. The main streets are wide—too wide, if anything—and the drainage ought to be perfect. The river is spanned by a handsome stone bridge of one arch. The streets are infested by enormous dogs, who thrive here on the cheap butchers' meat. Went to a very excellent hotel called the Prince of Wales, where I dined and slept.

July 11.—Received an intimation from the Melbourne Club that I was received as an honorary member. Dined there with my introducer, an old member, and six others. We sat down at six o'clock at a well-appointed table, lighted by many wax-lights, and we were waited upon by two men-servants, one in dress livery the other out of livery. At night, as I lay on an excellent bed at the hotel, I could not help making the following reflections. Here am I, after a voyage of thirteen thousand or fourteen thousand miles through the great ocean, arrived on a vast continent, the existence of which was unknown to the world until two hundred years ago, and which was not inhabited by white men until sixty-two years ago. More than that, I have been partaking of an excellent repast, served in a way which would be considered creditable in London or Paris, in the society of educated and wealthy men, in a portion of that continent which was only discovered seventeen or eighteen years ago, and in a city which sixteen years back was a savage waste, trodden by savage men in chase of the emu and the kangaroo. In this city there are 25,000 inhabitants, surrounded by all the necessaries and comforts of life; there are well-built houses; shops filled with everything one can require; two churches, besides chapels; active Ministers of all denominations; a well-managed custom-house, gaol, and post-office; numerous colonial trading vessels clustering at the river quays; while at the mouth of the Yarra, by William's Town, lie at anchor fourteen or fifteen full-rigged ships. What wonderful civilising tendencies the Anglo-Saxon race seems to have! Instruments are they of an All-Wise Providence to substitute in the remote extremities of the world humanising Christianity for savage Paganism, a pure code of morals for abominable impurities, government for anarchy, peace for bloodshed, industry for idleness, the certain fruits of agriculture for the precarious yield of the chase! An Englishman is never content to do anything that he undertakes, by halves; he will pull up all surrounding influences to his level; he never descends to them. It is the genius of the British colonist to reproduce in the most distant regions, and under the most unfavourable auspices, the minutest details of early associations, to surround himself at the antipodes with the atmosphere of home. With dogged energy he never rests till he has reduced to practice the great theories necessary to the birth and existence of commonwealths, which have been familiar to him from his childhood. And this imitation of 'Home' is carried into all the details of private domestic life, even down to the furnishing of a house or the arranging of a dinner. And why has Providence chosen England from all other nations to carry Christianity, and its offspring, Civilisation, into the faraway wildernesses of distant lands, inhabited by savage men, devouring one another? How does this come to pass? If we may, without presumption, canvass the designs of Providence, the question would be capable of the following

[185]

solution. It is, then, that every Englishman is brought up from his earliest infancy to read, learn, and digest the pure and undefiled word of God. He early forms a habitude of judging for himself in religious matters, biased, perhaps, but not peremptorily dictated to, by any man, or any body of men. And this independence of judgement, once formed, extends naturally to secular matters, and prevents the growth of vacillation of character. And more than this, he learns within the book of life that every man should consider himself a responsible being, gifted with certain talents by his Creator, of which he is to make use. This gives him early an idea that he has an object in life, and that he must not run to seed down here; and though the religious part of the matter is, alas! often lost sight of, yet the moral tone remains kneaded into his character, and begets in him a ceaseless activity, and a tenacious perseverance in carrying out all that he begins. To this, I imagine, must be attributed the superiority of the English national character over all other national characters; and this is why he is called upon by Heaven to accomplish that in which other nations, from want of moral ballast—fixity of purpose, would fail.

July 14 (Sunday).—Waded to church through mud four inches deep. St. James's is the first church that was built in Melbourne. Its external architecture is very hideous; internally it is, if anything, worse.

Sept. 4.—We have weather, the like to which, for beauty, I have never experienced. Mountains at sixty miles' distance seem but twelve away, and the air is so pure and fresh that one feels as if he were inhaling laughing gas. Took a long walk in the environs the other side of the Yarra. All is beautiful, but the parched-looking green colour of the trees is a great drawback. Attended a government land sale. The land is put up in lots, varying from two roods to six hundred acres, at prices varying from one pound to three hundred pounds an acre. It is a strange sight to see the rough-looking bushmen, mixed up with tradesmen and gentlemen, eagerly bidding in a room blocked up with stores, some sitting upon, others straddling across, barrels, cases, chests, and boxes.

Sept. 28.—After breakfast started for Gisborne.

Sept. 30.—Started for Melbourne after lunch, and rode there in four hours, stopping for twenty minutes or half-an-hour at the house of a rich importer and breeder of rams, situated on a plain of wonderful fertility. The last fifteen miles we rode in an hour and twenty minutes, without distressing the horses at all. Thus ends my tour in the Mount Macedon district, in which I was first initiated into the mysteries of squatting. In my childhood I always pictured squatters as a party of dirty people, squatting and lying round a large cauldron, full of inexpressible things, suspended from three sticks, and simmering over a fire. That idea has, I confess, a little haunted me since. At all events I never thought, until I went to Australia, a squatter's life to be an agreeable one; but now I am quite undeceived. I find well-educated and wealthy gentlemen squatting in the midst of their flocks and herds, surrounded by every comfort and luxury, and enjoying a delicious climate. They have nicely furnished dwellings; their dining-tables sparkle with glass and plate, and they ride the best of horses. Some of them are married, and the bush ladies make excellent managers, especially those that are gentlewomen by birth. They have good gardens, which yield them flowers and vegetables; and they are permitted to cultivate as much land as their home consumption may require. As they have vast tracts of fertile land given them by the Government for sheep and cattle-runs, at almost a nominal yearly rent, it would not be just towards the farmers, who buy land at a high price, that they (the squatters) should be allowed to sell the product of the soil. But every squatting has its drawbacks; the sheep are liable to three diseases, one troublesome and noisome, called the foot-rot, the cure of which is one of the most disagreeable operations that one can imagine; the other two mortal and ruinous—scab, and the terrible catarrh. Sheep with foot-rot and scab can be dressed with mercurial preparations and turpentine. Loss and trouble enough supervene with these; but for catarrh there has been no remedy—no alleviatory course of treatment discovered. The only plan is to cut the throats of those sheep that show any symptoms of the disease, and

[187]

draw off the unaffected ones to a distant part of the run, leaving that part tabooed for many a long day. If there be a boiling-down establishment near, the bodies of the victims can be converted into tallow; if not, they must be burned or buried, and then the loss is total. Thus squatters—particularly those whose runs adjoin the high roads—have always the sword of ruin hanging over their heads. They are subject, too, to drought, when the stock dies from the drying up of the water-holes. Their sheep, also, get rushed and worried by the wild dogs; and some times Government steps in, when the lease of the run is up, to take possession of the land, that it may be surveyed and sold in lots for the purposes of cultivation. In that case the squatter receives just compensation for the buildings he has erected.

Oct. 11, 1851.—Walked about Melbourne, which, owing to the *auri sacra fames*, has quite a deserted appearance. Many of the shops are shut, the occupants having given up sure and profitable trades that they may have a chance of getting rich suddenly.

Oct. 23.—People mad about the Mount Alexander Diggings. Four hundred Van-Diemonians have just arrived from Tasmania, on their way to them. Dined with a Mr. B——, one of the first merchants here. He takes a great interest in the religious and social progress of my district, and highly approved of my scheme of making every important head sheep-station a nucleus from which religious knowledge might be diffused.

Nov. 1.—On my way back to my district rode through the Black Forest to Kyneton, where the large inn is full of people going to and returning from the diggings, eighteen miles off. People drinking and making a great noise all night. No talk but of gold, and of the great yield of the mines. The maid-servant, an Irish girl, as savage as the surrounding aborigines, pulled out of her dirty pocket three or four nuggets of gold to show me, worth, at least, 12*l*., which a digger had given her.

Nov. 3.—Visited the Mount Alexander Diggings, accompanied by a mounted policeman. Rode along a mountainous road until we came to the locality where the gold was found. In a narrow valley between two ranges of lofty volcanic-looking hills were assembled, on the borders of a nearly exhausted stream, about three thousand men, some digging earth from pits eight feet square; others washing the earth in what are called 'cradles;' and others washing the bottoms of the contents of the cradles in tin dishes. In the background, away from the stream, were an infinite number of tents and shelters of every description. Looking by chance into one of the numerous pits I recognised a friend of mine, a young gentleman from Tasmania, who, with five others, were come here, hoping to make their fortune. After digging through four feet of gravel they had come to a stratum of decomposed slate, which they were washing to great advantage. I saw my friend pick with his penknife into a tin box from the sides of the pit a great number of small bits of very pure gold, about four times as large as a pin's head. On Friday last they got two ounces; on Saturday, three; and to-day they had already got five, when I was there. It is a very exciting occupation. The sight of a quantity of rich virgin gold just taken from the surrounding mould agitates the nerves strangely.

Nov. 8.—Arrived in my district across the Murray. Found a mob of drunken men and a conjurer in the public room at Maiden's Inn. This vice of drunkenness prevails to a frightful extent everywhere here. And thus it comes to pass. It is rarely the custom to keep wines, or beer, or spirits at the sheep-stations. So people when at home, whether masters at the chief hut, or shepherds at the remote outstanding hut, drink nothing but raking green tea, which I believe would be poisonous, if the effects of the copperas were not neutralised by an enormous quantity of sugar. Drinking several times in the day of this liquid, they get their stomachs into such a nervous, sensitive state, that when they have occasion to visit a public-house, requiring some tonic, they drink madly of spirituous and fermented liquors. And to drink moderately of wholesome drink would be advantageous to them, but as the rum is strongly tinctured with tobacco, the beer embittered with

[189]

strichnia, and the wine is some odious fabrication into which juice of the grape enters not, those who drink with comparative sobriety earn a headache, those who drink to excess subject themselves to *delirium tremens*.

Dec. 16.—Arrived at Deniliquin, having employed yesterday and to-day in travelling on horseback from Moolamon, a distance of seventy miles. Found all in confusion at the inn: the landlord and landlady are in bed ill; the ostler is tipsy; the whole population seems to be on the point of leaving for the diggings. And it is not to be wondered at; for I know to a certainty, that a labouring man, one of a party at the diggings, has gained for his share twenty ounces of gold in eight days.

Jan. 15, 1852.—To-day I asked a black fellow, called Peacock, if he had ever eaten 'black fellow'? As I said it laughingly, he was thrown off his guard, and acknowledged that he had; and from his look, the reminiscences of the fact seemed to be rather pleasurable to him than otherwise. 'What is the taste like?' I asked. 'Like pig,' he unhesitatingly replied. Then I changed my manner, and asked him how he could dare to do so horrible a thing? On this he declared that what he had just said was in jest, and that he had never eaten man. This is the first time I could ever get a confession of cannibalism out of a native. I have been told that the blacks cannot endure a white man's flesh. They say that it tastes very salt, and is highly flavoured with tobacco.

Jan. 21.—Rode through the Black Forest. The road resembled one of the great thoroughfares out of London, so full was it of waggons, drays, carts, gigs, equestrians and pedestrians, proceeding to the diggings. And no wonder; for a very common-looking person, who begged leave to ride by my side, thinking, perhaps, that my calling might be a protection to him, told me that he and three others had dug up sixteen hundred pounds worth of gold in nine weeks. He had a hundred and fifty pounds worth about his person then. He told me, that previous to leaving England he had been a helper in a stable in Yorkshire. There was immense confusion and drunkenness at the Bush Inn at Gisborne, where I slept. At night the chambermaid advised me to lock and barricade the door of my bed-room, otherwise she thought I may be intruded upon by drunken people; and it was well I did so, for during the night two men practised upon the panels of the door for at least an hour, and though they split them they could not get in.

Jan. 22.—Stopping to bait at a roadside inn near Melbourne, I spoke with a common labouring man, who had just dug up 800*l.* of gold.

Jan. 26.—The gold excitement is fast increasing. Seeing a crowd of people around a shop-door, I found that there was on show inside a lump of solid, purest gold, weighing twenty-seven pounds eleven ounces. The men who found it—four ill-looking persons— were in attendance, waiting to be paid for it. I heard that they had sold it for 1200*l.* The mass of gold had a very bizarre form, looking something like a Hindoo god.

March 11.—Gold is selling in Melbourne at 3*l.* the ounce.

March 18.—Took my first stage out of Melbourne towards my district. At night the landlord and his wife, both very drunk, fought so furiously, that I was obliged to separate them by force. During the fray, all the little children came clustering round the mother, taking her part. One sturdy urchin boldly attacked his father, by kicking his shins and the calves of his legs.

March 19.—Gave some serious advice to the landlord about the scene of last night, and afterwards rode to Kilmore to breakfast. Slept at the Mac Ivor Inn, where I heard from one of the diggers that the goings on there are lamentably immoral.

March 21 (Sunday).—Arrived at Maiden's Punt on the Murray, after a ride of thirty-two miles, in four hours and a half. Held Service immediately, and then rode on ten miles farther to another inn, lower down the Murray, and held a second Service.

April 10.—Went with two magistrates and the head constable of

[191]

the district to examine the corpse of a man, which had just been discovered on the banks of the Edward River. As we approached the spot, we came upon a dog, who, on seeing us, slunk into some bushes, frightened. Immediately afterwards we saw the body lying prone, with the head partially submerged in a little pool of water. As it had been dragged from a place some yards off, where two or three people had been camping, I suggested that it was possible there might have been foul play, although the corpse was so placed as to give a first impression that the man had, in the last state of exhaustion from want of food, dragged himself down to the water-side to drink, and there had died. On closely examining the body, we found that part had been devoured—probably by his glare-eyed, guilty-looking dog; and on turning round the head, which was resting on the arm, we discovered a tremendous fracture of the right parietal bone of the skull. Thus it is certain that a murder has been enacted here.

April 12.—Rode with a magistrate into Moolamon, to hold an inquiry with regard to the murdered man. We elicited the fact that, about ten days ago, three men from the diggings had passed the night here, and talked about having a quantity of gold about them. In the morning they went away together, accompanied by a dog, in the direction in which the body was found. We likewise were informed that the second day afterwards two men on horse-back, leading a third horse, and having no dog with them, were seen going at full speed across the spacious plain, which extends to the Murrumbidgee. Thus it is pretty evident that the three must have camped by the side of the Edward; and during the night, the two murdered the one for his share of the gold. They then arranged his body in a studied attitude, to make it appear that he had died of exhaustion; and placed his head to rest on his arm, so as to con-ceal the fracture. And this deceit would have succeeded, if I had not particularly requested that the head should be lifted up. The murderers have, however, got clean off; and in such wild, unsettled country as this, all researches will be useless.

April 20.—Hear that a hut-keeper, going from one hut to another on this run, has lost his way, and not been heard of. He started the day before yesterday in the morning.

April 22.—As I was mounting a horse, lately bought, he suddenly put his head between his legs, so as almost to meet his tail, and bucked his back up, so that I was shot off like an arrow from a bow. Luckily, I broke no bones. I believe that an inveterate buck-jumper can be cured by slinging up one of the four legs, and lunging him about severely in heavy ground on the three legs. It is called here 'turning a horse inside out.' No treatment can be too severe for a horse addicted to this abominable and incomprehensible vice.

April 26.—Went out with my friend to poison his run. It is thus done. When a beast is killed, a quantity of small bits are cut off the carcase. By means of a sharp penknife little holes are cut in these morsels, and into these little holes pinches of strichnia are introduced. These bits are put into a small bag and taken out on the run. The acting person then, as he rides or drives along, throws to the right and left this meat. At night the wild dogs come, eat it all up greedily, and ere long die. But the strichnia has not yet done its work. Wild dogs eat one another, and begin their repast with the entrails of their brothers. Now the entrails of the dead dogs contain the strichnia, which is so strong, that after passing into the second dog it will kill him too, and, as I have been informed, even a third. Thus the poor sheep call poison to their aid against their terrible enemies.

May 19.—The rain has fallen in torrents all day, and my condition is wretched enough in such a country, for there is no pastoral duty to attend to, and study and privacy in a poor little wooden hut is next to impossible.

May 20.—Rode to Mr. L——'s station, and there I heard of a shocking murder which has quite lately taken place in this neighbourhood. The actors in this horrible tragedy were Edward River blacks; the victim a man of colour from the United States, settled for some years as a pastrycook in Sydney. This poor fellow gave up a remunerative business that he might go to the Port Phillip gold diggings, and was travelling this way with a white comrade. He was unfortunately seen by some members of a tribe of blacks belonging to this neighbourhood, who followed him, chased him, and drove several spears jagged with bits of glass through his back, working them up and down in his body as he lay on the ground. His comrade, insane with terror, ran, or rather flew, to the nearest station, the blacks at first following him with his bundle which he had dropped, and begging him to take it, as they did not wish to hurt him. They then cut up the corpse of their victim into three or four pieces, buried them, and taking up his bundle, as well as the bundle of his comrade, walked very unconcernedly into the store at the Company's station, and gave them up to the store-keeper, saying that they had found them on the road. Now this dreadful crime has arisen from a most lamentable blunder. As I believe I have said before, all the tribes or families of the indigenes which are scattered over the whole face of the country, are in a state of natural warfare with one another. Sometimes alliances are concluded between them; but without such an alliance, every black who ventures into another territory is liable to be assassinated. Now these stupid blacks mistook this poor American black for one of themselves, and thus considered his life lawfully forfeited. They disdained to touch his property. A black expressed to me to-day great indignation at their stupidity, saying, that they ought to have known the difference between 'black fellow' and 'white man's black fellow.' It may be supposed that the whole country is much excited about this occurrence. The mounted police have been galloping about shooting the wrong people, and letting the guilty authors of the outrage escape. They have shot a lame old woman, I believe.

May 23.—Held Divine Service at the Doctor's hut at Maiden's Punt. Ten adults and fifteen children attended—quite a refreshing number, in comparison with the very few which usually attend my ministrations.

May 27.—After three or four days of heavy travelling over boggy ground, the horses having scarce anything to eat, I arrived at a station on the Barratta Creek, where I had a fine black swan served up for dinner, stewed. It ate very like rather tough fricasséed rabbit.

May 28.—After crossing the Edward River in a frail canoe of bark, and swimming my horse over two or three deep creeks, I arrived at the hospitable and superior head-station of Mr. G——.

June 1.—My horses have strayed away, so that I am doomed to remain here in a state of inactivity. In the evening I attended a native corrobery; or what would be called by the whites, a *soirée dansante*. The old men sat and smoked, the women drummed on skins, and the young men enacted pantomimic dances. These ballets were of diverse character; some were joyous, others warlike, others licentious, whilst one was funereal. According to their character, so the women chanted. Naked and painted as the dancers were, they looked like demons as they flitted to and fro among the watchfires.

June 15.—My horses came back of their own accord, so that I was able to get on; but the weather is atrocious, and the roads of melted caoutchouc. The longer I stay in this country the more hopeless does my position seem. The floods in winter and the droughts in summer render the life of a clergyman one of great difficulty and self-denial. It must be recollected, that riding a horse and leading another over boggy ground for twenty-five miles, is quite as fatiguing as walking ten. And the sole refreshment after such a day's exercise consists of poisonous green tea without milk, lean beef without vegetables, and heavy damper.

June 20.—Hear of some bushrangers on the Sydney side who robbed a gentleman, stripped him naked, and tied him across a nest of huge black ants, which ate all the flesh off his bones. He was their old master, who, by his severity, had caused them to take to the bush.

June 21.—It having been always the object of my wishes to visit the confluence of the Darling and the Murray, not only from being informed that the visit of a Minister would be very acceptable to the people of that district, but also on account of various objects of interest to be seen there, I started this morning at half-past nine from my head-quarters on the Edward River for the sheep-station of Canally, on the Murrumbidgee. Yet at the outset some difficulties occurred which might have affected a sensitive mind. My stipend is paid by a certain number of subscribers, among whom the names of the Darling squatters do not figure. My people then seem not altogether well pleased that I should venture a hundred miles away from the limits of the subscription list, although they know that there must be people to be married, children to be baptized, women to be churched, and, above all, a population growing up in a most far-off district, totally destitute of clerical visiting or of religious ministrations. But as I know that my health will not allow me to remain much longer in this extraordinary country, and that after me no one probably will dare to come for a long time, I have thought fit to set at defiance the half-smothered remonstrances of the subscription list, and to do the best I can for my neglected fellow-Christians during the remainder of my stay here.

Aug. 23.—Rode to Maiden's Punt, hoping to cross my horses; but the proprietor of the ferry absolutely refuses to attempt it. I baptized three children belonging to a man who is just starting for the diggings. He insisted on paying me. I said that our Church did not sell the Sacraments. He said that the clerk must be paid. I answered, that there was no clerk. He then said, roughly, that he did not wish anything from anybody, not even the Church, without payment. I told him that, in the present case, there was no alternative. He then went away in a rude manner.

Aug. 25.—Find that the man, whose children I baptized yesterday, has gone away at daybreak, and left a packet for me. On opening a very dirty bit of white-brown paper, tightly twisted, I found at least three ounces of small nuggets of pure gold in it. So he gained his point after all.

Sept. 18.—After sleeping at the inn called Vinges', and paying a pound sterling for a night's lodging for my two horses, I started for Melbourne, a distance of twelve miles. To describe the state of the road accurately would be impossible. Let us imagine four feet of pitch half cooled, and we should arrive at some idea of this dozen miles of black loam trampled into a deep mud by the hoofs of innumerable beasts. Woe to the rider who lets his horse stand still a moment with his forelegs together in this glutinous mass. It would be difficult to get him out, even with dismounting. And what dismounting! I met twenty-four bullocks drawing a dray, and with difficulty they slowly progressed. And quite pitiable it was to see poor families on their way to the diggings in a cart drawn by one horse. There were the children extended on the bedding, screaming, while the lean horse stood still in the mud, motionless as a statue, and the father and mother, bogged up to the knees themselves, were vainly pushing behind. Every now and then came showers of rain to damp the little remaining ardour of these searchers for gold. At times suspicious-looking characters passed me, armed to the teeth, who looked with a covetous eye on the quantity of baggage I had on my spare horse. This colony was the most desirable of all which the Crown possesses. How changed now! No more tranquillity and good-fellowship between the grades of society. All is confusion, selfishness, licence, and subversion of all respect for worth, talent, and education. Brawn and muscle are now the aristocracy, and insolently bear their newly-assumed honours. In fact, we have here the French Revolution without the guillotine. When I arrived in Melbourne, I found the streets full of a dirty, disorderly mob of people, many of them tipsy, who seemed to take a delight in setting the laws of decent behaviour at defiance.

Oct. 2.—Met in Collins Street a coarse-looking young woman, very gaily dressed, with a fine baby in her arms, who, to my surprise, recognised me with a loud voice, as the Minister who had baptized her child in the bush. She wore a French bonnet of a delicate lemon colour, with a white lace veil; a common cotton coloured handkerchief tied round her red neck; a new green silk dress, sufficiently short to show coarse, puffy legs and ankles, clothed with dirty socks, and thick winter boots laced up in front. She had a short and stocky figure, and from the redness of her complexion seemed to have just risen from dinner. When she found that I rather shrank from the warmth of her greeting, she said, 'Don't you recollect me as hut-keeper at the head-station of ——, and that you christened my baby, and wouldn't take anything for doing it? And now I have got plenty of money and wish to make you a present.' I interrupted her by asking her what she meant by walking about town without her husband, dressed in that way? 'Oh!' she answered, 'my husband knows all about it; he is gone to the diggings for the second time, to get some more gold.' 'Did he do pretty well on his first visit to the diggings?' I asked. 'Well, thank God, he did very fairly; he got 700*l*., and he has given it all to me to take charge of till he comes down again.' This young woman, six months before, was a raw, red-haired, savage Scotch maid-of-all-work, at a sheep-station 200 miles in the interior, married to one of the shepherds. Her husband and she had left service, gone to the diggings, and found this great prize. She was now roaming about Melbourne, amusing herself, and rendering herself entirely unfit for the only thing nature ever intended her for—hard labour. She finished a very voluble harangue in answer to some advice I gave her, by praying me to pay her a visit next morning, that she might give me a handful of nuggets. But this is one only of a thousand strange things which are occurring. A lady told me yesterday that she had just lost an excellent maidservant, who one day was followed about by a digger, who proposed himself off-hand to her, and backed his arguments so opportunely by a heavy bag of gold which weighed down his pocket, that the girl when she came back, showing her mistress the gold which the lover had given her to keep, confessed that she was engaged to be married so soon as a licence could be procured. And this marriage ceremony goes off thus. After the ceremony is over, and the officiating minister has received generous proofs of the prodigality of the contracting parties, the couple and their friends drive to St. Kilda or Brighton, with a suite of fortuitous applauding acquaintance. The toilette of the ladies is something preposterously extravagant. Their blue satin bonnets and white ostrich feathers oppress their heads; their crimson satin dresses blaze upon squat bodies, which have been submitted for the first, and probably the last time, to the screwing-in process of powerful stays. Next to the dress come the heavy boots laced up in front. The coachman wears blue and white ribbons; so do the horses; so even does the whip, nay, even the spokes of the wheels. During the journey, which takes half an hour to an hour, English porter, beer, and champagne are drunk by the driven and the drivers. On their reaching the inn, an expensive banquet is served, and the most expensive liquors which the colony affords are circulated in profusion. Evening comes on, and everybody accumulates drunkenness on himself. Night arrives, and the whole party gallop back to Melbourne in the most hopeless state of intoxication, having squandered a sum which I dare not here name, for fear of encountering incredulity. A week is spent by the married pair in all these delicate outpourings of first love, and then satiety having intervened, and the gold-bag having diminished, the new bride awakes one morning without her partner at her side and discovers that he has bolted to the diggings. She suffers great misery, and ultimately discovers that her partner having got more gold has married again in some other place, and that, in fact, he has had two or three consorts before herself. So she too, partly out of spite, partly from destitution, resolves to marry again. And thus the lower classes go on setting the marriage laws at defiance, to the utter despair of the clergymen, who see the inextricable social confusion prevailing around them, without the power to remedy it. It may be supposed that the publicans reap a rich harvest from so much social disorganisation. So fast are immigrants arriving, that this class of people have their houses crowded to suffocation, and sell their poisoned, adulterated liquors at fabulous prices. In the midst of all this social turmoil, the Colonial Government, although a little taken aback, acts, on the whole, with that firmness and good sense which British gentlemen always show in cases of emergency. And the press, too, setting apart a little too much party violence, nobly seconds the cause of order. The difficulty now is to get a sufficient police force on foot to check the disorder which prevails, for men who come to dig gold will not act as policemen unless very well remunerated. A horse patrol has been established, the privates of which receive 8*s.* per diem, exclusive of rations and lodgings.

Oct. 11.—Embarked in a steamer for Sydney, and paid 12*l.* for a passage of three days. As we steamed down the bay, we passed three vessels full of immigrants sailing up into the land of promise.

SOUTH AFRICA

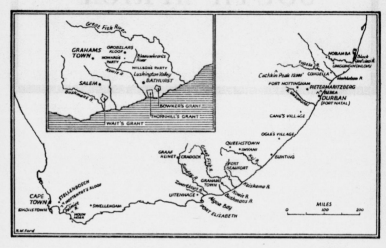

South Africa, with inset showing names mentioned by Goldswain

South Africa was known to modern Europe for over three hundred years before the British settled any part of it. And for a longer period still it was valued less for itself than as a stepping-stone to the far more important commercial area of the Indian Ocean.

The Portuguese found it when seeking to tap the source of Venice's Indian wealth. But the voyages of Bartholomew Diaz (1488) and Vasco da Gama (1497) induced no one to settle there. Both the British and Dutch used anchorages in the vicinity of Table Bay, but it was not until a Dutch ship was wrecked there that the enthusiastic accounts of the survivors caused the Dutch East Indian Company to set up a station.

This first settlement of 1652 was reinforced by successive parties from Holland and by three hundred-odd Huguenots, who had an influence out of all proportion to their numbers. The obstacle presented by the natives was quickly though, as we shall see, never finally overcome. Farmers spreading north and east from Cape Town first conquered the Hottentots and absorbed them as herdsmen, drivers, and domestic servants, and then, coming in contact with the Bushmen, set about their extermination.

For this purpose war parties, or commandos, were sent against them, and their organization remained the basis of local government, with its field commandant and field cornet, into Goldswain's time and beyond.

Already that prominent feature of Dutch South African history, the trek, had begun. The Great Trek of 1836 was but the best known and most impressive of a long series of such movements, for so much was Company rule disliked that there were always bands of settlers eager to move out of its range. The Company tried to keep up with them by establishing magistracies at Swellendam (1745) and Graaf Reinet (1786), but they were unable to protect as well as control their subjects so far from the seat of government; the Kaffirs harassed the farmers unchecked; and they in exasperation

[203]

chased away the Company's officials and declared themselves independent. They remained in this temper when Britain took the place of the Company, and it was responsible for outbursts against authority like that mentioned by LADY ANNE BARNARD in 1799.

From her account of the state of the country the evils of Company rule can be seen pretty clearly, though matters had improved just before her arrival in 1797. Conditions had been against the development of the Cape from the first. It did not produce the sort of things most needed in Europe; trade was completely closed save to the Company's ships, which usually had full cargoes when they arrived on their way home from the East. Since, then, there was no point in the farmers producing more than could be consumed in Cape Town itself, where they were away from the supervision of the Company, their lives were determined only in the very simplest way by economic factors. Hence part of their independent spirit, the rest being a revolt from the selfishness and narrowness of Company policy.

For it was 'in all things political, purely despotic; in all things commercial, purely monopolist': it is difficult to improve on the phrase of its historian, Watermeyer. The purpose of its rule was to preserve large dividends for a small number of families at home in Holland. All they wanted here was an efficient calling-place for their homeward-bound fleets—to the exclusion of those of all other nations. No initiative was left to the settlers—even their crops were prescribed—their numbers restricted, their desire for self-government checked at every turn. An air of frustration hung over a land ripe for development and drove the most vigorous into the freer atmosphere of the interior, in spite of the droughts and hostile natives waiting there.

The resulting division between the town-dweller and the Boer of the open country was further reflected in the system of government. The Boers managed their own affairs to some considerable extent. The chief official of each rural district, the landdrost, was appointed by the Company, but he was assisted by a number of elected heemraden. In the capital appointed outnumbered elected members of the main governing bodies.

Matters mended a little when French fleets often called there during the early 1780's. It was during this time, the period of war that followed the revolt of the American colonies, that Cape Town came to deserve its description as the gilded hostelry on the road to India, the miniature Paris. Commerce was stimulated and an irresponsibly extravagant Governor made the colony's wealth apparent, if it were not yet real, and it was during this time that the pleasant and luxurious houses of Stellenbosch, which Lady Anne Barnard so much admired, were built.

But the Dutch Governor, like Sir George Yonge later in the century, was living wildly beyond his and the Company's means. There was a financial crash, and he was recalled. Matters both in Cape Town and on the borders of the colony, where the Company was unable to give any protection, were such as to endanger the Cape's efficiency even as a port of call. There were at this time about 20,000 European colonists in the whole area between Cape Town and the Great Fish river.

This was the position when a British force landed in False Bay in the later summer of 1795. The armies of the French Revolution had overrun Holland; her ruler, the Prince of Orange, had fled to England; and the Cape was to be secured against France and the sea route to India safeguarded.

The rule of the Dutch East India Company was replaced by that of a British Governor, while local laws were maintained, taxes reduced, and trade encouraged. But this was amelioration rather than progress. The British, no less than the Dutch, looked upon the Cape as important from the point of view of the Indian connection, not as a country with a future of its own. Thus the trek Boers were never reconciled, the native question never settled.

There were, indeed, some at home who were in favour of keeping and developing the Cape. Lady Anne Barnard went there as the wife of the Secretary of the Colony as a result of the good offices of one of them, Henry Dundas, Secretary of State for War. But a new colony was not wanted; as Admiral Pringle said in one of his 'six-and-thirty-pounder corroborations,' 'as the Colony improved and peopled . . . it would to *us* only prove a second America, and would be more likely in time to rob us of India than to secure it for us.' This point of view won. At the Peace of Amiens, in 1803, the Cape was handed over to the Batavian Republic.

But hostilities broke out again, and when the scare of an immediate invasion of England had died down a fleet was sent to the Cape once more, and it was finally secured for Britain in January 1806, as Holland, in 1814, ceded it to her without reservation, thus confirming the conquest.

*   *   *

Even now emphasis was on the fortress, not on the colony. Only a few British settlers went out. What forced a change in this situation was a point of strategy.

To be an efficient fortress Cape Town had to be supplied with food. This food came from the interior and its producers were unable to concentrate on cultivation in the face of Kaffir raids. The Kaffirs were not stationary aborigines, like the Bushmen or Hottentots, but the advance guard of a great south-westerly movement of Bantu pastoral tribes meeting the north-easterly drive of the Boers, equally pastoralists. Stock raids were a natural consequence.

As far back as 1780 a treaty had fixed the Kaffirs' western border at the Great Fish river. As a result of warfare on varying scales of intensity it became necessary to push them back to the Keiskamma, and the country between the two rivers, with the newly built military centre of Graham's Town, was annexed to the colony. This done, the problem was to hold the frontier there.

The somewhat disingenuous solution was to plant the eastern frontier of the colony with immigrants, who would act as shock absorbers and protect the colony from Kaffir attacks.

To attract the necessary victims the Government evolved an emigration scheme, painting the land in question in bright colours and voting £50,000 towards its settlement. It was a complete change of face. No assistance had previously been given to emigrants to South Africa and the Government had protested that it did not wish to encourage them. Now free passages (subject to a returnable deposit) and provisions were granted, and each man on arrival was to be allotted one hundred acres of land at a nominal rent. The Government was so eager to populate the danger area that the scheme was made sufficiently attractive to divert those who would rather have gone to Canada or the United States.

The response was encouraging. From 90,000 applications less than 4,000 men, women, and children were chosen, divided into parties like the one JEREMIAH GOLDSWAIN joined. One he mentions, Thomas Willson's, comprised 307 persons. Twenty-four ships were specially chartered, many of them sailing from Deptford; though while the ships, as Goldswain describes, were 'almost readey to drop dow the river . . . they river Themes begun to freas' and a number of the emigrants lost heart and bolted for home.

After a ninety-day voyage they reached the Cape, the first stop.

> Then, midst the glories of an April day,
> They cast their anchor in Algoa Bay,
> Whose outstretched arms receive in their embrace
> Those dauntless Settlers of a Northern race,

as one of their successors was to write fifty years later. Tents were waiting as temporary accommodation; wagons and oxen had been hired from farmers wherever available, and, one after the other, the parties left for their locations, to combat nature and fight the Kaffirs.

These people, known to history as the Albany settlers of 1820, were given quarter by neither enemy. Rust spoiled the wheat harvest and murders became more and more frequent. The capital was moved from Bathurst, the 'Settlers' City,' to Graham's Town, where the discontented farmers had less of a voice, and failure and disgruntlement seemed to promise a speedy end to the venture. By 1823, 566 out of 1004 men had left their locations. Yet the country was to prosper. The ivory trade and the development of wool enabled the remaining settlers to turn their corner and to be celebrated as the most valuable and inspiring element in the South African community. Owing to their influence, English was introduced as an official language at the Cape in 1825.

*   *   *

Typical of the men they produced was JOHN MITFORD BOWKER, one of a family who spent active and often dangerous lives on the

[207]

Kaffir frontier coping with the vagaries of Government policy with regard to the natives. Sir Benjamin D'Urban came to be Governor at the Cape in 1834 and supported the settlers as far as he could against them, but Lord Glenelg, as Secretary for the Colonies, was strongly against any extension of British rule and sent Sir Andries Stockenstrom to the eastern provinces to see that the Kaffir chiefs were treated impartially. D'Urban, who had the full support of frontier farmers like Bowker, protested in vain until Stockenstrom's removal from office.

*   *   *

Missionaries were largely responsible for the humanitarian, as opposed to the economic, element in the Government's policy. They penetrated far ahead of settlers into native country, running, like FRANCIS OWEN in Zululand, very real risks.

By the time the Albany settlers had reached Africa the Zulu nation had been raised from an unimportant tribe to a powerful nation. Their ruler, Charka, who had contributed most to this transformation by reforming the military organization of his people (he introduced the short stabbing spear and the segregated army kraals), was by then Lord of Natal. In 1828, however, he was murdered by his half brothers, Dingaarn and Umthlangana. The latter was in turn murdered by Dingaarn, who (having rid himself of the opposition of a third brother) became king. It was to this bloodthirsty monarch that Owen, with his family, went to preach Christianity.

He had not been there long before he was brought, in horrible fashion, close to forces at work in Cape Colony itself. A complex of causes, though ostensibly the effect of Glenelg's Kaffir policy, had sent large numbers of Boers, eventually nearly 7,000, on the Great Trek away from British rule.

Many of them, of whom Piet Retief and his party were the first, entered Natal through the Drakensbergs in 1837. His negotiations with Dingaarn to obtain territory for his men ended in the massacre observed by Owen on what came to be known as the Hill of Slaughter. The Zulus advanced rapidly on Port Natal, forcing the surviving settlers to take to the sea. More trekkers arrived

though, and their counter-attack under Andries Pretorius drove
Dingaarn back into Swaziland, where, appropriately enough, he
was murdered himself. After this there was peace between the
whites and the Zulus until the war of 1879, that of Isandhlwana
and Rorke's Drift.

*   *   *

The British Government realized that on Pretorius' return there
was nothing to stop Port Natal becoming the centre of an independent Boer republic. To forestall this a detachment of the 72nd
Highlanders was sent from the Cape, who forced the Boers to keep
away from the coast; they founded Pietermaritzberg as the centre
of their new land. But as the Government still made no decisive
announcement on the question of sovereignty, the Boers were
encouraged to make an attack which was only foiled by Dick
King's famous ride for help to Graham's Town. It was not until
1843 that Natal finally became a British Colony. When this happened yet another trek took any recalcitrant Boers over the
mountains into the present Orange Free State and the Transvaal.
By the time JOHN SHEDDON DOBIE arrived, in 1862, there was a white
population of over 8,000, the greater number of whom were
British.

Lady Anne Barnard

For more than twenty years after her birth in 1750 Lady Anne Lindsay rusticated in her family's Fifeshire home while her 'excellent parents, having nothing else to do in the country, desisted not from their laudable aim of populating the castle of Belcarres, till their family consisted of eight boys and three girls.' But before going to Edinburgh and mixing with the brilliant literary society there, she had already written a work that was to perpetuate her own name—the ballad of 'Auld Robin Gray.'

From this time forward the wit that enlivens her letters was sharpened by contact with remarkable men. In Scotland there was Henry Mackenzie, the novelist, nicknamed after one of his own works 'The Man of Feeling,' the philosopher Hume, and Lord Monboddo, fascinated alike by legal puzzles and the anthropological one of man's relation to the orang-outang. Later on, in London, where she lived in Berkeley Square with a widowed sister, she entertained Sheridan, Pitt, Burke, and the Prince of Wales. But most significant of all was her friendship with Henry Dundas, later Lord Melville.

She had met him in Edinburgh, and it has been surmised that she kept her heart for him from that day. Certainly she kept her hand from anybody else until the age of forty-three, when she suddenly married a man not yet thirty. To her circle of acquaintance this was a surprise. Dundas was Right Honourable, was Home Secretary, was very soon to be Secretary of State for War,

Treasurer of the Navy, and President of the Board of Control. Andrew Barnard was only the son of the bishop of Limerick, a man with a position but little prospect of a career. Lady Anne got him one. She teased Dundas till he made Barnard Secretary of the colony at the Cape, to accompany Lord Macartney when he went out as Governor.

Lady Anne, as it turned out, had a position of more consequence than her husband, for as Lady Macartney stayed in England she was the first lady of the colony, whereas Barnard was by no means the second man. The letters which follow show with what good sense and courage she managed her responsibility—which, to her, meant carrying out what she knew were Dundas' wishes.

They are all written to him. They reflect his wish to keep the Cape, to explode the bogies that made it seem to some 'the "cussedest place" ever discovered,' and to placate the Dutch. They also reflect a determined and vivacious personality, confident on her own ground and only slightly uncomfortable when on that usually reserved for statesmen, credulous of marvels while hard-headed about facts, irritable and vain where her own position was in question. Clearly she had her heart as well as her head to thank for the fact that she was never without friends.

She returned with her husband to England in 1802, and was going to follow him to the Cape again in 1807 when she heard of his death. She sank back almost uncomplaining into the congenial social life of London, adding Sir Walter Scott, later to edit her ballad, to her list of visitors. And it was from this life that, in 1825, she departed, without having been called again to matrimony or to foreign lands.

These letters were edited by W. H. Wilkins in a book called *South Africa a Century Ago*, published in 1901 by Smith, Elder & Co. Letters to other correspondents dating from the same period will be found in *Lady Anne Barnard at the Cape of Good Hope 1792–1802*, by D. Fairbridge, Oxford, 1924.

The Castle, Cape Town: July 10th, 1797. Immediately on our

arrival Mr. Thornborn's house was filled with scarlet and blue
coats, who came to visit us and rejoice on our arrival. I should have
felt sorry, when I listened to the dislike every individual expressed
of the Cape without reserve, had I not hoped that many favourable
changes would soon take place from Lord Macartney's wisdom,
and from the acquisition society was gaining by a few good-
humoured people being thrown into the leaven tub, which at that
moment appeared to have too much acid in it. I plainly saw from
General Craig's manner that he was disappointed at not remaining here himself, but, since he was not to do so, it was very agreeable to him to go to India. He appeared, however, much less sanguine in his expectations of the benefits arising to England from
the Cape, or from the possibility of its being rendered flourishing,
convenient, or any *real acquisition* to us, than I had imagined he
would have been. He boldly said that the expectations formed
from it, and of it, were too high. One could only pause and listen
to this with a portion of regret, mixed with another little portion
of distrust of a judgement which, though a very tolerable one in
many respects, is not so extensive in its views or powers as some
others I wot of. Admiral Pringle, however, backed this gloomy
view with six-and-thirty-pounder corroborations. He said that the
Cape was the worst nautical situation it was possible for the devil
himself to contrive, with fewer possibilities of harbourings or
landing-places than could be conceived—no rivers, no water,
torrents in plenty from the mountain tops, but nothing in the
bosom of the earth. He imagined also that the Dutch policy was a
sound one when they checked all population or improvement, for
as the Colony improved and peopled he thought it would to *us*
only prove a second America, and would be more likely in time to
rob us of India than to secure it for us. He held all establishment
of manufactures to be dangerous and foolish, and said that no
pains should be taken with the interior of the country, but merely
with the skirting of it, which could produce comforts to our people
after their long voyages to and fro. All this the Admiral laid down
much more clearly, God knows, than I repeat it; and he wound
up by swearing that the Cape was the 'cussedest place' ever
discovered, with nothing good in it, and that even the hens did

not lay fresh eggs, so vile was every animal that inhabited the place.

There appeared to be no small mixture of prejudice, along with some reasonable causes of dislike, in all these explosions. I could only cry pause here also, and wait to hear the other side of the question; but this I was not likely to have from the military, who all to a man have disliked their quarters—nor is that much to be wondered at, as everything since the first capture of the Cape has been so extravagantly dear that the poor subalterns are both starved and undone. The private soldiers live well, and cheap, as beef, mutton, and bread are still reasonable, the first being only 2½d. per pound, raised to 4d. per pound now; and I suppose bread is not more, or so much, as in London, as our house bills for it amount to nearly the same sum as it cost us there. At first there was much drinking amongst the private soldiers, from the cheapness of the Cape wine, which could then be procured for about 3d. a bottle; but now I have heard there are wine-taxes laid on it, or some way is contrived to render its attainment less easy and counteract its pernicious effects in the garrison, it being now 6d. a bottle, or more. Every other article of life (the three excepted— wine, bread, and butcher's meat) is extraordinarily dear. An officer, who comforts himself on going to this distant destination by the thought of living within his pay, is therefore disappointed in the extreme to find that he is obliged to spend more here than if he were in London.

August 10th. I must begin this letter, my dear Friend, by telling you of the steps which have been taken to bring the people of the Cape into harmony with our English Government. There was a Proclamation to the effect that during a certain time, which was an ample one, they might come from all quarters and take the oath of allegiance to His Majesty. The gates of the Castle were thrown open every morning, and I was surprised to see so many come after what I had heard. Firstly came a number of well-fed, rosy-cheeked men, with powdered hair, and dressed in black. They walked in in pairs with their hats off, a regulation on entering the Castle on public occasions which, in former days, Dutch pride imposed. They were followed by the Boers from the country—farmers and settlers who had come some a very great distance. I think that many of them seemed very sulky and ill-affected; their manner seemed to say: 'There is no help for it. We must swear, for they are the strongest.' They are very fine men, their height is enormous; most of them are six feet high and upwards, and I do not know how many feet across; I hear that five or six hundred miles distant they even reach seven feet. They all come to the Cape in waggons, bringing a load of something to market at the same time. They were dressed in blue cloth jackets and very high flat hats. In fact, they struck me as overdressed, but the Hottentot servant who crept behind each, carrying his master's umbrella, on the other hand, was underdressed. He seemed to have little else to carry except a piece of leather round his waist and a sheepskin round his shoulders; one or two had a scarlet handkerchief tied round the head, sometimes an old hat ornamented with ostrich feathers, but very often they were bareheaded.

I must now tell you a little about a Cape expedition of mine. Having been told that no woman had ever been on the top of Table Mountain (this was not literally true, one or two having been there), and being unable to get any account of it from the inhabitants of this town, all of whom wished it to be considered as next to an impossible matter to get to the top of it, as an excuse for their own want of curiosity, and having found the officers all willing to believe the Dutch for ditto reason, laziness to wit, there was some ambition as a motive for climbing, as well as curiosity. And as Mr. Barrow is just one of the pleasantest, best-informed, and most eager-minded young men in the world about everything curious or worth attention, I paid him my addresses and persuaded him to mount the mountain along with me. We were joined in the plan by two of my ship-mates, officers, and my maid chose to be of the party. I had a couple of servants, and a couple of boxes with cold meat and wine. Mr. Barrow and I slung round our shoulders tin cases for plants, of which we were told we should get great variety on the top of the mountain. It is 3,500 feet in height, and reckoned about three miles to the top of it from the beginning of the great ascent, the road being (or rather the conjectured path,

for there is no road) necessarily squinted in the zigzag way which
much increases the measurement of the walk. At eight o'clock in
the morning Mr. Barrow and I, with our followers, set off. We
reached the foot of the mountain on horseback, and dismounted
when we could ride no more—indeed, nothing but a human
creature or an antelope could ascend such a path.

We first had to scramble up the side of a pretty perpendicular
cascade of a hundred feet or two, the falls of which must be very
fine after rains, and the sides of which were shaded with myrtles,
sugar trees, and geraniums. Wherever we saw questionable stone
or ore, Mr. Barrow attacked it with a hammer, which I had luckily
brought for the purpose, but he found the mountain through all
its strata, of which there are innumerable, composed of *iron stone*,
and that at least to the quantity of fifty per cent. The sun and
fatigue obliged me frequently to sit down; and as I had an umbrella
with me, a few minutes always recruited me. At last, about twelve
o'clock, the sun began to be so very hot that I rejoiced at the turn
of the mountain, which I saw would soon bring us into the shadow,
before we reached the great gully by which we were to get out on
the top. Redoubling my activity, at last we made the turn, but it
was wonderful the sudden chill which instantaneously came over
us; we looked at our thermometers, and in a second they had
fallen under the shadow fifteen degrees, being now 55, and before,
on the brow of the hill, they were 70. We had now come to a fine
spring of water, which fell from the top of the rock, or near it, over
our heads; we drank some of it with port-wine, but it was too cold
to have been safe, if we had not more way to climb. I saved a bottle
of it for you, *cher ami*. Opposite there was a cave cut in the rock,
which is occasionally inhabited by runaway negroes, of which there
were traces.

Once more we set off, and in three hours from the bottom of the
mountain reached the very tip-top of this great rock, looking
down on the town (almost out of sight below) with much conscious
superiority, and smiling at the formal meanness of its appearance,
which would have led us to suppose it built by children out of half
a dozen packs of cards. I was glad on this pinnacle to have a bird's-
eye view of the country, the bays, and the distant and near

mountains. The *coup d'œil* brought to my awed remembrance the
Saviour of the World presented from the top of 'an exceeding high
mountain' with all the kingdoms of the earth by the devil.
Nothing short of such a view was this. But it was not the garden of
the world that appeared all around; on the contrary, there was no
denying the circle bounded only by the heavens and sea to be a
wide desert, bare, uncultivated, uninhabited, but noble in its bare-
ness, and (as we had reason to know) possessing a soil capable of
cultivation, a soil which submits easily to the spade, and gratefully
repays attention. On the top of the mountain there was nothing of
that luxuriancy of verdure and foliage, flower or herbage, described by travellers; there were roots and some flowers, and a
beautiful heath on the edge of the rocks, but the soil was cold,
swampy, and mossy, covered in general with half an inch of water,
rushes growing in it, and sprinkled all over with little white
pebbles, some dozens of which I gathered to make Table Mountain
earrings for my fair European friends. We now produced our cold
meat, our port, Madeira, and Cape wine, and we made a splendid
and happy dinner after our fatigues. When it was over I proposed
a song to be sung in full chorus, not doubting that all the hills
around would join us—'God save the King.' 'God save great
George our King,' roared I and my troop. 'God save—God save—
God save—God save—God save—God save—God save—God
save—great George our King—great George our King—great
George—great George—great George—' repeated the loyal
mountains. 'The impression is very fine,' said Mr. Barrow, with
his eyes glistening. I could not say 'Yes,' because I felt more than
I chose to trust my voice with, just then, but I wished 'great
George our King' to have stood beside me at the moment, and to
have thrown his eye over his new colony, which we were thus (his
humble viceroys) taking possession of in his name.

If it was difficult to ascend the hill, it was much more so to
descend. The ladies were dressed for the occasion, else—I need not
say more after the word 'else.' The only way to get down was to
sit down and slip from rock to rock the best way one could. My
shoes I had tied on with some yards of tape, which had been a good
scheme.

September 12th. We have now quite settled down in our residence in the Castle, my dear Friend, and like it very much. I have arranged it all as best I can, a few things we brought out with us from old England coming in most useful, and really the effect is most pleasing to the eye. Since I got our house in order I have been busy carrying out a desire which I know you have much at heart, that we should conciliate as far as we could the factiousness of the Dutch here, which cannot be accomplished by any other means than by mixing them as much as possible in our society. To fulfil my position here as the woman, in the absence of Lady Macartney, at the head of the Government, it is my duty to show civility and hospitality to all the woman, Dutch or English, who live on good terms with their husbands, and to all the Dutchmen who have taken the oath of allegiance to his Majesty, and are of sufficient respectability to visit at the Castle. Mr. Barnard has invited the heads of the Departments to dinner, and the dinner went off in excellent style, our Swiss cook doing very well, assisted by three or four female slaves, whom his Excellency gave us permission to have from the Slave Lodge as servants. The balls and parties were left for me to settle as I thought best. Mr. Barnard, however, wished me to consult the Fiscal as to the proper mode of inviting the Dutch ladies. I did so, but found that, though an honest man, he was prejudiced, and if I followed his advice I should keep the friends the Government has already, 'twas true, but I should never make any new ones. When I went down the list with him he threw in so many objections to persons whom he called 'disaffected' that I feared none would be left, and said so. 'Oh,' he said, 'leave it to me, and you shall have at your parties true friends of the Government.' 'But remember,' said I, 'we are come out here not to call the righteous but sinners to repentance, if I may say so without being profane.' 'Well,' he said, 'if you are determined to bring the sheep and the goats together in one fold you must take the chance of your party becoming a bear-garden.' 'But I am going to give a ball,' I said, '*mon ami*; and music hath charms to soothe the savage breast.' He laughed and gave way, and so I had things as I wished.

The result is that I have given the most capital party on the 3rd of this month, and shall have one the first Thursday in every month. It is true, some of the Dutch fathers of families were sulky and stayed at home, being lukewarm, I suspect, to the English Government; but the mothers and daughters came, and to plough with heifers has always been reckoned a good means to improve reluctant soil. By-and-by I shall get the fathers, you will see. I had a fiddle or two and a bit of supper after; all went most friendly. I shall have a similar party on the first Thursday of every month, as I have already told you, but cannot have public days oftener, as everything is so very, very dear that I should be ruined. You will easily believe this, my dear friend, when I tell you that, amongst other things, my thirsty guests drank me up five dozen of porter, a little stock of which I had brought with me, but not enough to stand many such attacks. As to supper, three or four hams, some dozens of fowls and ducks, venison, and other game vanished in the twinkling of an eye, along with pastry of all sorts, for supper is a great meal here. I was able, however, to carry out the lighting on a more economical plan than at home. Our lamps, which were numerous, were lighted, and well lighted, with the tails of the sheep whose saddles we were eating. About these saddles of mutton, it occurred to me before leaving England that it might be useful to carry with me to Africa a map of a sheep and an ox, as I thought it likely that the Dutch butchers might cut their meat up awkwardly. I was not mistaken; my maps have been of great assistance to me here.

About the third part of the ladies at my party were Dutch— not more; but I shall have more by-and-by. Some of our Dutch ladies, in the town especially, are not all that they should be. The French, I am told, corrupted them; the English have merely taught them to affect virtue. I fear, alas! too, that some of our officers have led them astray from it. I cannot shut my eyes to the fact. So far as I hear, this is a great place for marriages, and our brides generally lay in with fine boys about two months after marriage, so rapid are things in this country. When I was told this, wishing to be polite, I said that I feared the children had come a little too soon. 'Not at all, madam,' said the Dutchman, answering literally, 'they came exactly at the proper time, but the marriages took place a little late.' I love a delicate distinction, but on his part the humour was quite unconscious.

October 15th. What a bold south-easter we have had these two days! How the wind raged, and how a tall tree which in the court-yard before my windows bent and tossed its great branches in at the casement, where the wind blew out a pane every half-hour! I shall feel more of these winds, I hear. How I long, my dear friend, for letters now, to tell me how you all are!—if safe and prosperous, or invaded by a foreign foe. I long also to know what is to become of us little mortals at the extreme point of Africa.

The last month has sent in from the country quantities of waggons chiefly loaded with wine, butter, skins, feathers and oranges,—grain is sometimes added as the farmer happens to have it. The waggons are very narrow, about the size of a large pipe of wine, and long enough to hold three in length. They are drawn by sixteen oxen, and driven by one man, a Hottentot besides generally walking at the head of the first pair. To govern their bullocks they have whips of immense length, which they lay on and produce no small effect; one lash is quite enough to set all the team into motion. These animals are much larger than our general breed of bullocks in England. I made a tallish man try the height of one of them—he guessed the team at sixteen hands and a half. The men who drive them are in proportion to their cattle, of a very large and robust stature, but their countenances gentle, and nothing rude or boisterous in their manners.

I long most ardently now to get up the country a little. I shall try hard for it when I am quite well, which I expect to be in a day or two. I have two offers—the offer of good living, lodging, car-riages, and civil hospitality from the Landdrost of Stellenbosch, and the offer of any empty house, two beds, and five chairs from the Fiscal, who has a house in that village, inhabited only by mice, and of course by no means uninhabited by *fleas*—the empty houses here being always richly stocked with that sort of wild animal. I love liberty, and I believe I shall prefer the mice and the fleas, a 'conjuror' for my cook, and the power of doing what I like, to the good things the Landdrost proffers me, with the hospitable attentions of his wife and daughters, which I shall gladly accept of now and then, but not all day long.

November 29th. As the little tour which this absence from the Cape permitted us to make is the first good opportunity I have as yet had of seeing the country and being able in any degree to form a judgement of the *Boers*, or real Dutch settlers—the people at Cape Town being scarcely to be named as such—I will give my dear friend a short account of things as they presented themselves to me, always trusting that you will forgive ten thousand inaccuracies and frivolities, while I repeat matter that, even at a distance, you have a more just idea of, I dare say, from your better information, than any I can give you.

The Landdrost of Stellenbosch, as I told you, had pressed us to come to his house. He has two pretty daughters and a good-humoured wife, but the ladies could neither *spraken* English nor French, and as we have never before found any necessity of speaking Dutch, we consequently are ignorant of it. I therefore preferred accepting of the Fiscal's empty house in the same village, where I thought we should be more at liberty, and give less trouble; consenting, however, to dine with the Landdrost and his family every day, and to accept of their carriage and horses, together with the most illustrious coachman of old Governor Sheiskin, now theirs, to drive us to all curious sights near or at a distance. We arrived in time to dinner, and had a plentiful one, really good, though in the Dutch style. The Landdrost's house we found more airy and spacious than any other I have been in here, having a sort of second row of rooms behind the first; but the division of every Dutch house in the Colony is the same—namely, a hall, a square room on either hand, and another family eating-room behind, with two bedchambers. Before the Landdrost's door there are the only two fine oaks I have seen, except the others in the village. They each measure eighteen feet round. But the perfection of this place consists in its extreme coolness in the midst of the most sultry weather; it is built in long streets, perfectly regular, each street having on each side a row of large oaks, which shadow the tops of the houses, keeping them cool, and forming a shady avenue between, through which the sun cannot pierce. Whatever way one walks one finds an avenue, right or left, and each house has a good garden. Stellenbosch, therefore, though there may not be above a hundred families in it, covers a good deal of ground, and is so perfectly clean and well built that it appears to be inhabited only by people of small fortune. But I am told there are many very poor people in it, without the means of ever becoming richer, as during the Dutch Government no manufacture was permitted there, and any person endeavouring to gain a livelihood by such means would have been severely punished. From this cause the place has few young people. It seems rather an asylum for old age than anything else, and I am told people live longer in it than in any other part of the Colony.

Being Sunday, we went to church here, though we understood not a word of the language. What amazing people for fat some of these good people are! A tendency to dropsy at the same time perhaps increases it, but after thirty years of age it is rare to see a woman, in the lower class of life particularly, weighing less than twelve to fifteen stone. The clergyman's wife, talking of the number of children christened in the parish, told me that the Sunday before this there had been twelve children baptized, and only five mothers to those twelve! Two of the mothers had three each, and three others two each. 'I thought, madam,' said I, 'that twins even had been rare in this country.' 'Oh no, madam,' she replied, 'I had two myself but four months ago.' These prolific mothers come from Overbergh; behind those mountains all sorts of good things are, I hear, to be found. I wonder the Dutch allowed such a race to live, their Government being equally against population and cultivation. I believe it is a bit of a reflection on people here to have no family. One or two Dutchmen, on hearing us say we had none, exclaimed, 'Oh, miserable! miserable!' in such a doleful tone, that I think I shall give myself credit for half a dozen left at school for the future.

Commissary Pringle told me just now that he had been advertising for a contractor to build chaff-houses, or some sort of public store for such matters as fall within his department. This has thrown the Dutch into great astonishment! '*Mon Dieu*, the

English then believe they still are to keep the Cape.' Not one of the Dutch believes it, and even amongst those of the English, who treat everything serious lightly, bets are laid of five to one that the place is ceded on a peace. All the world believe in the peace before Christmas but I, and I hear I am a fool for not believing in one. *Nous verrons.* I can't think that we will consent to all the French require to make a peace. If there is one, and there is still longer use for us here, well, we shall pass our time the more softly that we are on terms of the very best sort with the native Dutch. If there is no more for us to do, we shall see you all again the sooner. Come what will, I shall never regret having visited South Africa.

I must therefore conclude by saying that I hope it will be found possible to keep the Cape; that barren and ill cultivated as it now is, it strikes both Mr. Barnard and me to have great powers in itself to become one of the finest countries in the world. If the world was at peace, and I was a monarch, I should like to portion a younger son with the Cape, supposing him little, for a ten years' minority would produce a vast difference in this country, if it was as much encouraged as it has been repressed. Yet it is possible (if we keep it) that you may be obliged from policy to adhere to the same selfish considerations which governed the Dutch. The most enlightened of the inhabitants complain of the late *régime*. Their hands were tied up from being possessed of the riches they might so easily have enjoyed from their industry. They tell me there is nothing this place is not equal to, particularly if we can suppose the intercourse between the inner parts of the country and Cape Town rendered more easy. It is certainly a healthy climate.

June 6th, 1798. The enclosed journal, my dear Friend, will give you, I hope, some idea of the tour which I have made into the interior of the country since you last heard from me.

Our young cousin Jane preferred accompanying us to remaining at the Castle, and as a young lady, like a great general, is nothing without a proper staff, Mr. Barnard invited my cousin John Dalrymple to be her *aide-de-camp*. Johnny is somewhere from five to seven feet high; as he grows an inch or two every fortnight, there is no knowing where to fix him. As a cornet, he is fond of his gun, but fonder of his horse, and the prospect of being jolted in a waggon for some hundreds of miles with the beauty of the garrison, to the exclusion of all the generals, colonels, and field officers, filled him with rapture. We had with us also Mr. Barnard's servant, Pawell, the Brabanter, master of French, English, and Dutch, who is active, young, and fond of excursions.

So much for the company, now for the conveyance. Of course, it was a Cape waggon; any other sort of conveyance in this country it is impossible to think of for such an excursion. An ox waggon would have suited our pockets best, being exactly half the price of a horse one; but it goes very slowly, and as a month was all we could possibly afford, we could not cover half as much ground in the time. So we determined on horses, though we knew we should have to hire oxen also occasionally to take us over the *kloofs*, or steep passes in the mountains. The hire of our waggon, coachman, and eight horses, came to about three guineas a day. The waggon was long and narrow, after the fashion of those here, and had over it a stout sailcloth cover, very necessary in this climate. We then set to to add what was necessary to make our month as comfortable as might be. This, as a careful *haus vrow*, devolved on me. To begin with, I had a couple of sailcloth bags made to hold a pair of mattresses, two pairs of blankets, sheets, pillows, etc., in case we should find no beds at some of our nightly quarters, or perhaps very dirty ones at that. I also packed up some dozens of handkerchiefs to give to slaves and Boer servants, some ribbands, gold lace, needles, thread, scissors, tea, coffee, sugar, for the Boers themselves, etc., where people would not take money, a lot of pretty coloured beads for Hottentots, and some white pearl beads, some dozens of common knives, a large bale of tobacco, a bundle of candles, different things to eat, and a little bag of *schellings*, or bank notes of sixpence each, in my pocket. To these stores Mr. Barnard added two good hams, a large piece of beef, and two tongues, also a small cask of good madeira, a box of gin, rum, and liquors and plenty of powder and shot. We also each packed a box containing our special things, over which the seats were hung. By the time this was done we were ready to start.

Sunday, May 6th, 1798.—After making a tolerable breakfast from our own tea, just with the addition of some fresh eggs, which we bought, we started. We hired a team of oxen to carry us to the foot of the Hottentot Kloof, which we reached in about an hour, having passed but one farmhouse by the way, and not a single tree or bush. At the bottom of the ascent we found a Boer ready with twelve splendid oxen ready to be put to the waggon. They seemed to dislike the business they were going on, and lowed piteously when they found themselves in the yoke. The ascent is about two miles; for the first mile, wherever the eye turned there was heath, sand, sea, mountain, scarce a house to be seen, no cultivation, and, of course, no population. As we looked back over the wide prospect we were leaving, bay succeeded bay, and hill hill, carrying on the eye over a scene of infinite beauty. The path was very perpendicular, and the jutting rocks over which the waggon was to be pulled were so large that we were astonished how they were accomplished at all, particularly at one part called 'The porch.' At length we reached the summit, and the new Canaan opened to my eye; hillock upon hillock, mountain behind mountain, as far as the eye could reach, a slight thread of rivulet here and there winding through the valleys like a silver eel. Our descent was much easier accomplished. We went down on foot, and when we got to the bottom we found the waggon safe, and the horses put to it again. I was horrified to see how much the poor oxen had suffered in our service; their sides were streaming down with blood which the knives of the savage drivers had brought forth. They are very cruel here to their cattle—the whip is an implement of torture, and is sometimes supplemented by knives; the drivers are sufficiently good anatomists to know exactly the vital parts to be avoided. We travelled on over a tract of country still innocent of the plough, passing by three rivers, or *rivières*, as they are called here, of which the Palmite was the greatest. Then along a dangerous pass, which with a high loaded waggon and eight horses in hand was not very pleasant, but our driver was extraordinarily skilful. We at last reached the farmhouse where we were to stop for the night. The name of the farmer was Jacob Joubert, a mere Boer; his wife received us—a plain, stupid, but civil woman, strange to say without any children. We made a good dinner with them of some boiled fowls, with plenty of potatoes and butter—a repast fit for an emperor.

Monday, May 7th, 1798.—We started at seven o'clock in the morning, the weather glorious, and all our animals well. We had to engage a further team of twelve oxen to carry us over Howe-hook, another tremendous hill. These cattle were so strong that they pulled us with ease up perpendicular ascents, which made me think that they would pull us like Elijah up to heaven. The descent was two miles, and before us opened a wide desert, pathless, untenanted; one little bit of smoke only ascended to heaven—it looked like the fire-offering of Cain. Probably it was the fire of some poor Hottentot cooking his humble mess. We now got on to what is called 'The Great Road,' tolerably well beaten by waggons. We were going on to a Mynheer Brandt's, where we intended to pass the night; but we stopped halfway at a farm-house to rest the horses and have something to eat. I was very tired, and I thought the *stoep* in front of the house the pleasantest of all seats. We made the best meal we could, having as a table the top of an old barrel.

I wanted to stay here all night, but the coachman said he could go on and reach our destination before sunset. He was mistaken, for after we had gone some time the sun set with a vengeance. There is hardly any twilight here, and in this case there happened to be no moon, so within a quarter of an hour we were plunged from light into total darkness. The road was very rough, and though I made Hector walk at the head of the horses to be doubly sure, suddenly the waggon began to rock. 'Sit tight!' shouted Mr. Barnard. I felt the wheel sinking on the side I was, and, in a moment, down we came like a mountain. The waggon was over-turned, my head lower than my heels, and everything in the world, it seemed, was above me. Cousin Jane, Johnny, and I were laid low; Mr. Barnard escaped, and rushed to see how we were. I felt half suffocated with the luggage, and my arm seemed broken, but presently, when they had unpacked me, I crawled out safe on the heath. Presently Jane also emerged, and there we were, bruised, but with no bones broken; it was really a miraculous

s.—15   [225]

escape. While they were trying to get the waggon straight again, though they had great fear of doing it, I walked about to discover in the darkness where we were, while Jane sat on a stone, a statue of patience, condoling with herself for the bruises on a white marble arm, the rest of her being preserved, in a most literal sense of the word, for a cask of ginger had had its topknot knocked off in the fall, and had poured its contents in at Jane's neck and out at her toe, by which means she was a complete confection. I could not help laughing, and sat down to count my bruises with her, when we were startled by hearing a voice in the darkness behind us saying, 'Well, to be sure, this is the devil's own circumstance.' I found it proceeded from Cousin Johnny, who had embarked the whole of his fortune, amounting to thirty dollars, in Jane's netting case, which happened to be the only thing lost in our tumble. We all crept after it on our hands and knees in the darkness, but no-where was it to be found, nor had we a tinder-box to strike a light. 'Well,' said he, with a cornet's philosophy, 'here's for a light heart and a thin pair of breeches,' and he kicked out his foot to emphasise his words, and lo and behold! it struck against something which jingled. I leave you to imagine his transports. Every-thing was replaced in about an hour, and off we started. But fresh perils awaited us, for we had to cross the river; fortunately the ford was marked out by a stick or two, and we got over it safely. Never was anything so welcome as Mynheer Brandt's house. We entered through a kitchen filled with slaves, many of them with very little covering on. Under the guidance of Gaspar, who turned out to be a man of many talents, we made a most excellent supper, with a little hot wine and water to crown it. Decent beds rendered no trouble in unpacking necessary.

Sunday, May 13th, 1798. [Swellendam.]—After dinner we drove twenty miles without seeing a house, cornfield, or living creature, and at last arrived at the house of Jacob van Rhenin.

Tuesday, May 15th, 1798.—We asked van Rhenin how he came to settle so far away from human habitation. He said that he had spent a long time in Cape Town, but did not like it. 'My wife said she did not mind where she lived so long as it was with me. I have therefore chosen a place where, by breeding horses, I can always make a gain; and as I have a taste for sport, by hunting and fishing I keep my table well provided. I am perfectly contented and happy, and so is *meine vrow*. I am now independent, and away from rivalry, and I am beloved and respected. The first does not mortify, the latter does not flatter me. But we are forgetting to put to the horses.' 'That is the first bit of philosophy,' said Mr. Barnard, 'I have heard since I left Berkeley Square.' We both united in liking this man, his wife, his children, his horses, his fish, and everything to do with him.

The Castle, August 13th. By the way, I know not how it comes into my head *now*, what is an old story by this time—a very silly and ill-natured account of the races here, written and sent home by some dull wits with whom the Cape was a good deal infested at one time. There certainly *were* races here, but Lord Macartney, whose servant is stated to have broken his leg in riding one, not only had no horse, but privately disapproved of there being races at all, and did not subscribe. Mr. Barnard did the same. He declined being a member of what they call the 'Turf Club,' and out of a little pique they call him in the papers the 'life and soul of the turf.' This was untrue, for he went into the country to avoid them. I gave my ten pagoda's to the ladies' purse, as two other ladies of my own rank in society had subscribed their names to it without consulting me, and I did not like to throw a tacit stricture on them by refusing mine, or run the risk of being called shabby, though privately I liked no part of the business, thinking the Colony too much in its infancy for a sort of amusement which would be likely to introduce with it many other foolish things. But where there is a great body of idle young men, with a few ladies not ill-disposed to co-operate in any plan of amusement, one cannot be too cautious of appearing to set up as a reformer, if one wishes, as I do, to possess universal goodwill. With respect to the faro tables, to my great sorrow I found that the great good-nature of Colonel Hope (who is, sure, one of the best-conditioned good creatures in the world) had been over-persuaded by a Mr.

Bird, Deputy-Quartermaster under General Fraser, a young man who seems to love play, to hold a bank with him during these races. Mr. Barnard, I have reason to think, hinted this privately to the Governor, who sent a message to desire that it might be the first and last time he heard of such a thing in this Colony. In Lord Macartney's house there are no cards, and at my assemblies and balls only half-crown whist or casino, but no game of chance is allowed. If people don't like the rules of our house they will not come to it. As to the 'ostentatious splendour' of my appearance on the race ground, though possessed of the neatest chariot and four in the Colony, the only day I appeared there I was in the carriage of a Dutchman, with his wife and family, not in my own— very much quizzed indeed by my country men and women for being with the Dutch, but very well pleased to give this public testimony that the Secretary's wife wished to connect herself as much with the people of the country as they chose. In the course of the morning how angry I was often made by the folly and bad-breeding of the thoughtless John Bulls who were constantly galloping up to the carriage I was in, obviously a Dutch one, to bid me remark the figures that were to run the Dutch race. 'Lord, what a saddle!' 'Ye Gods, what a bridle!' 'I would give twenty guineas to see that one thrown—ay, and his neck broke!' 'How he would kick in his demipique!' etc. etc.—holding all the Dutch in such contempt, and forgetting that the company I was with were not *all* deaf, and some of them might understand English enough to comprehend an insult. I believe I remarked in a former letter that it is the supercilious mode in which the Dutch find themselves treated by the English here which makes them partly prefer French insincerity and French *politesse*.

September 24th.—A ship was lately driven in distress to a bay— I think they call it Algoa Bay—where some of the passengers left it and came by land. The captain and others have dined often with us, and the gentlemen who came by land arrived, and dined with us, yesterday. They describe the country (as it has also appeared to us in our time) as bare, but the soil good and the people hospitable and hearty.

[228]

Paradise, Cape of Good Hope: April 4th, 1799. First, my dear Friend, let me in three cheers express my joy on the late glorious event, which I daresay will form as bright a moment in history as England ever saw. [Nelson's victory of the Nile.] Light gains double by shadow, and dark indeed was the shadow which precluded these victories. I see the new peer is to be Lord Nile, or Lord Something of the Nile (I hope the eldest son won't be Baron Crocodile.) I should like to see a dozen more such creations.

While all goes fair and well with you in England we have got our little bit of insurrection here, at a distant part of the country, Graaf Reinet. The old bad news, I suppose (and none of the modern good yet), has travelled there, and inspired the Boers with the desire of kicking up a dust, and trying if they can't be masters still. It is nonsense for me to pretend to give you any account of matters, which the General, of course, must convey to you at length. Yet there is a possibility that this ship may sail without his dispatches, as I hear he is at Stellenbosch. So I will say what I can. These Graaf Reinet Boers have always been turbulent and unwilling to bend to any laws, or to the Landdrost. They particularly dislike their Landdrost, a very good sort of man, I hear, and affect to think themselves ill-used, now that they are British subjects, in not having an English Landdrost. General Dundas sent General Vandeleur there with a party of horse, also Major Abercrombie, and one or two small vessels with troops. It was the general idea that the seditious people would instantly be reduced to order by the sight of the scarlet coats, and would surrender their arms, but I hear that they have retreated, it is thought into the Kaffir country; and more men have been requested by General Vandeleur. I cannot say, however, that I feel at all alarmed at this; it will cost a few lives, and that is a pity, but I fancy some examples must be made to preserve peace in the Colony. One of the party having remained behind, and being desirous of joining the others by a short cut, almost lost his life, being pursued by a troop of buffaloes, who fairly hunted him like a hare, and the speed of his horse only saved him.

What a blessing, now that our white troops are called away to the above purpose, and others sent on to India, that the people of the Cape have that spirited old corps, the Cape Association, to trust to! A corps almost two months old, and commanded by Colonel Barnard, who of course is commanded by Lady Anne, that old and experienced officer! Her Ladyship, I hear, is soon to present the regiment with their colours, in which the Whitletomb (native of this country) is happily blended and united with the Royal Oak of Old England, a compliment her Ladyship means for Mynheer (if he has *nous* to understand it). The gentlemen volunteers who compose the corps had in the original plan professed themselves in readiness, should occasion require, to stand forward with any aid in their power, but General Dundas, very naturally thinking that *that* aid could not be properly administered, unless they were drilled into the knowledge of what was to be done on emergency, mentioned the Associations in England, and their conduct, as the model for this, which hint was of course adopted. The officers were chosen by ballot, and Mr. Barnard chosen Colonel, and as he is an old soldier, the business went on so much better. All were eager in the cause, a very few gentlemen excepted, who, shy of being smiled at by the military, and disliking the sacrifice of time necessary to the field days, are no longer of the corps, much to Mr. Barnard's regret, as they are good men, though bad officers.

May 14th, 1799.—Since I wrote last the disturbances at Graaf Reinet are happily terminated. All the seditious have submitted I hear, and two or three only remain untaken amongst the disturbers of peace and good order. The Kaffirs have expressed the strongest disposition to be on friendly terms with us; so too have the Bushmen, who, possessed of nothing, were robbers rather from necessity than choice, and who by the presents of cattle, etc., conveyed to them by Lord Macartney from the English Government, are won to the love of peace and good fellowship by having something to lose.

Jeremiah Goldswain

Great Marlow or plain Marlow, as it is now called, has little in common, save its lovely situation on the north bank of the Thames, with the small market town that Goldswain knew. The prosperity of the place depended largely on agriculture and there was always one and sometimes there was more than one annual fair at which cattle and horses changed hands. Visitors were few, though the local farmers and lace-makers must have had many opportunities of seeing the poet who wrote, in the year a number of them left their homes to emigrate:

> *Men of England, wherefore plough*
> *For the lords who lay ye low?*
> *Wherefore weave with toil and care*
> *The rich robes your tyrants wear?*

for Shelley brought his new bride, Mary Godwin, to live for a year in Great Marlow, though he had left by 1819, when the song was written.

Of Goldswain we know little apart from what he tells us. The emigration lists show that he was a sawyer and that the Eliza Debenham whom he married in South Africa had come over with her family at the same time as himself. His orthography shows that he had had some schooling, though it did not trench upon a baldly phonetic rendering of the Buckinghamshire dialect.

It is a little surprising that one of the reasons for his leaving home was to avoid 'gamblin and bad cumpney,' as his uncle put it, but perhaps evil habits had filtered down from the neighbouring Medmenham Abbey, once headquarters of the best known of English Hell-Fire Clubs. It is satisfactory to find that his later conversion was so effective that when he indiscreetly commented to a minister that the land over which they were riding was admirably suited for a racecourse, his 'hone conchion' immediately condemned him and caused him to give his horse 'such a jurk that it brought him allmost backwards.'

Anyway, he prospered, and having had four children and seen the colony survive the first difficult years and become the most vigorous element in South African life, he died in Graham's Town in 1871.

The text of the Chronicle is in the Cape Archives. The first part was edited for the Van Riebeeck Society in 1946 by Una Long (Mrs. Colin Gill). The editor has shortened it and added some punctuation: Goldswain only used an occasional comma and bracket, with full stops after abbreviations like 'Mr.' I have cast it into paragraphs where I thought the eye might be lost for ever. The whole diary runs from October 1819 to December 1858.

Tronk=gaol.

I was born in the year 1802 March 2nd in Great Marlow Buckinghamshier. Nothing purticler ocured in my Life untill October 1819 wen thear was a Great talk about the Cape of Good Hope and that thear was a Gentleman coming down from London to make up a partey to go to the Cape of Good Hope and all thoues that was willing to go was to go to Mr. Wm. Broocks and put our names down and to recve Sixpence as ernest money and at the later end of the Month Mr. Wm. Weait for that was the Gentlemans name and down to Great Marlow he came before the time was expired and we all ware worned to meet at they Gray-hown Inn at seven o'clock the same evening wen to my Great astonishment I found the Market roome quit ful. Thear ware meney Gentlemen present: thear ware the Overceares of the parish Dr. Hickman Mr. Givence: theas two Gentlemen tuck a great deal of intruest in the meeting as thear ware sum of thoues wich ware in the winter ceason depentent on the parish for surport but Mr. Wm. Wait asured them that it wold be thear hone faltes if they that did make up thear minds to the Cape of Good Hope if they did not make a little fortune in a verey short time. You see said Mr. Wm. Wait that they have nothing to pay: we pay all thear deposet and expences and agree to Give them half a bushel of wheat pur day, or other value. The houers that we ware to work for them ware from Eight oclock in the Morning untill four oclock in the afternoone and we ware to have half an acor of Land for us to cultivate and to build our house on and to serve him for Six years, and then we ware to have our fredom. This was all agread on and juest as we ware going away Mr. Weate requested that we wold com forwerd and signe our names again as he caled them out wich we agred to but to my Great cerprice wen my name was caled out my poor Mother steped forwerd and stated to him that her Son had promised her that he wold nott Go to the Cape of Good Hope: thearfore at that time my name was not put down with the others at that time but It was my intention to go, the time apointed for the partey to leve theare native Towns and vligeles was 26 of December and at the time and jest before the time mentined you mite have seen severel famleys coming in to Grait Marlow to be readey against the apointed time, on the evening of the 23rd. my dear Mother heard that It was my deturmation to Go to the Cape of Good hope: I met her in compney with a young feameal: they ware both weeping: I asked them what ware the matter. When my Mother could speak she said that I was a very unduteyful Child and I being her onley Child she said: a Jerey you will brake my hart if you are deturmnid to go and leve me for ever for if you do Go I shall never see you again: at this time I felt that my Hart was hard and semed to care for nothing. She wished me to go home with them and stop with her the short time thear ware befor I left them for ever: I said that I wold If they wold Give over weeping.

Wen we got Home thear ware meney of my relationes and

[233]

nabours ware com to know if it ware true that I ware going to the Cape of Good hope and wen I ancered them one and all be gun to weep and declare that the first thing that they should hear wold be that I was killed by the wild beast and that I was a verey undutiful Son. As swone as I was promited to speak I wished to know wether it was not better for me to leve my native home and Go ware I could do beter then stoping thear as I had got but little work to do and had no prospact of giting aney more and that Mr. W Wait had held out such Good prospetes to us and that the wages ware so Good and that we ware to have half an acor of Land and so much time to work for our selfes that I considred it a verey good opertunity and to have our psage paid for us and after serving him onley six years and then for we to have our liberty to do for our seleves in a Cuntrey ware we mite do so well for our selves and soon be able to return home Quite rich.

By this time my Aunt had colled down a little and we walked into the house and I purtuck of sum refreshment as my Aunt said that it wold be to long to wait for dinner and in the mean time she went and aquainted my Uncle Jeremiah that was living with them and had been living ever sence he had retired from bisness. Wen he came into the dining room he did not scole me as my Aunt had just been douing but he hoped that I should be a good lad and take care of myself: he also stated that he hoped that I should keep from Gamblin and bad cumpney. I informed him that that was one reasone wich I wished to leve Marlow for as I had often tried to keep from the Gamblen table but as shoure as I promissed myself to do so some of my companions wold com and purswaid me to Go with them but that once and it did not take verey strong words to purswaid me to Go with them. He Gave me sume Good advice and promised me that if I beaved as I ought to do that he wold not alter his will but that he wold help me. I wished him and my Unncle Richard and famley farwell and returned home ware I found my poor father and mother in verey lo sperites as they exptd to hear in the morning, I gave to my Mother half the money that my Uncle Jeremiah Gave me, the next morning 25th. Decr. I was informed that the pirson had com down from London: this was Mr. Adam Gilfillan Nesuw to Mr. Thornhill Mr. Wm. Waits

[234]

partner. He had provided a Good dinner and a pint of Ale to everey man and we ware ordred to hold our selves in redness to leave the following morning for London, 26th. Sunday we left Great Marlow about eleven oclock just as the Bells ware ringing for Church.

They town ware thronged with specttaters to see us start from the Greyhound Inn and menney of them brought us on our way as far as Bissum in Barkshiear a vilage anout one Mile from Marlow. At this place my Father and Mother left me and it was a verey hard strugle for me wen I recved my Mothers Last blessing and she reminding me that I was her onley Child and fealing her emotions wen she imbraced me for they Last time. They both off them reminded me off my promise of returning from the Cape of Good hope at the expiration of the time promised if I was spared from the wile Beast taring me to peaces: my Father and Mother weating untill I had Gon a short way on the road ware thear was a short turn in the road: at this point I was to hold up my hanker-shift as this wold be probley the Last time she wold see me for ever, I lost site of them and went on with a hevey hart. We rived at Madenhad a bout two oclock. Five of us tuck lunch at the Inn under the Town hall: the Landlord whould not charge aney thing for what we eat onley for what we drnk and at the same time wished that wen aney of us returned to England and came to Maidenhead that we wold give him a cale: off corse this we all promissed to do. We then recomenced our jurney and just as we had crosed hounslereath the evening was just closing in and as we ware waiting for the bagage wagons to cum up we ware serrounded by meney of the inabetence wanting to know what was the mater or ware we ware going and wen we informed them that we ware Going to the Cape of Good hope they exclamed one and all of them in one breth that if we ever got thear that our poor dear Mothers wold never see us aney more for the wild beast of the fields wold devour us for they had heard that thear ware people agoing to this place and that thear ware all sortes of wild animels thit wold teare us to peaces: but wen they found that we ware deturmened to Go and they wagons had now com up they with lifted up hands Gave us thear blessings and hoped that we should

[235]

not be cast away on they sea but that we mite rive safe thear and that they should hear of it, as soone as we came to the Inn we all halted as we thought for the night but we soone found that thear was not roome for all of ous in the Inn so that all the single men had to travel on to the neerest Inn wich was about a mile and a half frther on whare we purtuck of some refreshment and retired to beat. But thear was now sleep for me: I Looked back on the place of my birth and found that my mind was ocupied on former things and thous that I had left behind.

About Six oclock the wagones came up and we had to travel on untill we came to Branfort five miles from London: at this Town we haulted and Got brakefast: at this was the place ware Mr. Wait Lived and up to this peared he had carried on bisness as a wine Merchent. We then left and rived at hidepark turnpike ware we waited for about half an hour wen Mr. Hadam Gilfillen came and informed ous that we must Go to Dadfort dockyard ware we must go on bord the ship. We rived thear and Got on bord just as it was dark so that we that never saw a ship before we neve could think what place it was or ware we ware to sleep but we ware soon ordred down betwen decks but ware war we to sleep? we saw now no place or aney bading: the Stweard and his wife wa verey kind to ous and Gave ous sum Candles and pointed out to ous the births witch was prepared for our sleeping places and we ware the first partey so that thear was no one to show ous. We asked them: ware was the beading? You will get that tomorrow morning. This was verey pore conserlation for us as it was freasing very sharp but we soon Got a little close and the next question was: ware ware we to Git somthing for our suppers? This was soone ancerd by the stuard: you must waite untill the morning untill I Get orders to Give it to you: we all thought that this was a bad begining.

Well we all went to bead and rose at the first dorn of day to see ware we ware and what sort of place we ware in and what the vesel was like and wen and how we ware to have out foode served out to ous as thear ware severel about the same age as myself and our hapitites ware verey keen for had we been informed that we should not have had aney foode Given ous we could have surplied ourselves before we went on bord. About Ten oclock we heard the joiful newes: com and Get your rassons. Away we went and behold the first thing we had Given ous was a wooden Toub caled a kid olding about four Quartes. We ware ordred to form ourselves into messes 6 in number and then we had three quarters of a pound of busket for eich man sum Ote Meal a little meat and a verey little bit of utter and wen we had Got it we did not know what we ware to do with it or how we ware to coock it: but as our hapitites ware prepared to make aney shieft I set to at the busket but as it was not so soft as the bread that we had been acustome to for it was jaw braking work but we soon Got youse to it and then came pea soupe. Tword the close of the day eich of ous had one blanket and a matres and six of ous single young men had one birth for ous: and we had been about fourteen days on bord before we heard aney thing of our Master Mr. W Weat and then we herd that thear had been sum missunderstanding with him and Mr. Thornhill: at this time Mrs. Wait came on bord. The veasel was almost readey to drop dow the river but at this time they river Themes begun to freas and in a few days the hise was so thick that sum few men ventured to walk on it: the ice was strong anoff to bear allmost aney number if people. On a sunday morning about nine oclock we saw a grait meney people asembled togather: some of ous went down to see what it was and to our Great astonishment they had maid oles in the ice and had maid a bouth and was selling Gin and Gingerbread and thear ware a large circle maid by the pople and in the circle thear ware they fiddler and severel persons dancing.

[At Simon's Bay] The next morning som of ous went erley on dack to see if we could disern aney of they Sheep climen up the hills with thear Large tales as we had been told by old Solders and Salers that had been to the Cape of Good hope that they had seen the Sheep climen up they hills with thear tailes maid fast to a little truck with two weals for they stated that the hills that they Sheep had to feed uppond ware so steep that all thear fat run into the Sheeps tale but they ware noware to be seen but in corce of the day we saw one of thear tales waight about 5 lbs.

[237]

We landed on 27th. of May 1820. I had been on bord from the 27th. of Decr. 1819. Wen we rived in Port Elizabeth thear was not more than 12 or 15 houses and now at this time that I ham riting it is alarge sea port Town. After I rived at this place I soone gathered strenth: at this sea port we stoped six weakes and sum of ous went to work for two Rix Dollers pur day: a Rix Doller is one shilling and sixpence. Hear our Master recvd from the Commriseret Department all kind of tooles that was neserey. Our time of serves did not comence untill we rived on they Land that was alotted for ous. On the 8th. of July we left Port Elizabeth in compney with Mr. Arthur Barkers partey they Govement suplying the two parteys with 12 Wagons to take us and our Luggage: before we started we coocked cerfichent vitles to last ous two days and maid it fast under the Wagon behind thinking that it wold be quit safe. We left Zwartkops River on the forth late in the afternoon: we wished to travle by day so thay we could see the contrey but a long with evrey train of wagons thear ware a Field Cornet wich takes charge of the Wagons and us also and he told ous that they must travel by Night as well as by day as it may seute the masters of they wagons as he was a Goverment Servent an theas men ware prest by the Goverment with thear wagons to bring us up the Cuntrey to the sereval places ware we ware to be Loacated and if they did not travle at night so that thear Oxen could Graze by day. Dear reader I ought to have informed you that as soone as we came on shour that the Goverment gave ous Rashones or I do not know what we should done for I ham shour that our Master could not have found us in food: the Goverment gave to evrey man $\frac{3}{4}$ of a pound of Meal and 2 lbs of meat pur day the women half the mans a lowance and a Child one theard of a mans a lowance: this was not cerfishent for us to live on. When we came to the Bushmans River the Field Cornet was forst to git a farmer to show him the way: we ware a bout twelve days on our jorney: we came to our jurneys end a bout noon. This had been a Duch farmers place; thear ware meney of the postes of the Cattle Kraal still standing and the postes of the dweling House: they ware more or less burnt but we did not know the meaning of them been burnt at that time but we found out afterwards that the Kaffers had merdred they farmer and all his famley and had taken a way all his Cattle.

The morning after we arived on the Land we commenced sarching for aplace to build an House for our Master and also a place to plow and soe his seeds and we soone found the pleas ware the Duch farmer had had ploud and sowed his weat and barley as the stuble was still standing and quit fresh. . . . . and when we saw Mr. and Mrs. Wait comfutley situvatied in thear new Howes and everey thing ware planted we now thought it Quit time to ask for sumthing for our selves as we ware giting nothing nothing more then the ¾ of pound of meal (corn ground but not sifted) and two pounds of verey poor meat that had not fat on it to frie so that if it was beef we ware forst always to stue it and if we wanted if it ware but a half peneysworth of salt we had to pay for it to our Master. After we had been on the place a few days we heard that thear ware a Duch farmer liveing a bout Eight or ten Miles off ware we Could purch Bread and Butter &. so off four of us started and purched what ever we wished : this was a jurney of at least 16 miles under aburning Afrecan sun. Well we asked our Master if he could not pay ous our wages or sum part of what was coming to us : he informed us that he was not able to pay us aney part of it for he had before he left England printed simler papers to Bank Notes and that he found wold not pass in this Cuntrey so that it maid him quite unable to pay us. We then said whould he Give us our discharge : he posatively declard that he wold not : then we asked him if he wold give us more foode as the rashens was not serfishent for us to live on and to work so hard as we had don and more so thoues men that had wives and Children for the Children ware crien for vitles. At this time his ancers ware : I cannot for the Goverment donot alow you aney more and I cannot. At this time thear ware but seventeen of ous left for the other ten had left on account of not giting aney thing for thear work and at this time the Govermint gave us one Galon of Rum to Eich man : this also he wished to keep and give it to us wen and how he thought proper and this we wold not submit to as it was given to us as well as him and the rashing also. We found out that Mr. Wait was going to Grahams Town and that was the onley place to go to to have aney

disputes settled so on the folloing sunday morning we agreed that
six of us should go to Grahams Town and see if we could git our
wages or our discharge: this was a jorney of twenty eight miles.
We rived thear juest as the sun was setting with our feet blisterd
so that I could scasley walk: we sat down at the entrence of the
Town if it was worthey of that name for thear ware not more them
twentey five Houses in it that was worthey to be caled Houses:
thear ware a great part of three Rigements of Solgers the Cape
Mounted Rifels, the old 72nd and Royle Afrecnes.

We got up as well as we could for by this time we ware quite stif
with our jurney and with our blistred feet and got to Mr. Rafferty's
House and he gave ous for super such as his House aforded and a
tent to sleep in, and in the morning at a leven oclock we presented
ourselves before the offise of the Landrost of the distrest of
Albney Capn. Sumerset, of the Cape Mounted Rifels and Capn.
Trapes of the 72nd Rigements. They wished to know what we
wanted: we informed them that we ware com to complain of our
Master for not paying us hour wages and that we had fulfiled our
a Grement to the leter with him and that we had not recved one
farthing of our wages and that we could not git apromice of ever
Giting it, our Master was present and after along he promesed to
yous us better and Give us more rashens. We returnde and he
beaved to us well for about fortuen day and then he went on as he
had don before and they women agread to go to Grahams Town:
they ware six women and one womin was to stop on the place and
look after all the Children and the other five women went off to
Grahams Town and walked all the way, and when they saw the
Landrost Capn. Somerstet he wished to know what they wanted,
they informed him that they ware the wifes of sum of thouse men
that weated on him belonging to Mr. Waits partey and that he had
not preformed his promes twords his men and that they Children
ware crien for bread and that If they men cannot git thear wages
or sum compncation for thear labour that the Children wold be
starved to deth. [Eventually the court] decided that we ware all
to have our Discharge and that we ware not to have aney clame on
our Master or ware he to have aney clame what ever on ous and
that onley they marred men ware to Go to fetch our Boxes and our

things. Hear we ware fifteen of ous not a place to sleep in or a
blanket to cover ous, at last Captin Summerset gave ous lefe to
sleep in the trunt untill we could git ous a place of work.

I ingaged with Mr. Deates to saw for him and I was forst to Lay
on a box for sum time without aneything to cover me altho thear
was meney shopes but not one of them had Blankets on aney
thing that I could git to cover me with untill I met with aman that
had two Blankets and he sold me one of them and I ham sorry
to say that I met with a mate that youest to Drink most all that
we herned: we worked together a bout two month. Wen I had
recved from Mr. Wentworth 40 Rix Dolers I went to Cadles Races
at Howerds partey: I had not been thear Long before I had my
pocket picked and lost all my Money. I them returndd to Grob-
belaar's Kloof ware we ware sawing for Mr. Dietz: my partner he
stoped away from his work more them a weak wich made me
deturmed not to work with him aney Longer. On 23rd Decr. I
mounted a pack Ox and road over to Mr. Mahonys at the Clay
pites a bout 10 Miles having heard that he was in want of Sawers.
I had not gon more than four or five miles wehn I lost my way: I
had got into an Eelephents path wich went in a quit opersite
direction: at last I got on an ight hill and saw the place but how to
git thear I did not know: thear ware a verey deep Crance and a
verey Long range of Cloffs bush and rocks. I was forsed to dis
mount and lead my pack Ox and found a Wagon spur wich I
followed untill it lead me into a Wagon road: I was then a bout
two Miles from the place: this road tuck me direct to the House.
I found Mr. Mahony at home and we soone agread and I was to
com in two weakes: he wished me to stop and spend Christmas at
his place but I refuesed and as soone as I had taken sum refresh-
men I on kneeaulter my Ox and rturned to the Bush ware I rived
jest at dark. As soon as we had taken supper we laid down our
blankets on a flat rock and had an other that hung ove ous: we
ware five in number and aning rock was serfishant to keep ous
drie from the hevest thunder Storm. Wile we ware lien hear one
night about nine oclock a storme came on: the thunder and liten
was verey hevey and the rane decended in torents, it had not Lond

commenced wen a verey strong flash of Litening was seen and we hear in the Cloff belo ous they hevey crush of the trees that fell and soon after a verey large Torn tree fell cloce to ous so that som of the boues of it came onto our feet and in the morning we found that we was allmost inclosed so that we had to clime over the Large trunk of the falen tree, about 6th jeny. 1821 I left for Mahonys ware I worked thear about six weekes. One morning as we ware going to work about one Mile from the house and the wagon road running thrue som larg bushes and jest as we had come to one of them we ware startled by the blowing and scraping of a verey Large bul Buffellow. Had it not been for our Doge we should have been in a verey ocard purshion but the Dogs hearing the noise rushed forverd and away the went with Buffellow and the Dogs came to ous in about two hours after quite exausted.

[He decides to marry and goes in search of a minister.] As soone as I had taken a little refreshment I a gain mounted my poney: I had alreddey walked and road 20 Miles and wen I was leveing the House my intended father inlaw caled out to me stated that he hoped that I wold have mersey on the Horse: I said that I wold ride his tale off but what I wold find they Minester: so away went I spining over the flat and when I came to a hill I dismounted and walked along side of the Horse. At last I rived at Mr. R. Walkers. Mr. Kay came out and wished to know if I wished to speak to him: I said yes I wished to know if he had a licence to Marrey: he ancerd yes. I stated that thear was two persons at Hymans partey that had been disapointed by Mr. Boardman this Morning and have had to go from Hymans partey to Willisons partey and when they rived thear Mr. Boardman had left for Grahams Town and wold you be so kind as to oblieg them? He said yes. Should they com hear or wold he go over to Hymans partey? He then asked me if he went over thear did I think he could git a congregation to preach to: of corse my ancer was yes. How meney did I think he wold have to preach to? I said I thought from 16 to 20 or more: this number I could promise him. He said then he wold go with me if I wold wait for him to wright to Mr. Thornhill at the mouth of the Kowie Rivers as he had an apointment to preach thear that evening so

[242]

off corse I obaided and waited for him and in due time we both
mounted our steads and away we road: we had from five to six
Miles to go. We had not got more than one Mile when I stated to
Mr. Kay what a fine plane it was and a good place it was for a race
corce: Mr. Kay did not ancer me but my hone conchion condemed
me for what I had said and it caused me to Give my horse such a
jurk that it brought him allmost backwards.

When I reched home they wished me to wait and take sum
refreshment but I refeused to ender aney time and that I did not
need aney so off we went down into the partey and rived at Mr.
Trollipes about six oclock and was Marred at half past six oclock
and then we had to stop to the cervece and we rived at home at
half past eight at night: so my days work at last was finished and
from Six in the Morning to half past eight at night I had not
travled less then 40 Miles and the gratest part on foot and from
the time we left home to go to Grahams Town to pass the Matre-
momel Cort I had travled upwords of 160 Miles, this is a Duch
Law and a verey bad Law it is wich at this time meney a thief was
not brought to justes after commiting them selves on account of
the distence been so great it was imposable for the sufarer to
travel so fare to give evidence a gainst them, Bathurst wen we
first arived in this this Coleney was to be the Captle Town of this
Coleney but as it was not sentrel they seat of Govermint was
removed from Bathurst to Grahams Town and this caused all they
troops to be taken from Bathurst with all other goverment
departements. When theas ware all gon traid was put a stop to for
meny tradesmen that had left thear locations for to setle them
selves in Bathurst had bult them little Houses: sum of the Houses
was bult with turf others was built with postes and watled and
daubed with mud: sum few with brick and stone and thatched
with long grass, Goverment to incurage people to com and live
thear they gave everey one that maid appelaction to them a hearf
of ground to buld thear house on and to make a Garding: sum of
the hervings ware two acers but what was caled Mecanic Hearfs
was onley half an acer. Wile they troops and the goverment-
department and head Quarters was at Bathurst they people was
doing well but as soon as they was removed to Grahams Town,

[243]

Bathurst was forst to be derset by tradesmen and labours and the Land wich had been given to them the Govement with the Houses that had beein builded on it had to be sold for a mear trifel genrely for not more than what the land was worth. Of corce after such alterrations Bathurst decreced and Grahams Town increced in poperlation, a few days after we ware [?] Surcler Letters ware sent rownd to all the hemradens of Justes of the peace ordring all the Setlers to soornin as Soldiers. Soon after we ware worned by the Field Cornet Mr. G Dyason to com to his house in Lusherton Valey to recve fierharms and Ammunition. When we rived at Mr. G Dyasons he gave to eich man one gun and ten rounds of ball cartrages: this was a jorney of sixteen Miles. The gun wich I recved I lost no time in trying it as soon as I got home and I found it quit youslis at two hundred yards I could not hit a place six feet square: the this was a fine thing to be served out with if they Kaffers had com uppon ous. At this time it apears that the athorityis must have been afraid of then as we lernt after, that they Kaffers had been steling Cattle from they Duch farmers and that they ware afraid that they Kaffers wold com down uppon ous.

[1823] . . . at this time it went verey hard with meney of the Settlers for what of the October flood and having no Market for our produce fer our nerest Market was Grahams Town thirty Miles and meney of the Settlers having no convaince so that if they had aney thing for sale it was forst to be cept untill it got of no youce, at thime [this time] Goverment was lenden money to the Settlers on thear Locations or two good secureteyes to the amount of Rix Dolers 500 and to meney 1000 Rix Dolers—1000 Rix Dolers is £75: but of corce my having no Land I could not git aney of this Lone. I had severel pursons howing me money [1825] but was not shour wether I should be able to git serfishant two pay for my Cattle and at the same time my stock of provishans was jest exorsted and my wife and my self did not know what to do. At Last I went to one that had to pay me jest the amount that was due for they Cattle and the next day he brought me the Money. We had only Meal serfishment to make two little Cakes and this was to serve my self wife and two Children. My wife in the morning

that she wold make the two Cakes and that I should take one and
that she and the two Children wold have the other and they wold
trust to providence untill I returned: I said no I wold take adrink
of Milk and I will also trust to providence: she said what is a drop
of Milk for you that as got to ride thirtey Miles in such aburning
as It is to day? Feby. is the hotest Month in the year. I tuck my
drink of milk and mounted my horse and comenced my jurney:
I road the first forteen Miles without seeing aney one and at the
top of blukrance hill I met an Officer wisling a song tune: we never
spoke to eich other so I dismounted and led my horse down the
hill and rode on to the River. It was all most midday and it was
one of thouse burning scorching days wen the Sun was beeming
down on my head. I dismounted to Let my Horse drink: I thought
then that if I had not got aney foode for my bodey I wold go under
one of thous bushes in the shade of it and wile my horse is feiding
I well pray to they Lorde to feid my preshus Soul. I went and as
soon as I had nelt down I saw sum thing wite close to the stump of
the Bush in sum Grass. Before I comenced prear I puled it out and
to my astunishment wen I onfoulded a sheet of fulcap paper I
found around cut off of asixpeney wite lofe of bread spread with
verey nice freash Butter and then aslice of salted tung and an
other round of bread. My Hart was so fild with Gratude to God
for serplieng my wants in this wilderness I preaid as the Lod so
bountifully surplied me with temprel food that he wold feed my
preshus Soul with Spritule food and that he wold be so musaful for
Jesus sake to pardon my Sins: Glorey be to his holey name. He
did parden my Sins and wen I tuck up the refreshment wish he had
surplied me with o how I did rejois all that afternoon and dear
reader if you are not a converted carreter you cannot enter into
my fealings or can you rejoice with me but I wold in treat you to
seek the Lord wile he may be found and cale uppon him wile he is
neer for you must rember that life is un sertin and if it ware not so
in this world no comfort or hapeness out of Criest that man woman
or Child that as found the perel of great price and do know that
God as for Criest sake for given thear Sins is hapey and them a
lown.

Soon after this Congregation to large for the House to hold

them: we then beun to talk aboug build a Chaple. A commitee was formed and a subscription list was sent rowend to the Nabours: sum Gave bricks: sum beems and rafters: others wood for doors and windows: others gave thetch and labour so that with the subscriptions the Chaple was not much in depte. At the opning of the Chaple thear was preching in the Morning: Love-feast in the afternoon: preching in the evening and also the sacrement was adminerstred. The Chaple wold hold about two hundred and it was well filed and meney came from Grahams Town and severel from Salem thirtey Miles. Thear ware a Good dinner and tea in the afternoon for all. At this time the socirtey in creced and contuened so for a long time.

On the 25 [Dec., 1834] we recvd a Letter from Grahams Town stating that they Kaffers had killed severel of the traders and that they ware driving all the Cattle and sheep out of the Colney into Kaffer Land. . . . Sunday Morning 5 oclock they Duch-farmers that had colected to gather at provedence farm five Miles from Salem neer Bushmans River sent one of thear natives Servent into Salem wishing for us to com and help them as they Kaffers ware comming to atact them and they are not coming in hunders but in thousands. Mr. B. Wost the Field Cornet and seven of ous went up out of Salem to ware we could see the farm House. Mr. Woest tuck a Hottentot that was mounted with him leveing ous in site and he wold fier a shot if we was wanted. We wated the time apointed not hearing they shot. Wen we returned we found all the men standing readey for they Kathers to com down: five men ware sent into they Mission House to fier out of the windows and five into the Chaple five into the Scoleroom: this I thought was quite youseless. I wished to go out and meet them or could I stand in rank as they wished me to do: I thought on they farmers Cattle and expresed my wish to them. Mr. Bannan and ceverel others wished me to contain myself and never to mind they Duchmans Cattle: thear Cattle was gone out to Graze and if they Kaffers tuck them they must putup with it and the best is for ous to take care of our lives: they did not consider untill I informed them that all thear propertey was in thear Wagons and in thear Houses and

[246]

that they Duch farmers depended mostley on thear Cattle and if
they Kaffers tuck them they would have nothing to subsist on and
that I considered that if they wold not go was cowerds and was
afraid of they Kaffers. Mr. B. wished me to compose my self for
they Kaffers wold be hear in afew minetes: at this moment we
heard agreat noise jest above the Vilage and we reley thought that
the ware acoming. We soon found out that this was they farmers
Wagons bringing thear wifes and famleys criing and caling out to
ous not to stand thear but go and help to retacke thear Cattle for
they Kaffers had taken all of them more than Six Hundred head.
At this moment Mr. Woest came galoping down and calling out
for twentytwo men to go with him to retake they Cattle and that
the Kaffers ware running up to him: he shot one of them dead:
and that we must make ast as they wold soon be in the Bush. I
gave in my name: Mr. B Woest said that I had not a horse:
Mr. B offerd to lend me his Horse if I could git a Saddle and
Bridle.

We retuck all they Cattle that was on they left hand of the
Cloff: they Kaffers on the other side Caled out to ous that we had
got them but we should not have thouse that they had got. I
Caled out to the Field Cornet and informed him what they had
said: we then opned fier on them and retuck half the Cattle that
they had: two Englishmen and three Hottentots wear sent thrue
the Cloff to bring they Cattle thrue.

[January 31st 1835.] newes was brought into Town that Bathurst
was Burnt down and my House two Miles from Bathurst also was
seen in flames: I thought then that all my prospects was Lost: all
my Cattle had been taken by they Kaffers and all my propertey
destroyed. Two of my English Serventes came into Grahams Town
with the Bathurst people and the farmers that had flon to Bathurst
they brought me two Horses so that I conclueded that was all that
I had to comence the world with again with the ten Oxen and
one wagon. They also brought the sad newes of the murder of
Alixander Forbes: it was a verey fogey day and as we knew [not]
aney thing of a Kaffer war and as not one out of twentey had aney
fier harms Mrs. Forbes was washing at the spring and all the

Children Six in number was with her and her husband was standing at the House he loocking down to ware his wife and children ware he saw several Kaffers standing rownd his wife and Children. He left the House and run down to know what they wanted but he had now souner reached the partey then they Kaffers seased Mr. Forbes and stabed him to death with thear Asigies is poor wife and Children standing by and seeing faling down and Caling out for mersey and his Life but they heedednot his or his wife or Children Cries and intretes. I Cannot beter discribe thear feelings and thear sorrow then stating of it as folows

In the year 1834 when I think of
that eve it greves my Hart sore
when the blacks came on ous
that dwelt in the east
to burn and to murder
and to drive of our beast

when theas savages first
in our borders they came
they seased Mrs. Forbes that
dwelt on the plain
poor Alick he ruen the caues
to inquire they stabed him
to the Hart and set his House all on fier

ho think of her Loss her greaf
and her payn Six Fatherless
Babes and her House all in flames
no foud and no Clothing
and they Kaffers all in site
and nought but they woods
two sleep in all night.

[Debe River, April 1835.] Wile we ware lieing in Camp hear Mr. Driver got leafe from His Excellency for apartey of ous Waggoners to go under Slambie Kop to git sum Indian Corn and Pumkens but not less then twentey two ware to go with strict Charge not to go father then the Gardens wich we promised but

Jeremiah Goldswain

when we got to the Gardens we saw severel Horses greasen on the
Kop and thought that we could git them without danger: we
agread to go and if posable to capyure them but when we started
we did not think that it was so fare: but being deturmin we soon
got up almost to the top when we saw a verey fine Stable Horse
feeding not fare off us but by the help of our Talescope we saw
severel hundreds of Kaffers lien down in the Grass: at this time
they had not seen us. We maid good our retret by taken a neerer
path down the redge: we came to a hut maid in the Cloof and
found by a noise inside that thear was sume thing alive in it: we
not knowing what it mite be we serrounded it and one Standing
near to the door was ordred by Mr. Driver to push open the door
which he did and out sprung a large Grayhown. We found a grate
meney articles of crockrey ware and meney other things. We now
comenced giting the Indian Corn and Pomkens: som of the partey
had set fier to sume huts above the Bush which could be seen At
the Camp. As we ware going into one Garden we hat a shot fierd
at us and we returned it but could not see they Kaffers: we had
not been thear more then five minetes when two or three more
shotts ware fired at ous. Mr. Driver who had charge of the partey
caled out to sum that was higher up the field to com down: by this
time they Kaffers begun to cale out to ous to cum up and they
wold fight with us but we knew thear strenth and dold them that
if they wold cum down we wold alow ten to one of us but they
youssed sum vere busif langwage and said that we ware afraid of
them. By this time verey meney of them had com down off the
mounting into the wood close to the Gardens and comesced fireing
at us but being verey bad shotts they missed us. Mr. Driver
ordred the partey to move off: Mr. Driver and my self brought up
the rear. We had not gon more than two hundred yards—I was
walking on his wright—when a shott was fired at us by a Kaffer
from over they Garding hadge and nocked off my hat. Driver
loocked at me and said: have you got that Goldswain? I ancered:
no onley my hat as got it. He turned rownd and saw a Kaffer
agoing to fier at us: he caled out to me to take care. I turned rownd
and saw a Kaffer with his gun resting on the gardin fence with it
pointing wright at my breast: he was so neer to me that I cold see

[249]

his eye along his gun but before I cold bring my gun to my shoulder Mr. Driver fired and doun fell the Kaffer and I wishing to git his gun was going for it but Driver puled me back stating that the Garden was full of Kaffers and that we must make ast and git away from the wood as they wold be killing sume of us as we cold not see them and they cold see us so we maid the best of our way to the Camp. When we rived we heard that we had don rong by setting fier to they Kaffer huts and that Sir Benjeman was going to have us tried by a Cort Marshal and flog us so we started off Mr. Driver to beag pardon wich was Granted us. The night preves to our moveing forverd a Kaffer was atemteing to steal a Horse but one of the out Line Picket saw him and shott him dead: in the morning he was found to have a leather bag ful of honey.

[After two months activity as driver for the Commissariat Department] I left for home and reached thear the next day the 23rd. of June 1835 and found that everey door had been broken open and all the tables and chears had been taken out off the House and had been exposed with meney mor artleces of furniture to the sun rain and wind and sum of it broken and disstroid and all my Books off wich I valued verey much as at this time Books here are verey scarse: also all my papers Bills and recepts ware cast to the winds: meney I found along way off from the House and meney I never found and had it not been foe sum honest peaple that I had been dealing with I should have been agreat sufferer by the Loos of my papers. My Losses was 35 Oxen, 10 Cowes &. &. all most a mounting too to two Hundred poungs. My Gorden and fields all my cropes in them was distroyed. As this was the time to comence plowing and sowing as soone as my Oxen had two or three days rest I comenced plowing but I had not gon more then two furrowers before my plow braak all into peaces and what to do I did not know. At Last I deturmined to make a new one: I did so and it ancerd quit well.

In leaving Grahams Town I had to become ancable for 12 Muscates for 12 men that lived close to my farm and I had to muster the men everey night. We had not been home but afew days

when Capt. Forbbes came and ordred me wife and famley to Go
over to Mr. E Timmses Mill to sleep ware all the other 12 famleys
ware but I prosisted in not going as my famley was in a verey
delicate state of helth and if I had crouded in with thouse that was
in the Mill I should have lost sum of the famley. I had no dung to
Manur my Land with and was forst to go more then a mile for it.
My wife poor thing had to stand all the time that I was Loading
my waging with my Gun in her hand readey to give it to me in cace
aney Kaffer or Kaffers should trie to becrep us. One day I had to
go a short distance from the waggon when out came a Black man
out of the wood not far from the waggon and came up to the
waggen wich at his coming up to her and she could not discover
wether he was a Kaffer or not but jest at the moment I returned
and knew him to be one of the heards and had gon down into the
wood to look after a bees nest. At this time we was recveing
rashens from Goverment: 2 lbs of beef and threequarters of a
pound of Meal pur day wich bound us over so that if we ware caled
upon to go on padrole or aney other dutey that they may cale on
us to do. About this time the Comt. Department Advered for
Tenders for Lime per Bushel. I got the Contrect for it 3s. and 6d.
pur bushel and jest at this time Mr. T Goldeng came and asked
me to let him his wife and child to ocupie apart of my House. I
gave him leaf and also he wished as he had got a waggon to agre
to carrey Lime for me to Grahams Town or elce ware ware it may
be required by Govement: I agreed with him. We left one Morning
for Grahams Town and about Nine oClock the same Night the
Kaffers came to the House: the two women heard them walk
rownd the Hows and pulling the blind a little a one side Mrs.
Goldswain saw they Kaffers: they went rownd the Howse until
they came to the Kitchen door: they tried the latch but the door
was fast: they could not open it and a little Dog that barked at
them they beat it or kicted it so that Mrs. Goldswain thought that
they had killed him. Wile they Kaffers was trieing to open the
Kitchen door Mrs. Goldin wished to screamout to friten them
away for she was afraid that they wold set the House on fier and
then they wold be burnt to deth: but Mrs. Goldswain wold not
alow her to do it for if they did sit the House on fier they cold git

[251]

the Children down steares and all of them could go into the Kitchen and the other little rome and be safe: as the Kitchen was a flat rufe maid with Stone and Lime and the wood had no communication with the timber belonging to the other part of the House and they wold be quit safe all tho they mite be a little illconvenced by the smoke. Everey Night after this my Wife tuck her Gun upstares with her determine that if the Kaffers did com that she wold trie and shoot the first that entred into the House and then to put all the Children out at the window on to the flat roof and having a parapet wall rownd it so that if they all laid down the Kaffers could not see them. About this time Capt. Forbes came out from Bathurst and finding that I had left for Grahams Town and at this time thear ware onley my wife and five Children at the House he ordred them that moment to go over to the Mill. My wife informed him that she cold not do: he stormed and soore that she should go but she got the day. The Capt. mounted his horse and informed her that if the Kaffers came and killed all of them it wold not be his falt and that she cold not expct aney asistance from him so away he and the padrole rode they men loocking back and laughing at the braverey of my wife.

John Mitford Bowker

John Mitford Bowker's father was a wealthy farmer who had twice crashed in the difficult times following the Napoleonic wars. Seeing little probability of effecting a third recovery in England he, like Goldswain, went out to Albany in 1820. He took his family of seven sons and a daughter, while John, the eldest, being then nineteen, remained at home to dispose of the Devonshire estate.

Bowker senior did well in South Africa, dividing his time between making blankets at Bathurst and felt hats at Graham's Town, and John, after joining him, was made resident agent with the Fingo tribes and, later, diplomatic agent with various Kaffir tribes. But his over-independence and a partiality for frank and public criticism of his superiors led to suspension from office, and in 1841 he became a sheep farmer at Willow Fountain, Fish River Rand, not far north of Graham's Town.

In this district, for the five years before his death, he, like his brothers, played a prominent part in the political and military life of the country, alternately petitioning and abusing authority and fighting the Kaffirs. The following is an extract from the obituary which appeared in the *Cape Frontier Times* in 1848: 'He was a worthy illustration of Pope's definition of the noblest work of God. He was an honest man. He was more than this. He was a patriot in the true sense of the word. He braved public opinion in boldly advocating what he in his conscience believed to be the cause of

truth. In this cause he laboured disinterestedly. He was a thorough
Christian heart and soul, notwithstanding his opposition to the
cause of missions. Not even the most unprincipled of his opponents
will attempt to throw dirt on his remains by denying this. His
private character was without a blemish.'

These letters are taken from the anonymously edited *Speeches,
Letters, and Selections from Important Papers of the Late John
Mitford Bowker*, Graham's Town, 1864.

Willow Fountain, July 9th, 1841. My next neighbour Roux called
here yesterday on his return from Beaufort, whither he had been to
report the loss of eleven of his best cows. He traced them far
enough to satisfy himself that they were stolen by Kafirs and gone
to Kafirland, but night came on, and with it rain, and of course
in the morning they were the Kafirs' own, according to treaty, for
further tracing was out of the question. Three cows of Norden's
are gone too, and Jelliman's four oxen. P. Norton was one day
here looking for his cows, and the next for a Hottentot man, whom
he had sent to look for a span of oxen. He expected he was killed,
for he had seen the fresh spoor of two Kafirs just on the ridge
above his house, and his herds had said they saw the Hottentot
bringing the oxen the evening before; however, man and oxen both
turned up again. But I record the circumstance to show the
miserable insecurity and uncertainty in which we exist along the
frontier. Reynier Els and Stephanus de Lange took from three
Kafirs a few nights back, one span of black oxen. They had all the
appearance of having been stolen from some wagon travelling the
road, as they had very lately been in the yoke. I met three Kafirs
in native costume, that is nearly in *puris naturalibus*, and I asked
them for their pass, as they were neither in or near a road, and
after some hesitation they unwillingly produced it. It was signed
by the diplomatic Stretch. They were both Botman's people, and
it stated that they had TWO MONTHS' LEAVE to perambulate
the colony, 'to go see their brother at Uitenhage,' and here I met
them in the middle of our farm, going up the country as it were,

[254]

and at least twenty miles out of their direct road to Uitenhage, no
doubt making observations as to where were the best horses and
cows, and which were the worst looked after, and easiest carried
off; and thus it is, and so we live, thanks to the anile proceedings
or no proceedings of our Governors. My two horses were well
worth, and cannot be replaced, for £24. A pretty tolerable tax to
pay for living in the Kafirs' neighbourhood, and they may be here
again to-morrow for ought I know.

[End of 1842.] Since the time Sir Benjamin D'Urban's frontier
policy was so injudiciously overthrown by Lord Glenelg, and
superseded by the treaties brought out and put in force by Sir A.
Stockenstrom, a sense of insecurity, both of person and property,
has paralysed much of the exertions of the frontier settlers. They
are generally content to live in huts, knowing that if they expended money in the improvement of their homesteads, they
might be burned over their heads without a moment's notice. The
breeding of horses and cattle, for which the frontier was famed
before the Kafir war, is now in a measure abandoned, as the
Kafirs, under existing regulations, carry off annually nearly the
half of what is bred upon it, and the ineffectual and miserable
measures adopted by the Government to repress plunder and
murder, and recover property when stolen, have impressed the
ignorant and restless savages with an idea of the imbecility of the
British Government, which ought to make the cheeks of our
Governors tingle with shame, if they had any. But there, there lies
the grand root of the evils we experience. Our Governors are made
such, from fortuitous circumstances, and not chosen for their
activity and intelligence. But this is not all. The Boers, who are
horribly ignorant, and know little more of the power of Britain
than the poor sample exhibited daily before their eyes—in despair
of security under such a system, emigrated to the unoccupied lands
beyond the colony, well knowing they were capable of protecting
themselves when beyond the reach of the silly enactments in force
within it. And this they soon proved; for though our Governors
prophesied their speedy ruin, yet they were not long before they
made *themselves* respected and feared, having speedily humbled

[255]

the two great tribes of natives who successively and *unprovokedly* attacked them. Had they (the Boers) been destroyed, little sympathy would have been felt for them either by the Government here or in England. But having established themselves the Government then thought to bring them again under the pale of British law; this, by sane measures, might soon have been effected, but the strain of correspondence entered into with them by the Government here, was only calculated to irritate them, and the force eventually sent for their subjection was only sufficient to cause them to *despise* it, and quite in character with all that is doing here. The result of their insurrection we have yet to learn. *But unless the management of affairs here, like those of China, be speedily given over to wiser and abler heads than those we have here at present*, the worst may be feared. Some ten years ago a more peaceable, loyal, and well disposed set of people than these said Boers did not exist in any part of Her Majesty's dominions. The character given them for cruelty to the natives, they have never deserved. Individual cases of cruelty, such as may be found in *all* countries, have been industriously sought for to answer certain ends, and falsely held up as anecdotes illustrative of the general character and conduct of the people. But the philanthropists of England would be doing something towards the advancement of Christianity and human happiness were they to appropriate the thousands of pounds annually subscribed for missions amongst savages, and more than a million spent annually to repress the slave trade (with what effect let those philanthropists testify) to the education of such neglected people as the Boers of Southern Africa, and in assisting industrious, moral, and religious emigrants, to reach our shores. The effect of the expenditure of such a sum, or the tenth of such a sum, would soon be seen; whereas the present enormous expenditure of money, talent, and zeal, wasted on mission stations in Kafirland, I pronounce to be a *perfect failure*. A *savage* is not to be made a Christian of, and civilization (which was once begun under Sir Benjamin's system, and so injudiciously given up) must make great advances among them before they can ever understand or appreciate the doctrines of Christianity. A firm and enlightened Government on the Kafir

[256]

Waggon Train

Graham's Town

frontier, which would protect and encourage the industrious inhabitants, and aid in the diffusion of useful and religious knowledge among them, would speedily have more effect in civilizing
and Christianising the Kafirs, than all the mission stations in
Kafirland. I can assure you this colony is well worthy of the
attention of the Home Government, and the benefits to the mother
country that would accrue from the adoption of sane and salutary
frontier regulations would speedily be felt.

I have already stated that the breeding of cattle and horses, and
the improvement of our homesteads, have been abandoned
through fear of the Kafirs; the frontier inhabitants have, therefore, more decidedly turned their attention to the breeding of
woolled sheep, as Kafirs do not keep sheep, and, therefore, steal
no more than an odd one for food, whilst on their plundering
excursions within the colony. The export of wool has, therefore,
increased within these last few years more than twenty-three fold,
a fact which clearly proves the capabilities of this neglected
country.

December, 1844. With reference to myself as a country Justice,
further than contracting a few servants to their masters, I find my
office entirely useless to the country, and I have no 'detailed
statement' to make. I once committed a coloured person for sheep-
stealing. That man was afterwards tried before the sitting Magis-
strate, Martin West, Esq., and much to my annoyance and inconvenience, I was summoned to Grahamstown with the witnesses to
answer upon oath whether I considered the preliminary examination I sent in with the prisoner (wherein the evidence was noted
down from witnesses regularly sworn, and signed by myself in
proper form) was correct and true! This infliction was more severe
on me than the petty sentence was on the culprit, as I cannot
afford to lose my time in such a manner. It was the first and last
committal I have made since living in this neighbourhood, where
cases of theft escape daily with impunity, the distance from the
petty courts being so great, the farmers find it impossible to
prosecute as they ought. The evidence is generally *herdsmen*, who
cannot be spared for the length of time required, and the farmer

having so much to look to at home, sees it would be ruinous to give his time and attention to the case, and thus nearly all felony escapes with impunity, to the encouragement of roguery and vagabondism. I find no difficulty in dismissing complainants, as I have only to hint that if the case comes before me, and I commit, that I will swear in the plaintiff as special constable to take the prisoner into town, having no constable at command, and always a short account of servants, and none to spare for such purposes. I have no clerk, no constable, no lock-up house—in fact, no power whatever, and the only expense I am to the country is for a weekly copy of the *Government Gazette*, which may be safely saved, as from disgust at the inefficiency of my office, I have entirely neglected it, and it is posted to Bathurst, near which place I resided three years ago.

May 22, 1845. There are few frontier farmers who would not rather go and fight the Kafirs than write about them. Therefore, little is known concerning the actual life of a frontier farmer with all its harrassing anxieties; and the accounts filtered through the journals cause no sympathy on our behalf. Allow me, therefore, to bring to your notice a *true* history of frontier life in my immediate vicinity during the last three weeks. To begin with myself. I sent my oxen to my vee place on the 29th ult., to repair the kraals. As they were worked all day, they were obliged to be let run at night, or they would have been starved. And on the night of the 2nd inst., the three best of them were selected and carried off. The other seven were found in the morning near my neighbour Enos's house, and a good milch cow and calf and a heifer of his, were also missing. The day previous to the loss of these cattle, two Kafirs were seen in the act of driving off the horses on my brother William's place above mine. When seen they were busied in pelting a white horse out of the troop, as he was too conspicuous to suit their purpose. They escaped into the willow trees in the river, and no doubt contented themselves next night with the above mentioned cattle. I have not now actually oxen to draw my wagon, and two of the above I had just broken in myself with much labour and trouble, and they were the pride of my span. The horses I

John Mitford Bowker

purchased are in miserable plight with standing these longs nights in the kraal, and are of little service to me, as I can scarce take them from their food in the day time also. It may be said I might keep one in the stable; and so I would, but I cannot grow forage, and besides the expense of purchasing it, the Kafirs will not allow me to keep oxen to fetch it. And this is frontier life—the anxieties —the watchings—searchings—listenings—dog-barkings, &c., &c., I cannot describe, neither can you wholly conceive. This is the life that destroyed the loyalty of the Boers, and is ruining as fine a country as any under the Crown, and the chief means adopted to stay this is by subsidising mere savages, who cannot appreciate anything of the kind, but look upon it as a mere tribute from the weaker to the stronger, and our lenity is looked upon as the off-spring of imbecility and fear. Already are farmers beginning again to talk of trekking. Elias Nel told my brother yesterday he should sell out and leave. Half the Boers around here are Nels, and if one leaves it will only be a signal to all the rest

To the Governor at Fort Beaufort.

Thorn Kloof, Saturday, May 2nd, 1846.

Sir,—This evening, half an hour before sunset, some of our herds ran home from the Fish River Randt, calling that the Kafirs were among the sheep. Our cattle guard of five mounted men had just come in, and went off to save the sheep. The horses being still at a distance, six of us went also off on foot, supposing that the Kafirs were but few in number, the herds having only seen eight or ten. They had turned our sheep into a corner of the Fish River bush, and before we were aware we were hemmed in on every side by at least 100 Kafir cavalry, and 300 or 400 on foot. By keeping to-gether, and making a stand here and there behind bushes, we kept the Kafirs at bay, and retreated upon our camp cooly, and were met in time by another party of six or seven, which enabled us to get in. We had one of our party to carry, namely, Mr. Webb, who was early shot through the ancle, leaving at least 3,000 sheep in the hands of the enemy. The purport of this letter is to demand assistance. There are 40,000 sheep, 200 oxen, and 100 poor, scarce

[259]

serviceable horses, at this camp, with not more than twenty efficient white men and twelve Hottentots. I leave you to judge whether we, with those numbers, can do more than protect our lives. However, we will do our best until help arrives, which we implore immediately on the receipt of this.

(signed) J. M. BOWKER
W. M. BOWKER

Fort Beaufort, May 3rd, 1846.

Sir,—In reply to your letter of the 2nd inst., demanding assistance for the protection of property at your camp, I have been directed by his Excellency the Governor to inform you that he much regrets it is not in his power to spare a single man from this post to render you the aid of which you appear so much in want. Col. Somerset has, however, the Cape Corps, and the Burghers of Cradock and Beaufort, at his disposal for the protection of the farms in the colony, and the Civil Commissioner Cole has taken 190 men to the Somerset district, for the assistance of the inhabitants. His Excellency, therefore, suggests the expediency of your making application immediately either to Col. Somerset, at Grahamstown, or to Mr. Cole, or to both.

I have, &c.,
(signed) — SMITH,
Major and Frontier Commandant.

Maastrom, May 6th, 1846.

Sir,—Knowing your zeal and experience in the cause of your fellow-colonists, I beg of you to act as one of my deputies during the present emergency, and consequently to take the command in any sudden operation of a Burgher force when there is no superior officer present. On my return from the Tarka I hope to be able to communicate with you in more detail. In the meantime, in great haste,

I remain,
Your obedient Servant,
A. STOCKENSTROM,
Commandant-General.

Francis Owen

For the most extraordinary period of his life Francis Owen was indebted to a most extraordinary man, Captain Allen Gardiner, a naval officer of wild disposition and hitherto unimpaired frivolity, who resolved on the sudden death of his wife to 'devote his life to the service of his Saviour.' This was in 1834, and his resolution never faltered. The next year found him in Zululand, where his exhortations had little more effect on Dingaarn than Owen's were to have on that fleshly and humorous ruler. He was invited to stay, however, as a musketry instructor.

Undismayed, the cadaverous enthusiast, whose monocle was a source of wonder to the natives, returned to Port Natal and established a mission station on a ridge overlooking the bay which still has the name he gave it—Berea. And here, soon before he left for England to enlist help, he presided at a meeting where fifteen residents of the district resolved on founding a town to be named after the Governor of the Cape, Sir Benjamin D'Urban. Ogle and Cane, mentioned by Owen, were two of the members of the first Town Committee, but their plans were over-optimistic and the site remained uncleared. It is worth giving Gardiner's description of the occasion from his *Journey to the Zoolu Country* (1836):

'Tuesday, 23rd [June, 1835]—This afternoon a very characteristic meeting was held in one of Mr. Berkin's huts, for the purpose of selecting a site for a town. On my arrival I found the hut filled with the individuals expressly convened for this purpose.

Almost total silence was observed—the subject was not even hinted at, nor had any chairman or leading person been appointed to introduce the business. At length a voice cried out, "Now let's go and settle the bounds," on which I risked a question, hoping it might elicit a *programme* of the contemplated proceedings. "Are all present agreed as to the expediency of building a town?" To which it was replied, that their presence on this occasion was a proof that they were unanimous on this point. Thus began and ended this important conference, and off they all scampered in a posse to inspect the ground, some walking, others seated on the floor of a waggon without either tilt or sides, which was drawn at a stately pace by ten oxen. Short pipes, an indispensable accompaniment, were in full action on all sides. Being the winter season, it was a sort of reunion of hunters, who, tired of chasing sea-cow (i.e. hippopotami, Dutch and Colonial term. [G.'s note]) and buffalo, were now sighing for town-houses and domestic cheer. The appearance of any one of these forest-rangers would have gained the medal for any artist who could have transfixed his *tout ensemble* upon canvas. At length a pause was made,—"This'll do," cried one;—"That's the spot," exclaimed another. After some minutes of such-like random conversation, the whole party were compactly collected, and the business at length entered upon, and conducted in a rational manner, every proposition being subjected to the votes of those who were present, and carried or negatived accordingly. It was in this impromptu manner that the town of D'Urban was named—its situation fixed—the township and church lands appropriated—and, in short, as much real business gone through as would have required at least a fortnight's hard writing and debating in any other quarter of the globe.'

Back in England Gardiner set about gaining support, and he captured the imagination of a serious graduate of St. John's, Cambridge, then a curate in Yorkshire, persuading him to go out to set up a mission in Zululand under the auspices of the Church Missionary Society, for which permission had already been obtained from Dingaarn.

Owen sailed on the eve of Christmas, 1836, with his wife, sister and Jane Williams, their servant. He was totally ignorant of the country in which he was to spend four years, and, like most missionaries, never understood that natives were not merely unenlightened Europeans. He found, as Moffat found among the Matabele and Bechuanas, that the heathen, while from some points of view admiring the white man and eagerly taking advantage of his commodities, stopped short at accepting his religious beliefs, at which, indeed, they openly mocked. And Owen's position became untenable as soon as Dingaarn saw that he was not going to be assisted to the most valued commodity of all, gunpowder, for his hopes had been raised by a deal in which the unwitting missionary had obtained some for him in exchange for ivory. It speaks highly for his personal qualities that he was kept from harm during the Retief massacre—of which he was the only eye-witness to write a strictly contemporary account.

After the sack of Port Natal he did not immediately leave South Africa. He was a parish priest at Sidbury, near Graham's Town, for a time, and went on a mission to Bechuanaland. After that he returned home, to a parish near Sheffield. But the itch to travel was not now to be stilled, and it was in Egypt, in 1854, that he died.

But Gardiner never came home at all. Still missionizing, he went first to Chile, then to Papua, and finally died of exposure at Tierra del Fuego. He left a message behind him: 'I neither hunger nor thirst, though five days without food—marvellous loving mercy to me a sinner.'

The text of this diary, formerly in the possession of the C.M.S. in London and now in the Cape Archives, was edited by the late Sir George Cory in 1926 for the Van Riebeeck Society. He omitted some of the theology.

April 28th, 1837.—Commenced our long journey this day to Port Natal; having, during my residence at Graham's Town, purchased 2 waggons, 30 oxen, 2 horses and a tent. I had the waggons carefully fitted up and furnished with tools and a variety of other articles, necessary in African travelling. Two European drivers and four coloured men accompanied us: two of whom were Hottentots and the other two Zooloos, or at least natives of Port Natal, whom I met within a native village near the town.

May 3rd.—Crossed the Keiskamma river. Strict watch was kept over our oxen, by night and by day, in consequence of the sad character the frontier Kafirs bear for dishonesty. A large party of them overtook us, as we were walking at some distance behind the waggons armed with guns and assegais. They inspired a momentary fear, but quietly passed on, merely asking for tobacco; an article of which the frontier Kaffirs are passionately fond. It is the one subject of their requests. A heavy fall of rain, accompanied with thunder and lightning, prevented us from travelling above 3 or 4 miles to-day. As soon as we had spanned out, a company of natives who had been hunting, came running down from the heights with assegais and knobbed sticks. They manifested curiosity to know who I was, and being informed that I was a gentleman lately come from England, they asked me Wena Kona? Art thou the King? They afterwards noticed my glove, as something extraordinary and ludicrous and peeped into it, when I held it up, both old and young, with an ecstasy of delight, which was encreased beyond measure when they saw me put it on my fingers. I deeply regretted, however, that I was not able, for want of a suitable interpreter, to direct the unthinking minds of the accountable beings, to subjects more worthy of their regard. In the course of the day, my attention was directed to a company of native youths, whose bodies, but more especially their faces, were profusely daubed with white clay; and who, as an additional ornament, wore some hare tails dangling down on their foreheads. I could not suppose that this was anything more than a temporary frolic; but upon enquiry, learned that it is an important ceremony, which every Kafir undergoes, when he arrives at the age of puberty. By means of my driver and a native who understood Dutch, I asked these poor youths some of the plainest questions on the Divine Being and his works; but they were utterly ignorant or, at least, would not take the trouble to consider my questions, that they might answer them.

[264]

5th.—A party of natives surprised me whilst I was behind a bush dressing. Everything was an object of curiosity to them, particularly a small looking glass, by which they saw their faces reflected. Their behaviour however was perfectly civil, though somewhat troublesome, as one desired me to shave him, another to lend him my toothbrush, a third to try on my glove.

July 13.—Notwithstanding unusual care in my driver and leader, the waggon was again capsized in going down a difficult hill; the danger of which was concealed by the long grass. The driver who was on the box was thrown off, and narrowly escaped with his life. My family also had got out at the top of the hill, according to custom; otherwise they might have been seriously hurt. This was a new occasion for thanksgiving to the God of our life, who encompasses us about with mercies. Arrived by moonlight at the settlement of Cane, an Englishman. We now entered a country which was partially inhabited; the natives living under the protection of different English settlers, whom they regarded as their chiefs; these natives I understand, being the remains of various tribes.

14th.—Delighted to see the coast of Natal this day at noon, as we were travelling on the beach.

15th—The traces of three lions were distinctly seen on the sand this morning. Crossed the Umkomas river at low water. The descent was very difficult, but was accomplished without injury.

16th, *Sabbath.*—English service under the shade of a tree.

17th.—Arrived at Ogle's settlement, where we were detained by rain.

21st.—We completed our journey this day; arriving at Berea in the afternoon; having been about 12 weeks on our journey from Grahamstown, and six from Bunting. Took possession of the building erected by Capt. Gardiner for a school room.

August 5th.—Commenced my journey yesterday into the interior
of the Zoolu country, for the purpose of visiting the chief Dingarn.

18th and 19th.—Proceeded on our journey these days. On leaving
Congella, the road descends into the vale of the Umthlatoosi, after
crossing which stream it ascends some high mountains which form
a magnificent sight from Congella. The king being now at
Nobamba, his birth place, we proceeded toward that town. The
whole country there about is very populous, large towns being seen
in every direction. Immediately on our arrival and before we had
time to sit down, Dingarn sent for us. We were conducted into his
presence by persons duly authorised to perform this service. He
was seated inside of his Isikauthlo on a large chair. We stood
silently before him for about a minute. At length he saluted us in
the usual style and with a good humoured tone 'Dakubona' I see
you. He was clothed with a blanket not remarkable for its cleanliness and before him were strewed the presents which had been forwarded to him before our arrival, for his impatience to see them
was so great, that the bearers who carried them were directed by
Gambuji to go forward in advance. He began the conversation by
asking Capt. Gardiner many questions respecting the articles he
had brought with him. These engrossed for the moment his whole
attention. He told his women who were seated on some mats, that
I was the teacher who had brought him the cloth which they had
seen, for it had now been removed and deposited in one of the
King's huts. Everything was new and strange to me, and not being
called to speak, I had leisure to indulge my own reflections on the
character of that far famed despot in whose presence I now stood.
I observed the alacrity with which all his commands were obeyed.
On one occasion being in need of something which had been left
at Unkunginglovo, he said to his servant, 'Go, and be back before
the spit is dry in my hand,' and quick as lightning the order was
obeyed; the servant darting forth and vanishing in an instant.

20th, *Sabbath.*—I sent word to Dingarn in the morning to ask his
permission, as it was Sunday, to preach God's word to his people
in the large area in the centre of the town, or if he pleased to teach

in the Isikauthlo. He immediately returned answer that I was to
come to the Isikauthlo. Accordingly accompanied by Capt. Gardiner and our Interpreter I went. He was seated as yesterday on a
chair clothed with the same dirty blanket, his women came in and
sat on the ground. He was anxious that all his women should be
seated before I began. But having first learned [?] from Gambuji
the manner in which we pray, he begged me not to pray, but only
to preach as it would not be convenient for his women to kneel, the
design of my discourse was to show how God had given us his
word; first by plain instruction to a common ancestor—by whom
it was taught to his children—by them to their children and so
forth, till at last, mankind becoming forgetful of God, he sent
Prophets one after another, whom he first instructed that they
might afterwards teach the world. Last of all he sent his own son,
whose superiority to all former Prophets I shewed, both in regard
to plainess and fulness of his instructions and his Divine nature. I
then enlarged a little on our blessed Saviour's life, character,
doctrines, miracles and death. I then said he was laid in a grave
and on the third day God raised him up again—that he was seen
by his Apostles with whom he did eat and drink. At the mention
of the resurrection of Christ, Dingarn, who had been very attentive throughout smiled—it was a smile I have no doubt of
incredulity—thus did his incredulous mind lay hold of that very
doctrine, which in the first promulgation of the Gospel was
accounted foolishness and was the chief ground of opposition—
tho' the basis on which the truth of xtianity rested. He here interrupted me and asked what Hell was. I was proceeding to speak of
it in Scripture language, as a place where the fire is not quenched
—when he again interrupted me and asked where Hell was. I said
the word of God did not tell where Hell was, but only that there
was such a place. I then glided into the solemn account of the last
Judgement contained in those words 'when the son of man shall
come in his glory, etc.' After I had read a few verses, he said he
wanted to have the word more explained. I then enlarged on every
clause in this description. The design of Christ's second coming,
the glory with which he would come, the throne on which he would
sit and all nations coming before him. He asked what sort of a

[267]

throne? I said a great white one. He asked who were they that would rise up again, whether we, pointing to his women, shall rise again, what bodies we shall come with, whether we shall see one another and know one another again. Some of these questions he repeated and I gave such answers as the Ss furnished me with. He seemed to think it incredible that if the dead should be raised again, not knowing the power of God. Finally he said, why dont the dead get up now? that we may see them—to which I replied that God had appointed the day, and now he commanded all men everywhere to repent. I read also part of the 3rd chap of 2nd Peter, concerning the last day—and am persuaded that though he does not believe—yet he cannot venture to deny the truth of the resurrection. Not a word was spoken at this interview unconnected with the special design of it. Afterwards I sent word to the head Indoona, that I wished to have some conversation with him. He at first seemed rather astonished at my visit and at a loss to know what I could want with him. He was however very civil presently, but manifested thorough indifference to religious instruction. In the afternoon I sent word to the king to request he would give me permission to teach the same words publickly to his people, which I had taught him in the morning. To this message however no answer was returned. So passed the first Sabbath I had spent in the heart of a Zoolu town.

August 21st.—Dingarn sent for us early in the morning. He was now seated outside of the Isikauthlo, the cloth which I had brought being laid at his side. He promised that when the army returned a hut should be built at Congella, on any site to be pointed out to the Indoona of that town on our return home. Before finally dismissing us he sent forth his servants who with loud voices called all the men of the town together in a very short time. When they were all seated to the number of 300 or 400 he told me that I might now preach the same words to them which I had spoken yesterday, and begged me to go forward and stand in the midst of them. Dingarn on this occasion was not attentive and even drew away the attention of my audience by making sport with a blind man whom he *beckoned* in ridicule to come to him and presently bade

[268]

him go and look for something. The poor fellow stumbled about, run against me, and fell over my auditory, who I fear were little benifitted by my instructions. I felt grieved; but did not feel myself sufficiently at liberty to speak to Dingarn on the subject, He ordered bearers to carry our baggage to the Tugala and sent Gambuji with us to show me the hut which he had begun to build for me. It is on the top of a hill commanding a view of the whole town, from which it is distant about a mile and a half. A stream of water washes the foot of the hill; but trees, shrubs and everything conducive to comfort or beauty seem to be far away. Capt. Gardiner had selected a hill on the other side of the town, where there were some trees and which would have been a more pleasant and advantageous situation; but Dingarn changed the site on the plea that I should be too near the place where his women go to bathe; and he wishes me to be on an eminence, that he may view our buildings from the Isikauthlo, and spy with his telescope. The door of the hut is very high, so that it only requires us to bend our backs to enter and not to crawl on our knees and almost, in a manner, to break our backs as in the common huts.

Aug. 22nd and 23rd.—Pursued our journey homeward nearly by the same route which we came.

25th. Reached the Tugala which we crossed without difficulty, the water having subsided. The same hut was appropriated to us which we occupied before, but I had little sleep on account of the rats.

28th.—Arrived at Berea at 9 oclock in the evening, having been 12 hours on the road; my poor horse being completely knocked up by his long journey, but I had the joy of once more returning home to my family and finding all well. The distance from Port Natal to Unkunginglovo is estimated at about 150 miles.

Sept 10th, *Sabbath.*—Having given notice at Mr. Cane's store, that there would be a service today at Berea at noon and requested the attendance of both white people and black, as early as 9 oclock a considerable number of natives attended, enough to fill the large room which I occupied. Another body of natives assembled at 11 and at the specified time about ½ dozen white people arrived, to whom I read the English service and expounded. In the afternoon the natives assembled again. I was much pleased at the great readiness of the natives to be taught the word of God. I can scarcely doubt that at Berea, if due notice were given, there would be every sabbath day a large and quiet audience of natives from all parts.

14th.—Having been making preparations during the last fortnight for a waggon journey to the capital of the Zoolu nation where I had determined to fix my residence as well as employing myself by means of my Interpreter and a native servant in the study of the language, we commenced loading our vehicles this afternoon.

Oct. 10th.—Arrived at Umkunginglovo about noon.

Oct. 27th. Dingarn sent for me in the morning to read the letter from the Boers to Umthela who was seated at his feet. Neither of them made any observations on the letter in my presence, but Dingarn seemed more than ever to admire the mystery of writing and by the action of his fingers as if holding a pen intimated his great anxiety to be able to write. As he held the letter in his hand gazing at it with astonishment I offered to explain to him the antiquity of writing, in doing which I was led to remark that God had written his commandments on two tables of stone which he had given to his people, that they might observe them. I was in hopes that he would ask me what these commandments were, but he made no reply and took up his card which was lying on the ground and began to read. He had so far practised it by himself that he was now able to read every word without a mistake, tho' doubtless as all other beginners in a great measure by rote. He then called for some pictures and wished me to show him how they were drawn. By the messengers whom the king despatched to Capt. Gardiner, I wrote a letter requesting him to send the powder by them. In the evening Dingarn sent for me again, and as I guessed

[270]

that his object was that I might explain to him the art of writing, I took with me a volume of the Encyclopaedia, containing that article, shewing him prints of the eyes, ears, etc. of the human body, which I thought would satisfy him, but he asked if I had drawn them all today and hearing they were not my doing, he wished me to exhibit my proficiency in this art. I shewed him some plates in the encyclopaedia, particularly of the diving bell, and explained to him its principle and use. With this he was much pleased and told me to explain it to his women, for we were inside of the Isikauthlo. These poor creatures then gathered round, but being as destitute of sense as they are without God, instead of given me an opportunity of administering to them any sort of intellectual pleasure they did nothing but gaze on me and my dress: and whilst I was talking one of them succeeded in capturing a ribbon that was tied round my hat. Beyond their beads and ornaments they seem not to have a thought.

Nov. 19th, *Sabbath*.—Having erected a high pole yesterday near the station, at sun-rise this morning hoisted a white flag, to give notice that it was Sunday, but the wind blew so strong and cold from the South, that I did not think it advisable to go down to the king, to ask permission to preach to him as I intended.

Nov. 26th, *Sabbath*.—The most memorable at the same time most painful day since the commencement of the Mission. About 8 o'clock when I was preparing to go down to the town in order to preach the word of God (as I hoped) before the king, he sent a messenger to tell me that he was much displeased; that he expected the Teachers would instruct him in *all* things: however, they chose to select certain things which they would teach him, but would not instruct him in that which he most wanted to know, alluding to fire arms: therefore, I might indeed come down this once and preach God's words in the town, but this should be the last time the children might come to me on Sundays, but this was all he would grant. I thought this message strange, but made no reply to it, as I was myself ready to start to the king Dr. Wilson accompanied me. When we arrived he was sitting as usual in the

[271]

open area outside the fence of his Isikauthlo: a number of his servants sitting by him on the ground, and the rest of the men of the town at some distance ready to commence their breakfast, consisting of bowls of native beer, which the women bring every morning from a long distance. It was the first time I had seen the men partake of the beer, tho' I had constantly met the women carrying it on their heads, who as they proceed one after the other thro' the town to the Isikauthlo where it is deposited make a practice of singing. Instead of the Christian practice of giving thanks to the Father of all mercies before meals, these men praise their king for his bounty, shaking their fingers in the air, making a hizzing noise with their teeth and shouting out Bayet 'Our Father.' Dingarn having in vain endeavoured to extract from my Interpreter what my sentiments were on his message this morning, called me to him, and said that he was *very sore*. The white people, he said, were not *one with him*. They granted him some things, but other things they withheld (alluding to the gunpowder): yet he was ready to do all the white people asked him: first one teacher asked to instruct his people, then another, and he granted all! Yet he could not have his wants supplied in return! He said, moreover, that I was like the rest: that I was one with the white people; for when he asked me only to *lend* him a bullet mould, I refused, this shewed that I was like them. I told him that I was ready to do him every service in my power, consistently with my duty to my God, my king, and my country. He said it was no use for me to 'twist myself out' of the charge that he brought against the white people, for it was evident that I opposed his having fire arms as much as they did. I told him I did not mean to twist myself out of this charge, that I desired his good, chiefly the good of his Soul, which I had come in the first place to promote, and that I was prepared to teach him anything else besides God's word consistently with my duty to my country. He said it was in vain for me to shelter myself under the pretence that I desired his good, because I did not lend him the bullet mould. At length I told him it was Sunday, whereupon he bid me to address his people and teach them the word of God. At the same time he sent Masipulu, his head servant to tell the Indoonas that they were all to be quiet

Interior of Dingaarn's House

and listen to me. A dead pause immediately ensued. I went forward, feeling in my heart, that I was called to testify Christ publickly in this place for the last, and the only time! Having advanced within a convenient distance from the men, the king sitting a good way behind, I commenced by telling them that they all knew that there was a great chief above the sky. Dingarn now sent a message to us to tell us to speak up, as we did at Nabamba. Raising our voices I proceeded to say that this king was greater than all kings, greater than my king, greater than their king: that they ought to fear their parents, they ought to fear their king, but much more ought they to fear the great God; they ought to do what their parents bid them, what their king bid them, and also what God bid them! We have none of us, however, done what God has told us to do. We are all sinners before him: He is displeased at us: each of us has a soul that must live for ever when the body is dead, but that our Souls, by reason of sin, are filthy and that they must be *washed*. Until this moment the greatest stillness and attention prevailed, but now the contradiction began, and such a cavilling and stormy audience never did I before address. It is an impossible to give an adequate idea of the dispute which lasted for nearly 2 hours; one cavil succeeded another or was repeated 10 times, whilst no reply was made to my answers. The indoonas and the king were the chief objectors, the latter sitting at some distance behind and speaking low, his servant Masipulu shouted out to my Interpreter all his remarks. First I had to turn to the Indoonas, then to the king as they successively opposed me. When I had begun to speak of the need of spiritual washing in order to introduce the Gospel the subject was treated with scorn. One asked if we were to be washed in the river. I said not with water, but with blood! Whose blood was the natural reply. The blood, I answered of the Son of God, who was Jesus Christ. Where is he? they asked. In heaven, I said, but once he came down to earth, and . . . Whom did he leave behind to wash us? He washes us himself with his own blood. It is not our bodies that he washes but our Souls.—He washes all to come to him by faith. Away, its all a lie. I persisted in crying that Jesus Christ shed his blood, and that if they believed in him, that he came down from heaven, that he died for

s.—18 [273]

them, their souls would be saved. Dingarn asked me how many days Jesus Christ had been dead. If only 3 days (said he), it is very likely that he was not dead in reality but only *supposed* to be so! I said, that when he was on the tree a soldier pierced his side from which came forth blood, and that blood, I said, if believed in washes away sin. After a great deal more combat they told me I need not speak anything more about the resurrection, for they would not believe it. They had no objection to God's word, but they did not believe in the resurrection. At length they told me to say no more about the dead—leave them where they are, *go to the sick* and keep them from dying, for this is easier than to raise the dead. It is impossible to relate all that I said and all that they said. Whether all this contradiction was designed or not I cannot tell. Dingarn at length told me that the sun was hot and that I must tell him when I had done. I many times broke away from their cavillings and exhorted them to believe instead of objecting. The king once asked if all men would go to heaven? I told them plainly, if you believe the words which I now speak you will go to heaven, but if you believe them not you will all go to hell. They wanted me to give a proof that Christ was now in heaven; as who had seen him there. What the persons who took him up into heaven said when they came back again.

English service in the afternoon in the hut. In the evening I had a conversation with Shlay-kay-la, the king's servant who ordinarily comes on messages to me. He said he loved God exceedingly and he loved me too, and therefore it was that he now asked me for a cloak, tho' he confessed this was not so necessary for him as the forgiveness of his sins, and he did not mean to turn the discourse away from God. On the whole, however discouraging the day was, before I closed my eyes in sleep, I felt by the grace of God more disposed to remain at this place than ever. I realised the almighty power of Divine grace which is able to introduce the kingdom of the Redeemer, notwithstanding all the contempt and opposition of the rulers. The despotic Dingarn himself, who has so much con trol over his subjects and holds them fast in bonds of the most servile obedience cannot hinder them from embracing the truth if God's will, and the cause is his! Tho I despair of being able for a

[274]

long time of being able to minister public instruction to the people, yet I conceived that the indirect methods of conveying truth by private conversation with the natives are various, and I felt strongly disposed to seek and avail myself of opportunities for this purpose, waiting still to see the salvation of the Lord, and in what an unexpected way he will accomplish the purposes of his grace.

Feb. 2nd, 1838.—Dingarn sent for me at sunrise to write a letter to Mr. Retief, who with a party of the Boers is now on his way to the Zoolu capital. The letter was characteristic of the chief. He said that his heart was now content, because he had got his cattle again: he requested that the chief of the Boers would send to all his people and order them to come up to the capital with him, *but without their horses*: he promised to gather together all his army to sing and dance in the presence of the Dutch, who he desired would also dance: he said we would give orders that cattle should be slain for them in every place thro' which they passed on their road, and he promised to give them a country. The Dutch will be too wise to expose themselves in the manner proposed, but I cannot conceive that Dingarn *meditates* any treachery, which, however, he would have the power (if he chose) to exercise toward them, should they venture to come.

Feb. 3rd.—Large parties of Zooloos in their war dress were yesterday evening entering the town. This morning when we were at family prayers the unusual sound of muskets was heard from the west; this proved to be the arrival of the Boers who presently entered the town on horseback with their guns in their hands. An immense concourse of Zooloos were present to receive them. The deputation (in number about 60) brought with them the cattle which they had recovered from Sinkoyella. The Boers immediately shewed Dingarn the way in which they danced on horseback by making a sham charge at one another making the air resound with their guns. This was something the Zoolu chief had never witnessed. In their turn the Zooloos exhibited their agility in dancing. About noon I paid a visit to Mr. Retief, who with his party (after the amusement was over) were seated under the Euphorbia trees fronting the gate of the town. The answer he gave to Dingarn when he demanded the guns and horses was to show the messengers his grey hairs and bid him to tell his master that he was not dealing with a child. A tribe which has nearly been destroyed by the Zooloos has claimed the protection of the Boers. Three chiefs and about 650 men, the remnant of those who have at various times been slain, have been taken at their earnest request under the protection of the Dutch: it has been the practice of Dingarn to send an army against them every 2 or 3 years by which means all their young men have been cut off.

Feb. 6th.—A dreadful day in the annals of the mission! My pen shudders to give an account of it. This morning as I was sitting in the shade of my waggon reading the Testament, the usual messenger came with hurry and anxiety depicted in his looks. I was sure he was about to pronounce something serious, but what was his commission! Whilst it shewed consideration and kindness in the Zooloo monarch towards me, it disclosed a horrid instance of perfidy—too horrid to be described—towards the unhappy men who have for these three days been his guests, but are now no more. He sent to tell me not to be frightened as he was going to kill the Boers. The news came like a thunder stroke to myself and to every successive member of my family as they heard it. The reason assigned for this treacherous conduct was that they were going to kill him, that they had come here and he had *now* learned all their plans. The messenger was anxious for my reply, but what could I say? Fearful on the one hand of seeming to justify the treachery and on the other of exposing myself and my family to probable danger if I appeared to take their part. Moreover I could not but feel that it was my duty to apprize the Boers of the intended massacre whilst certain death would have ensued (I apprehended) if I had been detected in giving them this information. However, I was released from this dilemma by beholding an awful spectacle! My attention was directed to the blood stained hill nearly opposite my hut and on the other side of my waggon, which hides it from my view, where all the executions at this fearful spot take place and which was now destined to add 60 more

Francis Owen

bleeding carcases to the number of those which have already cried to Heaven for vengeance. There (said some one), they are killing the Boers *now*. I turned my eyes and behold! an immense multitude on the hill. About 9 or 10 Zoolus to each Boer were dragging their helpless unarmed victim to the fatal spot, where those eyes which awakened this morning to see the cheerful light of day for the last time, are now closed in death. I lay myself down on the ground. Mrs. and Miss Owen were not more thunderstruck than myself. We each comforted the other. Presently the deed of blood being accomplished the whole multitude returned to the town to meet their sovereign, and as they drew near to him set up a shout which reached the station and continued for some time. Meanwhile, I myself, had been kept from all fear for my personal safety, for I considered the message of Dingarn to me as an indication that he had no ill designs against his Missionary, especially as the messenger inflomed that the Boer's Interpreter, an Englishman from Port Natal, was to be preserved. Nevertheless, fears afterwards obtruded themselves on me, when I saw half a dozen men with shields sitting near our hut, and I began to tremble lest we were to fall the next victims! At this crisis I called all my family in and read the 91st Ps., so singularly and literally applicable to our present condition, that I could with difficulty proceed in it! I endeavoured to realize all its statement and tho' I did not receive it as an obsolute provision against sudden and violent death, I was led to Him who is our refuge from the guilt and fear of sin, which alone make Death terrible. We then knelt down and I prayed, really not knowing but that in this position we might be called into another world. Such was the effect of the first gust of fear on my mind. I remembered the words, 'Call upon me in the day of trouble and I will hear thee.' But of the Boers, Dingarn, the Mission, the Providence of God, I had other thoughts. Two of the Boers paid me a visit this morning and breakfasted only an hour or two before they were called into Eternity. When I asked them what they thought of Dingarn, they said he was good: so unsuspicious were they of his intentions. He had promised to assign over to them the whole country between the Tugala and the Umzimvubu rivers, and this day the paper of transfer was to be signed.

[277]

I have seen by my glass that Dingarn has been sitting most of the morning since this dreadful affair in the centre of his town, an army in several divisions collected before him. About noon the whole body *run* in the direction from which the Boers came. They are (I cannot allow myself to doubt) sent to fall or to join others who have been ordered to fall unawares on the main body of the Boers who are encamped at the head of the Tugala, for to suppose that Dingarn should murder this handful and not make himself sure of the whole number with their guns, horses and cattle would be to conceive him capable of egregious folly, as he must know that the other Boers will avenge the death of their countrymen. Certain it is as far as human foresight can judge, we shall speedily hear either of the massacre of the whole company of Boers, or what is scarcely less terrible of wars and bloodshed, of which there will be no end till either the Boers or the Zoolu nation cease to be.

Feb. 7th.—In the morning two Indoonas with an attendant called. One of them patted his breast, a common gesticulation of friendship. No Indoona had ever been to the station before and they asked to see the hut, waggon, etc. They were remarkably civil. They had been sent by the king to inform me that it was not his intention to kill either me or the other missionaries, for we had come into his country by *fews* and *fews*: he could live in peace with us, for we were his people. All George's people, meaning the British were his, i.e., he liked them, but the Amaboro were not his people: nor were they George's. He said that all the *armies* that came into his country should be killed, that the Amaboro were going to kill the king: they had come like an army and had fallen into a passion with him. I said little in reply to the king. I remarked that I had come into his country only to teach the Book: that I was not a fighting person, as those who taught the Book in my country did not handle the gun.

I did not give an adequate description of the dreadful carnage yesterday. I omitted to state that many of the Boers had children with them, some under 11 years of age, as I am informed, as these were all butchered. They also had their Hottentot servants and these were likewise slaughtered besides their Interpreter and his servant. The number of slain must have been nearer a hundred than sixty, but if there had been ten hundred it would have been all the same.

Feb. 11th, *Sabbath.*—The sacredness of the day did not I considered put any obstacle in the way of our departure.

Feb. 27th.—Arrived in the evening at the Tugala, which we found very full.

March 3rd.—A half pipe barrel having been fastened inside the empty waggon, the oxen swam across the river without a leader, drawing the floating vehicle after them.

March 4th, *Sabbath.*—The settlers at Port Natal intend commencing immediate war with Dingarn and to unite with them all the black people at the settlement.

March 8th.—Arrived at Ambanati, where we were joyfully welcomed by our friends and congratulated on our merciful preservation thro' the country, as the Natal expedition was in contemplation and might have reached the ears of Dingarn before we crossed the boundary.

March 13th.—In the afternoon the Natal army departed. It was a thousand strong, and headed by several of the settlers. Many, however, of these staid behind. About 100 of the natives carried guns. The black people are generally the remains of various conquered tribes. Many of them were formerly chiefs. A declaration of war has been formally declared by the Natal settlers against Dingarn.

April 17th.—A sad and awful day. I took a long walk in the morning chiefly with the view of visiting some more of Mr. Ogle's villages. On arriving at the first I saw a young warrior, and on my asking him and the women who were about whether they would like to be taught, he returned answer that the whole commando

[279]

had been destroyed by the Zulus and that all the white men were killed, particularly naming Cane. I pursued my walk to Mr. Ogle's own village, but ere I arrived the sound of weeping and lamentation met my ear. I entered Mr. Ogle's hut where a great number of natives were assembled. He himself had not gone out this time to fight and he now acquainted me with the various reports which he had heard which tho' differing in many particulars all agreed in this that there had been a great slaughter both of the natives and white people. He had scarcely begun to tell me what had happened when a native woman arrived bringing further intelligence at which all the women in the village set up loud cries and wailings, running in all directions crying in their own language. Alas! Alas! As yet no man had arrived from the commando who had actually seen the fight, but in a few minutes a warrior arrived with his gun, having fled 75 miles in a day and a half from the very scene of action. The intelligence he brought corroborated the former reports respecting the general massacre of white people and black and now the scene was heart rending beyond all example. The tumultuous cries of the distressed women whose husbands were supposed to have been slaughtered made the air to resound. One woman was seen walking with her hands at the back of her head crying mournfully 'Booya Baba,' return my father. An English woman among the rest was almost frantic with grief.

On board the Comet, Port Natal, April 26th, 1838.
My dear Sir,

It is with deep regret and great disappointment I inform you of the painful necessity which puts an end (at least for the present) to our mission at Port Natal. The settlers have most of them been killed, as I informed you in my last, together with about 400 of the natives. The Boers have invaded Dingarn's country, but failed of making that impression on him which they anticipated. Whilst I write the Zulus are actually at Port Natal, the whole country is at their disposal—there being no one to oppose them. They have been here since Monday the 23rd inst. We see them plainly from the vessel with our glasses. The natives having fled to the bush to conceal themselves from the enemy and escape death. They have been at Berea—but have not yet fired it. I expect to loose such of my property as is there and when the vessel goes, the store at the point which contains more will also be ransacked. Whatever is useful to the natives will probably be carried away by them—everything else fired. We have lost all our cattle in common with the other inhabitants, but thank God our lives have been preserved. If the gracious Providence of our God had not sent a ship into the bay, Mrs. and Miss Owen with Mrs. Hewitson must, as well as ourselves, have been concealed in the bush—but we are now safe in the ship. There is no course left for us to pursue but to take our passage to Delagoa Bay and from thence to the Colony.

John Sheddon Dobie

John Sheddon Dobie was a Scot. He was born in 1819 at Beith, Ayrshire, and, along with an elder brother, was destined for the law by his father, a Writer to the Signet and a Fellow of the Society of Antiquaries of Scotland. But law did not appeal to him, and neither, apparently, did veterinary surgery, which he tried as a substitute, and he soon left England on the first lap of a long and varied course.

He went first of all to New South Wales and took a run on the Yarra with a squatter's licence. But almost immediately a fall in prices forced him to sell. He passed on to California. Here he worked in the gold fields (it was 1851) for a while, but after a few months was off for the Hawaiian Islands on a trading venture.

By this time Australia had its own gold rush and in 1852 Dobie was back there. He combined gold digging and cattle farming with considerable success until bad luck hit him again. In 1861 squatting privileges were largely cancelled by the ruling that a farmer desiring land to bring it under actual cultivation could choose it where he liked, even if it were in the middle of a cattle run. So Dobie went to Natal, leaving, however, his name attached to a stone bridge across the Hopkins River on the Ballarat road.

A friend, Henry Bucknall, was a passenger on the same ship, and they decided to join forces. But even in Natal Dobie preferred not to stand still, and though he was deeply interested in the unsolved problems of sheep farming in Natal, he clearly enjoyed most of all the three journeys he made overland to the Cape in search of stock. And always this bluff, quick-tempered individualist was as ready to bring out his sketchbook before a good piece of mountain scenery as his gun at the sight of a springbok.

Circumstances beyond his control were once more an excuse to be moving. Over-speculation led to a slump in Natal, and in 1865 Dobie crossed to South America. He was on the point of settling down on an estancia in Uruguay when his mother inherited a property which she required his assistance in managing.

Back in Ayrshire again, he stayed there, dying in 1903 at the age of eighty-four.

The journal, with several of the black-and-white sketches that adorned it, was edited in 1945 by Professor Alan F. Hattersley for the Van Riebeeck Society. He had to cut it down by about one half. Dobie himself said that ' Along with my rifle, powder flask, bullet patch box and compass, small bags for collecting seeds, pencils, stump and india rubber, the notebook had its corner in my hunting wallet, and was always ready at a moment's notice.' The journal was written in a series of these notebooks.

Wednesday, 3rd September, 1862. [Approaching] Pieter-Maritzburg! Looks pretty well in the distance, situated on a low ridge underneath the high line of the next tableland. The rows of houses are broken and adorned by many tall dark spires, which my informant tells me are blue gum trees, not unlike Lombardy poplars in deep mourning! The other trees (seringas) being now bare of leaf give the city a rather naked appearance. As we approach nearer, the view of it is curtailed as our road descends gently into a broad flat valley leading us to a goodly stream of water, called Umsinduzi, which we cross on a suspension bridge, and we are in town about 5. It appears well laid off—streets at right angles, houses of brick, slated, tiled or thatched. Dismounted at 'The Crown' and walked to Pitcher's Hotel, where the two Bucknalls are to meet me, and they soon came in. The younger brother Fred, a pleasant looking lad. They think of renting a 6,000 acre farm about twenty miles further up country, which has been offered to them for £30 per annum; sheep are said to do well there. They have arranged to start with their own wagon and Kafirs, etc., through Kafirland to the Eastern Province of the Cape, where better sheep can be had and for half the price at which they can be bought here. Go through Nomansland, see that unoccupied country, which may do for squatting—buy sheep in the 'Old Colony' and, if the season gets too far advanced, return on the other side of the Drakensberg chain of mountains through the Free State, thereby avoiding the many rivers which have to be crossed on this side and become frequently impassable after the summer rains have set in. Proposed that I make one of the party, each to have his own horse and rifle, shoot, sketch, see the country, study the manners and customs of ye people and speculate in sheep, if I have a mind to do so. Agreed.

Sat. 6. The great difficulty here, appears to be labour; the supply of Kafirs cannot be depended on; they won't work, and the laws are too favourable, rendering them too easily independent. It is a serious offence to strike a Kafir. Loud outcries against the Governor and missionaries. At some of the mission stations Kafir girls are dressed up and treated as ladies while white women do the work for them! This, if true, is really preposterous, entirely reversing the order of civilization.

Mon. 8. Crossing the square the royal standard floated from a pole erected on what to all appearance seemed a very mediocre tomb, railed in with iron hurdles. On closer inspection it turned out to be the foundation stone laid by H.R.H. Prince Alfred on his visit in 1860, and of which eventful day this is the anniversary! For what particular purpose it was laid I could not discover; possibly, Natal-like, it might have come in handy some day! There it is, pretty much as he left it, a little *greener* perhaps. I say Natal-like. The whole Colony seems set agoing on the same principle. Farmers, or would-be farmers, rushed out and bought land. Speculators bought land, without knowing what to turn it to, or what it was fit for, on the chance of something turning up! Since the cattle were cleared off by pleuro-pneumonia, what have they done? Next to nothing! They have the land and the stone ready, but the structure has yet to be built! Sugar and coffee are on trial, sheep ditto, and I believe may do under proper management. But the farmers, properly so called, the agriculturalists, have as yet found little or nothing to do. Their standard crops are 'forage' and 'mealies,' otherwise called oat hay and maize, a marketable produce limited to the demand of the Colony. Wheat won't grow, at least it does not come to maturity as it ought to, being subject, owing to the constant rains in summer, to the affection called rust, which produces mildew and prevents the grain from filling properly. It is said that twenty bushels to the acre is considered a great return! This mainstay of the Anglo-Saxon has, in consequence, to be imported and is often at an exorbitant price. If sheep do not succeed here, the Colony to all appearance must go further to the wall.

Sun. 21. Up at daylight, greased wagon wheels and loaded up baggage. Had coffee, and started about 7. We three on horseback, two rifles, very imposing! Our party consists, besides our noble selves, of a young 'Africando,' Louis Norton, who speaks Kafir and Dutch, in charge of waggon, a Kafir, 'Phillip,' waggon driver, two other Kafirs, Skunguin and Lachan, foreloper and sheep driver when that time comes, waggon and span of five pair of oxen.

Wed. 24. Resolved, as there was some wood here, to spell and rig out the tent or tilt over waggon, without which it is not complete. This is generally done by the waggon maker and consists of a framework of wooden hoops with a neatly fitted canvas cover. The B.'s however preferred doing this themselves and make the framework of saplings with a canvas tarpaulin thrown over and lashed down to the sides as being better for roughing it and easier repaired in the event of a smash. Had a bathe in the little stream that joins the river at a pretty little fall. After breakfast tied a splice on the stock of my rifle, which had begun to show ugly symptoms of giving way at the knot in the wood. Then went fishing —lots of fish, but would not be caught. The stream reminded me of a Highland burn, with its rocks and falls and linns, but without

[285]

the ruddy wine-coloured water. Close to our camp a Dutchman's deserted house and orchard, in which were peach and lemon trees, from the latter got a specimen for our hot grog at night! A ruin in a new country; had a history no doubt and appealed to the imagination. Kafirs back with oxen, had strayed across river and a considerable distance homewards during the night. At mid-day assembled at waggon to dinner, after which and till night all hands employed in rigging tent. Waggon now looks ship-shape. The night however being very warm and fine took our sleep on the ground.

Fri.26. Waggon off a little after 3, but horses missing. Bucknalls after them while I mounted guard over saddles. When daylight came found them close to camp, and cooeed a recall! Travelled over like country and had shots at pau again, but no deaths. Camped for breakfast at a small stream and enjoyed a good wash. Altered sight of rifle and had a trial shot. On again, up a long hill, when I discovered to my great vexation that the bottom of my wallet had burst, had to turn back and search for lost contents. Luckily we had kept on the road and I found everything. Camped for dinner near top of tableland before descending to the valley of Umzimkhulu. Hot wind blowing strong,—fine view,—undulations more easy and longer than on Unkomanzi. Repaired wallet, which was a disgracefully rotten affair, dispensing with the thin leather bottom and sewing the two edges together, gives less room, but now strong. Guaranteed! On starting again rode to the highest point of the range and had a view of '*The Berg*' (Drakensberg) and 'Nomansland' as the tract of land adjoining Natal given up by the Chief Faku to the British Government, and still unoccupied, is called. Then descending into the valley, outspanned waggon and rode on to see Mr. Hancock, the resident official who inspects travellers, and reported ourselves. Asked to off-saddle. Found him a rather blunt and plain specimen, sort of half farmer, half policeman! Told us we would have bother with our guns and powder, but nothing more said about either. At tea, three more visitors arrived, a missionary-looking lot. Plenty of bread and butter, but no meat. H. has sheep here which he says do well, but don't increase their numbers much from cold and starvation in

[286]

winter. Saw them in the dusk, appeared to be a scabby lot and a great many old ones. Back to camp at 8, and all turned into waggon. The Kafirs now lie underneath, having a tarpaulin hung on weather side for a breakwind.

Fri. 17. October. Waggon off very early, and we lay down till daylight. Then on to another very pretty little plain. This plain like the other surrounded by the same picturesque outline of hills. H.B. had 2 shots at some springbuck about 150 and 200 yards off. Then through thorn wood and up a branch valley among kraals and mealie patches (maize plots) to a mission station on a little river called Bolota, very bare of feed, but mission shows a considerable amount of cultivation enclosed by turf-dykes. Camped for breakfast and had, as usual now, sundry great yabbers with the Kafirs! I called at mission and found it was named after St. John. Saw wool bales piled up and stored in verandah, and was shown a specimen of wool grown by Kafirs, pretty good but awfully short, sheer at all times to keep scab down. On up valley to the ridge, but could get no decided view of the plains, so did not stop. Down hill on a beautifully broad and smooth road, we will say nothing about the dust, and camped on the lee side of thorns. After dinner the farmer paid us a visit, a good-looking fellow, but decidedly like all I have seen, having a deuced seedy appearance, boots all worn out on the sole! Had been amusing himself playing cricket with Kafirs; says sheep are worth from 15/- to 16/-. Has some for sale for which he wants 14/-, a mixed lot up to four years old. Spell oh! for this day.

Sat. 18. Queenstown then hove in sight, prettily situated in a broad valley at the foot of ranges whose outlines would make a good sketch from any point, but such a beastly day for wind and dust it has never been my lot to experience. Got into town and to hotel with all my ideas blown clean away. Tried to walk out and see town life, but glad to get back again and at last gave it up altogether. Horses fed and we three dined at the table d'hôte, rather a rowdy lot, bowling bread from one end of the table to the other, very short of vegetables. Country getting into a state of famine from want of rain. It certainly looks a most forsaken land. After dinner managed to see the little place, which consists of streets at right angles, stone houses and willow trees lining the footpaths. A large church in course of erection. Altogether, though a good beginning, it is a very small potato affair. One sign attracted notice from its combining shoe making and hair dressing! Some boys shouted 'Oh Scissors!' at my trousers being drawn in and tied with string round the ankles of my boots. Otherwise I must say I was a seedy-looking cove with dirty white flannel coat, and what had been a white cocoa nut hat, but the tie round the ankles I consider a decided wrinkle to keep out the dust. Perhaps they have got to like it!

Mon. 20. Fine morning. Got myself up! putting on best blue, collar and peg-tops, so that young Queenstown should not ejaculate their slang at me! Saw some sheep, a mixed lot and small, 16/-, being shorn! Got horses very roughly shod, 10/-. Dined at hotel, a repetition of Saturday, behaving like ill-bred boys. Looked at shop windows and bought 6*d*. worth of dried-up-looking gum lozenges and 3*d*. worth of elastic bands. Dinner, drink and horse feed, 3/3. Then off to see another flock on our way back; proved a scabby lot, mixed and small also, some well bred, but great mixture. To camp and shifted waggon further up gully of some thorn wood close under hill: wind blowing from cold quarter earlier and something like rain coming.

Tue. 21. Got ready for a riding trip, leaving Norton and the waggon camped here while we take a survey round by Cradock, etc. Started first to the south, down an awfully stony gully, to see a flock that is for sale. Such jumbles of broken rock the hills are composed of, little tufts of grass between. Found farmer had a stone house, stone fence and stone kraals (sheep yards); went in and had a cup of coffee and chat with wife and family; people here look kind of woebegone. Then led our horses over the stony hills to look for sheep. Proved like the others. Ewes, rams, lambs, wethers, etc., 10/6 all round. They went on farther up the hill to see another flock while I most thankfully took charge of the

[288]

Portrait of J. S. Dobie

A New Zealand Settler's Hut

horses! Ended in a purchase however. H.B. off to see and find a
place on some farm on which to run them till he is ready for return
start. Fred and I down off these cursed stones as soon as we could,
he into town, I to camp. H.B. did not return till late, having had
supper with some farmer, but unable to *do* any of them out of
grass! They have not got it for themselves.

Wed. 17. December. [At end of return journey] Kept morning
watch for Fred, from 12 to 4. Sheep had been rushing a good deal
about, but nothing could be seen. Supposed to be jackals. Fire
sticks had been thrown about to scare them. During first of my
watch they began again, when I discharged rifle and neither saw
nor heard more of them, and sheep were undisturbed. One of those
provoking foggy nights when it is impossible to see anything,
among long grass, too Turned them out to the sound of the bugle-
horn at 4, and after breakfast away across some low ranges and
crossing Lion's river and tributaries for the farm—4 miles off. Got
first sight of it over a rocky range. A bare solitary-looking affair
with peculiar ends. Two Kafir huts in front broke the monotony!
Cotswold, something like that note above! By and by, however,
we shall make a sketch of it, after it has had some master touches
around it! When we got to it, found it in a very unfinished state.
Carpenter at work on floor, windows unglazed, and chimney top
not even carried through thatch. Has been very slovenly built.
Sandstone and loam for foundation, and sun-dried bricks for
upper walls. Makings of a nice place as it stands on a rise in a
gully with good slopes to carry off water and for a garden and
sheep yards, and there is a running burn and little waterfall on its
right front. Had a stroll, botanical, and picked up a few seeds of
old acquaintances. Got that of the little purple iris, but could not
see anything of that pretty graceful blue one. On coming back
found the poor waggon like some ship that has got into port, dis-
mantled of her canvas and reduced to her stumps. Stowed contents
inside house. Soon got enough dead wood collected. The 'yellow
wood' of the country, fine tall trees, a species of the yew, wood
very inferior, neither so close hard or tough or so prettily marked,
more like pine. Picked up seed of a pretty vine leaved like lime

tree growing a round flat, edible berry. Fog came on, and we gave up the intention of riding round farm. At supper, carpenter gave us 4 eggs, so we had cold mutton, bread and butter and eggs!!! Turned in on floor and did not feel at home with so much room to spare.

Thu. 18. Very foggy morning. Henry, Norton and Phillip went to bush to cut fencing stuff for the sheep yards. I tidying up, shovelling stones and rubbish into a big whole in front of verandah when Fred and Mr. Methley (owner of this farm) hove in sight. Seems a pleasant sort of man. Have had fearful thunderstorms and hail down below. Mr. M. went off home in afternoon, 30 miles, not bad for a Natal man and horse! Day been clear with wind. Fog again in evening. Settlement with Kafirs, great talk.

Fri. 19. House here in great mess between carpenter and plasterer. The whole of the work done in very Africando style, the walls above stonework very thin and uneven, the fireplaces all built of sun-dried brick and very small—kitchen one absurdly so—the beams warped all ways, and the woodwork in keeping with the masonry. Looks altogether a very tumble-down affair, a good Queenstown gale would lay it flat! Thunder in afternoon and then fog and drizzle, made a 'Noah's binnacle lamp,' an old lobster tin half filled with clay, wick rolled round a peg stuck in centre and filled up with melted tallow. Had a light to read the remains of a N.B. Daily Mail, containing summing-up of Judge Deas in Sandyford murder case,—but part gone.

Sat. 20. Nasty dull morning and kept so all day, the mist barely rising to show dimly McKenzie's bush. In afternoon fog set in again and thunder and lightning with rain at and after sundown. Bucknalls have also rented another farm from Methley, considerably lower down, near Noodsberg, for a winter farm. A number of Kafirs are located on it, who have to supply a certain number of young men for working at the usual wages. This afternoon three Kafirs arrived from the farm. A little boy 'Dot,' for house and cook's mate, at 3/- per month—a bigger lad for shepherd, 4/-, and a tall young man for all work at 6/-. Fred rode to McKenzie's for sugar and suet, out of meat, to have plum pudding tomorrow.

Wed. 24. Beautiful day, waggon arrived about mid-day. Great unpacking and overhauling of its contents, made our room like a store. Have had very wet weather in town, and, gratifying fact! some people enquiring what had become of me. Carpenter has made a table, and a sort of rocking unstable-footed bench for a seat gives a furnished look to the establishment! Great preparations for Christmas. Norton set to work as chief baker and a currant cake the consequence, lots of currants and raisins, but when we hunted for salt, which we are just out of, could find it nowhere: a lucky thought suggested the rock salt got for sheep and it was impounded accordingly. Set up the grindstone, Phillip assisting me, etc. Day kept up beautiful, clear and cloudy by turns. Fog at sundown.

Thu. 25. CHRISTMAS—dawned clear and bright and kept so all day. Had a great set to, plum pudding making. Had three visitors come to see sheep. Had a jolly good dinner, boiled corned beef and pudding, then raisins and almonds and a nip, oh dear, it wanted two! I felt quite unfit for any exertion and lay down on the floor of the house. Very warm; Henry rode out with the strangers to see the sheep, when they departed. Day kept fine till sunset, no fog, only a haziness from heat. Couldn't sleep at night, what between heat and pudding!

Sun. 28. Wet all day, principal occupations, gun cleaning, touching up sketches and eating! Phillip brought in remains of a sheep that he found in the sluit opposite, head down and all the body eaten bare.

Wed. 31. Sheep shearing begins! Some of the rams from Norton's not having their wool off, all hands set to work and got them done by dinner time, 24 rams to 4 shearers. Backs all very bad! Barking posts and rails in afternoon. Weather been cloudy, ending in

thunder and fog. Last night another sheep killed and eaten, supposed to be the foul deed of a leopard or panther, vulgarly called
tigers in this country, but on examination pronounced to be
jackals. Two jackals have been killed by the poisoned baits laid
for them. Footprint found in cowdung however seemed to argufy
the point in favour of 'tiger.'

Mon. 6. April, 1863. Took my departure for Gray's and Moncreiff's about 10. Over the low undulating style of country towards
a point of table land, the road turning round the point, divided
into three tracks. Two very large blocks of sandstone layers were
lying a long way from base of hill. Been detached at some earlier
shaky period and getting on their edge must have made a splendid
rolling! Called at sundry kraals to make sure of road but found the
Kafirs as usual a pig-headed stupid lot of brutes. Followed a fresh
waggon track, till crossing a stream, lost it, but an umfazi (married
woman) made me understand I was on the right road. Descending
into other valley got sight of gum trees (a sure mark of a farm) but
found it was 'David's' old place and had to go on a little further,
arriving at my destination at sundown. Found Gray a very decent,
well-informed and well-to-do Lanarkshire man, near Cathkin, after
which he has named the highest near point of the Berg. Gray
thinks this the cream of the country and good for sheep, no frost
here and in the valleys, under shelter of Berg, grass is in abundance all winter. What a bore this horse sickness is, a horse feeding
on grass at night almost sure to die, and here David has no stable
room.

Tue. 7. Up early but no breakfast till late. Note, in order to get
over ground, a morning's trek, after coffee, is decidedly advisable.
Gray branding cattle, stayed and saw *modus operandi*. Catching
performed by two Dutchmen aided by Kafirs, no posts, head
roped and leg roped, hauling and holding on by hand. One big
beast broke away altogether, and also another younger one; had
to get waggon into yard and make them fast to it; gave them a few
wrinkles about branding, as it ought to be done from former
experience among a herd of 3,000, which made them stare! On,

after a light repast, for Moncreiff's, nearly opposite and under
Berg, crossed Impafana and several small boggy-looking burns and
got to the place at sundown. Pretty situation in a basin at the foot
of one of the spurs of the mountain which is dotted over with
sugar-bush and clumps of bush, and waterfalls in the ravines.
Found Moncreiff, a tall young fellow living in the very roughest
style, a Kafir hut and not a morsel to eat. Would not live like that
if I were to get the whole of Natal, but he seemed to fancy it and
think he was doing a heavy trick! Had a drink of coffee and gave
him a smoke! which he relished amazingly, and after yarning
awhile turned in all standing, he having only one blanket which I
positively refused to take, and we lay down on the hard floor!
Poor fellow, when he thought I was asleep, he got up and spread
the blanket over me.

Mon. 17. August. [On another trip, arriving at Queenstown.]
Camped at the stony ridge in the valley. After breakfast had a
wash and rigged out for city, I putting on a neck-tie in addition
to usual toggery! Pleasant day and no dust, and got in about 1.
Dinner at 2, some of the old faces and still talking cricket! Town
decidedly duller than formerly. Knocked about and made some
purchases, etc. At P.O. found a letter from Cape Secretary;
Governor directs him to say that the Transkeian lands will be
thrown open soon and that the conditions will be published in the
Gazette. No others. Bit 7/6. Lollies 1/6. Dinner 4/-. Beer 3/6. Saw
Wright and Hulley, who have both given up farming and living in
town. Only heard of one flock for sale—Parker's, ewes and lambs
15/-, the same we saw at the Fort yesterday and pronounced a very
inferior lot!! Subscribed for a bottle of 'smoke' (Cape brandy)
and out to waggon, camped on the bare plain as formerly, but
tonight beautifully quiet and clear, with young moonlight.

Wed. 19. This is market day in town, saw sale of young stock, 2-
year-old bulls, 29/-. At dinner, the rowdies were numerous; was
going to eat salad till I saw one respectable-looking party help
himself with his own knife and fork. Dodging about after dinner,
and bought a lady's leather belt for a hatband, 1/6. Saw Parker,

who offered us his trap and a pair of horses to drive out to Imvani
and see those sheep, also another mob at Waldek's, agreed for
Friday. Fell in with a young fellow who had been a wool-sorter in
Victoria, who strongly advised us to go to Cradock and offered to
give us names of likely parties. Another party of a different stamp,
drunk, got his (word missing) kicked by Paton and afterwards my
whip across his nut. Waited to go to an amateur theatrical performance, supper noisy and no coffee. The theatre a very barn-
like arrangement, scenery after the low strolling player style, the
piece 'The Spectre Bridegroom,' very ill played. The 'Nicodemus'
very 'Glasgow' in his style and awkward in manner, like his
countrymen of the same stamp when trying to ape their betters.
Two men as females, dark in complexion and hoarse of voice, the
little one very straight up and down both fore and aft. By way of
interlude song of Lord Lovell, very ill done; for finale 'Bombastes
Furioso,' which was better. Did not expect much, but thought it
was to be amateurs of a better class. The poor performance was
nothing however compared to the disgusting behaviour of the
audience, such a noisy half-drunk set of beasts I never was among
before. Neither at diggings nor elsewhere have I seen men behave
so childishly and disgracefully. Saltmarket would be respectable in
comparison. One Dutch-looking beast kept playing with a lady's
ringlets till she was obliged to go to another seat. Throwing paper
balls about, yelling, singing in chorus to orchestra and endeavouring to cheer 'simultaneously together,' making themselves in short
as disgustingly noisy as they could well do, without using obscene
or profane language. Sat in disgust and left in contempt. After a
glass of grog at hotel, off by the waning moon to camp. Must, in
justice however to Queenstown, say that the noisy individuals
appeared principally to consist of the Cradock cricketers.

Sat. 22. Our wool-sorting friend showing us wool sales wherein the
Cape average was not so far behind, agreed with me in having
occasionally seen Cape wools quoted as high as any Australian,
and thinks there is no particular antagonistic cause why wool
grown in these colonies should not bring as good a price as that of
any other colony. Farmers here are too lazy and ignorant to look

after their sheep and careless about the scab, which is the cause of that brittleness and break in the staple of the wool so commonly complained of.

Mon. 24. Hurrah! Trek for Cradock. After breakfast, into town, made a few purchases, got letters, etc., etc.

Tue. 25. Late start. Called at a store and found Mrs. Stow, a very intelligent woman, who gave us leave to camp anywhere on the farm. In this Colony particular places are appointed along the roads for outspanning, and travellers camping anywhere else without leave are liable in trespass.

Wed. 26. Mr. Stow came to see us in and had a chat and coffee. After breakfast all went to call on him, see the papers and talk sheep. Gave us two letters of introduction, and off about 11, waggon having gone on before. Saw several flocks, scabby, and not particularly good. These plains make a long road to travel though looking short. Got to Mr. Millar's, to whom we had letters, about 3. Two-storey house, large orchard and cultivation. Found him a rattling old fellow with grown-up sons and daughters. Had gin and water, but nothing to eat. Our mates came up soon and we waited till sunset to see sheep—4 flocks. Very good sheep indeed, by far the best we have seen. One very nice lot of 1,100 yearlings, but wants to sell all together, wethers and ewes. Got forage for horses and the old cock sent on his Kafir with eight bundles to give them at night. Very nice girls, eldest busy making a muslin dress for a marriage party. This is a great country for balls and parties. Got leave to run oxen in hoek as long as we liked.

Fri. 28. Horrid windy morning. Started for Tarkastad. Got to the township in whirls of dust and glad to get inside hotel. After dinner called on Mr. Stow (brother of the other). Took Fred and I over to Mr. Venter's farm at quarter of an hour's walk and acted interpreter. Found he had about 1,000 maiden ewes which he offered for 15/-, but brought him down to 14/-. Left to return at sundown and see them. Got pony shod on fore-feet. All went over and were pleased with the sample, and Fred closed with him, to throw out all bad ones. Give him notice when we come back from Cradock, so that he may muster for drafting. Seems a very decent fellow for a Dutchman! Has got about 7,000 sheep, good house, but kept in rough fashion, extensive orchard and cultivation, a tall, over 6 feet, fellow; did not see wife, who it is said talks English. Fred in high spirits and excited about purchase. After supper had two rubbers at whist, P. and I partners, and came off equal. Beds had not the cleanest of sheets and felt an itching sensation, possibly the effect of imagination! Beautiful quiet night.

Sat. 29. And a beautiful quiet morning. Breakfast at 8, after which called for Mr. Stow. Found he was going to ride by a short road to Cradock, and offered to take us and introduce us to some farmers likely to sell sheep. Left at 11. Our road led through narrow poorts or gaps and defiles of piled up masses of huge blocks of trap rock, or broken up sandstone, the solid hill sometimes rising sheer up, very rugged, bold and grand. The water courses running through edged with rocks and thorns and willows. Mr. Stow showed us in one of the gorges where the trap rock was piled up in very heavy masses, forming cave-like recesses, some of the Bushmen's paintings in black and red colour of men and animals supposed to represent Kafirs, oxen, hartebeest, and horses. This diminutive race were at one time numerous here, and this style of country was well suited for them. These paintings are what Fred is in the habit of sploring about as showing wonderful talent, he having seen them on the Berg! Such things as children of three or four years old might daub! Strange however that the Kafir shows no talent whatever in this way. Then on to Mr. Marais, who had sheep and induced us to remain to see them. Got forage for horses and waited a long time before sheep came in, then walked up over these horrible gritty sandstone klinkers, or shivers, to meet them. No good, poor lot, no wool on faces or legs. Shook our heads and told Mr. Stow they would not do; wanted 15/-. Marais took the pet and went home, keeping ahead.

Sun. 30. Got to the great city of Cradock about half-past 1. It

lies low, on the border of Fish river, and is not seen till close upon
it, peculiar in its flat-roofed houses. Must be very warm here from
the glare of sun on rocks and stones. What a blessing we had a
quiet day; from the looseness of the soil it must be one cloud of
dust in a gale of wind. Put up at Beadle's, first rate house, and
had a good dinner, though past the *ordinary* time, to which did so
much justice that felt quite like doing nothing for some time after.
In evening had a stroll to see town, good houses, whitewashed and
with dodges for mitigating heat, such as green painted Venetian
shutters and shades, giving a decided Portugese look to them.
Streets wide and ornamented with fruit trees and various others,
peach and almond in full blossom. Along the open water sluit that
supplies the city, a fine row of thorns growing large and sweeping
to the ground; must be a fine shady walk in summer when the
leaves are out; inhabitants not particular about what they do
underneath. Had a look into bed of river, now barely running. The
population well sprinkled with different shades of colour. Hottentots and Kafirs and a great many well dressed 'Tottie' girls
flaming about in their crinolines. Back to supper at half-past 7, no
tea or coffee.

Mon. 31. Saw Scanlen, who, it was said, could tell us all about
those likely to have sheep to sell, he to call and see us at hotel,
and, at last, saw Mr. Tucker, who has sheep at his brother's farm,
but could tell us nothing about their number or ages! Introduced
us to Mr. Trollip, who has sheep, and he came up and had a talk
with us at night. Arranged that I start with him tomorrow morning at 6. He to drive me out.

Tue. 1. September. Started about 8, with Trollip and two children,
the road following up river and then over flat Karoo plains, the
hills encircling and sometimes forming pretty valleys in the distance. Main road to Middelburg and very good. Turned off to left
and got to farm about 12; large family; after dinner left for a time
to my own resources and walked down to river and did seed-pick-
ing, got some new kinds, and then back and had a walk with
Trollip. He picked up some seed of brackbush (considered good for

sheep) and enlarged upon fossils to an alarming extent! Any mis-
shapen lump of a stone became the ghost of a deceased speacies of
some sort! Sheep very long of coming in. Lambing stock, a fine
large and even lot, but scant of wool about face and legs. Put off
seeing young flock till morning. At supper the tutor, a delicate-
looking specimen of learning, opened out upon the mariner's compass. Afterwards he drummed upon the piano, trying to learn 'Oh,
it comes at last' in a spasmodic manner. Glad to suggest a visit to
the father-in-law, Mr. Collet, and had a talk about the Eastern
Province in general, and sheep. An old hand. Told me he had an
uncle who was lagged for forgery and had left a deal of money, but
he had never been able to get hold of it! Had a nip and then retired
to hear tutor descant upon the iniquity of killing snakes! Thankful to be shown to my dormitory, which contained an extensive
nuptial-looking brass posted four-poster, getting into which after
heaving a sigh or two, fell asleep. Stupid, forgot to mention having
seen a small mob of ostrich on a farm we passed, which are kept
for the sake of the annual return in feathers. They are accustomed
to run with the cattle and some of the young stock having been
sold and taken to a distance, the ostriches soon after disappeared
and could be seen or heard of nowhere and were supposed to have
been stolen. They were eventually discovered feeding along with
their old friends that had been sold, and could only be brought
back by bringing them and the cattle together. Ostrich farming is
now beginning to attract attention and, it is considered, will pay
better than anything else.

Sat. 12. December. Arrived at 'Cotswold' about 12. Henry looking
well. Found great improvements had been effected! Garden made
and fenced. Woolshed erected of corrugated galvanised iron, etc.,
etc. The house protected with a lightning conductor, and inside,
the chimney rebuilt and enlarged. Sheep arrived all right. Henry
been doing great things in garden and transplanting trees from
the bush. Wether flock shorn and sheep all looking well and comparatively free of scab; has been spotting with McDougal's com-
position, which seems to act well.

So here we are again, having traversed that wild uninhabited country said to be the abode of lions and lots of big game, without having seen a sign of the one and precious little of the other. Why that sandstone country should be in such a destitute condition in that respect puzzles me. Our old weather-beaten ship now deserted looks woebegone; it is the jolliest and most independent style of travelling ever I have tried, a prolonged picnic. Sorry it is over!

Tue. 22. Not in good working order; got a chill from the cold wind while looking on at sheep killing last night.

Wed. 23. Still out of sorts. Heavy thunderstorm and rain about mid-day. Very close to us, making the iron shed dirl and the rain beating into shed. In afternoon had a little talk about sheep and sold my lot to Henry and Fred at 20/- per head. *Statement*: Total amount of funds on hand at starting, £288. Deduct private expenses, £8 19*s*. 3*d*. Amount invested in sheep, £279 0*s*. 9*d*., which at 13/9 price paid per head gives my number of sheep at 406. From this falls to be deducted 3 p.c. for deaths, losses, etc., leaving 394 head at 20/-=£394. Add proportionate value of sheep skins saved during trek, 5/-=£394 5*s*. 0*d*. from which come to be deducted expenses of our own living, Kafirs' wages and grub, £7 7*s*., leaving a net balance of £387 4*s*. 5*d*. This on total money spent and invested gives a return of £100 or say 30 p. cent. *Finis*.

NEW ZEALAND

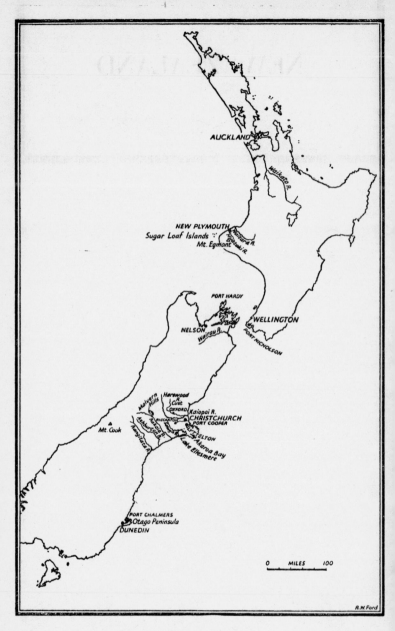

AUCKLAND

Waikato R.

NEW PLYMOUTH
Sugar Loaf Islands
Waitara R.
Waingongoro R.
Mt. Egmont

PORT HARDY

WELLINGTON
NELSON
Wairau R.
PORT NICHOLSON

Malvern
Hills
Harewood
R.
Cust
OXFORD
Kaiapoi R.
RICCARTON
CHRISTCHURCH
PORT COOPER
Rakaia R.
Mt. Cook
Ashburton R.
Selwyn R.
LYTTELTON
Akaroa Bay
Rangitata R.
Lake Ellesmere

PORT CHALMERS
Otago Peninsula
DUNEDIN

0   MILES   100

R.W.Ford

New Zealand

As early as 1769 Cook had annexed New Zealand to the British Crown, but his action was disavowed, and it was not till 1840 that sovereignty was formally established. By this time there were already two thousand white settlers there and more shiploads were on the way.

The intervening years show a gradual forcing of the Government's hand. When annexation came, it was again partly to forestall the French (as in the case of much of Australia), though the main motive was to put a stop to the dangers of unregulated intercourse with a rich land populated by vigorous and extremely warlike natives.

Early in the nineteenth century Australian sealers and whaling vessels took to visiting New Zealand and a desultory trade commenced. Its staple was timber, with tattoed heads as a luxury side line. The violent habits of the Maoris made them available in proportion to the demand until, in a flooded market, prices dropped from £20 a head to less than £2.

As trade grew brisker the British found it necessary to make frequent disavowals of sovereignty, and there was no one to keep order in the increasingly bloody free-for-all that was developing. White men took to living with the Maoris, helping them to trade (they were called Pakeha Maoris, from *pakeha*=stranger) and they in some cases became war leaders. One of the most notable episodes in this period was the attack made by Maoris on the 500-ton ship *Boyd* in Whangaroa Harbour. There were nearly seventy passengers, most of whom were killed and eaten. It was the cannibalism of the Maoris, more than anything else, that contributed to the evil repute New Zealand had for people at home, and which made it difficult for Samuel Marsden to enlist missionaries.

But missionaries went in the end and fought against the latest evil, the large-scale importation of fire-arms. The deaths resulting from endemic tribal warfare suddenly accelerated till they were numbered in thousands. The new weapon led to a breaking up of

[303]

the stability of the tribes and to migrations and enslavements that caused the greatest revolution in the internal economy of the country since the arrival of the first semi-mythical canoes in the fourteenth century.

Official opinion still held, however, that the solution was to leave the islands and the natives alone, and this hopelessly unrealistic view was shared by the missionaries at home.

But by 1840 speculators, impressed by the resources of the country, had bought, in a multitude of eccentric and extra-legal bargains, more land from various native chiefs than there was in the whole country. And in 1839 the first attempt to undertake systematic colonization was made by Edward Gibbon Wakefield's New Zealand Company. In the name of a large number of emigrants, the most respectable and representative group of men yet engaged on any colonizing venture, Colonel Wakefield set out to buy land on the spot. Though formerly involved in his brother's seduction plot and sentenced with him, he was a cool and resourceful person, and has been called the hand of the New Zealand Company, as Edward Gibbon was its brain.

The sailing of the *Tory* at last persuaded the Government to act, and they sent Captain Hobson to annex the country by agreement with the natives. So 1840 saw both protagonists in this drama of reluctant imperialism present, supported by a number of smaller figures, representing hard-headed Australian merchants, each waving an impressive legal conveyance with blanks left for the signatures of the illiterate Maoris.

Confusion remained, even after the signing by the chiefs of the Treaty of Waitangi, confirming them in the ownership of all the land of New Zealand but acknowledging the sovereignty of the Queen of England. The Company's purchases were whittled down and all others reviewed. Colonel Wakefield's claim of twenty million acres was reduced to a little over one million. The greatest snag was that all agreements were quite unreal unless they had been signed by every single member of the tribe concerned— usually an impossible provision, for the Maoris had no more conception of personal property than the aborigines of Australia.

An example of this is given by the colony of New Plymouth,

Harbour of Lyttelton, December 27th, 1850

The Last Day in Harness

where DR. HENRY WEEKES went to try his fortune. The New Plymouth Company bought 60,000 acres from the New Zealand Company, but it turned out that the purchase had been made by Colonel Wakefield from a tribe who had just conquered the real occupiers of the land, and when missionary influence had given a voice to the oppressed Maoris, they claimed their land again. And the unhappy settlers had all but 3,200 acres taken from them by the too dispassionate hand of Government.

*　　　*　　　*

Sometimes the settlers paid with their lives for these unsatisfactory titles to land. Such an occasion was the massacre of Wairau, where Edward Gibbon's other brother, Captain Arthur Wakefield, was killed along with several of the Nelson settlers, as William Deans describes. The fears engendered in settlers elsewhere were not unfounded. There were about 10,000 whites to nearly 110,000 Maoris. And for some years to come settlers tended to ignore the South Island, where there were much fewer of them.

The New Zealand Company's settlement at Port Nicholson continued to increase. This, with the Otago and Canterbury Settlements eight and ten years later, were the high-water mark of planned colonization in the century. Wakefield's ideal was to transplant a complete microcosm of English society far from the association of unhappy memories or evil practices into compact towns dependent on a defined area of cultivated land. He did not want people to scatter at once into independence, and he insisted on the price of land being sufficient to preserve the old relationship between master and man while giving the latter every opportunity eventually to become a master in his own right.

Things did not work out in such ideal terms, of course, and some inconvenience was caused by plans having been made delicately but at home. 'The country is more mountainous than I expected,' said Deans, and not surprisingly, for the Company had drawn out a plan for Port Nicholson on the assumption that it was all perfectly flat!

The letters of JOHN AND WILLIAM DEANS are significant in showing how, having realized that fortunes were to be won in New Zealand by the pastoral rather than the arable farmer, they turned from the forested North Island to the great expanse of flat land that has made the Canterbury Plains one of the finest grazing areas of the world. When they went to Port Cooper the name Canterbury had not yet been given to the land behind it, and they were among the first to realize its value, their nearest neighbours being a small band of French settlers who had been set down at Akaroa only to find that British sovereignty had been proclaimed six days before.

*   *   *

The next settlement on the South Island was made by a community of members of the Scottish Free Kirk at Dunedin in 1848. But the interest felt in it at home was quickly eclipsed by the fame of the Canterbury Settlement. Established in 1850, all the land there was taken up by 1858. The colonists were of an even better stamp than at Port Nicholson. 'The first body of colonists', wrote Wakefield, 'was made up by infinite painstaking. Nine out of ten of them were nursed into becoming colonists.'

The letter in which this passage occurs was written to CHARLOTTE GODLEY's husband, John. He and Wakefield were the prime forces behind the settlement, and Godley went out to receive the first immigrants and to steer them through the first two years. Conditions shortly after that cannot be better described than in an extract from another letter from Wakefield, who had come out to see how things were for himself, and died there. It is printed in Garnett's *Life*.

'At Canterbury I might have fancied myself in England, except for the hard-working industry of the upper classes and the luxurious independence of the common people. The upper classes are very hospitable, and very deficient in the pride of purse or mere station, and the common people are remarkably honest. Their entire independence is not disagreeable to me, who am accustomed to America, and like it. There is absolutely no servility. . . . There is an intense jealousy of new-comers; a state of feeling which always takes possession of young colonies, and holds possession of them till they begin to grow old. For every newcomer probably comes to be the competitor or rival of somebody. . . . When he is fairly planted he in his turn becomes jealous of other new-comers.

'But the worst feature, I think, of this colonial society is a general narrow-mindedness. Everybody's ideas seem to be localised in his own part of the country. I have not met with one person who is as well acquainted as I am myself with New Zealand in general. Thought abstract from the individual seems totally absent. The interests and amusements of each person are the only subject of his thoughts. This is partly owing to the want of intercommunication among the settlements, which are, and will be, until they get local steam navigation, as much cut off from each other as if separated by a thousand miles of ocean, so that each community is naturally as small in its ideas as in its numbers; but the evil in question has another cause, which is the cause of many more evils, namely, the total absence of popular power and responsibility . . . . It is a miserable state of things, and you will think that I must be very unhappy. But I am not so at all. On the contrary, I am sure that there is a good foundation to work upon in the best set of colonists that have ever left England in modern times; that poverty and crime (crime in the old country sense) are impossible; that the country is unrivalled in climate and productiveness; and that the mind of the people will be changed by the coming responsibilities of political power. Only there is heavy work for me, if I can but keep health for doing it. At present I am not in the least down-hearted.'

*　　　*　　　*

When SAMUEL BUTLER came out, in 1860, not only was the success of the individual separated settlements on both Islands assured, but the political muddles and struggles of the forties and early fifties had been followed by a calm. It was badly needed, for the population was to be multiplied by the Otago gold rush and there were yet to be wars with the Maoris. The much abused (for instance by Godley) autocracy of Sir George Grey had done the work for which he was called from South Australia. In 1852 the country was granted a constitution which was to give her self government, and by 1856 enough differences of opinion inside the country had been shelved to make it workable. Surely in the character of no other country is so much explained by the history of twenty years, the period covered by the writers of these letters.

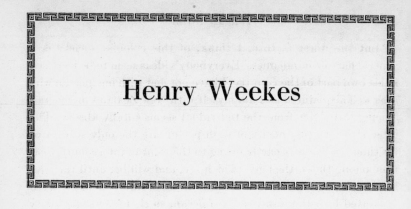

Henry Weekes

'In the autumn of the year 1840 I was attacked with the *emigration fever*, to which there had been evidently a predisposition in my system for some time. Instead of applying the proper remedies, I only increased the disorder by reading prettily got up works on the subject.'

When he wrote this Weekes was thirty-six years old. Born at Barnstaple, he took up medicine, adding M.R.C.S. and L.S.A. to his name and getting additional experience in Parisian hospitals. His chance to let his emigration fever run its course came in 1840, when the Plymouth Company of New Zealand, whose aims were 'to render available the resources of Devon and Cornwall, and to present to their inhabitants the means of participating in the favourable prospects offered by this new field of colonization,' sent a party out to the North Island. Weekes joined as Surgeon-Superintendent, having been warned that 'A deduction of 20*s.* will be made for every death on the voyage, and an addition of 20*s.* for every birth.'

The voyage was a prosperous one, but the first experience of colonization disappointing. He returned to England after two years, having left his name to an island off the Auckland coast. In 1848 the news of gold in California drew him across the Atlantic, and for five years he dug and washed in the intervals of stitching up knife-wounds, setting bones and removing bullets. But New Zealand drew him back and he was there to take part with the

[308]

Auckland militia in the Maori wars of the sixties. Nor did a move back to England prove final, for he went to live with the British colony in Barcelona, only coming back in 1889. Five years later, while still in England, he died.

These extracts are taken from Weekes' rough 'Journal of Common Things,' supplemented under the dates March 31st, April 11th and June 5th from the later version of the parts affecting New Zealand which he re-wrote later in life. The various MSS. are now in the possession of the New Zealand Government and are printed in *The New Plymouth Settlement*, 1841–1843, New Plymouth, 1940, edited by J. Rutherford and W. H. Skinner.

March 30th. 1841. A head wind yesterday in the Straits. A lovely day. Sighted venerable Mount Egmont at 5.30 a.m., the land sloping off from its base to a fine wooded and apparently level district much more agreeable than the mountains we have left behind us in Cloudy Bay.

P.M. After opening the Sugar-loaves we arrived off our 'el dorado,' and after firing a gun in answer to a cannon fired on the shore by Mr. Barrett, anchored to our great satisfaction about 5 o'clock. A boat shortly came off with the Messrs. Carrington, the surveyors. The anchorage is at best but an open roadstead.

31st. (Therm. 65°.) Being a fine day proceeded to land the emigrants without delay. Strange as it may appear, many of them had become so attached to the ship which displeased them so much at the early part of our voyage, that we had great difficulty in inducing them to make a proper despatch. But, acting on a slight knowledge of human nature, the children being placed in the boats first the parents were not long in following—in this manner all were landed safely before sunset.

Thus were disembarked, after being confined 140 days on board a crowded ship, without a single loss, every individual (including 70 children) who sailed from England. And this success may be mainly attributed to a strict and constant observance of cleanliness, ventilation, and order.

Whilst one party was engaged at the landing-place another was busy erecting tents and providing for the night. Fortunately, Mr. Barrett, who had recently arrived here for the purpose of whaling, had just built a row of native houses, part of which being unoccupied afforded us excellent shelter. By night every one had his place, and what with the delight of being released from the ship, and the fineness of the weather, every one was in first-rate spirits and every inconvenience overlooked. The next day the natives were bartering their potatoes and watermelons for biscuit, the children were throwing each other about, and gipsy-fires, washerwomen and soapsuds, were universal.

We found that the surveyor and his party had been here about six weeks; they amounted to eleven males and four females. We learnt that the banks of the Waitara, a river about twelve miles north of the Sugar-loaves, had been first selected as a site for the town but had afterwards been changed for a spot about two miles north of our landing-place. A vast deal of expense was consequently incurred and time lost by having to drag or carry everything this distance over a loose sand. Of course we took the first opportunity of visiting the 'town' as this part was now called, and as we walked along the beach naturally anticipated the great progress which eleven picked men had in six weeks been able to accomplish. We found everything in a state of nature with the exception of a pathway cleared of the underwood for a short distance up the Enui, and a piece of fern burnt on the Huatoki.

1st, 2nd, 3rd April. (Therm. 70° to 75°.) Fine. All hands engaged in landing the goods which was effected with more expedition than we had anticipated. Slept on shore in Mr. Cutfield's tent on Saturday night and found my clothes and shirt wringing wet in the morning. The dew falls very heavily at night and appears to penetrate the tents, while they are exceptionally hot in the daytime.

4th. (Sunday.) (Therm. 70°.) Fine. Dined on board with the Captain after having attended prayers by Mr. Wallace, who is a Wesleyan Missionary from Waikatu.

5th. (Therm. 70°.) Fine. Roofed in my house. The ship sailed for Port Hardy for ballast and will return in about a fortnight. We hope she will bring some pigs with her as they are very scarce here. The natives, who are few in number, bring us potatoes for biscuits, etc. The emigrants are placed for the present under tents but they are to have one-eighth of an acre each to build on near the town

8th. Fine. Slept 'at home' on Wednesday night—very comfortable. Rain came in.

9th. S.W. rain, which came thro' my roof of boards.

11th. The store house is now in progress and a wooden bridge commenced over the Huatoki. It has been slavish work for the men who have had to fell and drag trees from some distance for the bridge. Each labouring emigrant has had one-eighth of an acre allotted to him for two years, and with the assistance of the natives some *raupo*-houses (a typha, sort of bullrush) are springing up.

13th. A 'Mourai' or native thatched the house with a long grass called *toi-toi* for an old pair of trousers and a shirt.

18th. (Sunday). (Therm. 63°.) We have all been actively engaged in the past week, all the labourers for the bridge, store-house, etc., and the rest about their houses. The thatching has quite secured my board from roof rain; it has indeed had a fair trial for on Wednesday the rain was very great, just like thunder rain, and the whole week has been more or less wet. I am now engaged about a kitchen and fire-place, for our cooking is now all done gipsy fashion which is not *very* inconvenient in fine weather.

I put in some turnips on Tuesday, and mustard on Wednesday, and they have shown up this morning. Altho we are very quiet here, there being only a few straggling natives, yet there are rumours of war at Wanganui about 105 miles distant. Mr. Creed, our missionary, received a letter on Friday to request him to proceed to the seat of warfare in order to stop the fight if possible. A ship came in from the distance on Friday, fired a gun and sailed again—it is probably the *Wm. Bryan*, who does not anchor on account of the bad weather.

April 25th, (Sunday). The *Wm. Bryan* has not yet returned. The store-house is completed externally and is receiving a coat of paint. Some of the emigrants have brought up their tents, and we hope to get up the stores next week. We find it very disadvantageous to be so far from the landing-place. The past week has been a very stormy one—the break-up of the Summer. The rain fell more heavily at times than I ever recollect observing it in England, but yet the showers are of very short duration, seldom lasting more than ten minutes, succeeded by sunshine.

I had a native on Friday and yesterday about my kitchen, which with the chimney, is nearly finished. The chimney is made of supple-jacks woven in the basket fashion round slight posts and the interstices filled with clay. The nights have felt very cold and a fire of an evening will be comfortable. I have put in several seeds in my 'garden' or quarter-acre; the radishes, turnips and mustard were up in four days and peas in five and a half days, altho' they have had no hot weather, this being the end of Autumn.

May 31st to June 6th. After much delay the men have at last commenced the surveys, or are rather cutting roads by the rivers. This is rather hard work for the brush-wood is there very thick. The weather is mild with an occasional cold evening. Some of the days (this one among others) are as beautiful as the finest autumnal ones in England. Mr. Cutfield and myself have had a long ramble this afternoon into an unknown portion of the country and find everywhere abundance of water and soil of the richest description. We found it hard work getting through the fern, most of which is higher than our heads. Read prayers this morning.

June 5th. The annoyance we have experienced from the bite of the sandfly has been extreme. This small insect exists in such numbers as to make one believe almost in the doctrine of spontaneous generation; whereas their irritating bites cause you at once to dissent from the common, but vain opinion, that everything was made for the benefit of man. That they *enjoy themselves* is evident enough. They mostly abound in wet weather when they fill our rooms, and by making after a little time for the window, a clearance is partially effected by sweeping them into a dust-pan, or by opening the window and flourishing them out with a towel. They generate in the soil, and make the otherwise delightful occupation of gardening disagreeable. Children look as if they had had some serious eruption. After standing a little in the air they find their way up inside your trousers and the sleeves of your coat. At night they rest from their persecution except the candle fascinates them in which case scores of these flies, singed or dead, will drop into your tea or cover the table and books. Although we have had two months' 'experience,' they bite, draw blood, and leave the same itching swelling as when we arrived.

Rats. As if this plague were insufficient we have the additional one of *rats* in thousands. Traps, pits and poison have been unceasingly at work, but their numbers still appear undiminished—one man caught in a pit outside his door twenty-five in one night! They get at everything eatable and even descend the string by which you suspend the flour-bag from the roof so as to be out of their reach. And yet, strange to say, the numerous half-starved native dogs never think of destroying them.

While on the subject of 'annoyances' a dissertation on New Zealand *fleas* would not be ill-timed perhaps; but I will merely say that, (heaven knows where they come from), the greatest attention will scarcely keep them under, and being about as big again as the English species they bite so as to make you jump again.

July 5th to 11th. Mr. Barrett caught a whale on Friday with its calf. Several schools have been seen passing through the bay. Messrs. Chilman and King joined me on Saturday on an expedition to the Waitara river about ten miles up the coast. It is a fine river but has a bad entrance. At spring tides there is thirteen or more feet of water on the bar. The land is low, very fertile; some is very wet after rains and would require draining. We spent the night in an open shed with some natives who were very hospitable.

12th to 18th. Tho' not cold everything appears to be in a state of rest, not making any visible growth. Our stock of flour, etc. was exhausted; we fortunately obtained some from the *Lapwing*. We hope to see the *Amelia Thompson* in a week or two.

19th to 25th. No news or arrivals this week. The men struck for wages on Monday, not being content with 5/- a day. However, they soon found that the best plan was to resume their labours, which they were allowed to do on their working eight hours a day instead of seven. The morning gun is fired daily at seven a.m.

August 29th. (Sunday.) The *Amelia Thompson* not having arrived we are getting short of provisions. Our flour was expended last week, a few potatoes and peas being all the eatables, except salt meat, left at the stores. Owing to the peculiar manner in which we are living, drunkenness has lately much increased. This is the effect of the labourers having no amusements, there being a great sameness and want of excitement in this infant colony. They have more money than they can spend, and there being only one employer (the Company) no emulation exists among them, for an idle fellow gets just as much as a good workman.

My peas have stood the winter; those not eaten down by the fowls are in blossom. The tops of my onions were touched one severe white frost or two but are looking well now. I raised some melons, etc. in the chimney corner and planted them out in the early part of the month. Some raisin stones have come up to my satisfaction, and Mr. Barrett gave me some peach-cuttings yesterday.

August 30th to September 5th. The *Amelia Thompson* arrived here on Friday but has not yet come to anchor tho' she probably will tomorrow. She sailed from England on the 25th March—put in at Bahia and has been at Port Nicholson and about the Straits more than a month. Captain King rowed onshore (25m.) on Friday and many emigrants have been landed today. A large number of natives were on the beach to shake hands and welcome the *Pakias*. A great disappointment was felt on board when they heard there was no harbour here.

6th to 12th. Owing to the timidity of the Captain the *Amelia Thompson* anchored only last evening. We have had no blow, but keeping too much to the W. on the Saturday he could not beat up against the light Easterly winds. We had been busily unloading all day. Some of the Emigrants were nearly lost a few evenings since, having come on shore after dark and run on a reef of rocks. The natives stripped naked and went into the water with fire-brands, rendering the most important assistance.

13th to 19th. The ship returned this morning but has not yet anchored—she is unfortunate. A rather severe shock of an earthquake occurred on Friday night. It awoke me from my first nap and rather surprised me. The motion resembled that which we experience in the interior of a flour-mill, but in a greater degree; and the noise was very like the sieves at work. It lasted about a minute, and, as some say, terminated with a pop—but this I did not hear. No damage has been sustained. The rain has been excessive. The atmosphere was peculiar the evening before the earthquake, and an old Maori 'Huniko' told Lakeman at tea that we should have one, their name being *Mumu* for it.

20th to 26th. A lovely week but no vessel here to take advantage of the fine weather. There is no pork and but three barrels of flour left at the stores for more than three hundred people. The *Amelia Thompson* left on Monday and has not since returned.

September 27th to October 3rd. The *Amelia Thompson* returned on Thursday, and much was done on that day and Friday. The *Regina* arrived on Saturday and landed Captain Liardet to-day. He succeeds Captain King.

4th to 10th. Both vessels driven off on Monday morning and have not been seen since. Very stormy week. We have more than ever seen the disadvantages we labour under in not having a harbour. They have both returned to-day but are making off again.

November 28th. (Sunday). Moschitos very troublesome these two nights past. It appears they are felt principally in cloudy moist weather. No vessel has been here trading for some months. We hope they are not *afraid* to come. A party of men have been to the Waitara this week to mark the boundary of the Company's possessions, as the Waikatos threaten to come down shortly and take the Waitara and Waiongena for their own.

November 29th to December 5th. Very dull again—no vessel having been here for a long time. On Monday Captain Liardet met with a severe accident which nearly killed him. He was endeavouring to fire one of the cannons from the wreck of the *Regina*. After some difficulty in igniting the powder it went off unexpectedly whilst his face was almost close to the muzzle. He has suffered greatly and it is doubtful whether he will be able to see.

A slight shock of an earthquake felt about five o'clock this morning (Monday).

6th to 12th. A schooner here with some things for Barrett on Wednesday. No tea, coffee or sugar in the Colony! Flour getting short. Some of the houses practically unroofed to-day by the wind. My suburban section was marked out for me yesterday.

13th to 19th. A meeting held on Thursday to take some measure to provide necessaries—adjourned to Monday. A windy disagreeable week. Magistrates appointed last week—a lock-up house about to be built.

20th to 26th. Captain Liardet getting better. Colonel Wakefield blamed for not sending us flour. Selling my suburban in small parts.

December 27th to January 2nd, 1842. About a hundred Waikatos arrived here on Tuesday on a friendly visit. They met the Taranaki natives at Nga Motu, had a feast and much talk. On Wednesday they left having previously given us an amusing specimen or two of the war dance.

[316]

10th to 16th. Another beautiful week. The *Vanguard* has brought fifty barrels of flour for the Company. None to be sold except as rations to those who work for the Company. Col. Wakefield is rather hard with us.

17th to 23rd. Captain Liardet has been walking about this week with the help of being led. Cut my wheat yesterday—a fine sample. A meeting Friday to petition the Company for a harbour.

24th to 30th. Went to the Waitara on Friday in a boat, lost an oar and walked home in evening. No news for a long time.

February 21st to 27th. The *Timandra* arrived from Plymouth in one hundred and thirteen days, having been five at the Cape. Lost six passengers and had five born. Brings two hundred and one steerage and ten cabin passengers.

March 3rd. Set sail for Sydney at 5 p.m. on the brig *Caroline*, 150 tons.

Arrived in Sydney Monday 14th. Paid £12 for passage. Captain Liardet, King, Ware and Browse (of *Regina*) fellow passengers. Lodging at Vercoe's Coffee-house (25/- a week including good board and private bedroom).

William and John Deans

William and John were the first and third eldest sons of John Deans of Kirkstyle in the parish of Riccarton, near Kilmarnock. Both were educated for the law and had spent some time in their father's office before they became interested in emigration. Once convinced, they took up farming by way of preparation with the good-humoured and businesslike application they were to show all their lives.

It was agreed that William should take the actual plunge first and, having purchased land from the New Zealand Company in London, he sailed in 1839 for Port Nicholson, taking two servants, Gebbie, and Morrison, and their families. He was making stiff profits on the goods he had brought out within a few weeks, and when John came out to join him (the third brother, James Young, did not leave home in spite of their invitations) and they had moved to the South Island their prosperity was uninterrupted. They were pioneers in the sheep country later to be the site of the Canterbury Settlement—which they welcomed, as it meant a market for their products.

In 1851 William was drowned on a voyage to Sydney to procure still more stock. As Charlotte Godley wrote to her mother, 'His brother will feel his loss sadly; they were so united and happy together.' In the same year died Gebbie, who having set up as a dairy farmer on his own, left more than £1,000, which he had built out of an original capital of nothing.

[318]

William and John Deans

John returned to Scotland to conclude a courtship which had hitherto consisted of long periods of silence punctuated by a little gentle blackmail, for he was not prepared to let the farm suffer for time spent on the privileged duties of the gallant. He married plain Jane McIlraith in 1852 and brought her back to New Zealand, to the farm he had named Riccarton, which still belongs to his family and provides, like so many of the place-names of Canterbury, a link with those at home.

These letters, mostly written to their father, are printed from originals in the possession of the Deans family in *Pioneers of Canterbury Deans Letters*, 1840–1852, Dunedin and Wellington (1937), edited by John Deans.

William Deans.

Port Nicholson, 9th February, 1840. The *Aurora* arrived here on the 17th of January after a beautiful passage of 110 days from the Lands End with the loss of only one child by death; and she was said not to be able to stand the passage before leaving England. The climate is beautiful and the soil most luxuriant, but it will require a good deal of clearing. The land I am sorry to say will be a long time of being surveyed, and we are now located on patches of about an acre till such time as the Town Acres are surveyed. I have dug mine and am about to sow some seeds for the spring. I am likewise having a New Zealand house built on it—which is to be built for six blankets, and a more comfortable place I never saw. It is built of wood and large pieces of fern and is 34 feet in length by 17 feet broad, with three rooms—one for baggage, one for myself, and one for the servants. This letter is to go by a ship to Sydney and I have not more than ten minutes to write it in. I have not had an opportunity before, and have been so busy cutting and carrying wood that I have not had a moment to spare to write a long letter. My house is about ready and I have all my baggage carried from the beach, so I promise you a long account of the place. I will get Gebbie and Morrison employed by the Company at £1 a week with victuals and will be able to keep myself at about

[319]

3/- a week—plenty of potatoes for a small piece of tobacco, fish ditto, and a large pig for a blanket. I have bought six pigs in whole weighing about 500 pounds, and have made about £3 by them.

The ship by which this is to go is just leaving the Bay, and it has been so little known that I believe this is the only letter will go by her.

Morrison and Gebbie please me much. They were the best behaved men on board.

8th March. I mentioned in my former letter that our ship, the *Aurora*, had beaten all the others. Since our arrival all the ships that left England at the same time with us, have got here safe except the *Adelaide*. Besides we have the *Bengal Merchant* (by which I had your letter favoured by the Rev. Mr. Macfarlane) and the *Glenberrie*. The *Adelaide* has since arrived. The *Duke* took 126 days, and the *Bengal Merchant*, 106. There were six deaths on board the *Duke of Roxburgh*, the majority of whom were infants. There was one death, one birth, and one marriage in the *Bengal Merchant*, and in the *Oriental* there was one death amongst the cabin passengers, and two among the emigrants. You are aware that the *Adelaide* (the largest ship out) left England on the same day with us, or rather the day before we did. The lateness of her arrival caused strong fears to be entertained of her safety, and everyone was deploring her supposed loss as a sad blow to the early prosperity of the colony. Her arrival was welcomed by every-one, and particularly by those who had relations on board. The fact is that jealousies arose on board amongst the ladies. Parties were formed on board ship and the Captain put into the Cape to fight no fewer than four duels—he himself one of the principals; Dr. Evans another; Mr. Johnston, a Scotchman, another; Mr. Miller, another Scotchman, ditto, etc. Instead of having the duels fought, however, the doctor waited on the authorities, and had all concerned bound over to keep the peace. The quarrels are still kept up amongst them. We had few quarrels in our ship, although there was great occasion for many. However, we had two—one between a Major Baker and a Mr. Palmer which ended in an apology from the latter; the other between the Major and the

Doctor on board. The quarrels took place at sea, and there was a duel after our arrival here. On both occasions I figured as the Major's second. He is the son of the Middlesex Coroner, and is a most gentlemanly young man. He has been of some use to me here by mentioning me very kindly to Colonel Wakefield (whose bosom friend he is), and also to Captain Smith, the Surveyor-General.

Of the eligibility of Port Nicholson for settlement, or of what I have seen of New Zealand generally, I should not wish to hazard an opinion, which might turn out erroneous, without having some further acquaintance with the country; and will only now tell you what I have seen, leaving you to form your own opinion as to the merits. The country is more mountainous than I expected, and this may be a great drawback to its being an immense agricultural country. It is very much wooded and will take a great deal of money to clear. The climate is capital, vegetation most luxuriant, and the land the finest I have ever seen. Indeed it will grow anything. Cucumbers, melons, vegetable marrows, potatoes, maize, Indian corn, pumpkins, etc., etc., are most luxuriant. One thing we have been very much disappointed in is the capability of the rivers for navigation. It (the river at Port Nicholson) was represented as being navigable for 80 miles. It turns out not to be navigable for more than 15 or 20, and that only for boats drawing little water. Ours being the first emigrant ship here, of course we were first on shore, and engaged putting up our houses, on land allotted us by the Surveyor-General, on the beach. The *Oriental* passengers, although warned that the river might overflow, chose to squat on its banks, and have been followed by the passengers of the *Duke of Roxburgh* and the *Bengal Merchant*. The late floods caused them all great alarm, and many since have deserted their houses and come to the beach. We have been living very comfortably on the beach while they have been making themselves very miserable. You are aware that the instructions to Colonel Wakefield were, to look out for the best harbour, and the place best fitted for a mercantile town in New Zealand, and in its neighbourhood to purchase as large a tract of land as he could. In choosing Port Nicholson, he has certainly had an eye to his instructions, because I believe it is the best harbour in New

Zealand, and on its shores there is a place admirably fitted for a commercial town. Colonel Wakefield has chosen this place as the site of the town, but was absent from the Port on the arrival of the *Cuba* with Capt. Smith, the Surveyor-General. Captain Smith's instructions were somewhat at variance with Colonel Wakefield's, and on his own responsibility he commenced surveying a spot for the town, more connected with the place fitted for the agricultural district. This flood has caused the question to be mooted whether, from the probability of the river overflowing its banks, it was a place altogether safe and fitted for the site of the town. The place first chosen by Col. Wakefield lies on the opposite side of the bay from the river, and is about eight or nine miles distant by water and twelve or fourteen by the beach. Col. Wakefield has named that first chosen by him Thorndon, and the other Britannia. These questions having reached the ears of Col. Wakefield, he called a meeting which was held yesterday at which he stated the facts of the case, and wished to have the sentiments of the land holders as to whether they would have their town acres at Britannia or Thorndon, or half acres in each. He asked the meeting to deliberate amongst themselves and state their opinions to him. Dr. Evans was called to the chair and expressed himself strongly in favour of Thorndon, and after a six hours' debate in which the sides seemed pretty equally balanced, whether the whole town should be at Thorndon or Britannia or half acres in each (perhaps the advocates for the half acres were the majority) the Col. broke up the meeting by saying that he had sufficiently gathered the sentiments of the meeting from the debate, that he would not trouble them further, but decide the question by himself. His opinion is not yet known but is expected in the course of to-day or to-morrow.

29 March. Since writing the preceding, Col. Wakefield has come to a decision about the township, and the place fixed upon is Britannia. This has caused a great noise and a meeting was held, at which resolutions were moved protesting against the choice. These resolutions were very numerously signed and presented to the Colonel. Many are of opinion that it will yet be altered to Thorndon, and I am one of them. I think it will yet be altered.

Meanwhile the survey of the township at Britannia goes on quickly.

The New Zealanders are certainly a very extraordinary people, and may one day by means of education and the example shewn to them by Englishmen become the best mechanics, the best sailors and altogether the most ingenious people on the face of the earth. Indeed now it would astonish anyone to behold with how much ingenuity two New Zealanders, clad in a native mat, without hat, shoes or stockings, will construct a house, build a canoe and do many mechanical works. Besides they are most admirable seamen. You would be astonished to see with how much fervour they practise their devotions. They have prayers morning and evening and three times on Sunday. They begin now to see in a great degree the evil caused them by the very many fights they used to have amongst themselves, and they have been employed little in warfare of late and more in their potato and maize grounds. Indeed many of the tribes have made a compact to fight no more.

You will easily perceive that the £100 you were so kind as to say you would give me will be far more useful to me in goods than in cash here. I would therefore wish that you would send, say, 20 barrels of flour, a quantity of oatmeal, half a dozen bolts of unbleached No. 8 canvas. I had a bolt with me which cost a guinea and I sold it here for £3 5s. These things I expect to pay about cent. per cent. at least. Another thing I could sell here at 200 per cent. profit is Scotch whisky, and this I could do without any trouble. Indeed now I have got an agreement to purchase 20 gals. at 15/- per gal., I think I can get that for any quantity. I believe it can be bought for about 4/- or 5/- without duty. I had 20 gals of Geneva which I bought in London at 2/6 from Stayner, the Shipping Agent. I sold it here for 14/- per gal; the 2/6 included the commission for shipping and everything. I got the £14 for it, and the person who bought it unshipped it himself.

25th March, 1841. You will have seen the correspondence between the Deputies from the settlers here and Sir. Geo. Gipps, the Governor of New South Wales; by it we are insured our land, but are bound subject to the approval of the Home Government, to

[323]

take the 110,000 acres for the principal settlement in one continuous block, round Port Nicholson. It is the general opinion here that this will ultimately be better for the settlement than if the population had been divided by going to remote parts of the coast, and although some parts of the rural sections may not just be what could have been wished, yet I am confident it will be for the general advantage to have a block in the neighbourhood of a good harbour like Port Nicholson instead of being scattered over a country destitute of harbours and where the making of roads would have been either impracticable or too expensive for the resources of a new colony, where labour is so dear. At least it will render the settlement more desirable in the eyes of speculators and perhaps attract more capital to it, thereby keeping up its value.

In my last letter I advised that no relations of mine should come out to the Colony, principally on account of the heavy expense required for clearing the land. The Commissioners for the sale of the Crown lands in the colonies have since determined that a uniform price of a £1 per acre is all that is to be asked for land in the new colonies. Now in a country like New Zealand it is impossible to overrate the advantages of this arrangement; although in some places the land is not available, yet in many it is highly fertile and advantageously situated for the purposes either of commerce or agriculture, and the country being so recently resorted to by Europeans, only a few of these places are now occupied or claimed under anything like a valid or good title, or which will be recognised, and many more are not claimed or occupied at all. In these circumstances land either remarkably fertile, or in the neighbourhood of a convenient harbour or anchorage, or one of the larger settlements, where either merchants or agriculturalists are soon likely to resort, is worth over and over again the £1 per acre asked by Government. Few of the settlers have yet had time to look about for such places, and some time will elapse before they do so. Now I know several places within a reasonable distance of Port Nicholson and in the line of coasting vessels, admirably fitted for agriculture, where the land is easily cleared, or in fact already fit for the plough, and where only a commencement is required to draw numerous settlers together. Perhaps in another year I will sell my lease of Okiwi with stock and crop and my land here, and purchase land from Government and go and settle on it, where farming may be carried on on a larger scale and at less expense than in Port Nicholson. Hundreds will follow the example and thus be the means of enriching themselves and adding importance to the larger settlements in the neighbourhood, while the land is being yearly doubled in value. For these reasons and because of the proofs (which before were only prophecies) we have had of the great agricultural product of the land, I should advise most strenuously both Jas. Young and my brother John should come out here, and that as soon as possible. If they were to be farmers at home they would probably make nothing by it, while here their success with common prudence is certain. They can *buy* as good land here at £1 per acre from the Government as they can rent in Scotland for £2, with a ready and certain market for their produce at prices double those at home, and they will live in a beautiful and healthy climate where there are no taxes on native produce, and free from political discord. A sea voyage, far from being disagreeable, is pleasant, and in fact the only disagreeable part of it is the parting from friends and relations. I would advise therefore that John and Jas. Young come out here as soon as circumstances permit, bringing with them what capital they can procure, principally in money. But as they would go to a place where barter with the natives would be profitable they ought to bring a large stock of coarse, strong and big blankets and rugs of various kinds, with some double and single barrelled percussion guns and some common muskets, but without bayonets, caps and powder, some American axes, and Negrohead tobacco. If it is arranged that they will come out, I will go to the same place as they, and they will have the benefit of what experience I may have obtained. Let them bring nothing with them in the way of outfit, merely wearing apparel. Many things can be got cheaper here than at home. A Land Office will be established in the colony immediately and they can purchase their land here. Say they can procure £600 or £700 each, it will be enough for a large establishment in the place where we would go.

[325]

20th August. By the New Zealand *Gazette* which I hope you will receive regularly, you will see that the Governor has just paid us his first visit, and that he is anything but popular with the settlers here. Their principal cause of complaint is that he did not visit this place before making Auckland the seat of Government, thereby giving it the preference before seeing Port Nicholson, and that in many of his other acts he has shown a total disregard of our wants, and in fact a decided hostility to the place and to the settlers.

11th April, 1842. You would be surprised if you could just take a peep at Port Nicholson. It is now only two years and three months since the first emigrant ship arrived here, yet with the decided hostility of the Colonial Government towards us and the long and vexatious delays in the completion of the survey, our population now exceeds 3,700 persons. Our infant township commands the praise of most of those who visit it. In our store-houses can be purchased everything either of use or ornament. We have generally about twenty vessels laying at anchor in our port. News direct from England by the Company's or private ships generally twice in the month. One newspaper already and a second about to be established, and already we have canvassing from parties desirous to fill the office of Mayor or Alderman under the Colonial Municipal Corporation Act, and nothing would please you more than to see how soon we have become used to our new homes, for you could scarcely believe that you looked at a young community so far from home, their friends, and the mode of life most of them had been accustomed to, and that in such a short time and by their exertions and their means all this had been done. There is in fact no parallel to it in the history of modern colonization.

John Deans.

Port Nicholson, 16th January, 1843. I arrived at Nelson on the 25th of October after a passage of five months on a very leaky ship. My brother had been there waiting for me but left before the ship arrived. He advised me to leave Nelson as it was a very bad place After being there about a month I took his advice and came to this place. I let part of my land and left the other in charge of a gentleman

[326]

there to sell or let for me first opportunity, and I don't think I shall visit it again. The land at Nelson is not good and there is not enough of it for the settlement. This place is not very good for agricultural purposes either, but it never was my brother's intention to remain here permanently. He has been round a great deal of both islands looking for the best places. His surveys are in favour of Port Cooper which is on the other island, within thirty miles of the French settlement and about 150 from this place, and whither we mean to go in about a month. We are going to take with us a flock of cattle and sheep, a few working bullocks and a couple of mares, and take a lease of land from the natives, who are very willing to give us as much as we wish at a very moderate rent. I am going to Australia in a week or two for the cattle, etc. We mean to take about 50 heifers, 2 bulls, 300 sheep, with bullocks and mares, a lot of pigs, plenty of poultry, 5 dogs and as many cats. William is going down with the servants and baggage, provisions, etc., in the meantime to construct houses, stockyards, etc. I expect James Young with a wife and his sister out immediately. If he will go with us we will take a good many more sheep and horses.

Port Cooper is described by every person to be a splendid place for a settlement and I have no doubt there will be one formed there in a few years by which time we will have a pretty extensive stock and be able to supply settlers with butcher meat, working bullocks, vegetables and a great many little things. We will be the only settlers there except a few whalers who are stationed there. It is a beautiful port and of easy access, and there is a large extent of good land around it, and I have not the least doubt but that it will be the best settlement in New Zealand.

The natives are a queer lot. You would laugh to see some of them with their tattooed faces, wrapt up in a blanket, and occasionally a swell coming along with a shirt, coat and trousers on, making his arms go like a pair of paddles, and fancying himself a man of some consequence. A good many of the men are well-made fellows and if they had always been well fed would have been very strong, but the women are neither so well looking nor so good figures. They are in general lazy and love on a warm day to bask in

the sun. They are not fond of working at any one thing for any
length of time, but you will get them to work pretty hard for a
hour or so if you promise them some *ki ki* (food) when they have
done. They all smoke, men, women and some little children.
William is a great favourite with them, but he does not like the
most of them. They will do anything for him. He has been kind to
them, and they know as well as possible who is good to them. There
is generally a few of them living close to his place, and if he wants
to go or send to Wellington they would go with him in his canoe
any hour of the night. They are great cowards, although they fight
a good deal among themselves. Sometimes when William was going
into the country he has quarrelled with one or two of them in a
crowd of two or three hundred when he thrashed them without
any danger of the others interfering. Some of them are very unreasonable, and if you give them a good pummelling they will
behave better in future. There is one very good young fellow comes
here once or twice every month and stays a day or two. He is
always clean and well dressed; last time he was here he had on a
dark coloured surtout, a fancy vest, and pair of tweed trousers,
clean shirt with a due proportion of the collar and wrist bands
seen, and a pair of good boots, and over all a native mat. He always
sleeps on the floor of my bedroom. He speaks a good deal of
English and teaches me the Maori language.

William Deans.

Wellington, 6th September. On the 10th of February last I started
to the neighbourhood of Banks Peninsula for the purpose of
making arrangements for settling on land in that district, as the
letters I mention would pretty fully inform you both John and I
intended doing. We had a good run down to Port Cooper and soon
effected an arrangement with the natives and Mr. Robinson, the
magistrate of Akaroa, who had instructions from the Government
to give us what assistance he could. We have since been engaged
in putting up dwelling and farm buildings, which are now nearly
completed. We are settled behind Banks Peninsula, within a day's
walk of the French settlement at Akaroa, and about an equal
distance respectively from Port Levie, Pigeon Bay and Parake,

[328]

other harbours in the Peninsula, and only two hours' walk from Port Cooper, also a harbour in the Peninsula to which a cart and horse can now be driven, and to all the other harbours cattle can easily be driven. If you have the New Zealand *Gazettes* of about August or September two years ago, you will see the description Captain Daniel (who went out to look for a site for the Nelson settlement) gives of it; and on the chart you will see it marked 'Land very fertile.' It has been so marked since the days of Cook.

John arrived from New South Wales with the cattle, etc., on the 17th of June after a long and rough passage of 21 days; nevertheless only six steers and heifers and one mare died during the passage, although after landing the weakness consequent on the tedious and stormy passage caused the death of twelve more, so that we have now left sixty-one head of cattle, three mares and forty-three sheep. This is not more unfortunate than the average run of cattle ships, and John having made a very judicious selection they are much better than those generally brought here. We have had five cows calved since they were landed, but two of them from the knocking about in the vessel, had their calves too early, in consequence of which both the calves died, but the other three are fine strong healthy calves and doing well. The parties who were settled on this land formerly were sent down by some Sydney people, but their affairs getting disarranged in Sydney the parties whom they had sent down were forced to leave it after the first year, but during this time they had turned up about 20 acres of land with ploughs drawn by bullocks, part of which was sown with wheat and barley and produced excellent crops; part of some of their stacks still remain unthreshed, and what was not cropped of the plough land we are now again turning up. I am taking down a mill with me from here by which one man can grind about 40 lbs. an hour of flour.

I came here nine days ago for some supplies, and will return home again in three or four days. Everything here is rather dull, both from the settlers being kept in suspense about their land titles, and on account of the massacre at Wairau, near Cloudy Bay, full accounts of which you will see in the papers sent; twenty of the Nelson settlers were killed by a party of the natives in a dispute about some land, and amongst those were some of the principal people in the place, including Mr. Thomson, the Police Magistrate, and Captain Wakefield. It seems to be the general opinion here that the unfortunate sufferers were somewhat to blame in the matter by having first fired; by accident a gun went off it is said and killed some of the natives. It appears that although the Nelson party were armed, they did not go there to fight, and in fact never imagined it would come to that, but that after this musket went off, there was a skirmish in which the white party, forty in number, put to flight five times the number of the natives, but that Captain Wakefield or Mr. Thomson, not wishing to continue it in hopes that they might come to terms with the natives, who seeing this imagined that the white party were defeated, and orders were given to take them prisoners. A good many of the Europeans were then killed in cold blood. This party is very strong and will not allow themselves to be brought to trial except by force. Application was made to the Governor at Auckland for a force to do this and likewise to the Governor of New South Wales; from the former fifty-four soldiers (the half what were there) were sent down, and yesterday the *North Star* ship-of-war of 28 guns, arrived here from Sydney with sixty more, but they have no orders to land from the vessel or to go in pursuit of the native chief, but only to assist the settlers if they are threatened with any further attack. Indeed it does not seem probable that these 110 soldiers would be sufficient for the capture of the ringleaders who would be supported by their tribe, and it would be madness to send anything but a strong party after natives who are so well acquainted with the intricacies of the bush, as they might be taken at a disadvantage. Perhaps it may be necessary to wait for a further force from home, before the parties can be brought to justice, but surely sooner or later they will be so; both the survivors of the white party and the natives should be brought to justice, and the guilty punished. The Maoris are quiet enough now and seem to view the Wairau murderers in a very bad light, and in fact the murderers themselves are in great consternation about the affair, and many of them are in the interior under hiding.

William and John Deans

John Deans.

Port Cooper, 28th September, 1845. There is a very large lake or lagoon on this plain; it is said to be seventy miles in circumference, and I should say it is not much less; it is close to the sea beach and sometimes breaks through the sandbank that divides it from the sea. There are millions of eels in it; the natives make a sort of basket for catching them and they get tremendous quantities sometimes; they dry them in the sun and are almost the only food they have at times. In places like the lagoon and some of the still running rivers a good many of the eels are as thick as a man's leg and are very fat. We get them frequently and are very fond of them. We have got one of these eel baskets and William one morning last summer caught 32 lbs. in it, but that is nothing to what the natives catch sometimes. There is a sort of fish called trout in some of the rivers, but they are the worst fish ever I ate; they are never almost seen in the daytime, nor are the eels, and you cannot catch any till dark; the only other fish we get in the rivers are a sort of flounder and they are certainly very fine; the way we get them is to spear them on a clear day. There are a vast many sorts of salt water fish to be got in many of the bays, but very few are first rate. Of the feathered tribe, we have abundance of quail, very like the partridge but not much larger than the blackbird, they are very fine eating and would afford excellent sport to gentlemen who like the shooting better than the game. A great many description of ducks; the largest, called the Paradise Duck, is as large as two ordinary ducks, but has often a sort of fishy taste from feeding near or on the beach; they have very pretty plumage; the male has a black head, dark coloured grey and white feathers on the body; the female, white as far down the neck as the tame drake has green, then a mixture of white, reddish brown, and the back a beautiful bright grey for dressing flies. There is a very majestic bird somewhat like the heron in shape, but pure white in colour; they are very scarce. And a large bittern, which only cries in the spring, like the roar of a bull. Some of these when moulting cannot fly and a good dog can catch as many as you choose. The Paradise duck is more of the character of the goose than the duck, and is to be seen as often on dry land as water; when moulting you may kill

[331]

as many as you choose with a stick. When settlers first arrived at Nelson they were not the least afraid of them. There is a large kind of parrot called kaka, nearly as large as the pigeon; when fat it is very good. There is a sort of bird called woodhen which are abundant in some places; they cannot fly, at least very little, are rather like the corncraik but as large as a six months' old hen pullet; they can run very fast, but are generally caught by holding out a stick with a piece of red flannel on it which they come to devour, when with another piece of stick you stick a noose over their head as you would do a trout. One would think that it would be easier to give them a blow on the head, but they are too nimble for that. There are a number of small birds in the bush and a sort of lark on the clear ground. The robin here has not a red breast, he is black and has a white breast; every country has the robin, although of many different colours; their habits are exactly alike in all I believe. The most remarkable bird of the singing species is the tui, mocking bird or parson bird, by all which names it is called. Mocking bird because it tries to imitate a great many others, and parson bird because it is nearly black and has a white tuft of feathers on its throat very like a clergyman's bands. We had one tame for a short time; in the morning before it rose it commenced mocking, at one time coughing as a person would do that had a bad cold, then laughing as if he would have split his sides, and occasionally whistling his native notes; a stranger could not keep from laughing to hear him.

William Deans.

Port Cooper, 21st September, 1846. We have your and James' letters of the 22nd November last. The cause of our not writing sooner, as promised in my last, has been owing to the want of opportunities of sending from here to Port Nicholson, it being now five months since there has been any direct communication betwixt that place and Port Cooper, and although there were vessels in Akaroa we did not hear of them till they were gone.

Since we wrote to you last there have been great disturbances with the natives in the neighbourhood of Port Nicholson, and several white people have been murdered by them. The continual leniency that has been shown to them since the foundation of the colony had encouraged them to proceed from less to more, till at last they have begun to consider themselves stronger than the settlers and any force that could be brought against them, and consequently they have been continually increasing their extortions and annoying the colonists in every imaginable way. Our new Governor, on his first arrival in Port Nicholson, immediately went up the Hutt himself, to where some of the natives had settled, on land that they had previously sold, and having seen their proceedings personally, without being known to them, he gave orders for the troops to destroy their settlement. These natives did not belong to Port Nicholson, nor did the land from which they had driven the settlers, belong to them or their tribe, and they had merely come there for the purpose of extorting an additional payment to get them to remove. Ever since that time they have kept up a continual series of robberies from the outlying settlers and there have been various engagements betwixt them and the troops and Militia, and natives friendly to the Government, but without any very decided success on either side, till lately, when the Governor paid Port Nicholson a second visit and by his own example, marching himself along with the troops and cheerfully undergoing all the fatigue and privation that they had necessarily to do in the depth of winter, he had infused a fresh stimulus into every one and they had captured several of the natives concerned in the rebellion, had taken the pa of the principal rebel and had driven him into the bush; when on account of the meeting of the Legislative Council he was obliged to return to Auckland, when seemingly just on the point of completely defeating the rebels and putting a speedy check to the rebellion, but there is little doubt that within a short time they would be compelled to come to whatever terms the Governor may choose to dictate to them. The number of the rebels is quite insignificant, from all accounts not exceeding 300 or 400, and they have only been enabled to stand out so long on account of it being the winter season and from the difficulty of getting to them from the want of roads, etc. It has been long evident that it would come to this at last, from the continual yielding that has been shown to whatever demands the natives choose to make, and it is as clear now that there will be no dependence to be placed on their remaining quiet till such time as a severe lesson has been taught them sufficient to convince them of the utter hopelessness of gaining anything by force. The natives here are all quiet enough.

Our new Governor is very popular and it is expected he will do as much good as our former ones have done harm; South Australia when he was first appointed Governor of it was in about as bad a state as New Zealand, and when he left it, it was the most prosperous part of the colony in this part of the world.

This disturbance with the natives, although no doubt a serious drawback to all cultivation and improvement in the disturbed district, is the cause of a very large Government expenditure and consequently money is more plentiful in Port Nicholson than it has been for a long time past. We expect one of the parties who has a contract for supplying the troops with fresh meat at Port Nicholson down here daily to purchase what fat stock we have, and in this way we will probably sell between 30 and 40 bullocks and steers which we could not easily have been able to get disposed of down here at present. The price we will get for them will be 4*d.* a lb. The amount of our stock now is upwards of 130 cattle, two mares in foal, two fillies probably in foal, one entire horse, fifty sheep and about twenty pigs.

John Deans.

Newcastle, 19th August, 1847. I wrote you about six weeks ago from Sydney saying that I had arrived there for the purpose of purchasing some sheep, and I now write you this short letter to let you know how I have been getting on since. I chartered a small vessel called the *Comet*, and have now got 600 sheep on board, and all ready to put to sea. Vessels are very scarce here now or I should have got a larger one and taken more sheep. However, those I have got are very good ones, and if we should be fortunate in taking them down to New Zealand, they will be a commencement. I have not heard from William since I left Port Cooper, and I daresay he will be wearying for my return.

Port Cooper, 20th December. We had rather a long and boisterous passage with the sheep, but were pretty fortunate on the whole, having lost only forty-six out of 600 before landing. We have been rather unlucky since owing to rough weather; in one gale of wind we lost ninety-two, and the 600 have dwindled down to about 430, but even with these in a few years, if we have good luck, we will have a great number as they increase very fast. There is no great danger of our losing many more of them now as they are becoming acclimatised and some of them will commence to lamb in about a month. William had a passage of seven days from this to Port Nicholson with the cattle and lost four out of thirty, but those that were landed turned out very well, so that we consider ourselves fortunate in getting rid of them as they were all bullocks and were of no use in increasing our stock.

William Deans.

Riccarton, 8th December, 1849. The principal township of the Canterbury Association, to be called Christchurch, will be within a mile of our property, and, as John writes, a great quantity of the land around it will be laid out in suburban allotments. The Government surveying steamer *Acheron* has been at Port Cooper and made a complete survey of the harbour, of which the Captain and officers, some of whom are persons of great experience, speak in favourable terms. All of them are delighted with the country and will send to England most favourable reports of the district. The Bishop likewise has been here, and although it is believed that he was at first averse to having the settlement here, yet on his seeing the place he quite changed his tune and spoke in high terms of it. No one in New Zealand knows more about the country than the Bishop, and his opinion will go a great way with the people in England. Everyone who comes here is much pleased with our property, and in fact with the whole country. Mr. Tuckett is talked of in very disparaging terms for choosing Otago in preference to this as the site for the Scotch settlement.

We accepted the land here in full settlement of all claims we had against the Company. The reason for doing so was that the place we wanted was better than ordinary land, and we were allowed to choose it, different from the usual form.

There are about 130 natives with white overseers employed on the roads in this neighbourhood, and there are about sixty white people employed besides. There are six surveyors employed on the plain and this number will soon be increased. These last we supply with meat by the carcass at 5*d*. per lb. Most of our stock are young, but we have sufficient steers and wethers to go on supplying them at this rate. Perhaps we would make more off them to keep them on till the arrival of the settlers, but these are good prices, and we can import lean cattle for less than half the price the steers now fetch, which would be fat and fit for the butcher by the time the settlers arrived.

John Deans.

Sydney, 27th April, 1850. I arrived here on the 23rd and am just on the eve of starting into the interior to select the horses, cattle and sheep to take down to Port Cooper. I was led to believe before I left Wellington that it would be no easy matter to get a vessel here to carry them, on account of the great demand for shipping to go to California, but I am agreeably disappointed and I believe I will be able to get a ship on very easy terms, as the bubble about California is beginning to burst. I do not anticipate having any difficulty in getting the stock, as all the kinds I want are plentiful and cheap.

The California mania had spread as far as Wellington before I left, although not to such an extent as to some of the other colonies; although several vessels were loading with timber, potatoes, etc., etc., it was not expected that many people would go in them, and I think they would be unwise to do so.

It is long since we have heard any news of the Canterbury settlement. I hope it is still to go on; neither the *Clara* nor the *Monarch* had arrived before I left Wellington, although they were fully five months due.

Newcastle, New South Wales, 26th June. On the eve of starting for Port Cooper I write this to inform you that I have got all my

arrangements completed to my satisfaction; the day before yesterday we shipped 92 head of cattle, yesterday 78 head, all without
any accident. To-day we intend the horses, twelve in number, and
the sheep (611) will be put on board, and to-morrow set sail. Every
person that has seen the stock agrees in saying that they are the
best that were ever shipped from the colony, and that it would be
difficult to get as good from any other parties, than the Australian
Agricultural Company, even in this country. The ship is perhaps
the best that has ever been to New Zealand with stock, and I have
got good men to take charge of them on board, so that I may
reasonably expect to make the voyage without much loss, and that
they will amply repay us for all the trouble and anxiety they may
cost me. The stock when landed will have cost about £1,800, and
if they get landed without great loss I think they will be worth
twice that sum. I have no doubt William is looking for me very
anxiously at Port Cooper, as it is a long time since I left, but I
could not possibly have done the work sooner, and I am very
anxious to get back as soon as possible.

Riccarton, 20th September. I received your and James' letters of
the 30th March. Long before this reaches you I hope you will have
received a letter which I hurriedly wrote you on board the *Woodbridge*, after we had landed the stock. I therein mentioned that I
have received a letter from Miss McIlraith, as well as one from
her father. Since I first broached the subject I have written two
or three letters, and I am in hopes that she may still be induced to
come out here, but if on farther hearing from her, she is averse to
this step I shall make use of the first favourable opportunity of
going home to arrange matters personally. At the time you advised
me to take out a wife with me I intended to have asked Miss
McIlraith, but I again thought that in case she or I should not like
New Zealand, particularly as she was so young at the time, that it
might be a wiser plan to come out and see how I liked it in the first
instance, and if I determined to make it my home to get her out to
share it with me. You know how unsettled we were for the first few
years, and although I many a time thought how much happier I
should be with a helpmate, I could not bring my mind to ask her

to join me in so out of the way a place as this, where often for months we did not see a strange face. It was only on the arrival of the news about the Canterbury settlement that I could see my way clearly enough to induce me to make the proposals. Our prospects, in regard to worldly matters have much improved within the last eighteen months, and I am exceedingly anxious to get settled down in this place for life and with Miss McIlraith for my partner (if she is not very much changed indeed), I fancy I could make myself very comfortable. In case the settlement should go on this summer it would be a considerable loss to be obliged to go home to fetch her out, but if nothing else will satisfy her I will do so at all risks. I will, however, wait till I hear from her again, as she may be even now on her way out.

The cattle, sheep and horses are doing very well; we lost a few of the sheep and cattle after landing, but have been exceedingly fortunate on the whole. We got 156 cattle home a few days after landing and they are thriving very well. We lost none of the most valuable animals, such as mares, bulls and rams.

17th February, 1851. I have been very much perplexed at not hearing from Mr. or Miss McIlraith. I have never had but one letter from each although I wrote a good many. I am anxiously waiting for an answer to some of these before I decide whether it will be necessary for me to go home, or whether Miss McIlraith may be induced to come out under the protection of some respectable married couple. If she would consent to do this, it would be very advantageous to me, as it would be a very great loss to be obliged to leave this for twelve months or so at this time. If I do not hear from her soon I shall propose that she should come out in the same ship as Bishop Jackson, and were I certain that she would be prevailed upon to do so I would mention the subject to him before he leaves. I am sure he and his lady would act as guardians with much pleasure. Miss McIlraith says she is a very bad sailor, but in such a large ship as that the Bishop will return in, it will be quite different from any one she has ever been in. I am sure she would enjoy the voyage and laugh at the danger. If she should refuse to comply with this request, I am not perfectly

[338]

assured that she might not start some objections to come out with me, even were I to go home for her. I have now too great a stake in this colony to leave it with the intention of living in Scotland, at least for some years, however desirous I might be to do so, and I think I could be better employed in making preparations to receive her here than in going to fetch her at the present moment. I hope she will be induced to see the matter in this light. If she should do so, I hope you or James will advance her what money she may want for her outfit, and furnishings for the house, as it will be much better to bring out most of these things than buy them here. I attribute Miss McIlraith's silence more to ignorance of what vessels sail to New Zealand than any other thing.

William Deans.

Riccarton, 4th June, 1851. As the 2,000 acres of pasturage offered us by the Association would be quite inadequate for our stock, we have been making a stand with Mr. Godley on the lease from the natives. At first he would not listen to our claim. We then memorialised the Governor, who owes Mr. Godley a grudge on account of the prominent part he takes in politics against him. His Excellency laid the memorial before the Attorney-General for his opinion, which was that the lease being a contract prior to the Association's title, the production of such would be a sufficient answer to an action of ejectment at the instance of the Association against us. Still Mr. Godley would not listen to our claim. We then proposed to refer the case to an eminent lawyer practising before the Court of Privy Council, or that the Association should bring a friendly action of ejectment to try the question. Neither of these proposals suited him, and after a further long correspondence, it has been at last agreed to refer the whole case to Sir George Grey. If his Excellency is with us then we are to have a new run of 33,000 acres, about forty miles from here for the remainder of the term of 21 years, under the lease from the natives at £8 per annum; and in the meantime we are to take possession of the new run without paying any rent.

We have invested £2,000 in Government debentures, bearing 8 per cent. interest, and having some other spare cash, I am to go up to Sydney in two months hence to bring down a cargo of sheep to stock the new run. We propose shipping 2,000 maiden ewes.

The new settlers have generally not a large capital, but there are a considerable number of young men of good families and education, and we hear accounts of numbers more expected to arrive in the spring. There is no danger but the settlement will progress, but the new settlers, in a short time, will be far behind in the race. All the new settlers are pleased with the country, and unanimously admit that our accounts of it were not exaggerated.

Sir George Grey offered me a seat in the General Assembly of the Legislative Council now sitting at Wellington, but although I am quite with him on the subject of colonial politics and think that his government of the colony has been a most successful one, under the difficult circumstances in which he has been placed, yet the thing was quite out of my way, so I declined.

John Deans.

28th August. It is with a sad and heavy heart that I sit down to write you the melancholy intelligence of the death of our dear William. He sailed on the 20th July for Wellington from which place he intended taking the first chance to proceed to Sydney. On the fatal morning, the 23rd July, the ship was totally wrecked within a few miles of the entrance to Port Nicholson, when all on board, with the exception of a lad and a Lascar, perished. The first intelligence I received of this awful calamity was on the 20th instant. Mr. Lyon and his brother-in-law were making every exertion to find the body, but had not succeeded up to the 4th inst. I hope you will all be enabled to bear this sad bereavement; the greatest comfort I can afford you, and it has proved a great consolation to me, is that he was universally beloved and esteemed by everyone that knew him, both in the older settlements and in this place, in fact wherever he was known he was respected. He was everything one could wish in a son, brother or friend. Among the thousands that knew him he had not a single enemy, and surely we may hope that one who possessed so many good qualities, on earth, has found acceptance with God, through the redeeming blood of our Blessed Saviour, and that he is now looking down on us from Heaven. This hope has enabled me to support myself through this dreadful trial with more calmness than I could have believed possible, for how consoling it is to think that when our nearest and dearest friends are taken from us by death that the change to them is a great gain.

You may probably have heard of our loss before this reaches you. When I have in some measure recovered from the shock I will write you a longer letter.

Charlotte Godley

Charlotte Wynne was one of a large Devonshire family, and from her birth in 1821 until her marriage in 1846 lived the life, busy, crowded, yet serene, of a well-to-do country household. She gives us glimpses of it: the shooting parties, with their ponies and hampers, the end of the evening meal, with her father pouring out wine and her mother pulling up her scarf and giving her 'after dinner shiver.'

Her husband, whose name was to figure prominently in the history of New Zealand, was an Irishman from County Leitrim, educated at Harrow and Christ Church, Oxford. He gave up a legal career—of which an interest in general principles rather than in individual cases would have kept him from making a practical success—owing to ill health, and after travelling in Europe and North America returned to Ireland much preoccupied with sympathy for the hurts of that famine-stricken land.

With the colonization schemes of Wakefield he had for some time been in touch, and finally he became a collaborator in the project of planting a Church of England settlement in the Canterbury Plains of southern New Zealand. He became managing director of the Canterbury Association.

He decided to go himself to see the settlement on its feet, though he had been ordered to Madeira to fend off tuberculosis; and he, his wife and their son John Arthur (born 1847) left on the *Lady Nugent* in 1849.

[342]

They spent a short time in Wellington before coming down to Port Cooper to meet the first ships sent over by the Association. And for the two years of their stay there, Godley was virtually ruler of the new colony.

His wife emerges from these pages an irresistibly attractive person, the ideal complement of her serious husband. She did not have to work hard with her hands, perhaps, as Frances Stewart did, because she had the invaluable Powles, but as the wife of one of the foremost men in New Zealand she had an important part to play, and how well she played it a contemporary tells us. 'She left us the example, how it is possible, in the midst of harassing cares and unwonted discomfort, to be gentle and serene, and cheerful and uniformly courteous to all; and how little it needs of worldly wealth to create the purest type of an English home upon the shores of a scarcely inhabited island.'

They returned to England in 1853, where Godley became Assistant Secretary for War, and had great influence with the Government in their handling of New Zealand affairs. As during his stay in that country, when in opposition to the autocratic Grey, he was emphatic in the expression of views like this: 'May I earnestly and solemnly impress the one great fundamental maxim of sound colonial policy—it is, to let your colonies alone. . . . Do not be afraid to leave them to themselves; throw them into the water and they will swim.'

He died in 1861, eight years after saying these words. His wife lived to be eighty-six, and to see her Arthur become Secretary of State for India and Baron Kilbracken.

These letters to her mother are printed in *Letters From Early New Zealand written by Charlotte Godley*, Plymouth (N.Z.) (1936).

Lady Nugent. March 23rd. 1850. We came up within two miles of the shore with a sunset of golden haze over the New land and if we had had two hours more of daylight might have anchored that night. However that was not to be, and the Captain was obliged to be cautious, as we had no one in the ship who had ever been on the coast before. In the night we lay to, and then drifted too far

[343]

to the northward; the breeze freshened, and kept us beating about all Sunday the 23rd, and on Monday we had another gale, almost if not quite as bad as the Friday before, only then we knew where we were. Tuesday, we were all up early and in great spirits, with a fair wind blowing straight into the harbour, and at noon in we came, at a great pace. The entrance is very narrow as there are sand banks, covered at high water, which run nearly across the Bay. But it is *so beautiful*. It is eight miles from the point to Port Chalmers, which is a little bay in the harbour, and there *Lady Nugent* is now lying, in a perfect nest of beauty, and as snug as a ship can be. You must imagine wooded cliffs one over another like the scenery near Gwydir, only cliffs and wood all round, and instead of Llanrwst, to look down on the sea quite smooth. We were hungry enough to stay on board till we got some dinner, and then *such* a walk on shore! At Port Chalmers there are about a dozen little wooden houses, and after walking a little way through the wood above the port, we came upon such a salt water Lake! As clear as crystal, with the same sort of wooded cliffs all round, and pieces of rock standing down to the water like old towers, the colouring of which would drive you quite distracted; every shade of bright yellow and brown, and the foliage is very beautiful and so foreign, there is not one tree the same as any we have at home. The fern tree is very like the palm, with its bunch of leaves on the top, each about seven feet long, and there is a beautiful tall pine here and there, with a tall stem and tufts on the top, but very different in leaf from anything I have ever seen. There is every sort of wild bird's note, too, still to be heard in the woods. I believe even the parrots sing instead of screaming, and somebody shot two most beautiful little love birds. I cannot describe one-half of what we saw or felt at being again on land; any place would have looked beautiful to us just then, but it really is lovely, and would be still more so if we could still get a peep at any of the high hills which we saw from the sea; but that would require an expedition through the bush (as the uncleared parts are generally denominated here) to the tops of those now in sight, which we have not yet accomplished. The harbour of Otago is eighteen miles long from the flag staff at the entrance to the town of Dunedin (as you know, the old name for Edinburgh) which is the nucleus of the settlement. Port Chalmers lies about half-way up, and there wooded islands seem to shut the entrance any higher, and at present ships do not come beyond it; but with a pilot they may come up several miles further. The Captain, with his papers, rowed off to the town as soon as we had anchored, and returned in the evening with Captain Cargill, the New Zealand Company's agent here, who came to 'pay his respects' and to press us most kindly to come up and stay with him at the town until the ship is ready to sail again; which we were very glad to do, as it is a most disagreeable time to spend on board, and almost all the people about constantly drunk, in a little place like that, where our arrival is quite an event. We find the ship that sailed about a fortnight before us has not yet been heard of.

I must tell you though that I am writing from Dunedin now on Easter Eve! We came up on Wednesday, in a little open boat, wind and mist dead against us, a most uncomfortable sail of nearly five hours, and are now located very comfortably in a weatherboard house, the front half of which came out as it is from England. It consists of six rooms, three bedrooms, a pantry, kitchen, and sitting room, in which I am now writing, and it is a very comfortable abode for anywhere. It is weatherboard all round, but coated with single brick at the windy end, and rough cast, and the inside is *lined*, or as we should say pannelled, only roughly done, but with a pretty coloured wood, something like a very dark box, which takes a very good polish, if anyone had time to rub it at all. Quite an old fashioned fireplace with dogs for burning wood (but there is coal eight miles off when they have time to fetch it); a grand pianoforte, a brass inlaid clock, red twill curtains, and at least a dozen pictures in large gilt frames!

The situation of the town is of course very fine, at the head of the harbour, which opens out wider; but it looks rather bare and new, the clearings leave stumps and bare burnt branches, but it will look very different when good grass, etc., has time to grow, and the walks all about are most beautiful. There are perhaps 120 houses in the town, mostly of weatherboard; a little kirk, two butchers, three bakers, and other shops in proportion. I must say it is wonderful to see the progress made in two years, and the place looks about as grand as *Ysputty*, only the houses are all new and made of wood and rather further apart; and out of them come such smart ladies and gentlemen, what with lawyers, and doctors, and surveyors, and go-to-meeting clothes on other classes, there are heaps of them. Indeed the black spot in Dunedin to me is the state of society there. There is a Scotch and an English party, and half of them will not visit the other half, or approve of anything that is done. I believe it is so more or less in all small communities, and here *Scotch* and *English* of course makes a capital ground of offence. The whole place is at sixes and sevens, and I am a good deal alarmed at the idea of what may be my own fate at Port Cooper, being mixed up in anything like the same state of things; but I hope it may be possible to keep out of it. There are already a great number of people settled outside the town up every little valley and along the beach too, and *all* well off. Every thing is dear, wages 4*s.* a day, bread 9*d.* the 4lb loaf, meat the same as in London, and *very good*, milk ditto, fresh butter 2*s.* a pound, and such washing bills! about 3*s.* a dozen for everything, we pay, for a few things we brought up to have washed. The poorest people have fresh meat at least once a day, but still there are plenty of grumblers. The cows here would rather astonish our farmers. They run all day in the bush and attend to their calves, and at night, if possible, they are caught, shut up, and milked in the morning. But very often it is not possible, and it is funny enough to see a man, as I did, at the top of a tree with a telescope, looking for his cows, to be milked. Altogether it is much what I expected to find, except that I thought, in a colony, people would have been more friendly and fond of each other and less upon form. There is as much etiquette about visiting, and so on, at Dunedin as I ever saw anywhere at home, and the shopkeepers, etc., all dress most *expensively*. My husband is much distressed in the political economy point of view at finding the company providing work as charity while wages are 4*s.* a day, which is of course an absurdity, but I will spare you all that question.

April 8th. We left Dunedin on the 4th, and came back to *Lady*

Nugent with the Captain, in his gig, and sailed down under an impromptu piece of canvas in an hour and twenty minutes, with a perfect gale in our favour.

Port Chalmers is certainly a beautiful place, but I cannot admire its inhabitants; they are a very drunken set. We sailed out on the 8th, having been anchored a fortnight all but a day, and had a most lovely day for our start.

Lyttelton (the town, such as it is) lies quite in a little basin out of the harbour, and has risen into being, I should think, quicker than any town ever did; it looks almost as large as Dunedin, and has a far better jetty, etc. If there were as much wood as at Otago it would be quite beautiful, and so would the town, already, for the buildings, so far, are very good looking for this country. They are still of weatherboard, but not quite so much like little packing cases as the Otago buildings. There are several long-looking cottages together which are 'Emigration Barracks'; that is, houses ready for the emigrants to get into on first landing, while they make their selection of land and raise a house. Hotels or lodgings would be ruinous, of course. The only fear with these is, I think, that they will be too comfortable, and tempt the emigrants to remain in them longer than is necessary. They have all deep verandahs and lattice windows, and give you at once the idea of a hot climate, which indeed we found it for the two days we were there. Close to the barracks stands our house, built in the same style as the barracks, only with two stories, and to our great surprise we found it nearly finished, and the best looking house we have yet seen in New Zealand; six rooms and a kind of pantry. But the most magnificent feature of the place is the road, which is being made through the line of hills down into the great plains behind, which are about 40 miles in breadth, reaching quite up to the snowy mountains. It is very like our Holyhead road, and quite as good, wherever it is finished.

I was quite determined to see the plains if possible, but of course Arthur could not attempt to get up the hill; so I persuaded one of our passengers, who had been up once on his own account, that he would like to go up again on mine, and we found a very good, though steep, path to the top. The days too that we were there [at Port Cooper] were very hot and the Maori natives (Moury's it is called) had brought up melons from their village, grown like potatoes, which they sold us for sixpence apiece. They have a few huts on the spot which hold a *great* number of inhabitants, as they stow themselves away inside, literally as you would pack a box. Some of them, and especially the women, are frightful, but they look very picturesque, sitting about the place with a bright scarlet blanket and a deep black border spread over them. This is the favourite dress, but costs here about a pound more than a week's wages, for a Maori. Their faces are a fine rich brown with a mop of hair on the top, black, and generally as shiny as oil can make it. The near view however is not so well, especially with the blanket off. There is nothing but a *unique* garment of calico, always *couleur Isabelle*, which covers them, however, entirely, and their figures are most awkward. They really seem as if their only natural position was squatting, for nothing else describes it, with their chin on their knees and a pipe in their mouths, and they are horribly tattooed even on their lips. If anything obliges them to move, they slide along more like monkeys than anything human, and are down again directly. The men are generally better looking, and better dressed too, generally trowsers and shirts, etc.; there seem to be very few who still wear the blanket to go about in. I was among their huts in the evening, with Mr. Wakefield for my interpreter, bargaining for some melons which I thought would be acceptable presents on board, when a great tall man came home from his work, in a straw hat, and a blanket tied round his waist; which he immediately proceeded to take off, leaving only a very small garment behind. I began to think of the *Plume of Feathers*, and was near taking to my heels; but the next moment saw him down with the others, rolled like a ball in his blanket, by the fire in front of the huts, and his mouth full of hot potatoes; the women crawling about and screaming out their uncouth words. It was getting dark, and with the firelight glimmering on the whole scene, it would have made a good picture. To me it was like a dream, indeed I often feel inclined to say, like the old woman in the story, 'if I be I, as I suppose I be.'

[348]

April 28th, and in our own hired house at Wellington! Sunday too, and we have been to church for the first time since Antonie! To be sure the service was not very full, as both the Litany and Communion Service were omitted, and as we have another gale to-day, the weatherboard sides of the church were creaking so as to make hearing very difficult, and swaying about so visibly that it was difficult to imagine ourselves safe. I suppose there never was so windy a place as this; it is acknowledged to be the great drawback to the settlement, and in the town you get it all. This is the third *gale* we have had since we came, not yet a week, and if the house were not so well used to it I am sure it must come down; as it is, every board shakes, and between every board comes up a miniature hurricane; but then a house is *a house*, after 140 days of ship, and what can people want beyond a fire to sit by!

June 12th. I have spent a good part of to-day at Colonel Gold's with a view to Arthur's making acquaintance with the children. They seem nice children, and obedient to a word or look, but rather in the rough as to dress and so on, as may be imagined from their having, at present, only one nursery girl to wait upon them all, and poor Mrs. Gold, though she seemed rather overpowered with them all, said she had been so unfortunate in her last nurse (one of these very self-sufficient and independent colonial young ladies) that she would rather wait a long time, on the chance of finding something good, than take another in a hurry. You hear the same from every one here, and I should think the whole subject of maid-servants one of the great miseries of human life in N.Z. Every tolerably respectable woman has a husband and children, and does not wish to leave home. The men are not quite so rare or so troublesome, as far as I hear; they seem to do all the work in every house.

July 4th. This month, and August, are considered the worst here, and we may have even snow, though it is unusual; last winter they had it on the ground for three mornings, but it never lasts a whole day. How curious it will seem, too, to have a very hot Christmas Day, if we live to see it, and the windows ornamented with flowers something like lilac laburnums, (which is here a favourite for the purpose) instead of holly. So many things seem turned upside down; in expounding things to Arthur I often come to a stand-still. Sun in the north! etc., it makes our books all wrong. Further, with what face can I now teach him 'I hope I may never be tempted to roam, From England, dear England, my own native home' *vide* 'English Boy' Original Poems. All imported goods from England are about double their original price in the shops here; sometimes more. For instance, a piece of chintz I got, though only a little common blue and white stripe, is 1*s.* a yard, and our frightful Axminster carpet 4*s.* 6*d.*; crockery and glass the same, with some-thing additional from breakage. We are loudly lamenting that we did not bring more things with us. But people at home seem so little to know how you will really find things here, that even my husband, with all his opportunities, had formed no idea of what are the really useful things to bring out, and as for myself, not having been very available at the busy time, and moreover little disposed to turn my thoughts that way when I could help it, I don't think I at all realized that we should ever reach New Zealand at all, or that, if we did, we could ever aspire to anything beyond the barest necessaries of life, far less ever have to consider appear-ance; and so we brought a very slender stock of most things; for instance, spoons and forks (of which we have only enough for our-selves) and, except the pianoforte, nothing but our cabin furni-ture; if a thought of their necessity ever suggested itself so did my husband's usual maxim of '*doing without* them'; and yet, when-ever we go and *take up our station* at Port Cooper, even he says that we must have a dinner service, instead of a few willow pattern plates and dishes, which we now all use, so as to be able to ask people, at least to dinner, if not to stay in the house, as soon as they land after their long voyage, which will be expected of us.

July 15th. Arthur and I returned this evening from Mr. Petre's, where we found our way very successfully on Thursday last. Mrs. Petre, herself, is very young-looking and with wild spirits, and enjoys a ball, or a ride, or a scamper of any kind, and is sometimes very pretty. She is, like her husband, a Roman Catholic and was a Miss Walmsley, and brought up, though an only daughter, at a convent, till nearly sixteen. Then came home Mr. Henry W. Petre, to his Father's, Lord Petre's, *the great house* of the neighbourhood, from N.Z. in search of a wife. She was sent for from the convent, engaged before she was sixteen, married two months afterwards, (all of which I heard from herself) and after a short bit of London, and other gaieties, came straight out here to settle, eight years ago, and they seem as happy as possible. He is immensely tall and thin and looks like a set of fire irons badly hung together, and on the top a head that would be good-looking enough if the features had not that sort of lengthened look that you may see in your own by consulting the back of a silver spoon. He is very pleasant, though, and good-natured, and *quite* a gentleman, and seems moreover duly impressed with a high idea of her excellencies; which indeed are manifold, for there is nothing she cannot do, all learnt out here, from receiving company, down to cooking the dinner they are to eat; and all pleasantly and well, and so as to be very much liked.

August 12*th!!* How much, and how often, I have been wondering to-day what you are all doing? who is at Voelas? how many brace? Though indeed it is rather early to speculate on that, seeing that with you it is only about 8.30 a.m.; perhaps the ponies just gone from the door, and the breakfast things left in the hall! Perhaps too, it is raining, as it will sometimes, even on the 12th August. Is Sara there? and is Heneage? It is all very well for people to *say* that when you cannot live at home, or within a week of it, you may practically as well be in N. Zealand! but let them try being *always* four months, and generally six behindhand, in the most important news of their own people, and see whether they still think so.

August 27th. I shall be very sorry to leave Wellington, we like so much our little cottage all on the ground floor, with its garden which is quite private and then the beautiful view, and such nice walks in every direction, whenever it is dry. It is, by the by, rather descriptive of the climate here that the clothes are always quite in the summer style, such as white shawls with large bright flowers on them, straw bonnets with sky blue ribbons, and white cotton gloves; bright colours are quite 'the go' here.

I wonder who amongst you all will take pity on our benighted ideas, and send us a chapter on the fashions.

Port Cooper, however, is just now *quite the fashion*, quite the favourite idea here, so many people want to get land there, and are much disappointed to find that they must write to England to buy what is so near at hand, and so tempting to some people who are getting tired of being so *shut up* as they say, and feel, in a country like this, all of hills, without any ground where a plough can be used; even in the Hutt they are as yet very little used, I believe from the stumps in the ground left to *die* down, and which are still in high preservation; and labour so dear, besides the short colonial hours, that digging cannot be made to answer for corn. It all comes from Australia, Hobart town, etc.

August 29th. I am sure you would laugh if you could see the Maoris with their tops, not of the *humming* kind either, which are pretty amusements for anyone, but regular whipping tops; men with grey beards, women, and children, are all equally excited about them, and now that roads are getting dry the pathway through the town is really alive with them, more men, too, than children, laughing and talking about it in the greatest excitement. As the soldiers marched by the other day with the band, a full grown woman (dressed in nothing but a garment of brown cotton, like a pinafore with sleeves, and sewn up behind) was following them whipping her top along as an English child would a hoop. All the girls, too, are capital performers, and generally with pipes in their mouths, and so are the tiny children of six or seven, who are very funny figures, with a *piccaninny* of the smallest size on their backs, a little blanket over both, and the little bare brown limbs slipping out as they work away and scream with delight. A peculiarity of the Maori babies is that they don't cry; I did once hear a child of about two, that seemed ill, crying, but that is all. There is a Maori pah about a mile from the town and two more almost in it, being at each end of what is called 'the Beach',

that is the long street (about a mile and a half) if street it can
be called, that has houses only on one side, and runs along by
the sea.

October 1st. Again we slept at Pawatenui, and had the state
apartment. We had a very cold night there, quite thick ice on
the water next morning, to the great detriment of a flock of little
goslings, six of whom were killed, and another was found by Arthur
so numb with cold that it couldn't walk; however we warmed and
revived it so well that the landlord made it a present to him. It
took us seven hours to get home the twenty-one miles, walking up
and down hills, which was a great chance for the gosling, who had
got quite well, and enjoyed a little swim in a puddle at the roadside extremely; you can fancy Arthur's delight, and the number
of times that it had to be peeped at, under all its warm coverings,
to see that it was really alive, and 'singing its little song'. Next
morning it was found dead in its bed(!) and as he says 'its grave
is to be seen in the garden'.

Our kiwi was not much more successful. It was a most curious
beast, with a head and whiskers like a rat, a long, long bill like
a woodcock, but not so straight, coarse feathers, pointed and feeling like fur, legs like a miniature ostrich, and a short round body
with *make believe* wings as big as a just born chicken's. I defy anyone to see it run without laughing, its head swaying from side to
side at each stride, and a sort of *abandon* in its gait, that you see
in some of the little figures in *Punch*, running away from some
monster. It was a night bird, and quite stupid in the day, could
hardly see to eat its food, even worms and raw meat, and would
run its head into any dark hole it could find. We had it for about
a week and then one night it ran away, just after it had been fed,
and we could never find it. It was very cross, and would scratch
and peck anyone who came near it, but so very funny and odd
looking that we were sorry to loose it.

Port Cooper. On Monday the 16th December (I don't know how
to write large enough letters for the event), in the morning a *ship*
was announced early, in sight, and then at anchor!! But there is a

point of rock which hides them, where they usually anchor, from our view. Some people thought it might be an English ship . . . and then the matter was quickly settled by my husband's encountering Mr. FitzGerald, who was the first to step on shore, in the road down to the jetty; so altered by a sailor's dress, an immense straw hat, very hollow cheeks, a ferocious moustache, and I am sorry to say a lame leg, (which is well, though, now), that at first he scarcely knew him, and when he did, was so overcome as hardly to know whether to laugh or to cry, and I believe ended by doing both. He was alone, as Mrs. FitzGerald stayed on board for a headache, and the lame knee was from a most characteristic fall, got in snowballing the Captain in a gale, the decks all slippery from hail and ice. You may imagine the questions, etc., and the excitement of the whole morning. Mr. FitzGerald dined with us, and we talked as fast as we could, and that was not fast enough, and kept our eyes steadily fixed on his face, in the delight of seeing a real face, and hearing a voice, that we had seen and heard in England, a year and five days since we left it! and with all our arrivals he is still the only one I have ever seen before. 'It never rains but it pours', is a very old saying, and in the evening of the same day the *Randolph* anchored by the side of the *Charlotte Jane*, just as many hours after her here, as she had left Plymouth. We were full of wonder, and already thought it a remarkable coincidence, when next morning, Tuesday, 17th, in came the *Sir George Seymour*, making the third ship that had performed the voyage in such an unusually short time, for she had started from Plymouth again, twelve hours after the *Randolph*: was it not most curious? *Je n'en reviens pas!* and now I must thank for my letters, which came in by degrees, from one ship and then another, as the boxes came on shore, or *parties* carrying them, unpacked their goods.

On Xmas day we had a dinner party, to meet—a turkey and ham, that we had brought on purpose from Wellington, and a bit of roast beef that we got with some difficulty, and after rather a characteristic disappointment. The meat, of course, will not keep here, but must be cooked a day or two, at most, after it is killed, and on Xmas Eve our butcher (for there are two!!) came to tell us that he had *lost* the bullock that was to have died for the Christ-

mas dinners, and of which every joint was bespoken! He had
driven it successfully towards home, having some miles to fetch it,
but at two o'clock in the morning it had made its escape, and was
not to be caught. However, a fortnight after he was caught and
killed and we ate our bit of him. We had a plum-pudding, too, but
could not manage mince pies. It was very unlike Christmas Day, *so
hot*, even when we went to the early Service and Communion at 7.30.
We had a few greens for the Church, but not enough, and we had
a few up, too, in the rooms, but although they are evergreens, they
die like our ordinary trees, and will not last, like our good holly
and ivy and laurel, till Twelfth Night. At Wellington, the red
myrtle is just out in time, and makes a most beautiful decoration.
Our Church has been, so far, a large loft over the warehouse for
emigrants' goods, but we are going into a better one to-morrow.
One building of the Emigration Barracks, now that there is a little
more room, has been cleared, and thrown into one room, about
sixty feet long, and a good width; and, with the supporting pillars,
looks really *something* like a Church. They are waiting for Dr.
Jacksons' arrival to begin building a real one.

Mr. Cholmondeley has two tents, and a house, partly timber
and partly sods, but I cannot go through them all [the new
arrivals], and the workmen have all built little temporary places to
put themselves and their families in; some what they call here a 'V
hut', that is, a mere sloping roof of boards overlapping, set on the
ground without any walls to stand on, and of course removable
without loss, except of a little labour, when they know where they
will finally settle,—or by wind. Fancy one, the other day, from
having no door, caught up by the wind, and shoved bodily away,
and the people inside discovered eating chops! Some have 'cob'
houses, frames of poles filled in with clay; and some, merely a
frame of branches and poles, thatched with fern and grass.

And now I think I shall astonish you. *We* are going to give a
dance!! if all goes well, next Monday or Tuesday! It is intended
as a kind of friendly meeting, before the people all separate to go
to their selections of land on the plain, next month; and we are to
ask about one hundred, and give only tea, and the festivity is to
take place in the barracks, in some large empty rooms there, and

Mr. Wakefield is to *do it* for us. The music is a difficulty, but we hope to triumph over that. It is sure to be rather a bore, some such curious people must be asked; but I hope at least that a civil and even jovial intention on our part will be apparent, through pink calico, ship's flags, and 'patent composite' candles. I hope it may answer, but of that you shall hear (D.V.) by our next opportunity. We have been rather unhappy about the bread, 14*d.* the 4 pound loaf, but two ships came in yesterday, and at the sale this morning, flour was sold one-fourth cheaper than last week, which is very good news. Altogether we hope we are getting on pretty well, and there are already about a hundred people in the plains, all pretty comfortable and contented, and no one seems to be disappointed with that part of the scheme.

Lyttelton. February 5th, 1851. I must now enter on the melancholy subject of *our* Bishop, or rather, as I much prefer calling him, Mr. Jackson. (He says he is not Dr.) The *Castle Eden*, which had been sometime due, according to advertisements for her sailing, arrived on Friday, February 7th, and on shore came instantly in spite of a good blow, Mr. and Mrs. Jackson and two boys, twelve and nine. I had heard enough of him to alarm me beforehand, and when I saw and heard him, not even the idea, the hope, of letters on board his ship could make me tolerably happy to see him. So much of the tone and feeling of this colony must depend on the Bishop; being, as he will be, so completely the first person here in every way, besides his own peculiar vocation, that anyone who feels a real interest in it, must look to him as a sort of key to the whole affair. And then judge of our mortification and sorrow on seeing Mr. Jackson, a little fussy upstanding man, whose very bow and style of greeting, tone, manner, words, all have on them the very stamp of humbug (if I may make free with this gentleman-like expression) and forbid the idea of considering him what I have been used to call a gentleman. An outside of easy-going good-nature, not for an instant concealing a most careful watch over his own interest; and selfishness, even about armchairs, and the things he likes to eat; and a complete want of reverence in his use of sacred words and expressions. I asked him which of our four clergymen was to be incumbent of Lyttelton, and his answer was that I might choose. 'If you have a fancy (incumbent) for either of them, I'll put him here.' John really cannot bear him, and finds him as unsatisfactory as possible to do business with; always self-seeking and inaccurate. It is a deep disappointment to him, having such a man come out as Bishop, though he owns, and appreciates his great cleverness as a landsale commissioner and the remarkable eloquence of his sermons. His manners are most unpleasant; for instance, with his wife, he sometimes is so short and unfeeling to her that she has the tears in her eyes; and then it is 'Libby', 'Toto', 'love', and 'precious wife'; and Charles will appreciate the delight with which John stood by, the first night, to see him go up and kiss his wife, and in affected tones, say that she was 'welcome to his little diocese'. We like Mrs. Jackson very much, she is I think thoroughly good-natured and straightforward. Not very refined certainly, she calls people 'Wortley', 'Montague', is a little playful about her H's, and has a mouth rather like Miss le Loup; but we have quite got over this, and she is in some ways very good-looking.

March 1st. Near Ricarton. I have often thought that our letters from New Zealand described life in very different forms from the imaginings of our friends at home; no roughing, you will say, but balls, band-playings, morning visits, and tea-parties!! But I think you would say that we were tolerably colonial if you could see us all now, as I write; for the present located on the plains, close to Mr. Deans'. We had two pack-horses started off first, for our flitting, and then one of the riding-horses, laden with a few supplementary goods, to his very great disgust; he tried all ways, kicking, etc., to get them off, whenever we went down hill, and delayed us a good deal; and then the other, with my noble self, and Arthur on my knee. Powles walked, and got on so much faster than we did, that instead of dividing the distance, and letting me walk for two or three miles, she had half the things unpacked before we arrived. The day was beautiful, a blow of course we had, in crossing the hill, but it was very pleasant afterwards, and Arthur delighted to come and live in the bush, in a little V hut.

The first evening was very cold, when it came to sitting up with wind blowing between every board, but we managed to make the beds pretty warm and comfortable; and the next day, Sunday, was quite warm, and we went off to church at Christchurch. The service is performed in the unfinished rooms of the Survey Office, the largest in the place, at present; but a real church of stone is to be begun forthwith, and a parsonage house for Mr. Kingdon, who is, like everyone else, living just now in a V hut, but his has two rooms in it. It was very curious to me to see the plains actually dotted over with small houses, all round the site for the town, it is almost like Rosllan, only not, of course, so extensive, or such good houses; and when I was there two months and a half ago, there was just one built by Mr. Pollard, about a month before! Such funny buildings, or rather screens, some people have put up; just large enough to contain them at night, and all household operations, cooking, etc., are carried on outside, to the great edification of passers-by.

April 7th. I have not written in this letter for a week and now we have the *Travancore* in and such a number of letters and presents to thank you all for, and for all the good wishes for my birthday. You must be left to imagine my delight with all my parcels and presents. First came your hand-writing, a parcel from Mr. Evans, the night that the ship anchored, with my book from Louisa for Arthur; and my new collar, for Easter Sunday, it came most luckily, and my gardening gloves, with a little note from Mr. Evans promising to call; then, the next morning but one, my beautiful, perfect clock!—and long before I had done admiring that, my other parcels, presents for Arthur, and the *Ladies' Companion* from Sara, but not the gown she sent me; for we have such an advanced and superior custom house, that the gown had to be kept two days to be valued, and every other parcel opened thoroughly in search for letters. However, at last I did get it and everything else, and don't know where to begin my thanks. I am specially glad that there was a holiday on my birthday, only I am sorry you had such a small party. I can fancy I see you just at dessert, too, the dining-room door finally shut and my Father pouring out wine for everyone, and you just pulling up your scarf, and giving your after dinner shiver; Louisa and Francis, both, I guess, on the warm side of the table (such a shiny table, too, as we don't see in N.Z.), for your 14th November would not do very well for our festivity of tea out in the garden! It seems too happy to hope ever to see it again. I am now plotting deeply to get my husband sent home in disgrace.

May 27th. We had, on Saturday, a very gay day for the Queen's birthday. A Regatta, and English sports, and native dances, and a School feast. You will see it all in the papers which we mean to send, but it is a very bad account. The day was only too lovely, not a breath of wind all day, so that the sailing-boats never started. First thing in the morning, we had our visitors arrive from 'Pigeon Bay', two daughters of a Mrs. Sinclair there; they are very nice people and great friends of the Bishop's (of N.Z.). The boat-races, or rather rowing-matches, were very pretty. As there was no wind for the sailing-matches, we had to begin with them. The first was of five-oared whale boats, a sixth man steering, as they do in whale-boats, with a long oar out behind, and standing, which looks very picturesque. Five boats started, and four of them were Maoris'; only one white crew pulled against them, and they broke an oar, which was a very convenient excuse, for they were beaten very easily, and the Maoris were supposed to do it in remarkably short time and came in very fresh, and in great delight, as you may imagine, for they are very excitable. The start was really very pretty. The sun was very hot, and the sea like glass, and the boats full of brown figures, some quite good-looking, and with bare arms and shoulders; such eager faces watching Mr. FitzGerald, who stood by the great ensign on the jetty, with a gun, which was fired for the signal to start; and then off they went, working all over, and the steersman catching the arm of the man next him at each stroke, and lifting him back. The *Victoria* won, belonging to a chief, who did not go in her, but walked up and down, telling people he was just like Mr. Godley, and only looked on. Another boat was the *Captain Bailey*, owned and steered by 'Bigfellow'. They (the Maoris) have such curious names. Then we had some small sculling-matches, duck-hunt and so on, but not a

breath of wind all day long that would stir even Arthur's little
'cutter'; so my trouble was wasted, for I had made a lovely flag
for Mr. Wortley with the best white silk the town could afford
(persian, a little thicker than gauze), and some of my last remains
of cerise ribbon. He had got a boat, only for the race, that was
called the *Charlotte*, and had belonged to the Association, and so
he said I owed him a flag, as it was called after me. Let no one say
that is a small piece of trouble till they have tried to make one, or
until Persian ceases to stretch and ravel when cut on the cross.
Mrs. Russell had got a little vessel, smarter than the *Martha*, for
Arthur, and so she told him she would race with him, and this also
took place, but so little wind was there, that the vessels had to be
recovered by a little Maori boy walking into the water (for sixpence), as we could wait no longer; the war dance was to begin
and the best part to see, of that, is the beginning, when the chal-
lenger throws a spear, and they all run to pick it up. But the rest
of the dancing (?), especially when the women take it up, is very
unpleasing, and more like a clown in the pantomime, rolling his
eyes about to make you laugh, than any real dance. Then we had
luncheon, our own dinner, for about as many as could sit down in
our room, and then a soapy pig, and a greased pole, and a wheel-
barrow race, and then it was time to go to the school children,
whom we had invited to a tea party, in one of the empty barrack-
rooms that before served as a ballroom. There were to have been
seventy children (but some did not come), so we made the tea in
the boiler of a small furnace we have for washing, and ordered
twelve dozen buns and some plum cake from the baker's. I mention
this because I think it must be a satisfaction to you to know that
we can get buns here. Order was most strictly preserved by the
presence of our schoolmaster, a very tremendous gentleman, who
however rather took away from our joviality; and then the gentlemen of the glee club volunteered to give us some of their per-
formances (really very good), until it got dark, and we could have
the magic-lantern, which was to conclude the festivity. There is a
very good one among the innumerable things that Mr. Jackson
brought out, and the children received each new slide with loud
shouts of delight, and when they had gone home, and the big

children who came to watch with them, there was a second exhibi
tion for the Maoris, and we sent them tea and cake too. We had
only a few people at tea, and quietly to bed, but there was a very
gay party on board the *Travancore*, first dinner and then dancing.
There were eight ladies on board and about forty gentlemen, and
as seems always the case, the fewer the lady-partners were, the
more anxious were all the gentlemen to dance; in short it was very
successful, and everyone thoroughly tired next day.

August 5th. On Sunday we had a slight shock of an earthquake,
while we were sitting at breakfast; the first we have felt here. We,
who were accustomed to such things, knew instantly what it
meant; but most of the new-comers either did not feel it at all, or
thought someone had banged a door, or that a cart came by. So
you see it is not very bad. The ball at Messrs. Longden & Le
Creu's Store turned out very successful, in spite of pouring wet
weather, and such muddy roads. Miss Townsend went home that
morning, and so, hearing that the FitzGeralds had sent a refusal
on account of the terrible state of the hill up to their house, I went
up there myself, with Arthur and a long stick (without which you
must not expect to be able to stand upright anywhere but on level
gravel), and I suggested that, as dancing ladies were very scarce,
she ought to consider it a sort of duty to attend, and we did and
should go, even if it poured; and that she could come down by
daylight and dress and sleep at our house, and so it was arranged;
excepting that, as he is almost always late, they came sliding in
after I had dressed and just at tea-time. We were invited, you must
know, for eight o'clock, and we meant to go punctually, in spite of
the rain, which drizzled all the evening. There was a good deal of
groaning, as the time approached for the start; as was to be
expected, for it was a great effort! But it ended triumphantly;
virtue's reward appeared, in the shape of Mr. Townsend's cart,
which had cushions for the occasion, and we were conducted to the
door in great style; splashing through the mud, in which our
lantern made long lines of light. The upper floor of the warehouse
was our robing room, and the flags of all the ships tapestried the
lower one (which was the ballroom), round, and screened off

[361]

portions as a recess for the pianoforte, and for the tea room, which included a fireplace. Then we had loads of evergreens, and calico roses, pink and white; and a good many candles, and a tolerable boarded floor, and everything did as well as possible. One of the schoolmasters who is to be organist, played the pianoforte, and one of the policemen (late of the 65th's band at Wellington) played alternately on the flageolet and violin. At twelve we prepared for our walk home, and arrived most prosperously, only Mr. FitzGerald fell over flat on his side, and my husband lost one of his clogs in the mud.

August 14th. For two days we have had the *Labuan*, and its sad grievous news, [the death of her sister-in-law] of loss and sickness and sorrow; and for two days I have been longing to say, as it were, something to you about it all, and yet my hand seems tied; what shall I write? how will it find you all? who may read my letter? It is at such times as these that one feels the bitterness of so great a separation, so long and so very far away, and I have been writing to her for months; ordinary, stupid letters (I have one by me, luckily unsent), which I am sadly afraid may go straight to my dear Charles, and add one pain more to all he must suffer.

20th. I am sorry to say further accounts confirm the report of the *Maria's* wreck, all on board lost except one man, a Malay sailor, and one boy. It appears that they were in a tremendous gale; and, in trying in the night to get into Wellington harbour, they struck on a rock a little to the North, and the ship went to pieces. Seventeen bodies have already been washed on shore. Poor Mr. Deans is a great loss to us here. Not only from his unfailing kindness and good nature, but from the assistance that his advice and example, in all agricultural matters, gave to all the newcomers. His brother will feel his loss sadly; they were so united and so happy together; indeed I cannot tell what Mr. John Deans will do now; he was only waiting his brother's return from this voyage to Sydney (via Wellington) to get some fresh stock, cattle and sheep, to go home and be married in Scotland.

August 25th. I think I have always forgotten to tell you of a visit

[362]

we have about the middle of July from Mr. Enderby, the Governor of the Auckland Islands. He came up in one of his own whaling-vessels, *The Black Dog*—something especially smart and fast sailing, and he touched here on his way up to Wellington. He had with him a sort of aide-de-camp, or Secretary, much more gentle-manlike-looking than himself; a Mr. King from Sydney, and just going to return there, quite sick of his life at the Auckland Islands. Mr. Enderby himself is an absurd little mixture of a metropolitan, or rather Greenwich, soap-boiler, and a would-be rough tar, with a German-looking moustache, and no teeth, and rolling his r's just as Mrs. Hicks does. I do not envy him his governorship at all. The Auckland Islands are not really fit to be inhabited at all, until the world is a great deal more filled up than it is in these parts. They have a wretched climate, almost per-petual storms even in summer; and their soil is something like a passable bog, even then, and feels, they say, like walking on a sponge. Potatoes will grow there, when they are obliged; but everything else, including their supplies of fresh meat, must be brought from N.Z. or Sydney. They have about ninety-six adults, twenty-four of whom are women (and a very unmanageable lot), to compose their whole society. When anyone does very wrong, he is banished to a small uninhabited island two or three miles from the shore. Mr. Enderby, who is a tremendous talker, told us he had built a hut for his convicts to live in on this island. One day they came and told him that the convicts were unruly, and threatened to burn down the hut, of course by way of frightening him; however, he was quite resigned. The hut was burnt down, and now they live in a large cask with the head off, which they may burn too, if they like. There is one man there now, or at least there was when Mr. E. left, who is to remain for six months. They say that the Governor's life is sometimes in danger, there are so few respectable characters among them; but he is a most determined little man, and evidently not in any alarm himself.

December 29th. Mr. Wortley, I think I told you about, but as you ask after him, in case I did not, he is gone up to a station outside our Canterbury black, to the North, which he and Mr. Hanmer (who chose it) are to have and keep together, and we have heard from him there safely arrived, and setting up house, and so on. He went up in a boat with the man and his wife who are to be his servants, and was two days (two nights) on the road. To go by land takes much longer, I don't know how many days, for the road is bad, beyond the hills that bound our plain, and there is a bad river to cross. They will have, indeed, to make out something of a track, for as yet there is none. They are to keep sheep, etc., for some other people, taking them on thirds, as it is called here, besides what stock they can afford for themselves. They will not at all listen to our insinuations that they are going too far off, and will become semi-barbarous; and assure us that they will come down smarter than they ever appeared before, when they come down, once in a month or two, to get letters, or to bring in stock. I have begged them to have a lay figure of a lady, carefully draped, set up in their usual sitting-room and always to behave before it as if it were their mother, or some other dignified lady. They did not quite promise this, but they seem quite duly impressed with the necessities of attending somewhat to those little trifles which are very often altogether neglected by young gentlemen at stations; which neglect, by degrees tells upon their general habits, and even character, in a much stronger way than you might suppose.

January 14th, 1852. We went along nearly five miles of excellent road into Christchurch, all new since I had been on the Plains, and, much as I had heard, I was very much surprised, and not a little delighted, to see how very much civilized the country had become. There are houses, gardens, and cultivation, in sight all the way along; the patches, in some places, quite touching each other, and though the houses are small, they are tidy and weather-tight looking places. All people, too, doing so well, and looking so contented, and then when we got to the town, the number of houses seemed quite incredible to me, and the whole place so cheerful and so busy, that it has quite lost the dreary look which I own to have thought it had last year.

Our present locality is quite two miles from Christchurch, though the road is dotted along with houses, and is really very pretty, in its way. We have a wooden house with two rooms; one about ten feet square, which is bedroom for Powles, Arthur, and Elizabeth, and the other is for us, bedroom, sitting-room, etc.; then we have a hired tent, which is servants' hall and kitchen, with a fire out of doors, and a single tent, lent by Mr. Russell, which is our store-room and pantry, for we have to keep and bring everything we want, as we get nothing here but fresh meat, milk and butter. Even our vegetables we bring from our own garden, for there is no certain supply of them here, and the new potatoes are still 2*d*. a lb. We have the beautiful river in front, down only a few feet of bank, as deep, clear and cold as ever; we are never tired of admiring, and 'imbibing' it; and across the path, at the back of the house, comes the bush, full of such birds singing all day, *tuis*, and bell-birds, and N.Z. robins, which are little black and grey birds that light down close to you, like the tamest of English robins in cold weather—and such lovely little green parrots that look so foreign, far more so, to my mind, than anything else out here. Arthur and I counted a little flock of eighteen yesterday. This bush seems full of them, and of mosquitoes, I am sorry to say; however, they do not bite till the dusk, and then only if you sit still out of doors, or let your windows and doors be open too late; and then a few minutes will do all the mischief. A little care, so far, prevents their being any real annoyance; but it is, in a great measure, owing to our having so good a house that we can shut them out. Sleeping out-of-doors, here, they are sometimes very bad, and the remedy is scarcely much better; the best being to smear yourself perpetually with turpentine and oil, mixed, which is a very dirtying process, even if you don't mind the smell. Our sitting room is really quite a pretty room, with a high wooden roof, and the rough woodwork of the sides, which are not lined with anything, and admit a little light here and there, is quite picturesque. Then we have two large windows looking, one to the water, the other to the bush, with muslin curtains. Our bed disappears, being rolled up under an opossum-skin rug, and we have a shelf with books, a smart table and two chairs, lent by Mrs. Russell, besides three wooden ones of our own; and my little clock, on the chimney-piece, gives an air of grandeur to the whole. I

[365]

ought not to forget to mention that the fire burns remarkably well, and never smokes, whereas in our V hut last year, all the smoke, and some of the fire, came straight into the room, in all the bad weather.

January 21st. We are very unhappy at all the English yachts having been beaten by that *America*, which looks, too, such an ugly thing, in our *Illustrated News*, by the side of our English yachts. I suppose the Exhibition excitement is altogether over. I cannot help rather hoping that they will keep up the building for a garden, fêtes, and all such purposes. It seems a great waste to pull it all down. But I suppose it is rather an encumbrance in the Park. I must own that I am very sorry not to have seen it, though it will be a good thing when the *Illustrated* has done with it. We are so tired of the Exhibition pictures; first the building, as it seemed, each week, with the progress it had made, and then every conceivable inside and outside view, which, to the uninitiated, all look so much alike, we 'cannot tell t'other from which'. Everyone here, who saw it before coming out, agrees in telling how much we missed, but that is of course; and only one complains of a great squeeze. However, my regret at not seeing that forms such a very small part of my sorrow for being so long out of England, that it is not worth mentioning, and when we are to hope to go home seems just as uncertain, and a little further off, than ever.

March 23rd. Mr. Tancred is still going on well, and we have had a visit from the Governor. He has allowed £2,000 of our surplus revenue to pass into my husband's hands, for the purpose of making further roads into the plains, which we want sadly. In the meantime, this is a great gain to us; but I wish we had one or two shiploads of emigrant labourers arriving to help our labour-market. These Australian diggings are a sad temptation to men of that class. Although wonderfully few have left, as yet, to go there, we cannot help fearing that such continual accounts of fortunes made, must entice a good many at last, especially among single men, for it is almost always the bright side of the picture that travels here; and besides, it gives a feeling of insecurity; no one can calculate, with even ordinary certainty, upon how prices, etc., are likely to be.

May 31st. That is the great mistake that people make about this place. It must be a very steady young gentleman who can get on well here (unless under very favourable circumstances), and yet many people seem to imagine it a kind of training-school, of which the very air will reclaim those who can literally be made nothing of at home, and it is really quite painful to read the letters my husband gets constantly from parents, asking to have his private and confidential opinion of their sons, and of how they are getting on, when perhaps he has never seen them, and only heard of them in the most disagreeable way.

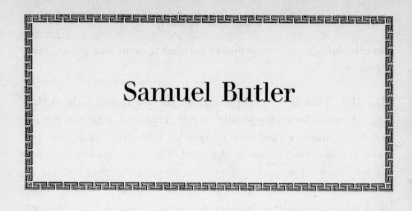

Samuel Butler

In the Preface to the Revised Edition of *Erewhon* Butler writes that 'the first part of *Erewhon* written was an article headed "Darwin among the Machines" and signed Cellarius. It was written in the Upper Rangitata district of the Canterbury Province (as it was then) of New Zealand, and appeared at Christchurch in the Press Newspaper, June 13th, 1863. . . . In passing I may say that the opening chapters of *Erewhon* were also drawn from the Upper Rangitata district, with such modifications as I found convenient.'

How much he was indebted to his early years in New Zealand will be clear to anyone who reads Chapter III, 'Up the River,' of *Erewhon* side by side with the extracts which follow. And he continued to remember with pleasure even very minute incidents of his life at the Antipodes. Readers of *Alps and Sanctuaries* will remember the solemn passage which begins 'Many years ago I remember thinking that the birds in New Zealand approached the diatonic scale more nearly than European birds do,' continues with two of their songs set out in musical notation, and ends: 'The rhinoceros grunts a good fourth, beginning, we will say, on C, and dropping correctly on to the G below.'

He went to New Zealand a year after leaving Cambridge, not wishing to follow his father's advice to enter the Church. After some time spent in looking round, he chose a place up the Rangitata river which he called Mesopotamia, 25 miles from his nearest

Samuel Butler

neighbour. The station comprised 8,000 acres and he soon had 3,000 sheep. In a few years, in spite of his inexperience, he doubled his capital of £4,000 and returned to England in 1864, selling his property before he left.

These letters home were published without his knowledge as *A First Year in Canterbury Settlement* in 1863 by his father, who omitted passages of the nature of which he did not approve, adding yet another to the number of grudges held against his parents by the author of *The Way of All Flesh*.

January 27 1860. [Port Lyttelton]—Oh the heat! the clear transparent atmosphere, and the dust! How shall I describe everything —the little townlet, for I cannot call it town, nestling beneath the bare hills that we had been looking at so longingly all the morning —the scattered wooden boxes of houses, with ragged roods of scrubby ground between them—the tussocks of brown grass—the huge wide-leafed flax, with its now seedy stem, sometimes 15 or 16 feet high, luxuriant and tropical-looking—the healthy clear-complexioned men, shaggy-bearded, rowdy-hatted, and independent, pictures of rude health and strength—the stores, supplying all heterogeneous commodities—the mountains, rising right behind the harbour to a height of over a thousand feet—the varied outline of the harbour now smooth and sleeping. Ah me! pleasant sight and fresh to sea-stricken eyes. The hot air, too, was very welcome after our long chill.

We dined at the table d'hôte at the Mitre—so foreign and yet so English—the windows open to the ground, looking upon the lovely harbour. Hither come more of the shaggy clear-complexioned men with the rowdy hats; looked at them with awe and befitting respect. Much grieved to find beer sixpence a glass. This was indeed serious, and was one of the first intimations which we received that we were in a land where money flies like wild-fire.

After dinner I and another commenced the ascent of the hill between port and Christ Church.

At the bottom of the hill we met the car to Christ Church; it halted some time at a little wooden public-house, and by and by at another, where was a Methodist preacher, who had just been reaping corn for two pounds an acre. He showed me some half-dozen stalks of gigantic size, but most of that along the roadside was thin and poor. Then we reached Christ Church on the little river Avon; it is larger than Lyttelton and more scattered, but not so pretty. Here, too, the men are shaggy, clear-complexioned, brown, and healthy-looking, and wear exceedingly rowdy hats. I put up at Mr. Rowland Davis's; and as no one during the evening seemed much inclined to talk to me, I listened to the conversation.

The all-engrossing topics seemed to be sheep, horses, dogs, cattle, English grasses, paddocks, bush, and so forth. From about seven o'clock in the evening till about twelve at night I cannot say that I heard much else. These were the exact things I wanted to hear about, and I listened till they had been repeated so many times over that I almost grew tired of the subject, and wished the conversation would turn to something else. A few expressions were not familiar to me. When we should say in England 'Certainly not,' it is here 'No fear,' or 'Don't *you* believe it.' When they want to answer in the affirmative they say 'It is *so*,' 'It does *so*.' The word 'hum,' too, without pronouncing the *u*, is in amusing requisition. I perceived that this stood either for assent, or doubt, or wonder, or a general expression of comprehension without compromising the hummer's own opinion, and indeed for a great many more things than these; in fact, if a man did not want to say anything at all he said 'hum hum.' It is a very good expression, and saves much trouble when its familiar use has been acquired. Beyond these trifles I noticed no Yankeeism, and the conversation was English in point of expression. I was rather startled at hearing one gentleman ask another whether he meant to wash this year, and receive the answer 'No.' I soon discovered that a person's sheep are himself. If his sheep are clean, he is clean. He does not wash his *sheep* before shearing, but *he* washes; and, most marvellous of all, it is not his sheep which lamb, but he 'lambs down' himself.

February 10, 1860.—I must confess to being fairly puzzled to know what to do with the money you have sent me. Everyone suggests different investments. One says buy sheep and put them out to terms. I will explain to you what this means. I can buy a thousand ewes for 1,250*l.*, these I should place in the charge of a squatter whose run is not fully stocked (and indeed there is hardly a run in the province fully stocked). This person would take my sheep for either three, four, five, or more years, as we might arrange, and would allow me yearly 2*s.* 6*d.* per head in lieu of wool. This would give me 2*s.* 6*d.* as the yearly interest on 25*s.* Besides this he would allow me 40 per cent. per annum of increase, half male, and half female, and of these the females would bear increase also as soon as they had attained the age of two years; moreover the increase would return me 2*s.* 6*d.* per head wool money as soon as they became sheep. At the end of the term, my sheep would be returned to me as per agreement, with no deduction for deaths, but the original sheep would be, of course, so much the older, and some of them being doubtless dead, sheep of the same age as they would have been will be returned in their place.

The question arises, What is to be done with one's money when the term is out? I cannot answer; yet surely the colony cannot be quite used up in seven years, and one can hardly suppose but that even in that advanced state of the settlement, means will not be found of investing a few thousand pounds to advantage.

The general recommendation which I receive is to buy the goodwill of a run; this cannot be done under about 100*l.* for every thousand acres. Thus a run of 20,000 acres will be worth 2,000*l.* Still, if a man has sufficient capital to stock it well at once, it will pay him, even at this price.

Another mode of investment highly spoken of is that of buying land and laying it down in English grass, thus making a permanent estate of it. But I fear this will not do for me, both because it requires a large experience of things in general, which, as you well know, I do not possess, and because I should want a greater capital than would be required to start a run. More money is sunk, and the returns do not appear to be so speedy. I cannot give you even a rough estimate of the expenses of such a plan. As for farming

[371]

as we do in England, it is universally maintained that it does not pay; there seems to be no discrepancy of opinion about this. Many try it, but most men give it up. It appears as if it were only bonâ fide labouring men who can make it answer.

February 13.—Since my last I have been paying a visit of a few days at Kaiapoi, and made a short trip up to the Harewood Forest, near to which the township of Oxford is situated. Why it should be called Oxford I do not know.

After leaving Rangiora, which is about 8 miles from Kaiapoi, I followed the Harewood road till it became a mere track, then a footpath, and then dwindled away to nothing at all. I soon found myself in the middle of the plains, with nothing but brown tussocks of grass before me and behind me, and on either side. The day was rather dark, and the mountains were obliterated by a haze. 'Oh the pleasure of the plains,' I thought to myself; but upon my word, I think old Handel would find but little pleasure in these. They are, in clear weather, monotonous and dazzling; in cloudy weather monotonous and sad; and they have little to recommend them but the facility they afford for travelling, and the grass which grows upon them. This, at least, was the impression I derived from my first acquaintance with them, as I found myself steering for the extremity of some low downs about six miles distant. I thought these downs would never get nearer. At length I saw a tent-like object, dotting itself upon the plain, with eight black mice as it were in front of it. This turned out to be a dray, loaded with wool, coming down from the country. It was the first symptom of sheep that I had come upon, for, to my surprise, I saw no sheep upon the plains, neither did I see any in the whole of my little excursion. I am told this disappoints most new comers. They are told that sheep farming is the great business of Canterbury, but they see no sheep; the reason of this is, partly because the runs are not yet a quarter stocked, and partly because the sheep are in mobs, and, unless one comes across the whole mob, one sees none of them. The plains, too, are so vast, that at a very short distance from the track, sheep will not be seen. When I came up to the dray, I found myself on a track, reached the foot of the downs, and crossed the little river Cust. A little river, brook, or stream, is always called a creek; nothing but the great rivers are called rivers. Now clumps of flax, and stunted groves of Ti palms and other trees, began to break the monotony of the scene. Then the track ascended the downs on the other side of the stream, and afforded me a fine view of the valley of the Cust, cleared and burnt by a recent fire, which extended for miles and miles, purpling the face of the country, up to the horizon. Rich flax and grass made the valley look promising, but on the hill the ground was stony and barren, and shabbily clothed with patches of dry and brown grass, surrounded by a square foot or so of hard ground; between the tussocks, however, there was a frequent though scanty undergrowth which might furnish support for sheep, though it looked burnt up.

After proceeding some few miles further, I came to a station, where, though a perfect stranger, and at first (at some little distance) mistaken for a Māori, I was most kindly treated, and spent a very agreeable evening. The people here are very hospitable; and I have received kindnesses already upon several occasions, from persons upon whom I had no sort of claim.

Next day I went to Oxford, which lies at the foot of the first ranges, and is supposed to be a promising place. Here, for the first time, I saw the bush; it was very beautiful; numerous creepers, and a luxuriant undergrowth among the trees, gave the forest a wholly un-European aspect, and realised, in some degree, one's idea of tropical vegetation. It was full of birds that sang loudly and sweetly. The trees here are all evergreens, and are not considered very good for timber. I am told that they have mostly a twist in them, and are in other respects not first rate.

March 24.—At last I have been really in the extreme back country, and positively, right up to a glacier.

As soon as I saw the mountains, I longed to get on the other side of them, and now my wish has been gratified.

I left Christ Church in company with a sheep farmer, who owns a run in the back country, behind the Malvern hills, and who kindly offered to take me with him on a short expedition he was going to make into the remoter valleys of the island, in hopes of finding some considerable piece of country which had not yet been applied for.

We started February 28th, and had rather an unpleasant ride of twenty-five miles, against a very high NW. wind. This wind is very hot, very parching, and very violent; it blew the dust into our eyes so that we could hardly keep them open. Towards evening, however, it somewhat moderated, as it generally does. There was nothing of interest on the track, save a dry river bed, through which the Waimakiriri once flowed, but which it has long quitted. The rest of our journey was entirely over the plains, which do not become less monotonous upon a longer acquaintance; the mountains, however, drew slowly nearer, and by evening were really rather beautiful. Next day we entered the valley of the River Selwyn, or Waikitty, as it is generally called, and soon found ourselves surrounded by the low volcanic mountains, which bear the name of the Malvern hills. They are very like the Banks peninsula. We dined at a station belonging to a son of the bishop's, and after dinner made further progress into the interior.

At night, and by a lovely clear cold moonlight, we arrived at our destination, heartily glad to hear the dogs barking and to know that we were at our journey's end. Here we were bonâ fide beyond the pale of civilisation; no boarded floors, no chairs, nor any similar luxuries; everything was of the very simplest description. Four men inhabited the hut, and their life appears a kind of mixture of that of the dog and that of an emperor, with a considerable predominance of the latter. They have no cook, and take it turn and turn to cook and wash up, two one week, and two the next. They have a good garden, and gave us a capital feed of potatoes and peas, both fried together, an excellent combination. Their culinary apparatus and plates, cups, knives and forks, are very limited in number. The men are all gentlemen and sons of gentlemen, and one of them is a Cambridge man, who took a second-class a year or two before my time. Every now and then he leaves his up-country avocations, and becomes a great gun at the college in Christ Church, examining the boys; he then returns to his shepherding, cooking, bullock-driving, &c. &c., as the case

[374]

may be. I am informed that the having faithfully learned the
ingenuous arts, has so far mollified his morals that he is an exceedingly humane and judicious bullock-driver. He regarded me as a
somewhat despicable new-comer (at least so I imagined), and when
next morning I asked where I should wash, he gave rather a French
shrug of the shoulders, and said, 'The lake.' I felt the rebuke to be
well merited, and that with the lake in front of the house, I should
have been at no loss for the means of performing my ablutions. So
I retired abashed and cleansed myself therein. Under his bed I
found Tennyson's 'Idylls of the King.' So you will see that even in
these out-of-the-world places people do care a little for something
besides sheep. New Zealand seems far better adapted to develope
and maintain in health the physical than the intellectual nature.
The fact is, people here are busy making money; that is the
inducement which led them to come in the first instance, and they
show their sense by devoting their energies to the work. Yet, after
all, it may be questioned whether the intellect is not as well
schooled here as at home, though in a very different manner. Men
are as shrewd and sensible as alive to the humorous, and as hard-
headed. Moreover, there is much nonsense in the old country from
which people here are free. There is little conventionalism, little
formality, and much liberality of sentiment; very little sec-
tarianism, and, as a general rule, a healthy sensible tone in conversation, which I like much. But it does not do to speak about
John Sebastain Bach's 'Fugues,' or pre-Raphaelite pictures.

After an early dinner, my patron and myself started on our
journey, and after travelling for some few hours over rather a
rough country, though one which appeared to me to be beautiful
indeed, we came upon a vast river-bed, with a little river winding
about it. We got on to the river-bed, and, following it up for a
little way, soon found ourselves in a close valley between two very
lofty ranges, which were plentifully wooded with black birch down
to their base. There were a few scrubby stone flats covered with
Irishman and speargrass (Irishman is the unpleasant thorny shrub
which I saw going over the hill from Lyttelton to Christ Church)
on either side the stream; they had been entirely left to nature,
and showed me the difference between country which had been

burnt and that which is in its natural condition. This difference is very great. The fire dries up many swamps—at least many disappear after country has been once or twice burnt; the water moves more freely, unimpeded by the tangled and decaying vegetation which accumulates round it during the lapse of centuries, and the sun gets freer access to the ground. Cattle do much also: they form tracks through swamp, and trample down the earth, making it harder and firmer. Sheep do much: they convey the seeds of the best grass and tread them into the ground. The difference between country that has been fed upon by any live stock, even for a single year, and that which has never yet been stocked is very noticeable. If country is being burnt for the second or third time, the fire can be crossed without any difficulty; of course it must be quickly traversed, though indeed, on thinly-grassed land, you may take it almost as coolly as you please. On one of these flats, just on the edge of the bush, and at the very foot of the mountain, we lit a fire as soon as it was dusk, and, tethering our horses, boiled our tea and supped. The night was warm and quiet, the silence only interrupted by the occasional sharp cry of a wood-hen and the rushing of the river, whilst the ruddy glow of the fire, the sombre forest, and the immediate foreground of our saddles and blankets, formed a picture to me entirely new and rather impressive. Probably after another year or two I shall regard camping out as the nuisance which it really is, instead of writing about sombre forests and so forth. Well, well, that night I thought it very fine, and so in good truth it was.

Our saddles were our pillows and we strapped our blankets round us by saddle-straps, and my companion (I believe) slept very soundly; for my part the scene was altogether too novel to allow me to sleep. I kept looking up and seeing the stars just as I was going off to sleep, and that woke me again; I had also underestimated the amount of blankets which I should require, and it was not long before the romance of the situation wore off, and a rather chilly reality occupied its place; moreover, the flat was stony, and I was not knowing enough to have selected a spot which gave a hollow for the hip-bone. My great object, however, was to conceal my condition from my companion, for never was a freshman at Cambridge more anxious to be mistaken for a third-year man than I was anxious to become an old chum, as the colonial dialect calls a settler—thereby proving my new chum ship most satisfactorily. Early next morning the birds began to sing beautifully, and the day being thus heralded, I got up, lit the fire, and set the pannikins on to boil: we then had breakfast, and broke camp. The scenery soon became most glorious, for, turning round a corner of the river, we saw a very fine mountain right in front of us. I could at once see that there was a névé near the top of it, and was all excitement. We were very anxious to know if this was the back-bone ridge of the island, and were hopeful that if it was we might find some pass to the other side. The ranges on either hand were, as I said before, covered with bush, and these, with the rugged Alps in front of us, made a magnificent view. We went on, and soon there came out a much grander mountain—a glorious glaciered fellow—and then came more, and the mountains closed in, and the river dwindled and began leaping from stone to stone, and we were shortly in scenery of the true Alpine nature—very, very grand. It wanted, however, a chalet or two, or some sign of human handiwork in the foreground; as it was, the scene was too savage.

All the time we kept looking for gold, not in a scientific manner, but we had a kind of idea that if we looked in the shingly beds of the numerous tributaries to the Harpur, we should surely find either gold or copper or something good. So at every shingle-bed we came to (and every little tributary had a great shingle-bed) we lay down and gazed into the pebbles with all our eyes. We found plenty of stones with yellow specks in them, but none of that rich goodly hue which makes a man certain that what he has found is gold. We did not wash any of the gravel, for we had no tin dish, neither did we know how to wash.

April 1860.—I have made another little trip, and this time have tried the Rangitata. My companion and myself have found a small piece of country, which we have just taken up. We fear it may be snowy in winter, but the expense of taking up country is very small; and even if we should eventually throw it up, the chances are that we may be able to do so with profit. We are, however, sanguine that it may be a very useful little run, but shall have to see it through next winter before we can safely put sheep upon it.

We started from a lonely valley, down which runs a stream called Forest Creek.

In seven hours from the time we started, we were on the top. Hence we had hoped to discover some entirely new country, but were disappointed, for we only saw the Mackenzie Plains lying stretched out for miles away to the southward. There we lay on the shingle-bed, at the top of the range, in the broiling noonday; for even at that altitude it was very hot, and there was no cloud in the sky and very little breeze. I saw that if we wanted a complete view we must climb to the top of a peak which, though only a few hundred feet higher than where we were lying, nevertheless hid a great deal from us. I accordingly began the ascent, having arranged with my companion that if there was country to be seen he should be called, if not, he should be allowed to take it easy. Well, I saw snowy peak after snowy peak come in view as the summit in front of me narrowed, but no mountains were visible higher or grander than what I had already seen. Suddenly, as my eyes got on a level with the top, so that I could see over, I was almost struck breathless by the wonderful mountain that burst on my sight. The effect was startling. It rose towering in a massy parallelogram, disclosed from top to bottom in the cloudless sky, far above all the others. It was exactly opposite to me, and about the nearest in the whole range. So you may imagine that it was indeed a splendid spectacle. It has been calculated by the Admiralty people at 13,200 feet, but Mr. Haast, a gentleman of high scientific attainments in the employ of Government as geological surveyor, says that it is considerably higher. For my part, I can well believe it. Mont Blanc himself is not so grand in shape, and does not look so imposing. Indeed, I am not sure that Mount Cook is not the finest in outline of all the snowy mountains that I have ever seen. No one can mistake it. If a person says he *thinks* he has seen Mount Cook, you may be quite sure that he has not seen it. The moment it comes into sight the exclamation is, 'That

[378]

is Mount Cook!'—not 'That *must* be Mount Cook!' There is no possibility of mistake.

I am forgetting myself into admiring a mountain which is of no use for sheep. This is wrong. A mountain here is only beautiful if it has good grass on it. Scenery is not scenery—it is 'country,' *subauditâ voce* 'sheep.' If it is good for sheep, it is beautiful, magnificent, and all the rest of it; if not, it is not worth looking at. I am cultivating this tone of mind with considerable success, but you must pardon me for an occasional outbreak of the old Adam.

[No date] I am now going to put up a V hut on the country that I took up on the Rangitata, meaning to hibernate there in order to see what the place is like. I shall also build a more permanent hut there, for I must have someone with me, and we may as well be doing something as nothing. I have hopes of being able to purchase some good country in the immediate vicinity. There is a piece on which I have my eye, and which adjoins that I have already. There can be, I imagine, no doubt that this is excellent sheep country; still, I should like to see it in winter.

June 1860.—The V hut is a *fait accompli*, if so small an undertaking can be spoken of in so dignified a manner. It consists of a small roof set upon the ground; it is a hut, all roof and no walls. I was very clumsy, and so, in good truth, was my man.

I should be loth to advise any gentleman to come out here, unless he have either money and an average share of good sense, or else a large amount of proper self-respect and strength of purpose. If a young man goes out to friends, on an arrangement definitely settled before he leaves England, he is at any rate certain of employment and of a home upon his landing here; but if he lands friendless, or simply the bearer of a few letters of introduction, obtained from second or third hand—because his cousin knew somebody who had a friend who had married a lady whose nephew was somewhere in New Zealand—he has no very enviable look-out upon his arrival.

[No date] The winter's experience satisfied me that the country

that H—— and I had found would not do for sheep, unless worked
in connection with more that was clear of snow throughout the
year. As soon, therefore, as I was convinced that the adjacent
country was safe, I bought it, and settled upon it in good earnest,
abandoning the V hut.

[No date] There was a little hut on my run built by another
person, and tenanted by his shepherd. G—— had an application
for 5,000 acres in the same block of country with mine, and as the
boundaries were uncertain until the whole was surveyed, and the
runs definitely marked out on the government maps, he had placed
his hut upon a spot that turned out eventually not to belong to
him. I had waited to see how the land was allotted before I took it
up. Knowing the country well, and finding it allotted to my satisfaction, I made my bargain on the same day that the question was
settled. I took a tracing from the government map up with me,
and we arrived on the run about a fortnight after the allotment.
It was necessary for me to wait for this, or I might have made the
same mistake which G—— had done. His hut was placed where it
was now of no use to him whatever, but on the very site on which
I had myself decided to build. It is beyond all possibility of doubt
upon my run; but G—— is a very difficult man to deal with, and
I have had a hard task to get rid of him. To allow him to remain
where he was was not to be thought of: but I was perfectly ready
to pay him for his hut (such as it is) and his yard. Knowing him to
be at P——'s, I set the men to their contract, and went down next
day to see him and to offer him any compensation for the loss of
his hut which a third party might arrange. I could do nothing with
him; he threatened fiercely, and would hear no reason. My only
remedy was to go down to Christ Church at once and buy the freehold of the site from the government.

The Canterbury regulations concerning the purchase of waste
lands from the crown are among the best existing. They are all
free to any purchaser with the exception of a few government
reserves for certain public purposes, as railway-township reserves,
and so forth. Every run-holder has a preemptive right over 250
acres round his homestead, and 50 acres round any other buildings

he may have upon his run. He must register this right, or it is of no avail. By this means he is secured from an enemy buying up his homestead without his previous knowledge. Whoever wishes to purchase a sheep farmer's homestead must first give him a considerable notice, and then can only buy if the occupant refuses to do so at the price of 2*l.* an acre. Of course the occupant would *not* refuse, and the thing is consequently never attempted. All the rest, however, of any man's run is open to purchase at the rate of 2*l.* per acre. The price is sufficient to prevent monopoly, and yet not high enough to interfere with the small capitalist. The sheep farmer cannot buy up his run and stand in the way of the developement of the country, and at the same time he is secured from the loss of it through others buying, because the price is too high to make it worth a man's while to do so when so much better investments are still open. On the plains, however, many run-holders are becoming seriously uneasy even at the present price, and blocks of 1,000 acres are frequently bought with a view to their being fenced in and laid down in English grasses. In the back country this has not yet commenced, nor is it likely to do so for many years.

But to return. Firstly, G—— had not registered any pre-emptive right, and, secondly, if he had it would have been worthless, because his hut was situated on my run and not on his own. I was sure that he had not bought the freehold; I was also certain that he meant to buy it. So, knowing well that there was not a moment to lose, I went towards Christ Church the same afternoon, and supped at a shepherd's hut three miles lower down, and intended to travel quietly all night.

The Ashburton, however, was heavily freshed, and the night was pitch dark. After crossing and re-crossing it four times I was afraid to go on, and camping down, waited for daylight. Resuming my journey with early dawn, I had not gone far when, happening to turn round, I saw a man on horseback about a quarter of a mile behind me. I knew at once that this was G——, and letting him come up with me, we rode for some miles together, each of us of course well aware of the other's intentions, but too politic to squabble about them when squabbling was no manner of use. It was then early on the Wednesday morning, and the Board sat on the following day. A book is kept at the Land-Office called the application-book, in which anyone who has business with the Board enters his name, and his case is attended to in the order in which his name stands. The race between G—— and myself was as to who should first get his name down in this book, and secure the ownership of the hut by purchasing the freehold of twenty acres round it. We had nearly a hundred miles to ride; the office closed at four in the afternoon, and I knew that G—— could not possibly be in time for that day; I had therefore till ten o'clock on the following morning, that is to say, about twenty-four hours from the time we parted company. Knowing that I could be in town by that time, I took it easily, and halted for breakfast at the first station we came to. G—— went on, and I saw him no more.

I feared that our applications would be simultaneous, or that we should have an indecorous scuffle for the book in the Land-Office itself. In this case, there would only have remained the unsatisfactory alternative of drawing lots for precedence. There was nothing for it but to go on, and see how matters would turn up. Before midday, and whilst still sixty miles from town, my horse knocked-up completely, and would not go another step. G——'s horse, only two months before, had gone a hundred miles in less than fifteen hours, and was now pitted against mine, which was thoroughly done-up. Rather anticipating this, I had determined on keeping the tracks, thus passing stations where I might have a chance of getting a fresh mount. G—— took a short cut, saving fully ten miles in distance, but travelling over a very stony country, with no track. A track is a great comfort to a horse.

I shall never forget my relief when, at a station where I had already received great kindness, I obtained the loan of a horse that had been taken up that morning from a three-months' spell. No greater service could, at the time, have been rendered me, and I felt that I had indeed met with a friend in need.

The prospect was now brilliant, save that the Rakaia was said to be very heavily freshed. Fearing I might have to swim for it, I left my watch at M——'s, and went on with the satisfactory reflection that, at any rate, if I could not cross, G—— could not do so either. To my delight, however, the river was very low, and I

[382]

forded it without the smallest difficulty a little before sunset. A few hours afterwards, down it came. I heard that G—— was an hour ahead of me, but this was of no consequence. Riding ten miles farther, and now only twenty-five miles from Christ Church, I called at an accommodation-house, and heard that G—— was within, so went on, and determined to camp and rest my horse. The night was again intensely dark, and it soon came on to rain so heavily that there was nothing for it but to start again for the next accommodation-house, twelve miles from town. I slept there a few hours, and by seven o'clock next morning was in Christ Church. So was G——. We could neither of us do anything till the Land-Office opened at ten o'clock. At twenty minutes before ten I repaired thither, expecting to find G—— in waiting, and anticipating a row. If it came to fists, I should get the worst of it—that was a moral certainty—and I really half-feared something of the kind. To my surprise, the office-doors were open—and on reaching that in which the application-book was kept, I found it already upon the table. I opened it with trembling fingers, and saw my adversary's name written in bold handwriting, defying me, as it were, to do my worst.

The clock, as the clerk was ready to witness, was twenty minutes before ten. I learnt from him also that G—— had written his name down about half an hour. This was all right. My course was to wait till after ten, write my name, and oppose G——'s application as having been entered unduly, and before office-hours. I have no doubt that I should have succeeded in gaining my point in this way, but a much easier victory was in store for me.

Running my eye through the list of names, to my great surprise I saw my own among them. It had been entered by my solicitor, on another matter of business, the previous day, but it stood next *below* G——'s. G——'s name, then, had clearly been inserted unfairly, out of order. The whole thing was made clear to the Commissioners of the Waste Lands, and I need not say that I effected my purchase without difficulty. A few weeks afterwards, allowing him for his hut and yard, I bought G—— out entirely.

APPENDIX

John Batman

John Batman's Letter describing his Bargain with the Port Phillip Aborigines.

By the time Batman's life had been set down on paper in 1867 it had already accumulated a good deal of legend, and we should perhaps disregard the story that, an Australian born (in 1800) and bred, he had to leave New South Wales in a hurry because of an unfortunate love affair. We are on firmer ground with his arrival in Van Diemen's Land in 1820.

Here he was not content with sheep farming but took to exploring, kangaroo hunting, and the pursuit of bushrangers. His most notable achievement in this last profession was the capture of the notorious Brady, who for years had been the terror of the island. The capture itself was marred for posterity by the gentle resignation with which the exhausted bandit gave himself up. For Batman, however, this was the culmination of services so valuable that the Governor asked him to name a boon. The romantic hunter, entering at once into the spirit of the occasion, requested the hand of a beautiful woman outlaw who for some months had been his companion, dressed in man's clothes. The boon was granted, a pardon given, and the marriage solemnized, though whether the Governor attended the ceremony or not, we are not told.

Batman took his wife to live on the South Esk river, in the Vale of Avoca, and there, in the intervals of farming, he took to hunting aborigines. This was for the purpose of segregating them in places of safety, and he took part in Arthur's £30,000 black line. He did, in fact, succeed in learning a lot about his quarry and making himself trusted by them.

In 1835 he became, for those who believed his story, the Founder of Melbourne, and they have the significant entry in his diary 'This is the place for a village' to point to. We have seen how his claims were treated. Disappointed and speedily forgotten, he died on the land signed away to him by Cooloolook and his brethren in 1839. His widow was turned off the twenty acres he had been allowed to keep, and not till 1882 did his name appear in any public place in the city of which he claimed to be the father.

This letter is shortened from the text in Bonwick's *John Batman*, 1867, and shows the cautious and ingratiating hand of lawyer Gellibrand, Batman's legal adviser.

[To the Lieutenant-Governor of Van Diemen's Land.]

Hobart Town, 25th June, 1835.

Sir,—I have the honour of reporting to your Excellency for the information of His Majesty's Government the result of an expedition, undertaken at the expense and in conjunction with several gentlemen, inhabitants of Van Diemen's Land, to Port Phillip, on the south-western point of New Holland, for the purpose of forming an extensive pastoral establishment, and combining therewith the civilisation of the native tribes who are living in that part of the country.

It occurred to myself and some of the gentlemen who are associated with me, that inasmuch as the Sydney natives who were living with me had become well acquainted with the English language and manners, and had acquired habits of industry and agricultural pursuits, they might therefore be considered partially civilised; and as the available lands in this colony were occupied by flocks of sheep, and fully stocked, it would be a favourable opportunity of opening a direct friendly intercourse with the tribes in the neighbourhood of Port Phillip, and by obtaining from them a grant of a portion of that territory upon equitable principles, not only might the resources of this colony be considerably extended, but the object of civilisation be established, and which in process of time would lead to the civilisation of a large portion of the aborigines of that extensive country.

In pursuance of arrangements based upon these principles I proceeded on the 12th day of May, 1835, in a vessel from Launceston, accompanied by seven Sydney natives, and proceeded to Port Phillip, on the south-western extremity of New Holland, where I landed on the 26th day of May.

On the evening of our arrival at Port Phillip, we saw the native fires at a distance of about five miles; I then made my arrangements for the purpose of opening an interview with the natives by means of those under my charge. I equipped them in their native dress, and early in the morning we landed. I desired the natives to proceed unarmed, and they preceded me a few hundred yards. When we had advanced within half-a-mile we saw the native huts and smoke. My natives then proceeded quietly up to the huts, expecting that we should find the tribe asleep, but when they had got to the huts it appeared that the natives had fled a few hours previously, leaving behind them some of their buckets and other articles.

My natives followed the track, which appeared to have been very circuitous, and after we had proceeded about ten miles we at length saw a tribe consisting of twenty women and twenty-four children.

My natives then made to them some of their friendly signals, which it appeared were understood, and in the course of a few minutes my natives joined the tribe, and after remaining with them as I judged sufficient length of time to conciliate them and explain my friendly disposition, I advanced alone and joined them, and was introduced to them by my natives, two of whom spoke nearly the same language, and so as to be perfectly intelligible to them.

After the strongest assurances on my part of my sincerity and

[389]

friendly disposition, and that no harm would be done to them, they proceeded to the huts, where I gave them a pair of blankets each, tomahawks, knives, scissors, looking-glasses; and I affixed, round the neck of each woman and child, a necklace.

As soon as I had distributed the presents, they were informed by the interpreters that they might depart and join their friends, and I left them and proceeded on board the vessel. They appeared, by my conduct towards them, highly gratified and excited, and showed by their manner that the fullest confidence existed.

Some conversation then took place between my natives and the tribe. The object of my visit and intentions were then explained to them, and the chiefs then pressed me to proceed with them to see their wives and children, which is one of the strongest demonstrations of peace and confidence. Upon my assenting to this request, the chiefs then inquired of my interpreters whether I would allow them to take up their implements of war, which I immediately assented to, and the principal chief then gave me his best spear to carry, and I in return gave him my gun.

We then proceeded towards the huts, and when a short distance from them, the chief called out to the women not to be alarmed, and I was then introduced to the whole tribe, consisting of upwards of twenty men; containing, altogether, fifty-five men, women, and children.

I joined this tribe about twelve o'clock, and staid with them until about twelve o'clock the next day, during which time I fully explained to them that the object of my visit was to purchase from them a tract of their country, that I intended to settle amongst them with my wife and seven daughters, and that I intended to bring to the country sheep and cattle. I also explained my wish to protect them in every way, to employ them the same as my own natives, and also to clothe and feed them, and I also proposed to pay them an annual tribute as a compensation for the enjoyment of the land.

The chiefs appeared most fully to comprehend my proposals, and much delighted with the prospect of having me to live amongst them. I then explained to them the boundaries of the land which I wished to purchase, and which are defined by hills, to which they have affixed native names: and the limits of the land purchased by me are defined in the chart which I have the honour of transmitting, taken from personal survey

On the next day the chiefs proceeded with me to the boundaries, and they marked, with their own native marks, the trees at the corners of the boundaries, and they also gave me their own private mark, which is kept sacred by them, even so much that the women are not allowed to see it.

After the boundaries had been thus marked and described, I filled up as accurately as I could define it, the land agreed to be purchased by me from the chiefs, and the deed, when thus filled up, was most carefully read over and explained to them by the two interpreters, so that they most fully comprehended its purport and effect. I then filled up two other parts of the deed so as to make it in triplicate, and the three principal chiefs and five of the subordinate chiefs then executed each of the deeds, each part being separately read over, and they each delivered to me a piece of the soil for the purpose of putting me in possession thereof, I understanding that it was a form by which they delivered to me the tract of land.

I have the honour of enclosing herewith a copy of each of the deeds executed by the natives to me, which I confidently trust will most clearly manifest that I have proceeded upon an equitable principle, that my object has not been possession and expulsion, or what is worse, extermination; but possession and civilisation, and the reservation of the annual tribute to those who are the real owners of the soil will afford evidence of the sincerity of my professions in wishing to protect and civilise these tribes of benighted but intelligent people, and I confidently trust that the British Government will duly appreciate the treaty which I have made with these tribes, and will not in any manner molest the arrangements which I have made, but that I shall receive the support and encouragement of not only the Local Government, but that of the British Government in carrying the objects into effect.

I traversed the country in opposite directions about fifty miles, and having had much experience in lands and grazing in New South Wales, and in this colony, I have no hesitation in asserting

[391]

that the general character of the country is decidedly superior to any which I have ever seen. It is interspersed with fine rivers and creeks, and the Downs were extended on every side as far as the eye could reach, thickly covered with grass of the finest description, and containing an almost indescribable extent of fine land fit for any purposes.

I have the honour, &c.,

BATMAN.

THE ILLUSTRATIONS: NOTES
AND SOURCES

EMIGRANTS ON DECK. From the *Illustrated London News*, January 20th, 1848.

AN INDIAN AND HIS SQUAW. From Lambert's *Travels through Canada and the United States of America*, 1816. This unterrifying pair will help to remind the reader that what was true of the Sioux was not necessarily true of the Indians living further east, in contact, to a greater or less extent, with the settled areas along the St. Lawrence.

CANADIAN LOG HUT. From *Five Years' Residence in the Canadas*, by Edward Allen Talbot, 1824.

BLYTHE, THE ORIGINAL SETTLEMENT. This is from a sketch by Anne Langton. The house still stands.

CROSSING BELL RIVER. A sketch made by Murray himself of an incident on his way to the Yukon. Published with the Journal. He is in midstream.

SOUTH VIEW OF SYDNEY. From George Barrington's *An Account of a Voyage to New South Wales*, 1803. The original is in colour.

VIEW OF TASMAN'S PEAK FROM MACQUARIE PLAINS. From Lycett's *Views in Australia*, 1824. The same book has an engraving of Macarthur's Elizabeth Farm. The original is in colour.

TITLE PAGE OF AN EMIGRATION HANDBOOK. One of a great number of similar publications.

SHEEP STATION POINT. From *What I Heard, Saw, and Did at the Australian Gold Fields*, by C. Rudston Read, 1853. These diggings are actually in New South Wales, not Victoria, but the scene represents accurately enough what Mereweather saw. The original is in colour.

Appendix

WAGGON TRAIN. The author concerned is The Rev. John Campbell, whose *Travels in South Africa* appeared in 1822. The original is in colour.

GRAHAM'S TOWN. This is taken from George Thompson's valuable *Travels and Adventures in Southern Africa*, 1827.

INTERIOR OF DINGARN'S HOUSE. From Gardiner's *Narrative of a Journey to the Zoolu Country in South Africa*, 1836. An extract from this book is quoted in the note on Owen.

PORTRAIT OF DOBIE. From a photograph taken in Glasgow, and printed in the Van Riebeeck Society edition of his journal.

A SETTLER'S HUT. From *The Women of New Zealand*, by Helen M. Simpson, 1940. The water-colour original is by William Strutt, a Taranaki artist of the '50s.

HARBOUR OF LYTTELTON. From *The Early History of New Zealand*, in Brett's Historical Series, 1890.

THE LAST DAY IN HARNESS. This picture is taken from *Crusts. A Settler's Fare Due South*, by Laurence J. Kennaway, 1874. The reader will not be misled by the charm of its simple pathos into underestimating the dangers of the situation it portrays.

Acknowledgements

I HAVE had to incur heavy obligations, and the list below conceals the unfailing kindness which I have received in letters from holders of copyright, from editors and publishers.

I thank, then:

Mr. H. H. Langton for permission to quote from *Early Days in Upper Canada*, published by the Macmillan Company of Canada, and to reproduce the drawing by Anne Langton.

Mrs. L. J. Burpee for permission to quote from the late Mr. Burpee's edition of Murray's *Journal of the Yukon* and the King's Printer, Ottawa, for permission to include Murray's sketch 'Crossing Bell River'.

The Macarthur family, and the publishers, Angus and Robertson, Ltd., for permission to quote from the first letters home of Mrs. Macarthur in *Some Early Records of the Macarthurs of Camden*.

Mr. George Mackeness, O.B.E., M.A., Litt.D., F.R.A.H.S., for permission to include letters in his possession from his *Some Private Correspondence of the Rev. Samuel Marsden and Family, 1794–1824*.

Mr. John Manifold of Purrumbete Station, Victoria, owner of the Barnes manuscripts; Mrs. John Biddlecombe, who sponsored the publication of *The Narrative of John Russell of Golf Hill*, in which they were printed; and the Oxford University Press.

Mr. Rendel Kyffin Thomas for permission to use passages from the letters in *The Diary and Letters of Mary Thomas*, published by W. K. Thomas & Co.

The officers of the Van Riebeeck Society for permission to make extracts from three of their publications: Goldswain's *Chronicle*, edited by Mrs. Colin Gill; Owen's *Diary*; and Dobie's *Journal*, whose editor, Professor A. F. Hattersley, University of Natal, allowed me to borrow without effort from his labours.

[395]

Acknowledgements

Professor J. Rutherford, Auckland University College, for allowing me to quote from his edition of Weekes' Journal in *The New Plymouth Settlement*, 1841–1843, and the New Plymouth Borough Council, who were responsible for this publication. Also Mr. H. D. Skinner, executor of the estate of the late W. H. Skinner, joint editor.

Mr. John Deans of Riccarton, Christchurch, New Zealand, and the publishers, A. H. Reed Ltd., for permission to quote liberally from *Pioneers of Canterbury* by John Deans.

Miss Eleanor Godley for permitting me to quote so extensively from her mother's letters in *Letters from Early New Zealand*. A new edition, edited by Mr. John Yardley, is appearing in 1950 (Whitcombe and Tombs, Christchurch, N.Z.).

The Alexander Turnbull Library and the Department of Internal Affairs, Wellington, New Zealand, for permission to reproduce the plate ' A Settler's Hut. '

And finally I must record the pleasure of working in a most humane and delightful place—the library at Rhodes House, Oxford. Its staff were uniformly indulgent, but I would like to note especially I appreciated the tolerance Mr. Frederick Madden, now Beit Lecturer in the History of the British Commonwealth, showed to a fish obviously very far from its own waters.

INDEX

Index

Italic figures refer to introductory matter

Index

D

Dadfort [Deptford], 236
Dalrymple, John, 222, 225, 226
Daniel, Capt., 329
Darling River, 196
Davis, R., 370
Dawes, Mr., *120*, 123
Deans, J., 356, 362
Deans, J., Snr., *318*
Deans, J. Y., *318*, 325, 327
Deans, W., 362
Deas, Judge, 290
Debe River, 248
Debenham, Eliza (Mrs. J. Gold-swain), *231*
Delagoa Bay, 281
Deniliquin, 190
Dennistoun, 94, 95
Desmarais, J. B., 20, 21
Dietz, Mr., 241
Dingaan, *208*, *261*, *263*, 266, 267, 268, 269, 270–279
Dod, Mr., 145
Douro, 39, 47, 65
Doyle, Martin, *151*
Drakensberg Mountains, *208*, 284, 286, 292, 296
Driver, Mr., 248, 249, 250
Dublin (Ireland), *150*
Duke of Roxburgh, 320, 321
Dundas, General, 229, 230
Dundas, Henry; *see* Melville
Dunedin, *306*, 344, 345, 346, 347
Dunsford, Lydia (Mrs. John Langton), *73*
Durban, *262*
D'Urban, Sir Benjamin, *208*, 250, 255, *261*
Durham, 96
Dyason, G., 244

E

East India Company, 121
Edgeworth, Maria, 37, 46
Edgeworthstown, 37
Edinburgh (Scotland), *210*

Edward River, 192, 193, 195, 196
Egmont, Mount, 309
Elizabeth Farm, Parramatta, 127
Els, R., 254
Enderby, Mr., 363
Ennismore, 63
Enos, Mr., 258
Enui (River), 310
Evans, Dr., 320, 322
Evans, Mr., 358

F

Faulkner, Mr., 43
Fenelon, 78, 80
Fenelon Falls, 94
Fifeshire (Scotland), *210*
Fingos, *253*
Fish River, 297
Fish River Rand, *253*
Fisher, Mr., 171
Fitzgerald, Mr., 355, 359, 361, 362
Fond du Lac, 29
Forbes, Alexander, 247
Forbes, Capt. E., 251, 252
Forbes, Mrs. A., 247
Forest Creek, 378
Fort Beaufort, 259, 260
Fort McPherson, 99
Fort Simpson, 99, 108
Fortune, T., 95
Fort Yukon, *17*, 99
Foster, Colonel, 39
Fraser, General, 228
Fremantle, 151, 153

G

Gage's Roads, 152
Gambuji, 266, 267, 269
Garden Island, 151
Gardiner, Capt. Allen, *261*, *262*, 265, 266, 267, 269, 270
Gatehouse, Mr., *142*
Gebbie, Mr., *318*, 319, 320
Gellibrand, Mr., 388
Gens-du-fou, 105, 108

Index

Gilbert, Mr., 172
Gilfillan, Adam, 234, 236
Gilles, Mr., 172
Gipps, Sir G., 323
Gisborne, 187, 190
Givence, Mr., 233
Glenelg, 171, 173, 176
Glenelg, Lord, *208*, 255
Godley, Charlotte, *318*
Godley, J., *306, 307,* 339, *342, 343,* 357, 359
Godley, J. A., *342,* 347, 349, 350, 353, 357, 358, 360, 361, 365
Gold, Colonel, 349
Gold, Mrs., 349
Goldeng [Goulden], Mrs. T., 251
Goldeng [Goulden], T., 251
Goldswain, Jeremiah (J.'s uncle), 234
Goldswain, Mrs. J., *231,* 251
Goldswain, Richard, 234
Gorgon, 120, 121
Gouger, Mr. (Colonial Secretary), 172
Graaf Reinet, *203,* 229, 230
Graham's Town, *207, 209, 232,* 239, 240, 242, 243, 244, 246, 247, 250, 251, *253,* 257, 260, *263,* 265
Grant, 20
Grant, Mr., 140
Gray, Mr., 292
Great Marlow (Berkshire), *231,* 232, 233, 235
Great Slave Lake, *99*
Greenlands, 128
Grey, Sir G., *118, 307, 168,* 339, 340, *343,* 366
Grobbelarr's Kloof, 241
Grose, Colonel, 130, *132,* 133, 134
Grose, Mrs., 121
Guardian, 120
Guildford, 155

Hamilton, Gawin [? = Major H.], 94
Hamilton, Major [? = Gawin H.], 93
Hancock, Mr., 286
Hanmer, Mr., 363
Harewood Forest, 372
Harpur (River), 377
Harrison, 31
Hawaiian Islands, *282*
Hawkesbury River, 125, 128, 129, 134
Hay, Lieut., 83, 84, 85, 86
Henry, William, 31, 35
Hesse, 28
Hewitson, Mrs., 281
Hickman, Dr., 233
Hilliar, Major, 39
Hindmarsh, Capt., 168, 171, 172
Hobart Town, *142,* 154, 352
Holdfast Bay, 171, 173
Holsworthy (Devon), *119*
Hope, 39
Hope, Colonel, 227
Hopkins River, *282*
Hottentot Kloof, 224
Hottentots, 214, 219, 223, 225, 246, 254, 264, 278, 297
Hounslow Heath (London), 235
Howard, 75
Howe-Hook, 225
Howerd, Mr., 241
Huatoki (River), 310, 311
Hudson's Bay Company, *13, 14, 15, 17, 99,* 108
Hughes, 35, 36
Hulley, Mr., 293
Huron Tract, *51,* 55
Hutchison, Dr., 44–45, 47
Hutt, Governor, *150*
Hutt (River), 333, 352
Hymans Party, 242

H

Haast, Mr., 378
Hair Hills, 21
Hamilton, 97

I

Ile de France, 148
Inman, Dr., 169
Irwin, Capt., 153

Index

Index

Sydney, *114*, *116*, 120, 123, 126, 128, 129, 138, 143, 147, 193, 200, 317, *318*, 319, 329, 330, 336, 362, 363

Syrius, 120, 121

T

Tamar (River), 144, 147
Tancred, Mr., 366
Tanner, Mr., 164
Tanner, Mrs., 156
Taranaki, 316
Tarka (River), 260
Tarkastad, 295
Tasmania; *see* Van Diemen's Land
Tench, Capt., 123
Texas, *99*
Themes [Thames], 237
Thomas, Frances, 169
Thomas, Helen, 170
Thomas, Mary, 170
Thomas, Robert, *168*, 169, 171, 172, 173, 174, 179
Thomas, William, 170
Thompson, Mr., 330
Thornborn, Mr., 212
Thorndon, 322
Thornhill, Mr., 234, 237
Timandra, 317
Timms, E., 251
Tinnakilly, 52
Tongue River, *19*, 28, 32–34
Toodyay District, 166
Toongabie, 128
Toronto; *see* York [Toronto]
Townsend, Miss, 361
Townsend, Mr., 361
Trapes, Capt., 240
Trauancore, 358, 361
Trent (River), 62, 75, 97
Trollip, Mr., 297
Trollipes, Mr., 243
Tucker, Mr., 297
Tuckett, Mr., 335
Tugala (River), 269, 277, 278, 279

U

Uitenhage, 254, 255
Umkomas River, 265
Umsinduzi (River), 283
Umthlatoosi, 266
Umthela, 270
Umzimkhulu (River), 286
Umzimvubu, 277
Unkunginglovo, 266, 269, 270
Upper Canada; *see* chaps. on Frances Stewart, Bridget Lacy, Thomas Need and John Langton, *14*
Uruguay, *283*
Utica, 71

V

Vandeleur, General, 229
Van Diemen's Land [Tasmania], *114*, *116*, *117*, 142–149, 154, 156, *182*, 188, 189, *387*, *388*
Vanguard, 317
Veale, Elizabeth=Elizabeth Macarthur
Venice (Italy), *181*
Venter, Mr., 295
Verulam, 62, 63, 78, 80
Victoria, *117*, 181–200

W

Waikatu, 310
Waimakiriri (River), 374
Waiongena, 316
Wairau, 329
Waitara (River), 310, 313, 316, 317
Wakefield, E. J., 348, 356
Wakefield, Capt., *305*, 330
Wakefield, Colonel, *304*, 305, 316, 317, 321, 322
Waldek, Mr., 294
Walkers, R., 242
Wallace, Mr., 310
Wallis, Mr., 94, 95, 96

[407]

Index